This book provides an economic historian's perspective on major questions that confront all students of Russian history: how stable were the economic and administrative structures of late-imperial Russia, and how well prepared was Russia for war in 1914? The decade following the Russo-Japanese War witnessed profound changes in the political system and in the industrial economy. The regime faced challenges to its authority at home from industrialists, caught in the throes of recession, and from parliamentary critics of tsarist administration. Against this domestic background, Russia participated in a frantic continental arms race. Peter Gatrell provides a comprehensive account of the attempts made by government and business to confront these challenges, examining the organization and performance of a key industry, and showing how decisions were reached about the allocation of resources, and the far-reaching consequences these decisions entailed.

D1564682

GOVERNMENT, INDUSTRY AND REARMAMENT IN RUSSIA, 1900–1914

Cambridge Russian, Soviet and Post-Soviet Studies

Series list continues after index

Government, industry and rearmament in Russia, 1900–1914

The last argument of tsarism

PETER GATRELL

Department of History, University of Manchester

CAMBRIDGE
UNIVERSITY PRESS

Published by the Press Syndicate of the University of Cambridge
The Pitt Building, Trumpington Street, Cambridge CB2 1RP
40 West 20th Street, New York, NY 10011–4211, USA
10 Stamford Road, Oakleigh, Melbourne 3166, Australia

© Cambridge University Press 1994

First published 1994

Printed in Great Britain at the University Press, Cambridge

A catalogue record for this book is available from the British Library

Library of Congress cataloguing in publication data
Gatrell, Peter.
Government, industry, and rearmament in Russia, 1900–1914:
the last argument of tsarism / Peter Gatrell.
    p.   cm. – (Cambridge Russian, Soviet and post-Soviet studies: 92)
Includes bibliographical references (p.   ).
ISBN 0 521 45263 5 (hc.)
1. Russia – Economic conditions – 1861–1917.
2. Industry and state – Russia – History.
3. Defense industries – Russia – History.
4. Russia – Armed Forces – Appropriations and expenditures.
I. Title.   II. Series.
HC334.5.G37   1994
338.947'009'041–dc20   93–11074   CIP

ISBN 0 521 45263 5 hardback
ISBN 0 521 46619 9 paperback

Contents

Maps

Tables

Preface

This study deals with the capacity of the tsarist regime to survive a challenge to its authority at home and to maintain its prestige abroad. The prerogatives of the imperial government to decide foreign and defence policy, as well as economic and fiscal policy, were called into question by the forces unleashed during war and revolution in 1904–5. After 1905, a struggle took place between state and society for control over fundamental issues of policy. This book concentrates upon one aspect of that struggle, by examining the organization, administration, finance and performance of the armaments industry in Russia from the turn of the nineteenth century to the outbreak of the First World War.

The first two chapters address the political, economic and defence imperatives before and during the years of upheaval in 1904–6. The final decade of the nineteenth century witnessed a series of important initiatives that had profound repercussions for the defence sector: Russia signed a military agreement with France, the tsarist government embarked on a programme of rapid industrialization, and significant reforms in the armed forces came to fruition. But none of these developments prepared Russia for what was to come as the new century dawned. The first crisis appeared in the industrial sector, where the basic industries that had flourished for a decade experienced instead a severe recession. Next, the war against Japan humiliated the Russian empire and exposed serious weaknesses in the system of military procurement. Much of the imperial fleet lay at the bottom of the Pacific Ocean. To restore Russian pride and military might was costly; and the price of rearmament had to be reckoned along with the costs of the war. Finally, the ensuing revolution provoked profound changes in the political system, leading to the establishment of a form of parliamentary government. The Duma had no constitutional right of control over the armed services, but its budgetary powers allowed its members to exert some influence over defence spending, as well as over the administration of the state-owned arsenals and shipyards.

The resolution of these components of crisis forms the basis for the following three chapters, which detail the rearmament programmes, defence spending, the reform of procurement and the behaviour of the arms industry. As in the first chapter, the treatment of armaments industry is set in the context of the basic industries which provided the essential underpinnings for modern warfare, namely iron and steel and machine-building, and which themselves produced goods that were either destined to be used by the military or that could be adapted to military use. These form the subject of chapter 4, which considers the mainsprings of industrial growth on the eve of the First World War. This chapter also charts the uneasy relationship between industry and government, in the light of budgetary conflicts, market uncertainties and shifting defence priorities. Chapter 5 discusses in detail the emergence of the private arms trade in Russia, as well as the problems that beset the established state sector. It also considers the place of the armament industry in the Russian industrial economy. In chapter 6, attention turns to defence procurement, where the theme of an 'internal arms race' figures prominently. The aim is to ascertain the claims made by their supporters on behalf of rival forms of enterprise, as well as the relative performance of the two sectors. The study ends with a broadly conceived assessment of defence preparations and Russia's readiness for war in 1914.

Acknowledgements

I take a great deal of pleasure in being able to thank the people who have helped me to research and write this book. My first task is to acknowledge the assistance of those archivists who kept me supplied with material. The staffs of the Central State Historical Archive, the Central State Archive of the Navy and the St Petersburg State Historical Archive, as well as of the Central State Military-Historical Archive, laboured under difficult conditions to meet many of my needs. Kenneth Warren gave me helpful advice about archives in the UK. I have also received assistance from staff at the John Rylands University Library, Manchester, including those in the Inter-Library Loans department, as well as from successive librarians at the Centre for Russian and East European Studies, University of Birmingham. In addition, the librarians and archivists of the Library of Congress, the University of Illinois Library, and Cambridge University Library dealt carefully with my requests for assistance.

I am pleased to be able to acknowledge financial support from the University of Manchester's Staff Travel Fund, the British Council, the Kennan Institute for Advanced Russian Studies, Washington DC, and the British Academy.

Several people read part or all of an earlier version of the manuscript. Two anonymous referees made numerous suggestions for improvements and prompted me to rethink my approach to the subject. Clive Trebilcock offered encouraging comments on the first draft. I am also very grateful to David Stevenson for sharing with me his thoughts about the diplomacy of the pre-1914 arms race and, more particularly, for commenting carefully and constructively on the entire manuscript. Edward Acton, now of the University of East Anglia, not only read a first draft and made helpful comments, but also never lost hope of my eventually finishing a revised version. No one could wish for a finer colleague and friend.

Several memorable trips to the USA, to Russia and Italy brought me into contact with a large number of historians and economists, who shared ideas with me, presented me with books and offprints and offered advice and encouragement. Chief amongst them are Charles Timberlake, Walter Pintner and John McKay in the USA: Boris Vasil'evich Anan"ich and Valerii Ivanovich Bovykin in Russia; and the participants in a Workshop on the European Armament Industry, 1860s–1939, organized by Luciano Segreto and Albert Carreras at the European University Institute, Florence, in November 1991. I also benefited from brief discussions with Kornelii Fedorovich Shatsillo and Leonid Efimovich Shcpclev, from whose work I learned so much, as will be evident from the footnotes to this book. I am grateful to Joseph Bradley for allowing me to read a manuscript copy of his excellent monograph on the Russian small-arms industry during the nineteenth century.

In the course of my research I have enjoyed friendship and hospitality at every turn. I much appreciate the warmth of the reception I received in the USA from Pat and Charles Timberlake, Sara and Walter Pintner, and from Frances, Ham and Rod Kenner. In Moscow, I could always count upon Leon and Ira Bell, Anya Bakhnova and Maya Rapoport. In St Petersburg, Iulia Mutusheva and family and Zina Skobeleva helped to keep up my spirits. Countless research trips to Cambridge and London were made enjoyable by the kindness and generosity shown by Kate and David Shoenberg, and by Peter Shoenberg, to all of whom I express my gratitude and love.

The completion of this book gives me the opportunity to thank Olga Crisp and Bob Davies, whose advice and support I have enjoyed for nearly two decades. I am also grateful to Michael Kaser for his encouragement. Nor do I forget those who taught me many years ago at the University of Cambridge: Neil McKendrick, Philip Grierson, Sydney Kanya-Forstner, Vic Gatrell and, above all, Norman Stone, Clive Trebilcock and Jonathan Steinberg who encouraged my interest in modern European history. I owe more than I can say to Keith Dawson, Haberdashers' Aske's School, Elstree, and to the late Tony Howarth. Their enthusiasm for history and their enviable gifts of exposition inspired me long ago and remain precious memories.

As always, my beloved parents and brother, Tony Gatrell, have followed my progress with keen interest.

It is hardest of all to find words to thank those who are so close and dear to me, and I shall not attempt to do this in print. I can do no better than to dedicate this book to Jane, David and Lizzy, with all my love.

Abbreviations

d.	delo (file)
f.	fond (collection)
GAU	Glavnoe artilleriiskoe upravlenie (Main Artillery Administration)
GIU	Glavnoe intendantskoe upravlenie (Chief Quartermaster's Department)
GUKS	Glavnoe upravlenie korablestroeniia i snabzheniia (Main Shipbuilding Administration)
l.	list (sheet)
LGIA	Leningradskii gosudarstvennyi istoricheskii arkhiv (Leningrad State Historical Archive)
ob.	obratnaia (reverse)
op.	opis' (inventory)
SGO	Sovet gosudarstvennoi oborony (Council for State Defence)
SOGD	*Gosudarstvennaia Duma: stenograficheskii otchet* (Stenographic report of the State Duma)
SOGS	*Gosudarstvennyi Sovet: stenograficheskii otchet* (Stenographic report of the State Council)
TsGAVMF	Tsentral'nyi gosudarstvennyi arkhiv voenno-morskogo flota (Central State Archive of the Navy)
TsGIA	Tsentral'nyi gosudarstvennyi istoricheskii arkhiv (Central State Historical Archive)
TsGVIA	Tsentral'nyi gosudarstvennyi voenno-istoricheskii arkhiv (Central State Military-Historical Archive)
VOGK	*Vsepoddaneishii otchet gosudarstvennogo kontrolera*
VDMM	*Vsepoddaneishii doklad po morskomu ministerstvu*

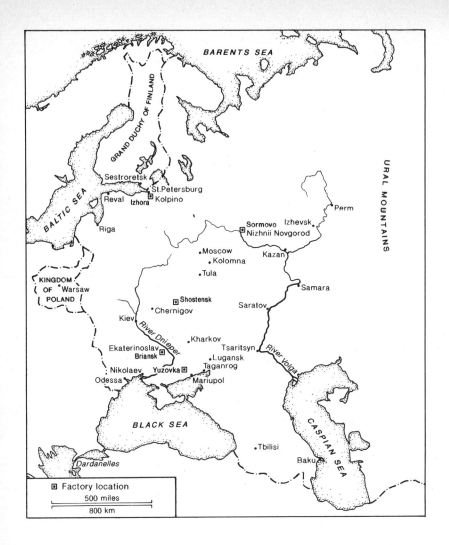

1 European Russia in 1914 showing the location of major enterprises.

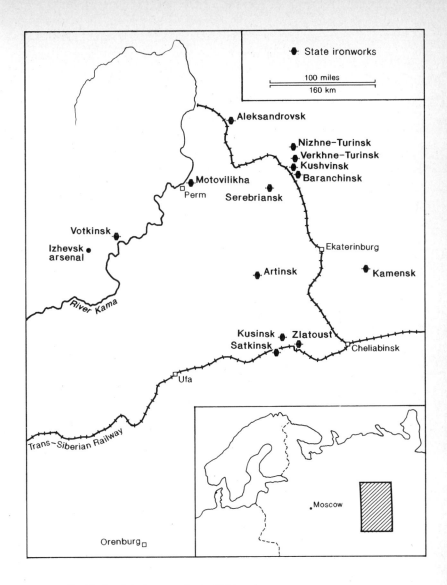

2　Urals state ironworks in 1914

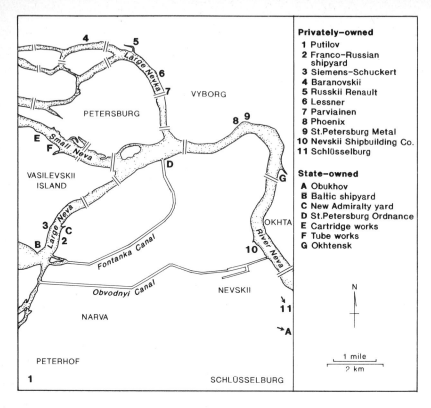

Privately-owned
1 Putilov
2 Franco-Russian shipyard
3 Siemens-Schuckert
4 Baranovskii
5 Russkii Renault
6 Lessner
7 Parviainen
8 Phoenix
9 St.Petersburg Metal
10 Nevskii Shipbuilding Co.
11 Schlüsselburg

State-owned
A Obukhov
B Baltic shipyard
C New Admiralty yard
D St.Petersburg Ordnance
E Cartridge works
F Tube works
G Okhtensk

1 mile
2 km

3 St Petersburg in 1914 showing the location of major shipyards and armaments factories

Introduction

An eminent scholar, surveying a century of Russian and Soviet development, once remarked that 'it always was a "political" economic history'.[1] This epigrammatical statement reflected the widely held view that the tsarist state actively promoted Russian economic development for geo-political purposes. The old regime, conscious of the disparity between its diplomatic pretensions and relative economic weakness, aimed to build a modern industrial economy. Russian industrialization and tsarist foreign policy were closely intertwined, as the regime sought to enhance the international status and influence which it forfeited in the years following the Crimean War. The pursuit of international prestige went hand in hand with a programme for rapid industrial development, which laid the foundations for economic and military security.

A generation after Gerschenkron wrote the words quoted above, many aspects of Russia's 'political' economic history remain contentious or unresolved. Scholars who disagree about key aspects of Russian history nevertheless agree that the tsarist state exercised a decisive influence over the course of economic development. But exactly what role the state played in the process of economic development and by whom economic policy was formulated are questions which still await thorough examination. The implications of a powerful state for private entrepreneurial initiative have attracted some attention, but many aspects of business policy, entrepreneurial practice and industrial performance remain unclear. The connection between foreign and defence policy, on the one hand, and industrial development, on the other, is opaque. What were the defence-related imperatives that Russian industry purportedly obeyed? What role did the state play in the production of defence goods, and what role did it assign to private enterprise? The interaction of government and business in the sphere of defence production is as yet imperfectly

1

understood. Did the tsarist defence effort promote economic growth, by mobilizing resources that would otherwise have remained idle, or retard it, by diverting resources from productive to unproductive ends?

Backwardness, businessmen and the tsarist state

Russian industrialization was of paramount importance to the tsarist state. Seeking to aspire to the great power status Russia once enjoyed, but had lost with the coming of the machine age, policy-makers had to overcome the legacy conferred by years of stagnation. Economic backwardness was deeply entrenched. But – according to Gerschenkron – having identified the ends, the tsarist state was forced to confront the limited means at its disposal. These included a preponderant and traditional agricultural sector, a dearth of funds for investment and a small and poorly qualified entrepreneurial class. The government was unable to devolve upon private enterprise the function of mobilizing resources for rapid industrial growth: the burden was simply too heavy, the responsibility too grave and the urgency of the task too great. In Gerschenkron's terms, the state 'substituted' for factors that were missing or in short supply, by purchasing industrial goods on a massive scale, supplying credit to selected entrepreneurs and encouraging the import of foreign capital and skills. Responding to these stimuli, Russian industrial development during the 1890s proceeded at breakneck speed.[2]

In Gerschenkron's scheme, war figured as an exogenous development, unrelated to prior socio-economic and political change. As a consequence, he never examined in detail the link between diplomacy and domestic policy. He raised briefly the possibility that Russian industrialists sought war, in order to secure lucrative contracts, but dismissed the suggestion, on the grounds that it tended to 'magnify the political significance of the Russian bourgeoisie out of all proportion'. Beyond this statement he refused to venture in print.[3] But the war did not emerge like an unforeseen bolt from the blue. As for the revolutionary process, Gerschenkron largely ignored its causes, preferring to concentrate instead on the stabilizing forces at work in the late imperial Russian economy.

The connection between government policy, industrial development and revolution figures much more prominently in the interpretation developed by Teodor Shanin. Shanin follows Gerschenkron in accepting the primacy of state initiatives in accounting for rapid industrialization. However, he offers a more explicit conceptualization of the tsarist state and posits a link between government policy and revolution. Shanin subscribes to the view that the Russian state underwrote rapid industrialization, in order to maintain its security at home and abroad. However, this programme accentuated the predominant features of a polity which is characterized by 'dependent development', namely 'a state machinery that has variously been described as "overgrown", "strong" and/or "state capitalist"'. The tsarist state possessed 'exceptional power' and maintained an 'extensive ... economic grip as owner, producer, employer and controller of resources ...'. Industrialization enhanced still further the scope of the tsarist state and its control over resources.[4]

Shanin's conceptualization of the state is accompanied by an interpretation of revolution. Industrialization helped to undermine the foundations of the state at the same time as it magnified state power. State-led industrialization antagonized and impoverished the bulk of the peasantry (Gerschenkron also saw this as a cause of revolution in 1905), and created irresolvable tensions between foreign capitalists, local capitalists and the government. Officials found it easier to handle indigenous capitalists than the foreign ones who flocked to Russia to take advantage of the growing opportunities for investment. The state, according to Shanin, was undermined by bureaucratic mediocrity and incompetence, by its dependence on foreign capitalists, by its exploitation of the peasantry and by an inability to reduce differentials of wealth.

Shanin's argument has the merit of addressing seriously the association between the economic system of tsarist Russia and its eventual collapse. According to Shanin, at the heart of Russian government initiatives there lay what might be termed a structural paradox, namely that the process of industrialization weakened rather than strengthened the old regime. But this paradox needs to be examined more fully. The latest research would certainly not corroborate the suggestion that state-led industrialization during the 1890s was fed by fiscal impoverishment of the peasant population; besides, the living standards of the peasantry improved significantly between 1905 and 1914. Nor should the professional competence of the bureaucracy be dismissed in so sweeping a fashion. The middle-level bureaucracy struggled reasonably well to reconcile divergent interests and constraints.[5]

Dietrich Geyer offers an interpretation which relates economic development both to domestic social and political conflict and to

international diplomacy. In his view, the tsarist regime found it difficult to come to terms with the changed realities following the Russo-
Japanese War. Internal problems remained acute in the aftermath of
the 1905 revolution. These problems included 'the disintegration of
pseudo-constitutionalism, an atmosphere of catastrophe charged with
strong social tension, the turbulence of a period of economic boom,
dissatisfaction in agricultural circles and the declining ability of the
government to assert its authority'. In these circumstances, deep-
seated fears about the future of the country 'were projected onto a
foreign enemy'. Although Geyer rejects the insistence of Soviet historians on the emergence of a 'revolutionary situation' in 1914, he finds
evidence of a profound rupture between government and people,
which the regime sought to disguise and even surmount by leading a
nationalist crusade against Germany and Austria-Hungary. Thus, the
structural weaknesses associated with economic modernization generated a foreign policy that was fraught with risk.[6]

A somewhat different argument is developed here. There is no
dispute that the search for imperial grandeur led the old regime –
more accurately, a modernizing faction within it – to embark on a
programme of industrialization during the 1890s. The industrialization
programme required for its completion a sustained period of peace
and stability, in order to promote business confidence and foreign
investment in Russia. But Russian heavy industry rested on fragile
economic and institutional foundations, and the industrial boom came
to an abrupt end at the turn of the century, when the frantic pace of
railway construction and capital investment slackened. The confidence of Russian businessmen received a nasty jolt. A welcome
upturn in the business cycle coincided with a reckless military gamble
in Manchuria, the result of ill-considered policies being pursued by
another faction within the regime. In the aftermath of the war against
Japan, Russia tried to pick up the pieces. The search for grandeur now
took on a different meaning, as the government struggled simultaneously to meet the costs of war in the Far East and to remain active on
the European stage. Russia hoped to share the burden of defence with
its French ally, but there was a limit to what the alliance could achieve,
when both parties ostensibly had little in common, save their mutual
suspicion of German predominance in Europe. In the industrial
sphere, the state used its control of industrial assets to counter a
potential increase in the power of capitalists, whether foreign or
Russian. Contrary to the claims of Shanin, the state did not succumb to
the dictates of foreign capitalism. Foreign investors, bankers and entre-

preneurs were kept at arm's length, either by design or by virtue of the mass of bureaucratic regulation which confronted them in the Russian empire and which made many businessmen wary of too deep an involvement in the tsarist economy. The story with regard to domestic capitalists was yet more complex, and requires a fuller elaboration of business-government relations. In this sphere, against the backdrop of renewed uncertainties about national security, is to be found a key component of social and political instability in late imperial Russia.

The economics of defence

The themes of industrialization, business-government relations and imperial diplomacy coalesce in a study of defence industry. In any modern economy, as in tsarist Russia, several distinct branches of industry contribute to the market for defence goods. The armed forces require weapons and naval vessels, which are supplied either by specialist armouries and dockyards or by metalworking and machine-building industries. Engineering firms also supply defence equipment, such as military vehicles, whilst at the same time producing a range of other goods for the civilian market. Other industries, too, are involved in the construction and furnishing of military installations, such as fortresses, barracks, depots and ports. Explosives are produced by the chemicals industry. The armed services also require food, fodder, footwear and uniforms. Thus, the market for defence products is very varied and draws upon the productive capabilities of a range of industries. Here, in pragmatic fashion, defence industry is used as a convenient shorthand to describe those heterogeneous branches of industry that supply goods for the armed services. In practice, the focus is largely on those branches of industry that produce semi-finished goods and finished military hardware.[7]

'Defence industry' is not, however, an artificial construct, created simply by amalgamating a number of discrete branches of manufacturing industry. Defence industry is possessed of specific features that relate both to its structure and to the nature of the defence market.[8] The production of military hardware is distinguished from other branches of industry in that the goods are destined to be used, neither as investment goods nor as the means of satisfying household consumer needs. The defence industry is 'a component in an international system of threat and conflict, as distinct from all other industries whose relation is one of international exchange'. Its products are either used as the means of destruction or are stockpiled until their potential military usefulness has expired.[9]

Its strategic significance gives defence industry a potential leverage that is likely to be denied other sectors. Decision-makers may attempt to influence the course of foreign and defence policy, in order to enhance its prospects. In a classic article, first published in 1933, the German historian Eckhart Kehr argued that this behaviour was a functional necessity for the survival of the industry. When business is slack, he asserted, the industry's leaders advocate rearmament, in order to protect their investment. The government may be unwilling to respond, but the failure to accede to their demands carries the risk that factories will close and skills will be dissipated. Corporate pressure by the arms trade would, for these reasons, be difficult to resist.[10] Kehr's conclusions hardly command universal acceptance amongst scholars who have studied the prewar arms race. Evidence from other societies, where Kehr's views might have been expected to be confirmed, weakens his case. For example, the zaibatsu did not wholeheartedly support the Japanese arms build-up during the 1920s and 1930s, fearing that the programme would lead to higher taxes and international instability. Although the expansionist policies pursued by Nazi Germany had the active support of leading German firms, notably in chemicals and non-ferrous metals, Hitler's foreign policy was driven by a range of social forces, of which big business was only one element.[11] More generally, the concept of a 'military-industrial complex', which Kehr was the first to scrutinize in depth, has lately been reassessed. Defence economists have demonstrated that modern capitalist economies do not rely heavily upon defence production for their survival, and they are sceptical of the view that modern governments are strongly influenced by defence firms.[12]

Other distinctive attributes of defence industry command attention. One outstanding feature is that governments are the sole customers for its products. Government is directly involved in issues of defence production and procurement, and will be at pains to establish some degree of control and supervision over the industry, in order to ensure that suppliers adhere to the terms of the contract. This means that government agencies pay close attention to questions of price, product quality and delivery date. A close relationship thus develops between government and industry. But it does not follow that government, as sole customer, is able to exercise the power implied by monopsony. The defence industry is often structured in such a way as to prevent competition.[13]

Defence economists have specified the conditions that hinder competition and foster a tendency towards concentration, contrary to the competitive tendencies which purportedly exist in other branches of industry. The potential for oligopoly (a market dominated by a handful of firms) is created in two ways, namely by the barriers to entry of new firms and by the tendency of existing defence contractors to collude and combine, in order to protect themselves against their client. Barriers to entry operate because potential newcomers do not have the necessary specialist expertise in defence production. They find it prohibitively expensive to invest in the lengthy research and development required to enter the industry. Existing defence firms, for their part, will tend to join forces in order to realize economies of scale, such as pooling their technical knowledge and expertise in order to share R&D costs and thereby keep pace with the high rate of technological change, on which their future depends. These oligopolistic tendencies may be offset by other developments. Barriers to entry operate less effectively where the technology is itself undergoing change. In these circumstances, new and existing defence firms are in the same position, neither having been able to accumulate the necessary expertise. In addition, the complex and constantly changing pattern of military demand may allow a plethora of small firms to secure a niche, by concentrating their limited resources on one element of the market.[14]

How relevant are these considerations to Russian defence industry at the beginning of the twentieth century? Most of the attention of economists who have studied defence industry has been devoted to the principles governing the behaviour of private enterprise. This emphasis is unfortunate. Before 1900, the contribution of state-owned enterprise to armaments production was more important than the contribution made by private industry. In Russia, state enterprises had been established by Peter the Great. By the second half of the nineteenth century they had built up a skilled and loyal labour force.[15] The tsarist government had no wish to depend on the private sector, when firms might combine, in order to dictate terms to government, or suddenly cease trading. There was no question of abandoning state-owned defence industry. However, the realization of this strategy depended, in part, upon the distribution of large subsidies to state shipyards and armouries. Whether this support could be justified after 1905, in view of new political and fiscal pressures, was another matter.

A significant private defence industry came on the scene relatively late, at a time when government-owned enterprises were well established, particularly in small arms and artillery. In the manufacture of small arms, a high degree of precision engineering was required, far more than in other branches of civilian engineering, such as locomotive manufacture. Here, a technological barrier certainly hampered the entry of new enterprises. The entry of private firms in other branches of defence industry coincided with a profound shift in armaments technology. In artillery, heavier calibres were adopted, the machine gun became more widespread and, above all, shipbuilding was transformed by the introduction of the dreadnought. Now, private enterprise offered the Russian government the opportunity to tap advanced technology, by means of the technical agreements concluded by new firms and their foreign associates. The barriers to the entry of new enterprises in defence industry began to come down.

There were nevertheless risks involved in entering the defence industry. First, private firms might invest heavily in new plant, designed with a specific product in mind, only to find that the procurement agencies changed the specifications attached to the order or, more worrying still, that the government transferred future contracts to the state sector. It must be said that some risks were no more serious than the risks attendant in other branches of manufacturing industry: fluctuations and uncertainty afflicted the defence market, but the same was true of the Russian market as a whole. In practice, as we shall see, private firms dealt with the problem by maintaining a diverse product mix. Until the eve of the First World War, only a small number of firms specialized exclusively in defence products.

Another key issue relates to the defence effort more broadly conceived. To what extent were patterns of defence spending during the early twentieth century linked in a coherent fashion to changing conceptions of strategy? What kind of military preparations were being formulated by the military leadership of the European powers: were they designed to equip countries for an offensive or defensive war, for a long or a short war, for a land or naval engagement? By what means, and with what success did these military conceptions translate into defence spending and armaments programmes? These issues have attracted a substantial literature, particularly in regard to German preparations for war during the 1930s. The Blitzkrieg strategy was designed to enable Germany to adjust its military goals to resource endowment, in particular to shortages of raw materials. This strategy in turn imposed the need for rearmament 'in width', that is a programme based upon stockpiling tanks and other weapons. Economic realities and military ambition thus corresponded closely. A discussion of economic and strategic planning before the First World War reveals that Admiralty strategists capitalized on Britain's geographical position and naval power to prepare for the starvation of German civilians, dependent as they were on imported foodstuffs, into submission.[16]

This kind of analysis has not been pursued very far with regard to imperial Russia. Only rarely have military strategy, domestic politics and economic policy been considered together.[17] K. F. Shatsillo argued that the personal preference of Tsar Nicholas for a strong fleet led to cut-backs in planned spending on territorial forces. His approach is more subtle than the crude judgements made by other former Soviet historians. One eminent historian of late tsarist Russia condemned tsarist military preparations in sweeping fashion: 'the government of Nicholas II, in the ten years after the Russo-Japanese War, did *nothing significant* to prepare for the coming war'.[18] Given the resources at Russia's disposal, including the prospect of sharing the costs of defence with its French ally, did the country's military planners obtain adequate security? Could they have done better?

The clear implication of one well-informed study of the imperial defence budget is that Russia substituted manpower for capital equipment.[19] This policy economized on the relatively scarce resource. It tallied also with the expectations held by French military planners, who dearly hoped to maintain a huge contingent of Russian troops on Germany's eastern frontier. As Russia's ally, France could have been expected to exercise influence over the allocation of military manpower and thus, indirectly, over the allocation of resources in the defence budget.

Domestic politics should have the final word, because the combined impact of international and domestic economic variables ultimately impinged directly on the conduct and structure of domestic politics. Possible sources of strain in the imperial polity included the politicization of defence spending. Taxpayers, with some access to a parliamentary assembly after 1905, might not be expected to tolerate the burden of taxation, particularly if rearmament made it heavier still. On the other hand, their criticisms might be offset by a commitment to the overall strategic goals of the Russian armed forces: the containment of Europe's other empires and the protection of slav minorities on the territory of Austria-Hungary and the Ottoman empire. A more serious problem derived from the attitudes of Russia's military leaders, who baulked at the constant expectation that troops were expected to repress the 'enemy within' as well as to defend the empire from external aggression.[20] Other sources of conflict – between Duma and government, between state and private enterprise, between government and businessmen – also posed challenges to the old regime. Whether it could handle them, at a time of rapid economic change and international uncertainty, is the subject of this book.

Part 1

Defence imperatives and Russian industry, 1900–1907

Ultima ratio regum
(The last argument of kings)
(motto inscribed on French cannon during the seventeenth century)

1 Defence and the economy on the eve of the Russo-Japanese War

Introduction: Russian imperialism and industrialism from Crimea to Manchuria: economic foundations of a search for imperial grandeur

The pursuit of imperial grandeur – the desire to recapture the international stature that Russia enjoyed during the eighteenth century – occupied much of the time, energy and resources of the tsarist regime. It was, however, a pursuit fraught with difficulties and contradictions. The humiliation that autocratic Russia had endured at the hands of democratic England and France during the Crimean War convinced thoughtful contemporaries that future catastrophe could best be avoided by some measure of political and economic reform. Hence the decisions between 1860 and 1874 to modernize the banking system, to dispense with the institutional prop of serfdom, to create organs of local self-government, to modernize the Russian army and to overcome deep-seated prejudices against that most modern and democratic of nineteenth-century inventions, the railway.[1] But these institutional reforms neither guaranteed stability at home nor enhanced the external security of the Empire. Partly, this was because any reform created opportunities for new social groups to operate and for political ideas to be articulated in opposition to the prevailing orthodoxy. In addition, exogenous forces undermined tsarist Russia's attempts to regain imperial hegemony. By 1870, Germany threatened to dominate Europe, as Austria and France had recently discovered to their cost. The weakness and enforced isolationism of Russia implied that Britain, as a great naval power, alone stood in the way of Germany's complete subjection of the continent. In this respect, the decaying empires of Austria-Hungary and Turkey counted for nothing. Thus, the fate of Europe seemed to hinge on Russia's prospects. If Russia went the way of the Ottoman Empire, there was little to prevent the abandonment of Europe to German domination. But if Russia could develop the appropriate economic foundations to meet the challenge of German blood and iron, all was not yet lost.[2]

By 1900, tsarist Russia had completed more than a decade of rapid economic growth. Between 1889–92 and 1901–4, total output grew by around 4.7 per cent per annum in real terms, or by around 3.4 per cent per capita. These rates were high by international standards. Although the performance of Russian agriculture continued to give cause for concern, other sectors of the economy were more dynamic and promised a still greater contribution to national wealth. A modern iron and steel industry had been established, and in addition Russia had the makings of a modern engineering industry. Newer branches of industry, such as basic chemicals, had also begun to appear. Consumer goods industries thrived, largely on account of the growth of urban population. The construction of a huge railway network offered the prospect of further economic gains, by reducing transport costs, improving inter-regional trade and stimulating population movement to areas of greater economic opportunity. The process of industrialization seemed to be irreversible, notwithstanding the misgivings of populists about Russia's long-term capacity for industrial development. The government had recently (in 1897) taken Russia on to the gold standard and, against the background of fiscal orthodoxy and monetary stability, the 1890s witnessed a massive inflow of foreign capital, in the form of private direct investment in industry. In per capita terms, Russian national income remained well below that of other industrial economies, such as Germany, Britain and the United States, and the fruits of industrial progress had still to trickle down to the bulk of the population, many of whom continued to live in abject poverty. Nevertheless, there can be little doubt that Russia had achieved the status of a major industrial power by 1900.[3]

The rapid growth in industrial production during the 1890s rested in part upon a programme of railway construction, induced and financed by the tsarist government. Between 1890 and 1900, the total length of track in the Russian Empire increased from 30,600 to 56,500km. During the quinquennium 1896–1900, railway investment as a whole amounted to between one-quarter and one-third of total net investment. The railways did not by themselves create the conditions for industrial growth, and should be seen against the background of a more broadly-based process of capital formation. Nevertheless, annual additions to the transport capital stock usually exceeded additions to the industrial capital stock between 1890 and 1905, and it was the investment in rails and rolling stock that generated demand on a scale broad enough to sustain the new iron and steel industry and the nascent engineering industry.[4]

The broader repercussions of industrial growth must also be remembered. To espouse the cause of industrialism, in the interests of great power status, was to abandon much accumulated wisdom about the economic foundations of the Russian empire. To promote industrial expansion was to introduce a Trojan horse into the camp of imperial Russia, in the shape of new social forces, possessed of their own agenda and aspirations. In due course, Russian businessmen would demand to be heard in the corridors of government, whether in support of their immediate economic interests, or in defence of the rights of capital *vis-à-vis* an interventionist bureaucracy. Some kind of strategy would also have to be devised to accommodate the demands of the growing industrial labour force. Tsarist Russia had to confront another difficult problem before 1905, namely how to sustain the interests of businessmen without sacrificing the traditional noble estate (*dvorianstvo*) on the altar of industrial supremacy. The problem of reconciling imperialism and industrialism was resolved by maintaining a substantial degree of direct or indirect control over Russian industry. This managed to satisfy those in the bureaucracy who had never lost their hostility to industrial enterprise and whose aversion did not diminish with each passing year. They were assuaged by the recognition that industry was held in check by the Treasury, by officials who controlled tariff policy and by the maintenance of state-owned enterprise. That these conditions would not persist for ever appeared not to cloud the thoughts of most tsarist officials and contemporary observers.[5]

If industrialism raised a number of difficulties for the tsarist polity, so too did imperialism. To engage in adventures beyond the borders of the empire was to risk disorder in the state, partly because of the higher taxes that might result from foreign adventures, and partly because of the expectations of reform that might be raised among the civilian population and then dashed. The bulk of educated society had been in favour of energetic action during the so-called war of liberation in 1877; whether this support for military action would be forthcoming if other imperial interests were at stake – in central Asia or in the Far East – was by no means certain. In Manchuria, for instance, the only liberation at stake was the freedom conferred on a handful of speculators to make a quick killing. Some Russian businessmen stood to gain from an adventurist policy in the Balkans, but there is no evidence of ministerial susceptibility to the blandishments of these merchants. Most industrialists had a vested interest in peace, rather than in bellicosity.

Of all the continental powers, France had most to gain from the restoration of Russia to its proper place in the European firmament. The cultivation of a serious rival on the eastern borders of the German Empire offered France the hope of eventually exacting revenge for the defeat it had suffered in 1871. For two decades, Germany's leaders did their best to cultivate the Reich's eastern neighbour, by including Russia in the Dreikaiserbund. However, the German grain tariff threatened Russia's trade surplus and Bismarck's manipulation of the money markets against Russian interests drove Russia into the arms of France. In 1893–4, much to the delight of the Quai d'Orsay, the French succeeded in persuading Russia to sign a military convention confirming the close ties established by the political agreement in 1891. Preparations for the alliance with France had already begun to unlock the Paris capital markets to Russian customers. The inflow of French capital unleashed a decade of rapid industrialization, unprecedented hitherto in world economic history.[6]

In addition to the many favourable economic indicators which contemporaries could identify at the turn of the century, tsarist Russia enjoyed the advantages of international peace. This was an essential background to the movement of capital, goods and specialist technical advice on which the industrial boom of the 1890s depended. Russian public opinion did not need reminding that the situation had been very different during the 1850s and 1860s. In the aftermath of the Crimean War (1854–6), Minister of Finances Mikhail Reutern had embarked on a campaign designed to restore the currency, shattered by the inflationary consequences of war. But these efforts were quickly dashed by the Polish uprising in 1863, which destroyed foreign confidence in the ruble and, by implication, in the tsarist government itself. The government struggled to restore the currency to a semblance of stability, but Reutern was frustrated in similar fashion by the Russo-Turkish War in 1877–8. It was left to his successors, notably N. Kh. Bunge, I. A. Vyshnegradskii and S. Iu. Witte, to make use of the peace in Europe during the 1880s and 1890s to lay the foundations for budgetary expansion, monetary stability and foreign investment.[7]

Towards the end of the nineteenth century, the achievements described above seemed secure. At the turn of the century, however, they were threatened by a slump in industry, a loss of confidence on the part of foreign investors and a decline in industrial, municipal and railway investment. The crisis led in 1903 to the dismissal of Witte, who was held responsible for the impoverishment of the Russian consumer and thus for the inability to generate an alternative source of demand to compensate for the decline in government orders for investment goods. While Russian industrialists struggled to survive this recession, the tsarist government more easily overcame the political crisis associated with the departure of Witte. But within two years, the government faced a much more serious reversal in its fortunes. A short, yet disastrous war against Japan – itself the consequences of a wholly misguided and, in many respects, dishonest attempt at 'peaceful' economic penetration of the Far East – proved once more, if proof were needed, that war was a costly business for the tsarist state to undertake.

Foreign and defence policy

For much of the nineteenth century, it made sense for Russia, as a predominantly agrarian country, to concentrate diplomatic attention on the Balkans. Economic interests dictated that the passage of grain through the Straits of Constantinople should be protected. But the rise of industrialism dictated other considerations, such as the need to protect the Russian market from German competition and to find export markets in China and the Near East. These considerations might not loom large whilst Russia was itself an infant industrial power. But they could hardly be postponed indefinitely. At the same time, the inflow of foreign capital to finance government commitments, notably railway construction, and industrial investment, required a fine diplomatic balancing act in order to maintain peace and stability in Europe, and thus safeguard capital flows.

The delicate balance of European great power relations during the last decade of the nineteenth century could be disturbed in a number of ways. One possibility was that Russia might come to an understanding with Germany, thereby wrecking the best-laid plans of French diplomacy. A somewhat different issue arose in the Balkans, where slavic populations suffered under Austrian and Ottoman tutelage. Russia had intervened in 1877 in support of 'pan-slavism', but at heavy cost to state finances and (as War Minister Dmitrii Miliutin had feared) to military pride. No less disheartening were the tactics subsequently pursued by Britain and Austria, which revised the terms of the peace treaty agreed with Turkey. The Balkan problem, and with it the vexed question of Russian access through the Straits, remained a powder keg. Still more uncertain was the diplomacy of Russia beyond the European mainland. Russia had huge territorial borders to defend. In addition, elements within the imperial bureaucracy tolerated and (in some instances) demanded that Russia extend its influence into Persia, Afghanistan and the Far East. The burden of maintaining a high profile on the European mainland could be shared with Russia's new-found ally. But the costs of engaging Britain in the Near East and Japan or China in Manchuria would inevitably be incurred by Russia alone.

After the humiliating experience of the Crimean War, the tsarist regime sought to avoid further military operations in Europe. The War Ministry concentrated instead on army reform. During the early 1870s, Miliutin set in motion a series of changes in military organization and administration, slashing the normal term of military service to five years and creating a trained reserve. These far-reaching reforms did not reach fruition before Russia became embroiled in war against Turkey. Russia's armed forces revealed themselves to be woefully unprepared. Their poor performance in battle reflected abject generalship, chronic deficiencies in military procurement and supply and the poor quality of Russian small arms – all of them problems that had been in evidence during the Crimean War. The Miliutin reforms had been designed to create a better trained army: clearly, they had a long way to go before they could bear fruit. Only the greatly inferior opposing forces saved the Russian army from the beating it could otherwise have expected.[8]

A widespread belief in Russia's relative economic weakness and potential political instability, together with the memory of recent military humiliation, compelled Russian decision makers to counsel moderation in Russian diplomacy. The Minister of Finances also quashed any hope of re-equipment, rearmament and further military reform. The 1899 conference at The Hague represented the high-water mark of this disengagement from the 'struggle for mastery' in Europe. But new diplomatic initiatives threatened to call forth fresh military commitments. The alliance with France was the cornerstone of Russian defence policy in Europe during the last decade of the nineteenth century. The protocols stipulated that Russia would come to the aid of France, if France were attacked by Germany. The French government agreed to assist Russia in similar circumstances. Both parties committed themselves to mobilize their troops in the event of a German attack. The military convention also required the French and Russian general staffs to liaise over military strategy. During the final years of the nineteenth century, Russia strengthened its defences on the western border with Germany as best it could. However, Russian policy was driven by nothing more ambitious than a desire to keep the French reasonably happy. Successive ministers of war reminded anyone who would listen of the commitments into which Russia had entered, but political circumstances deprived them of serious influence in goverment. Russia's defence policy in Europe was driven by budgetary policy, not the other way round.[9]

It was a different story in the Far East, where Witte's policy of economic expansion brought imperial Russia face to face with Japan, which had ambitions of its own on the mainland. Conventional wisdom in St Petersburg held that the considerations that dictated caution in central Europe did not apply in the Far East, because Japan was not a power of any significance. The prospect of conflict with the European powers over Manchuria seemed remote, and this perception gave the tsarist government the kind of freedom of action which it was denied in the west. China's weakness during the 1890s enabled Russia to gain a foothold in the Liaotung peninsula. In 1895, international pressure forced Japan to give up its territorial conquests there, and Russia obtained a long-term lease on the cherished warm water facilities of Port Arthur. But these diplomatic gains brought with them further responsibilities that could not easily be shirked. By the mid-1890s, resources had to be found to defend these new interests in the Far East. This meant additional troops in Manchuria, stronger fortifications at Port Arthur and a bigger Pacific fleet. The government also projected a railway that would link the trans-Siberian line with the heartland of Manchuria. Unlike some of the commitments into which Russia entered in Europe, the burden of financing these developments could not be shared with France.[10]

Diplomatic manoeuvres in Europe during the late nineteenth century gave rise to a new wave of militarism. By the early 1890s, Russian military experts had excellent knowledge of the scale and character of European rearmament. The supply of magazine rifles to the continental armies made corresponding improvements in the Russian army imperative. Between 1888 and 1891, the War Ministry began to implement a plan for the re-equipment of the Russian army with modern rifles. The change proved to be a great success: the new Mosin rifle revealed itself in trials to be far superior to the alternative versions available. The military also planned to modernize field artillery, by introducing pieces that had a longer range, and to install new, large-calibre ordnance in the fortresses on the western frontier. Minister of War P.S. Vannovskii instituted a competition to find an improved version of field artillery. By 1900, production of the new artillery pieces was well under way, at the Putilov factory. The War Ministry also increased the number of artillery batteries per battalion. In fortress artillery, the main innovation consisted in replacing old pieces with steel guns (1895), but progress was held up by a lack of funds. These were not half-hearted measures, although they neither compensated for a decade of relative neglect nor matched the advances being made in western Europe.[11]

General A. N. Kuropatkin, who replaced Vannovskii as Minister of War in 1898, had strong reservations about the impact of Witte's policy in the Far East: 'this diversion of funds to the Far East is now a great obstacle to the satisfaction of many essential needs of our army, and hinders our taking measures towards the further strengthening of our military position on the western front, which is most important to us'. Kuropatkin argued that naval rearmament had already begun to siphon funds from the urgent programme to reconstruct the land forces in Europe. If Witte were allowed to pursue an expansionist policy in the Far East, he at least had the duty to provide additional funds for troop deployments on the border with Manchuria. The Minister of Finances conceded this point in a report to the Tsar in 1895. The implications of Russian expansionism soon made themselves felt. In 1900, Russia dispatched troops to pacify Manchuria and protect Russian property against the Boxer rebels. Four years later, war broke out against Japan.[12]

Whether or not Russia developed diplomatic ambitions beyond the mainland of Europe, the possession of a navy implied a willingness to engage with the supreme maritime power, Britain, and to protect Russian interests in its Far Eastern territory. Initially, however, the rationale for a Russian navy was defensive: that is, the objective was to secure the Russian capital from attack. The Straits posed more complex problems. Russia unilaterally embarked on the construction of a Black Sea fleet, in contravention of the terms of the peace settlement that followed the Crimean War. Not surprisingly, this decision provoked the British into flexing their maritime muscles. In 1878, Britain declared its readiness to send warships into the Black Sea, with or without an invitation from the Turkish authorities. By the end of the 1890s, British ships moved freely through the Straits. The possibility always remained that Russian vessels would find themselves in confrontation with British and Turkish naval forces.

The catastrophe that befell the Russian navy at Tsushima in 1905 might lead one to suppose that little had been done to improve the

Table 1.1. *Size and complement of the Russian fleet, 1899–1904*

	Battleships		Armoured cruisers		Light cruisers		Destroyers	
	A	B	A	B	A	B	A	B
1899	20	190	7	54	3	12	87	15
1904	20	221	14	111	9	22	118	22

Col. A: number of vessels; col. B: total tonnage (000 tons)
Source: *Rossiia v mirovoi voine*, Moscow, 1925, p. 95.

quality or quantity of military vessels in the preceding period. But this was not the case. Ever since the Japanese incursion into Korea and China in 1894–5, Russia had made plans to strengthen the Far Eastern fleet. Furthermore, the imminent modernization of the German navy, as a result of the initiatives taken by Admiral Tirpitz, lent additional urgency to the naval programme envisaged by the Tsar. Between 1895 and 1899, the Tsar approved additional expenditures on the fleet. The programme of naval rearmament provided for the construction of 12 destroyers (*eskadronnye bronenostsy*), 19 cruisers and up to 42 torpedo boat destroyers (*minonostsy*). Two-thirds of the total order went to Russian factories, as part of a deliberate policy to favour domestic suppliers. In 1898, exceptionally, the government ordered vessels from abroad, at a cost of 90 million rubles. In the thirteen years after 1894 the Russian fleet increased by nearly 680,000 tons, compared with 225,000 tons in the years 1881–94. The fleet became much more powerful. The total horsepower embodied in the new ships that entered service between 1894 and 1907 was four times greater than those completed between 1881 and 1894.[13]

The navy set a deadline for completion of the programme in 1904. By that time, the building programme had made considerable progress. But it had not proceeded without a hitch. Much of the addition to naval strength actually took place during 1904, reflecting the hurried completion of orders that should have been completed sooner. The government appointed a special commission under Vice-Admiral Ver-khovskii, a previous director of the Main Administration of Shipbuilding (GUKS), with a brief to accelerate the programme's completion. Meanwhile, the Japanese fleet prepared to launch a pre-emptive attack on Russia's Far Eastern fleet.[14]

The completion of the programme did not guarantee that the vessels would be put to effective use in battle. In theory, the navy was adequately provided with the vessels it required. But the training of officers and men left a lot to be desired. In a typical instance of mismanagement of resources, the navy enforced stringent economies on the use of coal and on the expenditure of artillery ammunition. These shortsighted measures deprived officers and men of the practical experience that might have saved them from catastrophe at Tsushima.[15]

The defence budget

The competing claims of defence and the economy were never more apparent than during the last two decades of the nineteenth century. The Russian army suffered a decade of relative underfunding during the 1880s and even the increased appropriations of the 1890s failed to compensate entirely for this fiscal neglect. The army budget increased in absolute terms, from an average of 261 million rubles (1890–4) to 302 million rubles (1895–9). Allocations to the navy increased from 47 million rubles to 71 million rubles, excluding an extraordinary appropriation of 90 million rubles in 1898. Taken at face value, the growth of the defence budget during the last decade of the nineteenth century suggested that spending was more than sufficient to meet the needs of the military. However, this level of expenditure represented a declining proportion of state funds. The military share of the total budget fell from 24 per cent during the first half of the decade (28 per cent, if we include the navy) to 19 per cent during the second half (24 per cent, including the navy). This proportionate decline reflected other pressing government commitments, notably expenditure on the construction and maintenance of the railway network. The construction of the trans-Siberian railway was but the most dramatic manifestation of railway mania, which testified to the superior bargaining power of the ministries of Finances and Transport. Whilst Russian military leaders stood to gain from the anticipated improvements in the speed with which troops could be mobilized in the railway age, this did not compensate for what they took to be a neglect of traditional priorities. The final straw came in 1899, when the government reimposed a ceiling on the War Ministry's budget, to remain in force over the next four years.[16]

The size of the Russian military budget was largely dictated by the number of conscripts. In 1890, the army comprised 878,000 officers and men, but within five years, as a result of growing commitments in the

Far East, it had grown to more than a million. This large army was a function of the sheer size and backwardness of the Empire: apart from the extensive frontiers to defend, to say nothing of the need to maintain troops in 'hostile' areas of the Empire, the huge distances involved made it difficult to mobilize men as quickly as Russia's potential adversaries. Only correspondingly greater numbers of men in uniform could compensate for these disadvantages. In addition, Russian conscripts were kept longer in uniform than their counterparts in western Europe, on the grounds that they needed longer training in the ways of war.[17]

The War Ministry incurred a significant cost in maintaining an army of this size. The military budget was severely stretched. Financial constraints meant that a far smaller proportion of Russian manpower received military training than elsewhere. Those men who were conscripted received a relatively meagre allowance. In an attempt to inflict on soldiers the burden of feeding and clothing themselves, the ministry supplied raw materials to the troops and obliged them to prepare food and manufacture boots and uniforms. In the absence of military accommodation, many men found whatever billets they could with local residents. In short, the War Ministry cut corners.[18]

Nor did the War Ministry manage the resources at its disposal in a manner that inspired confidence. Typical of this incompetence was the management of funds for the acquisition of raw materials. A great deal of money found its way into the pockets of a small circle of suppliers, who charged extortionate prices. The State Auditor urged the intendance officials in the Chief Quartermaster's Department (GIU) to enlist a greater range of suppliers, in order to stimulate competition and keep prices down, but without evident success. Collusion between suppliers was not the only problem. Officials in the GIU, like their counterparts in other agencies, received no special training and lacked interest in such matters as the quality of cloth and leather. An unscrupulous supplier did not find it difficult to bribe ill-paid officials. With the scarcity of resources available, the War Ministry could hardly afford the waste implied by this level of incompetence and corruption.[19]

The Russian army faced difficult choices when it came to defining spending priorities. In 1891, the War Ministry received funds to acquire the new Mosin rifle; appropriations were subsequently approved to strengthen the fortresses on the western frontier. The army also obtained extra funds – notwithstanding the financial straitjacket imposed in 1899 – for artillery and barrack construction. However, the army suffered in other respects, notably in the supply of heavy field artillery and fortress artillery, in which there was a shortfall by 1900 of more than 1,000 guns, or 15 per cent of the required norm. The average annual amount spent on fortresses between 1880 and 1900 came to no more than 18 million rubles, far below what was necessary to maintain all 23 fortresses in an adequate state.[20]

Yet, to argue that the tsarist defence effort as a whole suffered from underfunding before 1905 is to underplay the significance of spending on the imperial navy. During the 1880s, the naval budget increased steadily. After 1890, it increased at a much faster rate. Between 1891–5 and 1896–1900 total appropriations for the navy grew by around 52 per cent. Over the course of the next quinquennium the naval budget grew by a further 40 per cent, reaching the impressive sum of 107.4 million rubles by 1901–5. Unlike the army budget, which was divided between expenditures on manpower, horses, uniforms, equipment and armaments, the naval budget went overwhelmingly on the acquisition, repair and operating expenses of naval vessels. Yet, as with the War Ministry budget, poor accounting procedures meant that the imperial navy could have got better value for money from these appropriations. There is no evidence that naval officials pursued this possibility with any vigour, or even thought in these terms at all.

The cost of funding these defence programmes, as well as the expansion in troop numbers, was that the material living standards of officers and men failed to improve. Civilian ministers remained indifferent to this state of affairs, and argued that the quality of military life mattered less than the maintenance of civilian morale and living standards. Vyshnegradskii summed up the prevailing viewpoint in 1888, arguing that 'the welfare of the people, even if it implies a certain imperfection in the military establishment, will render more use in wartime than the most complete military preparedness of the army'. The Russian soldier, he went on to say, could only lay down his life once and would make a bigger contribution to the nation by developing its productive forces, thereby improving Russia's material foundations for war. Such men (Vyshnegradskii might have added) would also have a greater vested interest in the defence of their country. This was a valid argument and in the long term had much to commend it, but it hardly corresponded to the immediate problems of the Russian army. Given that Russia's military leadership was preparing for a brief war, a strong case could be made for spending additional resources on the improvement of conditions for the relatively small contingent of men who were likely to be exposed to the battlefield.

Instead, on the eve of the war against Japan, Russia ended up with the worst of all possible worlds. Men whose living conditions in civilian life left a lot to be desired, but who nevertheless played a crucial part in the peasant family economy found themselves abruptly immersed in a military world whose harshness owed much to the underfunding of basic facilities and services. Meanwhile, the men already in uniform saw no improvement in their conditions. In a society whose military commanders stressed the morale and commitment of the individual soldier, the Russian army suffered from an unhelpful allocation of resources.[21]

The defence industry: armaments and shipbuilding before 1904

The tsarist government spent substantial sums on food for the army, on fodder, pay, transfer payments and uniforms, as well as on barracks, equipment and military hardware. Confronted with this varied menu of requirements, one might be forgiven for thinking that Russian manufacturers supplied a wide range of goods to the armed forces. Nothing could be further from the truth. Before 1900, the Russian government did not normally supply its soldiers with manufactured goods, whether they be blankets, belts or biscuits. Russian troops were expected to feed and clothe themselves. Armaments and military vessels constituted a relatively small part of the total defence budget. However, they assumed disproportionate significance in discussions about defence capability, partly because the government exercised direct control over the manufacture of hardware and partly because military prowess in the machine age was so closely identified with armaments. To focus on armaments and shipbuilding is, therefore, to reflect the attention given to hardware in the corridors of the defence establishment.

The resources devoted to armaments impinged directly on the emergent industries of metalworking and machine-building, lending further justification to the study of military hardware. True, the impact of military spending on manufacturing industry and employment was not confined to the production of armaments and military vessels. Resources were also absorbed in the construction and maintenance of military installations, such as port facilities, military fortresses and barracks. In 1900, more than 60,000 workers were employed in these tasks. None the less, the substantial workforce engaged in military construction did not possess the significance that attached to armaments, the manufacture of which absorbed large amounts of fixed capital and engaged the energies of a more skilled and settled work-force.[22]

As elsewhere in Europe, a good deal of armaments production took place in state arsenals and dockyards. The state employed around 66,000 workers in shipbuilding and armaments production in 1900, making defence second only in importance to railway transport in state-owned enterprise. The role of the state in Russian armaments production had been consolidated over the course of two centuries. Between 1712 and 1719, Peter the Great established two shipyards, an armoury at Tula and a gunpowder works on the river Okhta, in the city that bore his name. For a century and a half, these enterprises, supplemented by the Izhevsk arsenal in the Urals, remained the cornerstone of the Russian defence industry. The government also procured artillery pieces from several privately-owned metallurgical factories that were scattered around the Urals.[23]

The administration of production was divided amongst three separate agencies: the Main Artillery Administration (GAU), under the aegis of the War Ministry; the Department of Mines (*Gornyi departament*), a branch of the Department (later Ministry) of Trade and Industry and thus part of the Ministry of Finances; and the Admiralty Administration, within the Navy Ministry. The GAU administered 18 separate enterprises (*tekhnicheskie artilleriiskie zavedeniia*), including 6 state armouries (*arsenaly*). The Department of Mines had overall charge of 13 ironworks, all but one of them located in the Urals. They included armament factories at Perm (Motovilikha) and Zlatoust. The navy maintained four shipyards, the Admiralty, Izhora, Obukhov and Baltic yards, as well as wharves and workshops in Kronstadt, Sevastopol and Nikolaev.[24]

At the beginning of the twentieth century, only a small number of specialist defence firms were to be found in private hands. Without doubt, pride of place before 1900 belonged to the Putilov Company. Its primacy was unaffected by the fact that a number of other general engineering firms also accepted military contracts from time to time. None of them specialized in armaments work. In shipbuilding, only the Nevskii Company and the Nikolaev Company could claim to be of any significance. Both enjoyed mixed fortunes: as we shall see, the Nikolaev yards struggled to stay afloat, and eventually fell into receivership, whilst a question-mark always hung over Nevskii's long-term viability as a private venture. To survive in the fragile Russian defence market required patience, good fortune and a level of government largesse that could not be taken for granted. For these reasons, state-owned enterprise had the field virtually to itself.[25]

Occupying centre stage in the tsarist defence industry for much of the nineteenth century were the renowned state armouries of Tula and Izhevsk. They had not always been owned and administered directly by the state. Izhevsk had been leased to private entrepreneurs for a brief spell during the 1870s and early 1880s, before returning to state control. The Tula armoury also had a somewhat chequered history, having been leased to military officials during the 1860s. These arrangements proved short-lived and by the 1870s the Tula factory was also back in state hands. The state armouries were joined by other government-owned factories producing shell, ordnance and cartridges, as well as special steel. In 1900, Tula employed just over 7,000 workers. The Izhevsk works was slightly larger, employing around 8,000 workers during the 1890s. The Sestroretsk armoury, close to St Petersburg employed 1,725 men in 1900, but the labour force shrank to just over 1,000 three years later.[26]

The Tula armoury was exceptional in being located in the central industrial region: most state arsenals and armouries were situated either in the Urals or in or near Russia's chief port and capital city, St Petersburg. Tula enjoyed a high status both in Russia and further afield. Its reputation depended largely on the ability of the local labour force to retain their skills under varying management regimes. The manufacture of rifles took place in a centralized plant. Management had experimented briefly with a putting-out system, under which rifles were produced by craftsmen in surrounding villages. However, the complex tasks associated with the production of the Mosin rifle during the 1890s made it imperative for management to exercise closer supervision over the labour process, the implications of which are considered below.[27]

It was difficult to envisage a more isolated plant than that of Izhevsk. The nearest rail link was 150km away (on the Perm–St Petersburg line) and even the nearest navigable river could only be reached after a trek of over 40km. Location in the Urals offered reasonably convenient access to supplies of iron, but the distance from central Russia made it difficult and costly to send finished products to their destination. Inhospitable conditions also made the Urals an unattractive posting for government officials. Management had the unenviable task of ensuring that adequate stocks of materials and other supplies were on hand during the long winter months, when the factory was virtually cut off from the outside world. Coking coal arrived from south Russia and pig iron from the Urals ironworks; only fuel and construction materials were in abundance, provided by the forests that surrounded the factory. The construction of a proper rail link did not take place until the First World War, when a new line connected the factory with the towns of Kazan and Sarapul. Notwithstanding these difficulties – perhaps even because of them – the factory worked reasonably smoothly and developed an excellent reputation. The steel mill produced a high-quality product, which laid the basis for a reliable and effective finished product from the ordnance shop. Wherever possible, the plant concentrated on mass production: Izhevsk 'never chased after private work under the influence of a temporary shortage of work, but instead specialized in the mass manufacture of a definite range of munitions and brought this production to perfection from a qualitative and technical-organization point of view'.[28]

The state ironworks in the Urals, administered by a different authority, supplied shell and steel to the army and navy. Most of these factories had been in existence since the eighteenth century. They had extensive tracts of forest land, and therefore charcoal, at their disposal. Between them, the twelve ironworks supported a huge number of workers. In 1900, more than 35,000 men and women lived on plots of land to which many of them had received title during the 1870s. The armaments factory at Motovilikha and the ironworks at Votkinsk and Zlatoust employed almost three-fifths of the total labour force.[29]

Motovilikha was in many respects the jewel in the crown of Russian ordnance factories. It found itself in an anomalous position. Although administered by the Department of Mines, it had no iron foundry and purchased bar and billets from the other state ironworks. As a major supplier of ordnance and artillery ammunition, logic dictated that it should have come under the control of the Artillery Administration, but the Department of Mines was reluctant to relinquish control. In 1900, it received one-quarter of all orders given to the state ironworks, a position it retained in the early twentieth century. Its location gave it great advantages over comparable factories. Unlike Putilov and Obukhov, for instance, it did not depend on imports of coal and deliveries of iron and steel from distant parts of the Empire. The disruption of foreign trade by a blockade or the dislocation of transport would not directly affect production at Perm. In addition, Motovilikha produced high-quality guns and an advanced armour and deck-piercing shell, manufactured under licence from Krupp. The other significant armaments producer at Zlatoust, in the south of the Urals, produced shell and rifles, accounting for 14 per cent of orders allocated

to state ironworks in 1900. The remaining factories were not in themselves of great significance to the defence effort, although some of
them supplied iron and steel shapes to Motovilikha and Zlatoust and
to other defence producers in the state sector, such as Obukhov and
the nearby armoury at Izhevsk.[30]

Ordnance production offered the main outlet for private enterprise,
in the shape of the world-famous Putilov Company. Putilov had been
established during the late 1860s, largely to supply the growing market
in rolling-stock. The industrialization boom during the 1890s marked
the turning point in the fortunes of the firm. New share issues brought
total share and bonded capital up to a massive 20 million rubles by
1900. The labour force vitually quadrupled, reaching 12,400 in 1900.
Putilov was traditionally identified with government orders. Railway
products accounted for more than half the total output. But the firm
maintained an interest in other types of government contract work. By
1900, Putilov had begun to manufacture new artillery pieces, borrowing from government to finance the expansion of plant. The State
Auditor entertained the hope that orders for new 3-inch artillery
would go to Obukhov, which promised to undercut Putilov by at least
13 per cent. But Putilov offered a superior product. Hedging its bets,
the War Ministry ordered guns from both suppliers.[31]

The example of ordnance production demonstrates that the tsarist
government did not willingly renounce control of armaments production. Putilov had to share its contracts with the state-owned St
Petersburg Ordnance factory, as well as with Motovilikha and
Obukhov. A similar story emerges in the supply of cartridges. Complaints during the war against Turkey about the quality of the product
from the state-owned cartridge works in St Petersburg created an
opening for private enterprise. In 1880, the Tula Copper and Cartridge
Company appeared on the scene, helped by a generous advance from
the GAU. No doubt, the owners of the new company hoped to recruit
skilled workers from a town already familiar with armaments production. But initial expectations were quickly dashed as the firm ran
into difficulties, and only substantial government aid helped it to
survive. Before long, the company moved into civilian products.
However, the adoption of the Mosin rifle in 1891 obliged the army to
order new cartridges, and the Tula Cartridge Company seized this
fresh opportunity. Finding the government less than receptive to its
overtures (the government decided to build a second state factory, at
Lugansk), the firm reconstituted itself as a joint-stock company. By
1900, with fresh capital at its disposal, the Tula company had the

capacity to manufacture up to 50,000 cartridges per annum, fewer than at St Petersburg, but greater than Lugansk. Another relatively new firm, the Schlüsselburg company, entered the field during the 1880s, trading on its ability to provide a new product, smokeless powder.[32]

The defence market did not provide sufficient work for state enterprise, let alone for the private firms. The three armouries were kept busy by the manufacture of the new rifle, but it was a different story elsewhere. Government regulations permitted the Urals ironworks to take on civilian contracts, provided that they did not interfere with work on government contracts. In 1900, trade orders generated more than a quarter of total output. The proportion rose to two-fifths at Votkinsk, which supplied locomotives to private railway companies.[33] In the private sector, several engineering firms offered their services during the last quarter of the nineteenth century, but they could not afford to specialize in defence production. Major companies, such as Sormovo, Kolomna and Phoenix, as well as newcomers, such as Lessner, dabbled in the manufacture of shell. Even Putilov found it impossible to specialize in defence production. These firms had to bide their time until they could become more than part-time members of the arms industry.

The Russian shipbuilding industry had a still more chequered history. At the end of the nineteenth century, as at the beginning, the industry was dominated by state-owned yards established by Peter the Great. Private enterprise flourished briefly after the Crimean War, but by 1900 most of the ventures had either collapsed or been taken into state hands. Many officials within the navy remained ill-disposed towards private enterprise and were inclined to ignore its claims to be taken seriously. By 1900, only one firm, on the Black Sea, had emerged as a genuine rival to the state yards.

During the first half of the nineteenth century, state shipyards gradually ceded their position as suppliers of military vessels to foreign yards. The Crimean War shook the complacency of the Admiralty and released the shipbuilding industry from its lengthy torpor, because the navy switched from sail to ironclad vessels, with steam and screw propulsion.[34] Instead of reviving the flagging fortunes of the state yards, these opportunities encouraged new firms to enter the market. The Baltic Shipbuilding Company and Nevskii Shipbuilders were both founded in 1857, the former by Russian engineers and the latter by a Scottish engineer and his partner, an English sugar merchant. But their hopes were dashed when orders dried up during the later 1860s. The Baltic yards sank deeper and deeper into debt. The government allowed a new private owner to take over, but the volume of orders once again proved insufficient to sustain profitability, and the firm collapsed ignominiously in 1876, with debts of three million rubles.[35]

This time the government was forced to step in. New statutes, approved in 1877, announced the formation of the Russian Baltic Ironworks and Machine Company, three-quarters of whose shares were owned by the Admiralty. The new company limped on year after year, with contracts to supply thirty torpedo boats. During the 1880s, it recorded a profit for the first time and began to supply a range of products, including armoured cruisers and marine engines. Throughout this period, management made no claims on shareholders for additional funds; instead, the firm relied upon a flow of government orders to provide the resources to fund operations. Eventually, the Admiralty took the yards over completely in 1894. Subsequently, after three decades of fluctuating fortunes, the Baltic yards enjoyed some prosperity, thanks to the stimulus given to Russian shipbuilding by the programmes launched in 1895 and 1898. Between 1894 and 1903, investment in new buildings, machinery and other items amounted to close on five million rubles. Simultaneously, the factory settled its outstanding debts and created a substantial reserve and amortization fund. The value of capital stock in the Baltic yards more than trebled during the 1890s (table 1.2). By 1900, the Baltic yards were equipped with a modern engineering shop, a foundry, and a new slipway. The yards produced high-quality steel forgings and boiler fittings. By producing virtually all auxiliary items on site, management avoided the necessity to subcontract, allowing management to maintain a much tighter control over costs. At the beginning of the new century, the Baltic yards were the most powerful and modern in Russia, testimony to the fact that government administration was not incompatible with economic progress.[36]

The fortunes of other state yards were equally mixed. During the 1880s, two of the oldest shipyards ('Galernyi ostrov' and 'New Admiralty'), had been leased to the privately owned Franco-Russian Company, whose owners required a shipbuilding facility to add to their boiler-making shops. However, they reverted to state control during the following decade.[37]

The instability that characterized the Russian shipbuilding industry was nowhere more clearly revealed than in the case of Nevskii Shipbuilders. Nominally in the private sector, Nevskii had few genuine claims to be regarded as a private venture. Most of its shares had been

Table 1.2. *Baltic Shipbuilding Company, 1877–1903: selected indicators*

	Average annual tonnage completed (tons)	Assets* (million rubles)
1877–84	3,100	
1885–93	3,550	
1894–1903	10,122	
1894		1.67
1898		5.75
1902		5.94
1906		6.63

* Insured value
Sources: col. 1 from N. I. Dmitriev and V. V. Kolpychev, *Sudostroitel'nye zavody i sudostroenie v Rossii i za granitsei*, St Petersburg, 1909, p. 902; col. 2 from TsGAVMF, f.420, op.1, d.188, 1.111.

held since the 1880s by the State Bank, whose representatives sat on the board of directors. Nevskii's difficulties were largely caused by its geographical setting. Located on the left bank of the river Neva, the ships it built had to negotiate the bridges in St Petersburg, before making for the open sea; the construction of large vessels was out of the question. None the less, the yards were kept busy, building 21 destroyers and 36 other vessels, mostly high-speed boats, between 1890 and 1906. From a technical point of view, the factory was reasonably well equipped. Originally built as a 'universal' factory, it manufactured steel, in addition to marine engines and ship hulls. But the flow of work from one shop to another was haphazard, and there was a good deal of potential for improved productivity.[38]

The tsarist government also maintained a dockyard at Nikolaev on the Black Sea, but this yard stagnated in the aftermath of the Crimean War, the victim of government cutbacks and closure of the Mediterranean to warships. In 1895, however, a group of Belgian financiers set up a rival venture, the Nikolaev Shipbuilders, Engineering Works and Foundry, with an initial investment of five million rubles. The new firm benefited at once from the shipbuilding programme, rapidly establishing a reputation as a supplier of vessels to the Russian navy, as well as other items to private customers, who accounted for a quarter of all output in 1900. The Nikolaev factory, like Nevskii, boasted an integrated set of facilities. Apart from the dockyards themselves, Nikolaev consisted of six separate workshops: a bridge and boiler shop, a

Table 1.3. *Nikolaev Shipbuilding Company, 1897–1904: selected indicators*

	Gross output (million rubles)	Labour force
1897–8	2.80	3,000
1898–9	3.45	2,650
1899–1900	4.01	2,250
1900–1	3.42	2,140
1901–2	4.06	1,906
1902–3	4.38	2,344
1903–4	5.70	2,492

Sources: TsGAVMF, f.512, op.1, d.1781, 11.9ob., 21ob., 29ob.; f.512, op.1, d.1782, 11.1–2ob.

forging shop, a castings section (copper and pig iron), a steel mill, an engineering section (for the manufacture of turbines) and a wagon-producing facility. Arranged in sequence, these workshops were served by a single railway track, unlike most of the yards in the Baltic, where different shops were often laid out in a chaotic fashion. The Nikolaev yards were also served by a single power generator, unique in Russian shipbuilding in 1900. The slipway was modern and well-equipped and the docks could handle two large or four small vessels at any one time.[39]

Investment, coupled with sharp cuts in the labour force after 1897 held the key to the impressive financial performance at the Nikolaev yards. Between 1897 and 1902, the company reduced its labour force by a third, whilst the value of output began to rise. As the shipbuilding programme reached a climax, labour productivity at the Nikolaev yards more than doubled (table 1.3). However, as the new century dawned, a question-mark hung over the future of the entire industry, given the limited tasks envisaged for shipbuilders, once the 1895–9 construction programme was completed. Cutbacks seemed inevitable in state and private yards alike.

The creation of the kind of capacity described above generated considerable potential for armaments production. Whether that capacity could be exploited efficiently was another matter. Material inputs might be supplied to customers in the required amounts – the growth of basic industries helped to overcome this uncertainty – but the effective utilization of those inputs was a different matter. It might not be difficult to recruit workers from the pool of migrant labour in Russia. But to train and supervise them, in order to maintain the quality of work required in a modern armament industry was likely to prove a much more daunting task. How well did those responsible for armament production at enterprise level use the resources at their disposal before 1904?

The organization of the industry did not make the tasks of management any easier to confront. The armament industry did not form an integrated whole. Although owned and administered by the tsarist state, arsenals and government dockyards demonstrated no tendency towards collaboration; nor did officials encourage them to do so. The regulations by which the managers of these enterprises were forced to abide made no reference to formal cooperation. Admittedly, the three state armouries coordinated activity to the extent that the parts produced in one workshop were interchangeable with those produced at another. Links were also established between the armouries and the Izhevsk works, which supplied them with steel shapes for the manufacture of rifle barrels. But other factories do not appear to have coordinated their affairs to anything like the same extent, let alone to have standardized their products. The two factories that manufactured cartridges, in St Petersburg and Lugansk (established in 1895), instituted little or no technical collaboration. The two major armaments factories in the Urals, at Motovilikha and Zlatoust, were administered by the Department of Mines, and no mechanism was in place to encourage the manager of one enterprise to liaise with his opposite number in another, even if both factories were engaged on similar programmes. This vacuum hardly made for rational decision-making in the Russian armament industry.[40]

Such striking indifference towards collaboration, let alone integration in the state sector stood in sharp contrast to the bureaucratic efforts that were made to prescribe the functions and responsibilities of management. The regulations published by the Main Artillery Administration (GAU) set down in elaborate detail how its enterprises were to be managed. The GAU appointed directors (*nachal'niki*) to manage its factories. The director in turn appointed an 'economic committee' which was responsible for the day to day management of the enterprise. Its members were not permitted to serve for more than three years, a provision designed to lessen the chance that suppliers would establish a familiar and potentially corrupt relationship with members of the administration. By the same token, of course, any expertise that had begun to emerge was rapidly dissipated. The rights and responsibilities of the committee were strictly limited. It supervised work in progress, but had no right to discuss technical questions, such as the design and specification of weapons, which were the province of a separate committee. The economic committee could also propose and prepare plans for the extension of the plant. Its other main function was to arrange for the purchase of raw materials. In order to demonstrate how seriously it took this particular issue, the GAU placed its own nominee on the committee, to ensure that committee members adhered strictly to the War Ministry's guidelines on the prices at which raw materials might be procured. The economic committee could thus take little initiative in procurement of raw materials.[41]

Other boards were charged with responsibility for technical questions and for the supervision of the labour force. The technical committee, chaired by the director, controlled all matters directly relating to the production and testing of finished goods, as well as the care and refurbishment of tools and other equipment. The personnel committee gave the director the right to hire and fire workers, to determine wage and piece rates and to fix the hours of work. His autonomy in this sphere contrasted sharply with the constraints to which he was subject in respect of procurement prices.

These regulations created a number of difficulties. One concerned the lack of clear demarcation of responsibilities between the technical and the economic committees, regarding such matters as work in progress and the acquisition and use of tools. This hardly promoted the smooth running of the business, which likely depended upon the authority and competence of the director. Another problem derived from the regulations on the procurement of inputs. Where large sums were involved, the administration had to get prior approval from the relevant department of the War Ministry. Only in the case of small orders, where sums of 5,000 rubles or less were involved, did the economic committee have slightly more scope for independent initiative. This provision encouraged the factory to order supplies in small quantities, the source of much friction between the management and its suppliers, who regularly complained about lack of forward planning (*planomernost'*) among their clients. Finally, the regulations afforded the director only limited room for manoeuvre. He received his annual budget from higher authority and could not deviate from the accompanying schedule of expenditure. In normal circumstances, this lack of flexibility might be irritating, but not damaging to the medium or long-term performance or viability of the enterprise. But the frustration felt by managers can easily be imagined: a piece of equipment that broke down could only be repaired or replaced if and when the following year's estimates provided the necessary funds. The directors of the GAU enterprises, who were poorly rewarded for their services, had a thankless task. They were inundated with paper-work: the GAU regulations were accompanied by 250 different forms that the director was expected to complete, some of them daily! Few of these procedures contributed to the efficient operation of the armouries and factories under GAU control.

The Urals ironworks were administered by the Department of Mines, not by the GAU. This arrangement made little administrative sense where the armament factories at Perm and Zlatoust were concerned. The bureaucratic regulations under which they laboured did not differ in essentials from those that applied to state arsenals. Management exercised little scope for independent judgement in such key areas as finance and supply, and kept no proper check on production costs or the value of work in progress. The use of capital equipment was badly supervised. Enterprises made no allowance for the depreciation of capital equipment, simply notifying repairs and replacements to the central administration, in order to obtain the necessary credits in the following financial year.[42]

As the century drew to a close, questions began to be asked about these procedures. In particular, the internal organization and performance of the state shipyards excited a good deal of critical comment. The Admiralty yards, for example, comprised two quite separate facilities, for no good reason. Each yard had an engineering and shipbuilding section, separately managed, giving rise to excessive overhead costs. In practice, work in progress constantly passed between the two yards, but this only caused protracted delays. The director with overall administrative responsibility failed to address this chaotic state of affairs, displaying more interest in the condition of the surrounding gardens than in the affairs of his shipyards. In 1900, the government remedied this confused state of affairs, by appointing a Chief Ship-building Engineer, with the task of ensuring that the two yards adopted similar methods of work. This initiative reduced production costs by 10 per cent and cut the time taken to complete contracts by an even greater margin. Here, surely, was a model for the defence indus-try as a whole. But the need to find jobs for retired army officers as managers, and the bureaucratic fondness of regulation, were powerful inducements to maintain the status quo.[43]

The acquisition of private yards during the 1890s posed problems for the imperial government. Would they be incorporated into the exist-ing regulations for state enterprise, or would they retain elements of commercial management? In 1898, the State Auditor pressed for commercial principles to be maintained at the Baltic and Obukhov yards and to be extended to the Izhora and Admiralty yards. The Baltic yards operated within a prescribed budget, receiving no further assistance from the Treasury during the financial year. However, the reform cut little ice with the mandarins in the defence ministries, who abided by regulations that specified different priorities: 'the state requires of its factories not dividends, but good quality products'. The Baltic yards, with their tradition of self-finance and independence of the Treasury, might represent the ideal to which other government dockyards should aspire; but this ideal corresponded more to the wishes of the finance departments than it did to those of defence chiefs. As the new century dawned, those in charge of government enterprises were bathed in a glow of complacency. To be fair, this attribute extended to virtually all elements of the old regime.[44]

The Russian armament industry had, since its inception in the eighteenth century, relied chiefly on unfree labour. The state directed military recruits to its arsenals and dockyards and required that their children serve in turn. Workers conscripted in this way were liable to be discharged once they had completed their military service. In practice, many of them stayed on. Most workers retained plots of land which they had been granted, in return for being attached to a particular armoury or ironworks. To leave one's place of work, therefore, disrupted a well-entrenched family economy; understandably, few workers were prepared to make that sacrifice. The formal emancipation from compulsory labour at government enterprises took place in 1862, at which time around two-thirds of Russian shipbuilding workers belonged to the category of bonded labour. Notwithstanding the abolition of unfree labour, some of its features – notably a sense of obligation towards the labour force – persisted.[45]

The Russian armament industry employed around 75,000 workers in 1900, making it one of the largest sectors of the industrial economy.[46] This total included 27,000 workers in factories and arsenals administered by the GAU, around 25,000 workers in the Urals ironworks and 14,000 workers in government dockyards. The labour force employed in the private sector barely amounted to 9,000 workers, most of them in private shipyards. Fewer than 2,000 were employed on armaments work in general engineering plants. Armaments accounted for about one-fifth of the labour force in metallurgy, metalworking and machine-building combined, or around 4 per cent of the entire industrial labour force. This appears to have been a much higher proportion than in armaments industries elsewhere in Europe. The labour force effectively engaged across the entire range of defence production was considerably higher than these figures indicate. A further 60,000 workers were occupied in various military construction and engineering projects, including work on barracks and fortresses. But even the inclusion of these workers does not exhaust the numbers actually employed in defence production at any one time. No one stopped to count the contingents of soldiers who manufactured basic military equipment, such as uniforms and boots. If these items had been factory-made, total employment in defence production would have climbed much higher. For present purposes, however, it is the permanent labour force in defence industry that claims our attention. What accounts for this high level of employment, and to what extent did workers' experience conform to that of their counterparts in other branches of industry?[47]

One explanation for the high level of employment in armament production is that the poor level of labour productivity compelled employers to substitute quantity for quality. Generally speaking, labour productivity in manufacturing industry compared unfavourably with other European economies. Basic education left a lot to be desired, and the dearth of training programmes did nothing to improve the aptitude and skill of successive generations of workers, as contemporaries noted. Employers and work supervisors tended to see things differently, pinning the blame on the 'pre-industrial' work habits of the Russian workers, who took too many holidays, drank to excess and treated materials and equipment far too casually.

Nevertheless, the causal link between manning levels and labour productivity is not clear cut. Russian entrepreneurs might have gone out of their way to employ large numbers, in order to offset the poor quality of new recruits. But low labour productivity – defined in this context as gross output per person – may have been the result of a high employment regime, not its cause. In the uncertain world of Russian industry, where supplies were erratic and production schedules difficult to plan, employers retained large numbers of workers to cope with sudden upsurges in the pace of production. Furthermore, it was cheaper to employ unskilled labour in various tasks (such as fetching and carrying materials within the enterprise) than to mechanize these auxiliary processes. Russian enterprises tended for these reasons to be larger than their equivalents elsewhere in Europe.[48]

These considerations apply still more forcefully to the armaments industry. As in other branches of industry, unskilled workers could be used in abundance to transfer work in progress from one part of the factory to another. But the specific characteristics of armaments production tended to promote a high employment regime. A 'reserve army' offered managers a means of insuring themselves against a sudden influx of orders or an abrupt change in specifications, and enabled them to handle a sudden consignment of raw materials. By recruiting and retaining a large labour force, management could maintain a cushion against such emergencies and reduce the risks of incurring a penalty for late delivery.

There were other reasons for the high level of employment in this sector of industry. Some workers in the state sector exercised considerable power on the shopfloor, enabling them to inflate manning levels. Contemporaries noted that workers at state shipyards habitually slowed down the pace of work, lest they be laid off when the administration had exhausted its annual credit from the Treasury. At Motovilikha, workers reportedly organized tasks in such a way as to maximize the number of positions available to workers: 'all power [wrote an inspector in 1906] is in the hands of semi-literate artisans'. The famous Tula armoury was probably an exception: towards the end of the nineteenth century, management had been able to confront the power of labour, and work practices became a byword for close supervision. Elsewhere, workers enjoyed greater autonomy, affording them scope to influence employment levels.[49]

State enterprises, in general, were suffused by a culture of patriarchy. This patriarchal tradition had its roots in eighteenth-century practice, which dictated that workers should be kept on, in good and bad times alike, subject to the availability of funds earmarked for the completion of a given project. Even when such funds were depleted, workers were transferred to other tasks, including the maintenance of factory buildings. The persistence of this doctrine inevitably tended to inflate levels of employment, particularly at the state ironworks.[50]

One further consideration needs to be mentioned, in connection with the prevailing paternalist ethos. The tsarist government restricted the number of hours worked in state industry. Regulations introduced in 1861 limited the working day at the state shipyards to ten hours. No equivalent limitation was placed on the number of hours worked in the private sector. On average, Russian factory workers spent between twelve and thirteen hours on the shopfloor during the 1880s. The government only intervened to regulate hours of work in 1897, when the government stipulated a maximum of eleven and a half hours in factory industry. None the less, this legislation continued to confer a clear advantage on employees in the state sector. In rejecting the punishing routine that applied to workers in the private sector, the government deliberately committed itself to a high level of employment in many of the enterprises under its jurisdiction.[51]

The numbers employed in armament production imply a considerable effort in recruiting and retaining factory labour. The recruitment of unskilled workers posed relatively few problems. Young men were often drawn from the locality: at the Sormovo engineering plant, close to Nizhnii Novgorod, two in five workers arrived from nearby villages. Others came from further afield. The rapid expansion of factory employment in St Petersburg between 1897 and 1900 was made possible by immigration from the adjacent provinces of Tver, Yaroslavl and Novgorod. These men, who retained significant links with the family farm, were initially given ancillary and mundane tasks, such as carting and loading materials. Many workers bribed recruiting agents or foremen, in the hope of being taken on.[52]

The recruitment and retention of skilled labour posed far greater problems. In order to maintain the flow of skilled workers, managers set up craft schools on factory premises and took on children as they completed their education. The management of government arsenals attached particular significance to this initiative, and instituted vocational schools at Izhevsk in 1877, Tula in 1894 and at Sestroretsk in 1899. Izhora shipyards established a similar school in 1889, offering five years' basic education to employees' sons, as well as giving them priority when vacancies arose. Not that these schools necessarily offered an adequate education. Petitions presented to the management of the Sestroretsk arsenal during the 1905 revolution indicated that these schools were staffed by poor teachers, who had failed to find jobs elsewhere. The fact that workers contributed financially to the maintenance of such schools only served to intensify the grievance. Elsewhere, those in charge of state arsenals, cartridge and tube works instituted factory schools for the children of workers. Children who enrolled at these schools pursued a less vocational curriculum.[53]

These arrangements created a constantly replenished pool of semi-skilled labour upon which the plant managers could draw. Recruiting the children of factory workers also helped to overcome problems of adaptation that bedevilled management elsewhere in Russian industry. The law allowed children to start work at the age of fifteen. In 'exceptional circumstances', children as young as twelve were employed, provided that they could read and write, that the work was not dangerous and they worked alongside their parents. Government dockyards also provided training for the children of employees, who were given preference when job vacancies were filled. The need to recruit young workers already in possession of basic skills remained the paramount concern. By contrast, only a handful of factories in the private sector established schools for workers' children.[54]

Managers of state yards traditionally tried to retain workers from one year to the next, particularly if their skills made them difficult to replace. Prolonged lulls in armaments production made this a difficult strategy to sustain. During the 1880s and late 1890s, the state armouries tended to lose labour to the private sector or to construction projects. In 1882, having completed work on a new rifle, workers at Sestroretsk departed for jobs in the engineering industry in the Russian capital. Workers left Izhevsk and took labouring jobs on the trans-Siberian railway. Tula's armourers turned to the manufacture of iron goods, samovars and musical instruments. Some of these workshops became familiar and well-established landmarks, such that when master craftsmen returned to the armoury they continued to employ workers on their own account. Workers who had little or no skill fared worse, being forced to take poorly-paid jobs in St Petersburg or other towns and cities, unless they could persuade the foreman to retain their services.[55]

The managerial strategies described above tended to induce in workers a sense of loyalty to particular enterprises. A survey of the Baltic shipyards in January 1906 revealed that only 14 per cent of the labour force had served for less than twelve months. More than half had been employed for between one and five years, whilst more than a quarter had worked for between five and ten years. One worker in ten had been with the yards for more than a decade. The enquiry uncovered a higher degree of loyalty amongst fitters, lathe operators and joiners, in common with other parts of the St Petersburg engineering industry. The relative loyalty at the Baltic yards compared very favourably with other factories in Russia, where only 10 per cent of workers formed a permanent core, defined as five years' service or more. At Baltic, the equivalent figure was 35 per cent.[56] In the private sector, material incentives appear to have provided the chief reason for workers to remain with a particular company. At Sormovo, there was a close correlation between wage rates and length of service, longstanding employees being rewarded with higher wages.[57]

Welfare legislation and benefits confirmed the superior entitlements (and, therefore, status) of workers in the state sector. Since 1862, workers in military shipyards had been insured against accidental injury and death. A further four decades elapsed before the government, having overcome the objections of industrialists, legislated a compensation scheme for industrial workers in the private sector. According to the standard Soviet account, only one in ten factory workers was covered against accidental injury before 1903. If a worker in the government shipyards was injured as a result of an accident at work, the law required management to compensate the worker or his dependants. No attempt was made to apportion blame, and thus claims could not be dismissed by management on grounds of the worker's 'negligence'. Payments were made in accordance with a series of separate sliding-scales for masters, journeymen and apprentices. Provision of a slightly different kind existed for workers employed in the state ironworks. In 1857, the government agreed to compensate these workers for industrial accidents. Mutual benefit societies were established in 1861, to which all state workers were required to belong. Fresh legislation in May 1901 confirmed the relatively privileged position of workers in government employment: henceforth, they were covered against diseases contracted at work. If a worker submitted a claim for industrial injury, his own 'negligence' did not constitute grounds for dismissal of the claim. Finally, disability amongst this group of workers was judged in accordance with the more rigorous health standards required by the state; the claimant did not have to prove that he was unable to perform any kind of physical work. His claim for disability was therefore more likely to be settled.[58]

Some workers in the state sector were also provided with an old age pension. At the state ironworks, a scheme had been in force since 1861. In 1898, the Obukhov and Baltic yards introduced a compulsory pensions scheme. Management deducted three per cent from wages each month and created a fund from which payments were made to workers who retired after more than ten years' service. These provisions were extended to other government dockyards in April 1903. No equivalent statutory provision for old age existed at state armouries, but the Popov commission (see below) recommended that this anomaly be rectified. Managers of the armouries strongly supported this proposal, on the grounds that an old age pension would enable them to pay off elderly retainers (they failed to mention that it had not produced this result at state ironworks). In the private sector, meanwhile, the prevailing assumption was that the extended family would support retired workers, an attitude that reflected an increasingly outmoded view of the links between workers and the village.[59]

Government concern for the welfare of state employees surfaced in two extensive commissions of inquiry: the Kolokol'tsov report on shipyards, in 1896, and the Popov commission on state arsenals, which sat between October 1902 and March 1905. Both commissions recommended further improvements in conditions of work at state enterprises. The government responded to Kolokol'tsov in 1897, by stipulating a minimum and a maximum age for employment, setting increased wages and instituting a right of appeal over piece-rate payments. Significantly, the government also began to supervise workers more closely, by enforcing penalties for lateness or absenteeism. General Popov, the former director of Izhevsk, advised the War Ministry to cut the length of the working day to eight hours, to introduce a minimum wage and pension entitlements, to improve and extend basic facilities, such as accommodation, schooling and leisure provision. The outbreak of revolution in 1905 quickly resolved matters in Popov's favour.[60]

Thus, at the beginning of the twentieth century, the old regime provided a range of benefits for workers in government employment. Meanwhile, the government eschewed welfare legislation for workers in the private sector. Underlying this inaction was a belief that conditions of work ought to be a private matter, forming part of the contract between a worker and employer. A small number of factory inspectors had the right to monitor the observance of this contract, but their powers and numbers were limited. *In extremis*, the government might intervene, using force to deal with any serious outbreak of labour unrest in the private sector. But in its own enterprises, the culture of patriarchy proved resistant to change. In this respect, as in others, the government maintained a clear demarcation between the two forms of enterprise.[61]

Defence production and supply

In the decade prior to the Russo-Japanese War, the main tasks of the defence industry consisted in supplying the army with new rifles, manufacturing new calibres of artillery and producing vessels in accordance with the shipbuilding programme of 1898. Russian industry coped well with the first two tasks, but the last taxed the abilities of the domestic shipyards almost to the limit. Russian factories devoted little time to the manufacture of basic finished goods, such as uniforms, for which the Russian soldier himself was expected to assume responsibility.

The cornerstone of the rearmament programme during the 1890s was the re-equipment of the Russian army with the new Mosin rifle. In

1891, the three state armouries at Izhevsk, Tula and Sestroretsk contracted to supply half a million new rifles annually. This ambitious task
entailed huge outlays. The government set aside 155 million rubles to
instal new machine tools, most of them imported from Britain, France
and Sweden. Production of the new rifle continued throughout the
1890s. Ten years later, in 1901, the programme was finally completed, at
a total cost of 270 million rubles. The army hailed it as a great success;
so, too, despite the expense involved, did the State Auditor. None the
less, the three armouries only managed in one year to meet the target
they had originally embraced.[62]

More complex armaments posed a greater challenge to domestic
armouries. The manufacture of machine guns was a case in point.
Kuropatkin vigorously espoused the new weapon. In 1896, the army
ordered demonstration models from Vickers and from the leading
German producers. After lengthy negotiations, Vickers finally agreed
to allow the manufacture of its new Maxim gun under licence on
Russian soil. However, technical difficulties held up production at the
Tula Armoury until 1904.[63]

The supply of field artillery proceeded rather more smoothly.
Putilov designed a new 3-inch gun, which embodied improved
manoeuvrability, greater range and a lower recoil. In 1900, the army
ordered 1,500 pieces from Putilov and from the state-owned St Petersburg Ordnance factory to be delivered in two years' time. Putilov
agreed to take a half share in the contract, as well as to supply all gun
carriages and shell. This contract was completed on schedule. In 1903,
Putilov and Obukhov received a second order, for 400 and 750 guns
respectively, worth a total of 1.55 million rubles. But Obukhov failed to
deliver gun barrels and carriages on time, blaming technical problems
for the delay. This failure threatened the completion of the 1904
programme, under which the army hoped to take delivery of 1,050
guns in 1905 and a similar quantity in 1906.[64]

The completion of the shipbuilding programme left a great deal to
be desired. Only four of the ten warships destined for the Far East
were launched before the agreed deadline. Naval procurement
officials laid the blame squarely on poor work practices at the yards.
There are good grounds for believing that productivity at the state
yards failed to improve before 1905, in contrast to the performance of
the privately owned Nikolaev yards. Workers deliberately slowed
down the pace of work, in order to secure their jobs in the short term.
But this explanation hardly accounts for delays in the shipbuilding
programme during 1898. Work was abundant and employment more

likely to expand than to contract. A more plausible explanation for the delay is provided by the constant changes that were made to the specification of vessels by the Naval Technical Committee (Morskoi tekhnicheskii komitet). Complaints on this score surfaced time and again in the correspondence between defence contractors and government departments.[65]

Given these shortcomings, the government found it necessary to order military vessels from foreign suppliers. The foreign share of the addition to total tonnage between 1881 and 1894 stood at 6 per cent; in the following years it increased to around 15 per cent. Nevertheless, thanks to the naval rearmament programme, the total tonnage supplied by domestic yards increased dramatically. Russian firms had made a significant inroad into the market for warships and even marine engines.[66]

Only in exceptional circumstances did the Russian army supply its troops with the products that added to their comfort, health and hygiene, rather than to their immediate fighting potential. The state displayed little interest in the production and distribution of finished uniforms and boots. During the 1870s, Miliutin had planned to establish a range of centralized factories and workshops, in order to produce uniforms and similar items, but the reform foundered – typically – because of a lack of resources. Instead, regiments were supplied with the raw materials and the troops were expected to manufacture their own boots, uniforms and food.[67]

The funds allocated to regimental officers for the purchase of cloth and leather were invariably insufficient, for reasons outlined earlier. Troops were obliged to use their meagre earnings from side-employment in the civilian economy, in order to pay for additional raw materials. The system was frequently criticized, because it provided plenty of scope for fraud on the part of officers, who bought and sold goods on behalf of their men. The impact on the morale of the troops hardly needs to be laboured: soldiers were 'convinced that the state (or, rather, the commissariat) gave them the very worst'. These time-consuming tasks sapped the energy of the common soldier and undermined faith in his superiors; worse, they reduced the time that could be devoted to training. The Quartermaster's Department (GIU) had neither the resources, the expertise nor the inclination to monitor the quality of the finished product. Whenever the GIU did decide to distribute boots, manufactured by peasant craftsmen (*kustari*), all manner of complaints surfaced about their poor quality. Government-issue boots were supposed to last for a year, but they reportedly fell to pieces within four months. Soldiers preferred to make their own boots and to sell the others to local merchants, who promptly sold them back to the procurement authorities.[68]

The War Ministry maintained a small number of workshops (*oboznye masterskie*) that supplied carts, harness, belts and buckles. The labour force consisted of hired labour or military conscripts. At one stage these workshops had been leased to private entrepreneurs, who sold their product to the state at an agreed price. By 1900, however, they were back in state hands and funded from the state budget. Regulations in force since 1867 stipulated that they had to be capable of supplying semi-finished goods for up to 25,000 men per annum, or finished goods for up to 15,000 men. But they would find it impossible to respond to frantic demands for their product in the midst of the war against Japan.[69]

The Russian defence industry entered the war against Japan, confident that its main obligations to the defence departments had been discharged. The expectation was that any additional demand for military items in wartime could reasonably be met without disrupting normal work routines and without calling upon new domestic sources of supply. In the main, military production remained the preserve of state arsenals and dockyards. Not even war was expected to disturb the comfortable government monopoly.

The basic industries: iron and steel

Two branches of industry, ferrous metallurgy and machine-building, underpinned the efforts to establish a modern armaments industry. The emergence of Russia as a modern industrial power owed much to the creation of a dynamic iron and steel industry. During the 1890s, foreign investors took advantage of government inducements to establish new ventures or subsidiaries on Russian soil. Strictly speaking, their activities were confined to Ukraine. The long-established iron industry in the Urals remained immune from Russia's industrial revolution. This regional contrast in economic vitality corresponded also to differences in ownership. In Ukraine, the new firms all belonged to Russian or foreign capitalists. The Urals ironworks remained in state hands or belonged to noble landlords. Hence, the struggle for supremacy in iron and steel was also a tussle between competing forms of enterprise. The changes outlined below foreshadowed a later confrontation between the state sector and private enterprise.

By the beginning of the twentieth century, Russia had joined the ranks of the world's major producers of iron and steel. Russia contributed around 6 per cent of total world output of iron and steel and occupied fourth place after the United States (42 per cent), Germany (18 per cent) and Britain (14 per cent). Between 1890 and 1900, the production of pig iron in Russia more than trebled, from 0.93 million tons to 2.93 million tons, while the production of rolled iron and steel increased from 0.79 million tons to 2.67 million tons, representing in both cases an average annual rate of around 1.5 per cent, well above the rate of growth of industrial production as a whole.[70]

Most of the growth in output was contributed by the new iron and steelworks located in Ukraine, where iron and steel production grew nine-fold between 1890 and 1900. By the end of the century, the Ukrainian industry accounted for almost half of total steel output in the Russian Empire; in 1890, its share had been below one-fifth. The Urals, which had been virtually synonymous with Russian iron production since the early eighteenth century, forfeited its leading position in 1896. By 1900, this region contributed one-fifth of total production, half the share of the market it held ten years earlier. While the Urals 'slept' – as the dismissive contemporary phrase had it – Ukraine forged ahead, literally and metaphorically.[71]

Iron and steel producers in Ukraine had a competitive advantage over producers in other regions of the Empire. Foreign entrepreneurs installed new Bessemer converters and Siemens-Martin open-hearth furnaces, capable of producing high-quality steel. The capacity of blast furnaces increased, albeit modestly. Although the average capacity of blast furnaces was smaller than in Germany or Belgium, the difference was offset by the higher quality iron ore supplied by mines in Krivoi Rog, and more pig iron was produced per ton of ore than in western Europe, to say nothing of other parts of the Russian Empire. New rolling mills, supplying steel rails, structural shapes and steel sheet, represented another breakthrough. As a result, Russia possessed an integrated iron and steel industry that stood the test of comparison with best practice elsewhere in Europe. Other parts of the Russian Empire were left behind.[72]

By 1900, the iron and steel industry in south Russia was dominated by a dozen large works. With the exception of John Hughes' New Russia Ironworks (1870), these factories were established after the imposition of high tariffs on iron and steel in 1887 and 1891. There were no barriers to entry during the heyday of expansion. The five largest, namely the New Russia Ironworks, the South Russian Dnieper

Ironworks (established in 1891), the Briansk Ironworks at Aleksandrovsk (1887), the Russo-Belgian Metallurgical Company (1895) and the Donets-Iurevsk Metallurgical Company (1895) accounted for 50 per cent of pig iron production in south Russia and 25 per cent of production in the Empire as a whole. With a few exceptions – Briansk and Donets-Iurevsk, and the Nikopol-Mariupol Company, Hartmann and Taganrog Steel – the industry was in the hands of foreign entrepreneurs. Makeevka Steel was controlled by the Société Générale of France, and Donets Steel at Druzhkovka and Huta-Bankova both formed part of the French Bonnardel Group. Less important than the question of corporate nationality, however, is the fact that modernization and growth went hand in hand.[73]

However, this expansion came to an abrupt halt at the beginning of the twentieth century. The value of iron and steel production fell sharply in 1901 and again in 1902. The production of rails fell by nearly half between 1900 and 1903. Steel producers worked at only three-fifths of capacity. Stocks of unsold pig iron increased from 11 to 25 per cent of production. The value of shares plummeted. Several companies suspended dividend payments altogether. Profits fell sharply (see table 1.4). Other evidence supports this picture: the high dividends available to shareholders in iron and steel companies during the late 1890s, averaging around 12 per cent of nominal capital, fell to 4 per cent in 1900–4.[74]

Individual firms had their own story to tell. The New Russia Ironworks made a profit of 25 per cent on capital in 1898 and 1899; between 1901 and 1904 the firm still achieved profits of 10 per cent, largely as a result of its participation in the rail syndicate (see below). Other companies, without the benefit of government orders for rails to keep them afloat, were in dire straits at the beginning of the century and their situation remained bleak well beyond 1904.[75] But reported profits disguised as much as they revealed of companies' financial position. Firms may have been at pains to emphasize their difficulties, in order to improve the case for financial assistance and to minimize their tax liabilities. The possibility that the situation was less bleak than indicated above is suggested by evidence of declining costs of production. A report prepared for the Crédit Lyonnais found that costs of pig iron production fell by 20 per cent between 1899 and 1905, because of a fall in processing costs, attributable to improved labour productivity, because of a decline in input prices and because of the abolition of the excise tax, previously levied on iron. The cost of producing semi-finished products also fell, by around one-half. It is against this background that entrepreneurial tales of woe should be judged.[76]

Table 1.4. *Net profits reported in iron and steel, 1901–1906 (per cent of capital employed)*

1901	2.26
1902	0.40
1903	1.61
1904	1.75
1905	1.24
1906	0.20

Source: *Stenogramma soveshchaniia o polozhenii metallurgicheskoi i mashinostroitel'-noi promyshlennosti*, St Petersburg, 1908, pp. 6–7.

The dynamism of the iron and steel industry in south Russia contrasted sharply with the fortunes of the industry in the Urals, where the state ironworks were an albatross around the neck of government. Their main function was to supply the government with iron and steel and finished goods, including armaments. They were entitled to produce for the civilian market, provided that this did not interfere with government contract work. In 1900, civilian orders generated more than a quarter of total output, a proportion that rose to two-fifths at Votkinsk, which supplied locomotives to private railway companies. The lesser ironworks relied no less heavily upon civilian contracts.[77]

But these ironworks were notoriously unprofitable. The State Auditor attributed their recurrent losses to the inability of management to reduce production costs. In part, this was a result of a failure to innovate; whilst other regions introduced the hot-blast method of smelting pig iron and installed modern rolling facilities, factories in the Urals remained comatose. As we have already seen, the government insisted on tying the hands of its managers. A commission of inquiry took evidence during 1903 and made several suggestions for improvements in accounting procedures, but results were slow in coming. Technical innovation and managerial initiative were not characteristic features of this industry.

The Urals enterprises were inevitably affected, like other iron and steel producers, by the industrial slump at the turn of the century. Output reached its lowest point in 1902. The chief cause was the decline in government orders for shell. Some enterprises did weather the storm. Baranchinsk continued to produce shell, and the ironworks at Zlatoust kept going by diversifying its product mix. Satkinsk was more successful than most, because demand remained buoyant for its

Table 1.5. *Total output and shell production at state ironworks, 1900–1908*

	Total output (million rubles)	Shell production (per cent)
1900	13.12	34.5
1901	13.73	27.5
1902	11.33	26.4
1903	12.53	28.2
1904	15.65	39.4
1905	14.77	37.6
1906	12.03	55.1
1907	11.96	44.0
1908	12.76	32.3

Sources: col. 1 *Otchet gornogo departamenta za 1900–01*, St Petersburg, 1902; *ibid.*, *za 1905*, 1906; *ibid.*, *za 1908*, 1909; col. 2 derived from G. K. Miftiev, 'Artilleriiskaia promyshlennost' Rossii v period pervoi mirovoi voiny', kandidatskaia dissertatsiia, Leningrad, 1953, appendix 2.

low-cost and high-quality pig iron. Others were less fortunate. Serebriansk continued to lose money throughout the years 1900 to 1904. Artkinsk produced simple agricultural implements, for which demand was sluggish; unlike Zlatoust, it failed to diversify. However, the stuttering recovery that took place in 1903 was followed by a spurt in output, associated with government demand for military goods during the Russo-Japanese War. The Urals ironworks enjoyed brief windfall profits.[78]

As all enterprises in the iron and steel industry struggled to come to terms with the slump at the turn of the century, it became apparent that the private sector suffered especially severely from its consequences. Government subsidies helped to insulate the Urals ironworks from the effects of recession. Granted, private entrepreneurs possessed a degree of freedom of manoeuvre that enabled them to respond more creatively to the pressures they encountered. But they faced an uphill struggle, if they were to convince tsarist bureaucrats of the need to launch a government-led recovery programme.

The basic industries: machine-building

The engineering industry, so crucial to the modern industrial economy in peace and in wartime, comprised a large number of product groups. Five broad categories may be distinguished: transport equipment, agricultural machinery, industrial equipment, electrical products and non-military shipbuilding.[79] In practice, the largest engineering firms had a stake in at least two product groups, and the apparent diversity of these branches should not be allowed to obscure the fact that they faced common problems, notably exposure to a fragile market.

The origins of a modern machine-building industry in Russia can be traced back to the 1860s and 1870s. Russian factories began to produce more complex items of agricultural machinery, ships and railway equipment. In 1869, two firms, the Kolomna Engineering Company (founded in 1863) and the Nevskii works, along with the state ironworks at Votkinsk began to produce locomotives. But the limited market compelled these firms to diversify. Nevskii supplied rails, rolling-stock and ships. Sormovo Engineering (founded in 1849) produced steamships, steam engines, boilers and shell, as well as locomotives. Kolomna built bridges and other products. Nor did the government encourage firms to supply a standard product, for example in locomotive construction. As a result of frequent changes in product specification and the short production runs, costs remained high. Many leading firms, having taken the opportunity provided by the first railway-building boom to acquire corporate status, subsequently found it difficult to reward shareholders and to meet their obligations to creditors. During the 1880s, the government stepped in to rescue many of the larger firms from bankruptcy, with a mixture of loans and subsidies.[80]

The expansion of railway construction during the 1890s revived the flagging fortunes of the engineering industry. Between 1887 and 1900, Putilov and Sormovo enjoyed a five- and six-fold increase respectively in the value of their gross output. The railway building boom, accompanied by the high rate of protection given to domestic industry in 1885 and 1891, encouraged firms to produce locomotives once again. New firms entered the industry, such as the Kharkov Locomotive Company (1897) and the Hartmann Ironworks in Lugansk (founded in 1896). Both newcomers possessed adjacent steel mills and were self-sufficient in steel castings and forgings. Again, the production of locomotives added one more product to the diverse range produced by Russian machine-builders. Few firms looked upon the supply of locomotives as their main activity.

The boom of the 1890s demonstrated the potential for improvements in productivity that could be derived from a larger volume of output.

Between 1890 and 1894, Russian factories supplied 163 locomotives on average; during the next quinquennium this figure increased to nearly 600. The largest producers could set up long production runs, and with impressive results. In 1892, the price of locomotives fell by 18 per cent compared to the price charged in the late 1870s, and the price of wagons fell by 13 per cent.[81]

The production of steam engines, electrical equipment, textile equipment and, especially, machine tools remained weak spots. The largest firms, such as Putilov, Lessner, Nobel and Sormovo, normally manufactured in-house. The new shipyard at Nikolaev was equipped with its own tool-making shop. Imports filled most of the remaining gap. A handful of specialist manufacturers supplied simple products by 1900. The Moscow firm of Bromley supplied drilling and turning lathes to the rapidly proliferating railway workshops. Gerliakh and Pulst of Warsaw supplied milling machines to factories that produced munitions or sewing machines. In St Petersburg, Phoenix supplied state dockyards with metal-cutting tools. But, as these examples suggest, the market for machine tools remained small and specialized. Few Russian workers had the opportunity to acquire skills in the manufacture of machine tools. To compound the problems of market demand, the government offered this infant industry little protection.[82]

Russian merchant shipbuilding developed haphazardly and sluggishly in the period before 1900. This did not reflect a dearth of possibilities in terms of coastal and river navigation. On the contrary, the number of steam-driven vessels on the Volga increased from 1,015 to 1,783 between 1890 and 1900 and the volume of freight more than doubled. But most new vessels were imported. The main Russian shipping company, Russkoe obshchestvo parokhodstva i torgovli (established in 1856), received a government subsidy, but was not obliged to order ships from Russian suppliers; instead, the subsidy covered operating costs on routes in the Black Sea and Mediterranean. Only after 1900, under pressure from the Ministry of Finances, did it order from the Nevskii factory.[83]

The production of merchant vessels was hampered by the high cost of raw materials. The tariff of 1891 did not assist the domestic industry, because it maintained high duties on inputs. In 1898, the government even abolished the tariff on finished vessels, with the promise of a review in ten years. Larger firms switched to other products, leaving specialist suppliers to struggle as best they could. In this unsympathetic environment, domestic producers barely maintained their share

Table 1.6. *Machine-building production, 1885–1913 (million rubles)*

	Current prices	Constant (1913) prices
1885–9 (annual average)	56	56.4
1890–4 (annual average)	69	67.1
1895	98	98.0
1896	148	159.3
1897	174	182.8
1898	202	214.7
1899	198	210.0
1900	191	199.2
1901	218	227.1
1902	202	213.8
1903	219	226.0
1904	230	247.3
1905	249	268.0
1906	231	249.2
1907	233	221.3
1908	214	218.6
1909	225	224.1
1910	252	255.6
1911	271	271.8
1912	317	318.9
1913	418	418.0

Note: figures include output from small-scale industry
Source: P. R. Gregory, *Russian National Income, 1885–1913*, Cambridge, 1982, pp. 276–9, table I.1, col. A.1, deflated by an index of equipment prices, recalculated from table I.1, col. D.3a and D.3b. The original data on machine-building output derive from S. G. Strumilin, *Ocherki ekonomicheskoi istorii Rossii i SSSR*, Moscow, 1966, pp. 442–53, with the pre-1897 data converted to Empire territory. The price deflator is discussed in Gregory, pp. 272–3, 280–1.

of the market. Nor did tariff policy constitute the sole difficulty. As happened elsewhere, merchant shipbuilders were bedevilled by customers' tendency to change specifications each time they ordered a new vessel. Costs of production remained high. For these reasons, Russia – like France but unlike Britain, Japan and Germany – developed only a small merchant shipbuilding capacity.[84]

The total market for Russian-built machinery grew rapidly between 1885 and 1900, by around 9.7 per cent per annum. However, this growth took place from a low base, and much of it was confined to production for the railway transport sector (see table 1.6).

The increase in output of the metalworking and machine-building industries that was such a marked characteristic of the 1890s came to an abrupt end in 1898. Output stagnated during the next two years. A brief recovery in the value of production in 1901 was immediately followed by a renewed slump. During the years 1903–5, output increased steadily, but growth was interrupted once more in 1906. The recovery in 1907 saw output virtually return to the 1905 peak, but the hopes of the industry were quickly dashed. By 1908, the value of output had fallen to its lowest level since 1902.

These phases of growth, stagnation and slump in the engineering industries did not coincide precisely with the experience of Russian industry as a whole or of ferrous metallurgy in particular. The stagnation in metalworking and machine-building between 1898 and 1900 coincided with a phase of continuous growth in total industrial output, whose growth continued uninterrupted until 1905. Similarly, the sharp fall in engineering output in 1902 hardly shows up in the aggregate production index, which actually records a slight increase in that year. By contrast, total industrial production fell during 1905, whereas output of metalworking and machine-building reached a fresh peak. However, the situation was reversed in the following year: a sharp recovery in industry as a whole coincided with a slump in metalworking and machine-building.

Stagnation at the beginning of the twentieth century concealed important differences between the various sub-branches of the industry (see table 1.7). The value of rolling-stock output fell by seven per cent between 1900 and 1908. Production of boilers – a major element of industrial equipment – plunged dramatically. By contrast, the value of agricultural machinery output more than doubled between 1900 and 1908; in 1908, it accounted for 13 per cent of total engineering output. The production of gas, diesel and electric engines increased substantially. So, too, did the manufacture of flour-milling, butter-making and oil-processing machines, and refrigerators. On the other hand, the production of lifting equipment, sugar-refining machinery and distilling equipment fell slightly. More significant was a fall of around one-third in the value of machine tools and textile machinery. Broadly speaking, the market for industrial equipment in this phase of the business cycle left a lot to be desired.[85]

Underlying these shifts in industrial production were important changes in the labour:capital ratio and in the productivity of labour. The recession improved the technological level of the industry, by weeding out some of the less well-equipped firms and leading to a

Table 1.7. *Gross output of machine-building, 1900–1908*

	1900			1908		
	Units	Output (million rubles)	% share	Units	Output (million rubles)	% share
Rolling-stock	14	92.0	46	18	85.3	41
Vessels	32	6.1	3	18	4.6	2
Boilers	52	24.6	12	56	11.7	5
Agricultural machinery	162	12.1	6	216	26.5	13
Other	279	67.1	33	244	83.3	39
Total	539	201.9	100	552	211.5	100

Source: V. I. Bovykin, *Formirovanie finansovogo kapitala v Rossii*, Moscow, 1984, p. 61.

concentration of capital. The amount of horsepower per worker increased by one-third, with a still greater rate of increase in the branch supplying rolling-stock. Furthermore, it is clear that some older steam engines were being replaced by newer forms of motive power, such as electrical and internal combustion engines. Output per worker increased by 18 per cent, an increase that conceals substantial improvements in the agricultural machinery industry. This seems to have been a period in which new and technologically more advanced firms entered this branch of industry, attracted by the prospect of taking advantage of the fall in the price of iron and steel, which accounted for a larger share of total input than in other branches of engineering. As a result of these changes, the labour productivity differential narrowed between agricultural machinery and rolling-stock producers. Whether corresponding advances could be made in an industry such as armaments, where different technical standards prevailed, and rigorous quality controls were in force, remained to be seen.[86]

Industrial depression, reorganization and business–government relations, 1900–4

The unprecedented slump in heavy industry at the turn of the nineteenth century served to remind Russian industrialists of the underlying vulnerability of the ventures they had created. Foreign financiers, no less than Russian businessmen, were alarmed by the sudden onset of recession and accused the Russian government of doing nothing to protect their investment. In fact, this was a specious claim. Having been the midwife of growth in heavy industry during the 1890s, the government was not about to renounce responsibility for its offspring. Officials took a number of steps to alleviate the critical position of iron and steel producers. The State Bank extended long-term credit facilities to the zemstvos, enabling them to purchase agricultural equipment from Russian suppliers. In 1902, the Ministry of Transport placed a large order for rails with the steel companies. But the most significant measure was indirect, namely the decision to countenance the formation of a syndicate in the iron and steel industry.[87]

The initiative for the formation of a syndicate in the iron and steel industry was taken by the directors of a handful of metallurgical firms, most of them operating in south Russia. These firms had close links with French financial institutions, notably the Société Générale and the Banque de l'Union Parisienne, as well as with Belgian capital.

French investors, the value of whose stock was falling during the industrial crisis, clearly supported any measures to stem a further decline, and the banks took their interests to heart. The planned venture also had the support of Witte, who saw a syndicate as a means of reassuring investors that he had no intention of using the crisis to acquire French-owned assets at a cut price. To the firms concerned, the formation of a syndicate had a more direct appeal: it would help to create a more unified sales system, thereby reducing the leverage of merchant houses, which imposed onerous credit terms on suppliers of metal.

Twelve firms agreed to establish a 'Society for the sale of output of Russian metallurgical factories', known by its Russian abbreviation as Prodamet. In July 1902, the statutes of the new joint-stock company were approved by the tsarist government. By 1905, Prodamet had concluded agreements with firms outside its base in south Russia. Prodamet apportioned orders amongst its members, in accordance with pre-determined quotas. Initial agreements covered sheet iron (July 1902), tires and axles (November 1902), beams and channels (June 1903), pipe (1905), and structural shapes, strip iron, profiled iron and spring steel (1909). Finally, in December 1909, Prodamet fixed quotas for rails. There was no formal agreement to syndicate pig iron, because this was largely consumed by the steelworks themselves. Each party agreed to sell its output through Prodamet, under threat of financial penalty in the event of refusal to comply.[88]

What impact did Prodamet have on the consumer of iron and steel? The immediate effect of the syndicate was to force up the price of products, such as sheet iron, which in 1901–2 had sold for approximately 1.40–1.45 rubles per pud. By the end of 1902 it sold for 1.50, and the price in 1903–4 had risen to around 1.7 rubles per pud. The price of structural shapes (sortovoe zhelezo) increased from 1.40 to 1.70 rubles per pud within a month of the agreement to syndicate output. Furthermore, there were several ways in which Prodamet could charge consumers more than the rate stipulated in the basic schedule of prices, for example, by charging consumers for the 'theoretical' weight of iron, rather than the actual, heavier weight, but at the same rate. Prodamet also charged consumers at the higher freight rate in force on the railways, even though the syndicate itself paid a reduced tariff.[89]

Yet it would be wrong to give a one-sided impression of the behaviour of Prodamet. There were tendencies that worked in the opposite direction to those described above. In particular, differences in technology, labour productivity and location between one firm and another within the syndicate meant that it was difficult to enforce a unified price on all members. Some firms in south Russia objected to the schedule of prices that applied to output from members in other regions. As a consequence, there was a tendency towards lower prices in certain regions, with a complex scheme in force to compensate those producers, predominantly in Poland and the Baltic regions, who had to accept a lower price. Consumers, for their part, benefited from the lower prices and from the reduction in commission charged by the syndicate. Transport costs also came down, because Prodamet's office ensured that a customer received iron from a neighbouring factory. In areas where Prodamet competed with outsiders, prices would be forced down. Once competition had been eliminated, Prodamet could raise prices in order to subsidize its efforts in other markets.[90]

In the circumstances, the iron and steel industry had much to gain from measures that imposed closer control over the market. The government took other measures, for example extending to foreign-owned corporations the law on receivership, which allowed them to suspend debt payments indefinitely.[91] But government assistance also went down the road of direct intervention. The main instrument was a committee to allocate railway contracts. Government orders had formed a crucial part of the output of the rapidly-growing iron and steel industry, especially in south Russia. In the middle of the 1890s, these contracts amounted to two-thirds of all output of south Russian metallurgical firms. By 1900 they had dropped to 25 per cent, at which level they remained stable for the next few years. In normal circumstances, suppliers of rails and other items were invited to submit bids at auctions organized by the local offices of the Ministry of Transport. But in 1899, as the crisis deepened, the government established an official commission under Count D. M. Sol'skii. The commission broke with convention, ordering rails from a select handful of factories over a three-year period. At that moment, five iron and steel companies were planning to form a syndicate for the allocation of orders for rails that they received from the government. Both actions were motivated by the desire to prevent other firms from entering the market for rails.[92]

In 1902, the government decided to make the above arrangement permanent, 'to enable the most reliable factories to survive this difficult moment without perturbations and losses'. Having successfully concluded two large loans, with France in 1901 and with Germany in 1902, Witte drew upon these funds in order to finance additional railway construction. The new committee purchased rails from six firms in south Russia (the New Russia Ironworks, the Briansk Ironworks, the

South Russian Dnieper Company, the Russo-Belgian metallurgical Company, the Taganrog Metallurgical Company and Donets Steel), and three firms in the Urals. Each firm's contract corresponded to the volume of work it had carried out in recent years, the price being fixed for three years. The advantages of this arrangement were considerable. During 1902 and 1903 the market price of rails fluctuated between 1.08–1.12 kopeks per pud, falling at one stage to 90 kopeks. The government agreed to pay 1.25 kopeks to its chosen suppliers. The Moscow industrialist Jules Goujon, who – as an outsider – bitterly opposed the deal, reckoned that the firms concerned reaped a total of 8.5 million rubles from the government. In addition, they could force down the price of other iron and steel products and, by competing with non-privileged producers, exercise enormous influence in the industry. Other advantages accrued to companies involved in this arrangement. The traditional regulations on procurement required firms to leave a deposit with the government office as a mark of good faith, but the new scheme freed the privileged few from this obligation, as well as providing them with government loans and subsidies. No wonder that the iron and steel producers who found themselves excluded from these arrangements protested at the treatment they received.[93]

The impact of the depression was not felt immediately in those branches of the engineering industry that produced industrial equipment and rolling-stock. The manufacture of locomotives fell sharply in 1902, but over the next three years the volume of production fluctuated around the peak reached in 1901. Newly built lines required rolling-stock, and the lag between orders for rails and for rolling-stock created a degree of buoyancy. The relative insulation of these manufacturers from the effects of the slump, at least until the end of 1906, also owed much to the willingness of government to offer subsidies. That advantage was compounded by the fact that producers of rolling-stock (with the exception of those, such as Briansk and Hartmann, who had substantial iron and steel capacity) could benefit from the fall in the price of raw material inputs. For these reasons, the financial position of producers of transport equipment held up relatively well.

Nevertheless, the writing was on the wall for Russian producers of rolling-stock. If, in 1900, it was apparent that the feverish railway-building boom had come to an end, by 1906 it became evident that the government would no longer order rolling-stock on anything like the scale of the 1890s. Nor would private railway companies, with only a fraction of the total track between them, be able to plug the gap. As a

Table 1.8. *Net profits reported in Russian machine-building 1901–1906 (per cent of capital employed)*

	All engineering	Locomotive and wagon producers	Other engineering
1901	1.18	1.49	0.99
1902	2.27	4.0	1.22
1903	2.67	5.53	1.05
1904	3.53	6.49	1.93
1905	2.78	6.37	0.83
1906	2.19	4.64	0.95

Source: D. P. Il'inskii and V. P. Ivanitskii, *Ocherk istorii russkoi parovozostroitel'noi i vagonostroitel'noi promyshlennosti*, Moscow, 1929, p. 91; *Stenogramma soveshchaniia metallurgicheskoi i mashinostroitel'noi promyshlennosti*, St Petersburg, 1908, pp. 6–7.

consequence, leading firms shed their workforce with brutal rapidity and revived the informal selling agreements that had been instituted during previous lean times.[94]

Negotiations for a syndicate of producers of locomotives were completed in December 1901, when six leading manufacturers agreed on joint action. Unlike Prodamet, the newly-formed 'Society for the trade in products of Russian locomotive factories' (Prodparovoz) did not acquire the formal trappings of a joint-stock company. When the members of Prodparovoz did seek corporate status (in 1908) the Russian government refused to give permission, its hostility demonstrating the extent to which tsarist officials maintained their distance from 'monopoly capital'. In March 1903, a similar agreement was reached between eleven companies that traded in railway wagons: Putilov, Briansk, Sormovo and Kolomna were once again involved, along with Lilpop (Warsaw), the Russo-Baltic Wagon Company, Maltsov works, the Moscow Wagon Company, Verkhne-Volga, Phoenix (Riga) and Dvigatel' of Reval. However, Prodvagon conducted few transactions before 1906, and only in 1908 did its members conclude an agreement that determined quotas. As with the locomotive syndicate, Prodvagon failed to make much of an impact on government. Its members lobbied unsuccessfully for additional orders and failed to force up prices for finished goods. The government had its own reasons for not wishing to see major locomotive producers go to the wall; hence the element of subsidy in the trickle of government orders. But these were hardly the stuff of industrialists' dreams. Some Soviet scholars used to argue that both Prodvagon and Prodparovoz dominated the committee for the allocation of rails, but the evidence for this is inadequate. All one can say is that the two syndicates liaised with government officials, enabling the firms to plan their production schedules in a more rational manner than hitherto. This hardly smacks of government subordination to big business.[95]

The syndicates played a broadly positive role in the industrial economy. In a memorandum to the Ministry of Trade and Industry, a spokesman for Prodvagon made the point that

> unifying the activities of wagon manufacturers ... has influenced the quality of the finished product, because their agreement has brought together the individual technical offices, their designers, builders and specialists. The factories exchange drawings for new types of rolling stock (which economizes on effort), collectively appraise their worth and shortcomings, and seek to unify and standardize the separate parts of rolling-stock, in order to simplify and cheapen production.

Shorn of the somewhat idealized claims made on their behalf, this element of the syndicates' activity has been underestimated in the literature.[96]

The depression provided engineering firms with an opportunity to reassess their product mix. In the initial phase, producers of rolling-stock, who dominated the industry, were able to survive perfectly well. Most of them could continue to reap advantages from bulk production, as they had done during the 1890s. But, by 1907, they were forced to cut back on the volume of output, and only the creation of syndicates enabled them to maintain some degree of technical progress. In the medium term, they were likely to look elsewhere for custom. Armaments, as we shall see, provided one outlet. For the present, they turned to the production of iron and steel castings, agricultural machinery, even laundry and gymnastic equipment. Production of agricultural machinery flourished on a wave of land settlement in western Siberia and the vast prairies of south-eastern Russia. The relative buoyancy of consumer goods industries created a demand for the corresponding types of equipment, such as textile machinery. Finally, firms in all sectors of industry began to instal new kinds of motive power, replacing older steam engines with machines powered by gas and electricity. Many of these developments, however, lay in the future. Between 1900 and 1908, the engineering industry as a whole simply marked time.

Conclusion

With the exception of a brief flurry of military activity during the Russo-Turkish War, Russia enjoyed a half-century of peace between 1856 and 1904. This breathing-space provided the tsarist regime with the opportunity to embark on a remarkable and wide-ranging programme of administrative reform. The prolonged peace also helped to create a climate in which foreign capital could be tapped to help finance the construction of a railway network and modern enterprise in mining and metallurgy. Industrialization was associated with the emergence of powerful new firms in private ownership. Some of the leading firms began to develop expertise in armament production, but this tendency did not as yet yield significant results. One reason was that other lines of production appeared to hold out better prospects, transport equipment being the obvious instance. Another was that the government retained a strong grip over defence production. This did not make the tsarist regime unique – other states, too, maintained dockyards and arsenals in public ownership. But in Russia, this practice bore all the hallmarks of a deliberate ideological choice to retain state control over the most sensitive area of industrial production. The emergence of a dynamic private sector in iron and steel only served to demonstrate what would be in store, were the government to open the gates to the arms trade: lobbying by and collusion amongst suppliers, and the vulnerability of established state enterprise to organized capitalism.

Russian entrepreneurs as yet paid little attention to the presence of state armouries and dockyards. But their indifference could change – and did change – when market conditions became less favourable. Having grown fat on a diet of government orders before 1900, industrialists felt entitled to a similar level of support when the recession began to bite. This implied a reduction in the government commitment to state enterprise. To strengthen the case for the private sector, it would be necessary to marshal arguments against state-owned enterprise; hence, as we shall see, the genesis of complaints about 'inefficient' state arsenals and shipyards. If industrialists could devise and utilize a public forum in which these views could be articulated, so much the better.

The defence industry on the eve of the Russo-Japanese War excited adverse comment from those who advocated a more commercial approach to administration. But the deficiencies of the armament industry did not signify peculiar shortcomings of Russian enterprise and public administration. Critics of British and French dockyards and arsenals also complained that accounting and management procedures needed to be reformed, in order to allow for a proper calculation of production costs. Industrial managers in these societies, like their counterparts in Russia, could be heard to lambast procurement officials who changed their mind about specifications in the middle of a production run or whose behaviour in other respects made life difficult for the modern armaments enterprise. But it did not follow that the way forward necessitated the extension of private capital into defence production on an increased scale, even assuming that capitalists were willing to take the risk of becoming involved.[97]

In certain instances, the tsarist state did yield ground to the private sector before 1905. However, before this process could advance very far, certain conditions had to be met. The most important condition required that private enterprise offer a substantially new product. Innovation, as in the manufacture of smokeless powder, light artillery and new cartridges, encouraged the government to turn to private enterprise. But this was a necessary, not a sufficient condition. The availability of a new product did not in itself imply that the state would tolerate the extension of private enterprise in this sphere. The sense of responsibility to the labour force under government control, the widespread bureaucratic aversion towards private enterprise – despite more than a decade of capitalist industrialization – and the realization on the part of private investors that defence contracts offered an insecure future, all conspired to limit the role of the Russian arms trade. Whether its modest scope would survive the impending recession, let alone the crucible of war in the Far East, remained to be seen.

In retrospect, Russia's defence preparations did not suffer from evident weaknesses in the organization of the armament industry. Nor did the so-called underfunding of the defence effort during the 1890s create serious shortcomings. Much more alarming was the use to which available resources were put. Russian infantry entered battle with inadequate training, because they were obliged to devote so much time to other tasks. Fiscal starvation offers only a partial explanation for the persistence of the regimental economy. Other considerations predominated. Officers and men alike remained wedded to their traditional way of life. Procurement officials had neither the training nor sufficient motivation to change this state of affairs. The navy, too, suffered from the misallocation of resources. Sailors were expected to engage the enemy, without having put to sea in naval trials, because the Admiralty did not regard this as a priority. Not for the first time, and certainly not for the last, the besetting problems of Russia's armed forces resulted as much from conceptual myopia and rudimentary decision-making, as from economic backwardness. The adjustment to modernity, whether it manifested itself in the guise of industrial syndicates, business ambition or the availability of new military technologies, proved painfully slow.

2   War and revolution, retrenchment and recession

Introduction: the emergence of a new agenda, 1904–1907

Sergei Witte, the deposed Minister of Finances, argued that the war against Japan proved a turning point in the fortunes of imperial Russia. The war, he said, 'even if it did not create the revolution, brought revolution forward by decades'.[1] The events in the Far East unleashed a torrent of criticism of the old regime by liberal members of the Russian intelligentsia, the nobility and the merchant estate. These disparate social groups urged the Tsar to concede some form of national assembly that would oblige him to listen to the voice of 'society' (*obshchestvennost'*). Some liberal activists demanded a parliament, elected on the basis of universal, equal, direct and secret suffrage. They were not alone. As news reached St Petersburg in December 1904 of the fall of Port Arthur, workers in the capital took to the streets in protest against living conditions and behind the banner of radical reform. The following year and a half of revolutionary action by workers, peasants, soldiers and sailors affected all realms of political and economic life. In October 1905, the Tsar was obliged to issue a manifesto, conceding a form of parliamentary government. Country-wide elections led to the convocation of the First Duma in May 1906.[2]

The loss of human life in the war against Japan was accompanied by the destruction of capital, notably the loss of military vessels, amounting to three-fifths of the value of the imperial fleet. The ensuing revolution yielded its own harvest of capital depletion, in the form of serious damage to oilfields in the Caucasus. This was an extreme, although not unique, example of the destructive impact of revolution on the industrial economy.[3] In addition, the wave of strikes disrupted production and called forth punitive measures from the authorities. The continued revolutionary ferment drove a wedge between liberals, who welcomed the October Manifesto, and the radicals, who saw in the newly formed soviets an alternative form of government. The revolutionary experiment in urban Russia collapsed, amidst the arrest of soviet and strike leaders. A general strike in Moscow during December 1905 was suppressed with great ferocity.

From an economic point of view, the loss of output and the destruction of productive assets were, beyond the short term at least, less significant than the effect of war and revolution on state finances. Witte maintained in 1907 that the war 'completely destroyed the entire economic organism of the country'. His main point was that the war bequeathed Russia a heavy burden of debt. Germany and France extended credit to Russia, partly because of diplomatic considerations and partly because international financiers took a sanguine view of Russia's underlying financial resilience. The end of the war confronted Russia with the need to service these newly-incurred debts.[4]

V. N. Kokovtsov, Witte's successor as Minister of Finances, sought to convince his colleagues that the country could not afford any additional commitments beyond the measures required to stabilize the economy. In straitened times, government departments that traditionally made heavy demands on funds, particularly the ministries of Transport, War and Navy, had to cut back their claims. The pressure on these spending stalwarts was made yet more intense by the appearance of a fresh claimant on the post-revolutionary scene, in the shape of the Ministry of Agriculture, which drafted an expensive programme of land reform.[5]

Retrenchment thus became the keyword of economic policy after 1905. What of the implications for defence preparations? Kokovtsov, whose name was synonymous with this policy, took much the same view as his illustrious – and embittered – predecessor, namely that war and preparations for war were inimical to economic prosperity. In itself, this view might not antagonize the military establishment, who in the aftermath of the defeats in the Far East were hardly in a position to go looking for trouble. But to deny the armed forces funds to re-equip and reorganize – to fail, in short, to do the minimum required to salvage military pride and restore basic defence capabilities – would certainly not commend itself to the Russian military leadership. Here was scope for a divergence of opinion between government and the military.

In this context, the attitude and behaviour of Russian industrialists were especially critical. Some sections of industry, in particular those connected with military supply, did well out of the war, which temporarily alleviated the worst consequences of the recession. But the outbreak of revolution early in 1905 shattered the dream of a sustained upturn in economic fortunes. The peace treaty with Japan, signed in August 1905, brought to an end the frantic pace of work in Russian arsenals, shipyards and engineering shops. The defence sector was faced with all manner of problems: increased costs, resulting from the concessions made to workers earlier in the year; depleted order books, which left equipment idle; and falling profits. Considerable entrepreneurial initiative would be required to address these difficulties. What resources did industrialists have at their disposal as they sought to come to terms with the aftermath of war and revolution? During the revolution, the fledgling business political parties had a short life: evidently, the Duma would not become a refuge for distressed businessmen. On the other hand, industrialists did devise new forms of association during the revolution, which offered them better scope to exercise leverage upon government.[6]

The revolution altered business perceptions of government, but it also created in the Duma a parliamentary body that would claim the right to pronounce on business and government affairs alike. Parliament provided a forum for liberal politicians to criticize the existing arrangements for the administration of armament industry and to question the procedures for the management of the defence budget and military procurement. By so doing, the Duma challenged the long-standing prerogative of the Tsar to oversee all matters relating to the defence of the realm, a responsibility which he did not intend to renounce. A threat to this prerogative would test the new political system to the limit.

The war against Japan, 1904–1905

The Russian war effort in the Far East was bedevilled by shortcomings in military supply which to a significant extent reflected the location of the theatre of operations. The supply of military matériel, food and fodder to Russian troops in Manchuria (100,000 of them in February, twice that number by October 1904), over a distance of 9,000 km, posed enormous problems. At the outbreak of war, the carrying capacity of the trans-Siberian railway was limited to ten trains per day in one direction, and although this capacity more than doubled during the war, its limitations inevitably caused bottlenecks at stations along the line. Furthermore, no track yet ran around the southern side of Lake Baikal; in winter, a light track could be laid across the ice to transport troops and goods quickly, but in summer the authorities had to make use of whatever boats were at hand to make the journey. By contrast, Japan could ship troops (150,000 of them in February 1904) and equipment across to the Korean peninsula within twenty-four hours.[7]

The war cruelly exposed the inadequacy of existing arrangements for military supply. Contemporary critics of the Russian war effort, anticipating the accusations that were levelled at the procurement agencies ten years later, pointed to the failure of the Main Artillery Administration (GAU) and the Chief Quartermaster's Department (GIU) to supply the army with stocks of weapons and equipment in adequate quantities and at the appropriate time. A subsequent investigation uncovered deficiencies in artillery supplied to the fortress at Port Arthur and to the army in the field. At the outbreak of hostilities, the fortress was equipped with guns based on the models of 1867, 1877 and 1886 ('there are even brass guns'). There were other instances of failures to keep abreast of modern technology. The GAU continued to place orders for older versions of mountain artillery, even though contemporary Russian arms producers had begun to produce more sophisticated versions. Officials seemed to be in no hurry to place orders for new guns; thus, 'the excellent quality of the rapid-fire field guns, built by Putilov, could not be exploited, because of delays in supply of the new guns to artillery batteries'.[8]

Serious deficiencies in armaments and equipment manifested themselves once they arrived in the Far East. The firepower available to the army was limited by the shortage of artillery appropriate to the terrain. Field artillery pieces were too heavy to move in the rugged and often muddy conditions that the army encountered: when troops retreated, they simply jettisoned these guns. Military equipment was transported on wheeled carriages, which proved vulnerable for the same reason: pack animals would have been better suited to the terrain. The army suffered, too, from a lack of adequate stocks of mountain guns and fortress artillery. Officers complained of shortages of high-explosive shell, compared to shrapnel, as well as a dearth of machine-guns. To add to these problems, radio communication between army units hardly existed, and messages were relayed by soldiers on horseback.[9]

Other problems emerged with the supply of uniforms and boots. In peacetime, Russian troops themselves manufactured uniforms and footwear. Unfortunately, a system that operated tolerably smoothly in peacetime broke down under the sudden increase in demand. The Quartermaster's Department hastily abandoned any attempts at procurement by auction. Nor could it require front-line troops and reservists to supply their own uniforms, in the midst of hectic preparations for mobilization and military training. Instead, the GIU hurriedly placed contracts for finished goods with local authorities, wholesalers and other potential sources of supply. The army constantly complained about delays in the delivery and about the quality of goods, fuelling the discontent of the already over-stretched and despondent troops. In some regiments, more than half the boots (*valenki*) disintegrated after a fortnight, forcing soldiers to patch them with pine and fir bark.[10]

If Japan had the advantage over its adversary in terms of geography and quality of weaponry, the same could not be said of troop strength. Japan never possessed a commanding numerical superiority over Russian troops. For example, at the battle of Liaoyang in August 1904, 125,000 Japanese troops, with 485 guns at their disposal, faced 160,000 Russian troops, with 592 guns. However, the Russian army was unable to convert this quantitative advantage into military success. Shortcomings in military supply and qualitative deficiencies in armaments do not tell the entire story. Many soldiers were inadequately trained. A candid assessment of the lessons of the Russo-Japanese War concluded that, 'manifesting astonishing stubbornness and perseverance in defence, our armed forces are unable to display similar qualities in attack ... The reason for this must be found in inappropriate training, a lack of understanding of local conditions and of weaponry, the lack of any internal connection in the actions of different elements in the armed forces and an inability to agree upon those actions'.[11] Subsequent research has tended to corroborate this assessment. Soldiers were inadequately prepared to use the artillery at their disposal, because they had been given no prior opportunity to practise manoeuvres. Training placed a higher premium upon routine drill procedures than it did upon techniques and skills that could be deployed on the field of battle. In addition, Russian officers failed to inspire confidence in their men. Their background had instilled in them a preference for routine and an unwillingness to take initiative.[12]

Morale inevitably suffered from the constant strain imposed by shortages of food and equipment. The more fortunate soldiers succeeded in obtaining meat from regimental herds and bread from the regimental bakery. Other troops were not so lucky. Sanitary and medical facilities appear to have been fairly primitive, but not woefully inadequate by the standards of the time. An American observer gave a broadly positive assessment of attempts to cater for wounded and sick men, and applauded the army's programme to protect horses against anthrax, which was endemic in Manchuria. The army's own medical service was supplemented by the zemstvos, who provided doctors, *fel'dshera* (heath-care auxiliaries) and hospital beds in the field and in the rear. Unfortunately, the consequence was a protracted conflict between official and voluntary personnel, typified by complaints that zemstvo doctors were paid twice as much as army personnel.[13]

If the two sides were fairly evenly matched on the field – Russian superiority in numbers helping to compensate for inferior munitions – the same cannot be said for their relative naval strength. Japan enjoyed a clear advantage in the quality and quantity of its ships and armaments. The Russian navy lacked sufficient cruisers and torpedo boats to deal with the threat posed by the Japanese. At the decisive battle of Tsushima, Japanese torpedo boats outnumbered Russian by seven to one. Furthermore, Japanese ships were better protected by armour plate; and their guns could fire three times as much shell (by weight) and fifteen times as much (in terms of explosive power) as the Russian artillery. Russian ships were poorly endowed with radio equipment and telescopes, leaving them ill-informed about the movements of their Japanese counterparts. In addition to these material differences, the quality of personnel left much to be desired. A contemporary report suggests that both navies had much to learn about the deployment of mines and the use of artillery; however, in contrast to the Russian fleet, 'the Japanese were learning all the time'. Many naval commanders lacked experience of the vessels for which they had responsibility. Naval ratings were not encouraged to display any initiative; in any case, the sailors who made up Admiral Rozhdestvenskii's fleet had been forced to endure a rigorous and unbroken seven-month voyage from the shores of Latvia to the Korean Peninsula. As a result, they arrived in the Far East in a demoralised and exhausted state. 'Of all the lessons taught in the war [wrote an astute American attaché], the most important is the value of trained and patriotic personnel'.[14]

The naval engagement at Tsushima on 14 May 1905 effectively sealed the fate of the Russian war effort in the Far East. The irony of this outcome has sometimes been lost on historians. The campaigns which they engaged in during 1904 and 1905 had decimated the Japanese army. Japan began the war with an army of 320,000 soldiers, but by the beginning of 1905 around 230,000 men had been killed. By early summer, the Russian army outnumbered the Japanese by one-third. Tsushima rescued the faltering Japanese war effort, which explains why the Japanese government was not averse to the peace settlement proposed by Theodore Roosevelt. However, Russia's military leaders, and especially its naval commanders, derived little comfort from this state of affairs. After Tsushima, only one cruiser and two torpedo-boat destroyers limped on to Vladivostok; the rest of Rozhdestvenskii's fleet was either sunk, captured or interned. In all, the tsarist navy sustained the loss of seventeen battleships (including two coastal defence vessels), eleven armoured cruisers, five light cruisers, twenty-two torpedo-boat destroyers, four transport ships and eight dock vessels. The Russian navy lost virtually its entire complement of battleships and cruisers, and around one-fifth of its destroyers. The implications of these losses for the defence of the Baltic littoral were not lost on Russian observers. In addition, 284 officers and 6,227 men from the Far Eastern fleet lost their lives, representing one fifth of the total complement. It is hardly surprising that contemporary publicists spoke of Tsushima as an unparalleled tragedy for the Russian fleet.[15]

The latter part of the Russo-Japanese war coincided with mounting unrest in the main urban centres of European Russia. Against the background of revolution and of Tsushima, the War Council entertained the continuation of war. Some participants spoke in favour of a further effort to defeat the Japanese ground forces. According to War Minister Sakharov, additional troops could be deployed in the Far East. Inevitably, however, this decision would jeopardize the maintenance of public order in cities such as St Petersburg and Odessa. From his vantage point as commander-in-chief of the St Petersburg military district, Grand Duke Vladimir Aleksandrovich, uncle to Tsar Nicholas, insisted that 'internal welfare [*blagosostoianie*] matters more to us than victory against Japan'. This view was not shared by other military men, notably Sakharov, who complained of the damage to Russian pride, and Kuropatkin, who insisted that a victory over Japanese troops remained a real possibility. Appropriately enough, the Court viewpoint prevailed: just as the Tsar's entourage pressed him to confront Japan in the first place, so they now encouraged him to bring the war to an end.[16]

The conclusion of hostilities after a succession of military defeats brought with it the search for scapegoats. Post-war investigations conducted by the Russian army admitted to shortcomings in military training and expertise, but concentrated their criticism on the system of weapons procurement. The main commission of inquiry berated the various procurement authorities for failing to order an adequate range of products: machine-guns, artillery ammunition, communication and observation equipment. Although military personnel were poorly placed to make use of the equipment at their disposal, the army managed to shift much of the blame for military setbacks on to the procurement agencies. Peace brought them precious little respite from bureaucratic invective and public opprobrium.

The impact of the war on the defence industry

Russian arms manufacturers saw the war against Japan as an opportunity to put idle plant to use. They can hardly have been prepared for the flurry of orders that were showered upon them. Even the readiness of the procurement agencies to order armaments from foreign suppliers did not prevent intense activity throughout the defence industry. In this respect, as in much else, the Russo-Japanese War prefigured developments a decade later: charges of profiteering were levelled at industrialists, while the government procurement departments stood accused of procrastination, corruption and disorganization.

Only the readiness of the procurement agencies to place orders with foreign suppliers stood between the domestic defence industry and full order books. According to a spokesman for the arms trade, the navy alone spent more than 200 million rubles on foreign vessels and related items during the war (included in this total were contracts placed with overseas producers in earlier years and delivered in 1904–5). The defence departments placed substantial foreign orders during 1904 with German firms such as Krupp and Blohm und Voss, in a desperate rush to secure armaments and vessels.[17] The two ministries between them spent 175 million rubles on imports in 1904–5, including 72 million rubles on military vessels, troop transport ships and naval accessories and 58 million rubles on artillery and other weaponry. Orders for coal and coke for the navy, worth 25 million rubles, accounted for the remainder (see table 2.1). These contracts amounted to one-third of total orders for weaponry, but up to four-fifths of all new orders for military vessels during the war.

This level of dependence on foreign sources of supply was enough to justify the fears of domestic manufacturers that they would be overlooked in the scramble for military hardware. They looked on in despair as the French sought to link Russian contracts to negotiations for a Russian loan. Russian industrialists claimed that domestic factories were quite capable of supplying these goods and would have

Table 2.1. *Foreign orders for military goods, 1904–1905 (million rubles)*

	War Ministry	Navy
Weapons and ammunition	57.5	5.7
(incl. 3-inch shell)	(23.0)	(–)
Explosives	1.2	0.4
Coal and coke	1.7	25.0
Metals	5.0	1.4
(incl. aluminium)	(2.5)	(–)
Communications equipment	3.0	0.7
Optical equipment	0.5	0.2
Searchlights	–	0.7
Balloons (aerostats)	0.6	0.2
Ships and accessories	–	72.0
Total	69.5	106.3

Source: TsGIA f.1276, op.4, d.530, ll.198–202ob.

done so, if only the procurement authorities had made adequate preparations for war, by ordering more vessels and armaments from domestic suppliers in the years before 1904. The urgent need for military vessels in 1904 only underscored, in their view, the short-sightedness of procurement policy. Government officials defended the decision to order from foreign suppliers, pointing out that Russian firms were unable to deliver on time or at a suitable price. In the case of new weapons, such as the machine-gun, domestic industry had no manufacturing experience on which it might draw. The Tula armoury had only just begun to produce machine-guns on the eve of the war. Officials also argued that it made little sense to deal with Russian firms which simply assembled parts manufactured abroad. The government might as well obtain the finished product quickly and cheaply by ordering direct from a foreign source.[18]

An outburst of voluntary initiatives to deal with shortages of military goods also anticipated later events. In February 1904, Russian industrialists and professional people established a 'committee to strengthen the fleet by voluntary donations', with funds raised from the sale of securities. Within a year, the committee had placed orders for eighteen torpedo boats and four submarines, at a total cost of 14.4 million rubles. In a move calculated to demonstrate to official agencies its confidence in domestic industry, the committee spent most of its resources in Russia and Finland. For instance, the Latvian firm of Lange and Son obtained a contract for eight torpedo boats. This 'patriotic' initiative went some way towards alleviating the effect of the official procurement policies.[19]

The procurement authorities certainly did not overlook domestic suppliers. State-owned armouries were especially hard pressed. The production of rifles was almost entirely entrusted to the factories administered by the GAU. The three armouries at Tula, Izhevsk and Sestroretsk between them produced 204,000 rifles in 1904 and 312,000 in 1905, albeit with much lower completion rates during 1905, when they were seized by revolutionary ferment. At the Tula arsenal, whose labour force had been cut from a peak of 10,000 in the 1890s to 3,600 in 1903, extra workers were recruited, bringing the complement back to 10,000. Employees worked overtime to cope with orders for small arms. The three cartridge works, in St Petersburg, Lugansk and Tula also worked round the clock to keep pace with military demand. Output at the Tula works increased from 4.2 million rubles (the average figure in 1899–1903) to 14.8 million rubles in 1904 and 10.0 million rubles in 1905. The workforce increased at a staggering rate, from 1,400 to 4,700 during 1904, and reached 7,000 in 1905.[20]

The manufacture of artillery and shell followed a rather different course, in so far as the volume of production was maintained throughout 1906. During the war, three factories (Putilov, the St Petersburg Ordnance factory and the Perm Cannon Works at Motovilikha) produced 1,400 3-inch guns. In 1906 and 1907 production increased to 1,700 pieces, as the army replenished its stocks. The Perm factory received a stream of orders from the Admiralty, as well as from the GAU. Other ironworks in the Urals restored their fortunes by taking additional government defence contracts. Most of them concentrated on the manufacture of shell, which accounted for two-fifths of their output by 1905.[21]

The war led to feverish attempts to complete the shipbuilding programme initiated during the 1890s. The average annual displacement tonnage completed in 1895–99 had been 264,000 tons. In 1900–4 the figure rose to 340,000 tons, and in 1905 alone it reached 416,000 tons.[22] At Obukhov, the impact of the war was reflected in a sharp rise in gross output, and management reported a modest – and merely temporary – improvement in profits. The Baltic yards also worked at fever pitch, producing and repairing vessels. Additional workers were taken on to cope with the volume of orders, bringing the total workforce to just under 7,000 in 1904, compared to 4,200 at the beginning of the century. The value of gross output swelled to 13 million rubles (yielding profits of 2.7 million rubles), compared to four million rubles ten years earlier, when the yards had been in private hands. Not all state yards reported such healthy results. The war exposed serious shortcomings at the Izhora works. Izhora continued to produce high-quality armour-plate throughout the war, but its cartridge shop left a lot to be desired. In 1904, the navy – urgently in need of artillery ammunition – found that Izhora was four years behind the current production schedule. Inspectors attributed delays to a lack of specialist technical advisers at the factory and inadequate techniques for brass-moulding.[23]

In the private sector, too, the war provided a much-needed boost. Putilov embarked on its career as a specialist arms manufacturer. In 1900, military production accounted for 15 per cent of its output; by 1905, this had risen to 27 per cent. During the war, Putilov received orders from the GAU worth nine million rubles. Contracts for artillery were accompanied by a loan worth 1.5 million rubles for the expansion of the gun shop. Putilov's products commanded the admiration of the army and other interested observers, and the firm occupied a position of virtual parity with the great state ordnance works at Perm and Obukhov. Other private arms producers were able to restore their labour force to the levels of the 1890s. At the Nikolaev shipyards, the workforce reached 2,700 in 1904–5, having fallen below 2,000 in 1901–2. During the war, output reached 6.67 million rubles, one-fifth higher than in 1903–4 and twice as high as in 1901–2. However, this revival in the fortunes of the beleaguered company was to prove shortlived.[24]

In the short term, factories coped with the volume of orders by working additional shifts. But there was a price to be paid: the pace of work meant that equipment was subjected to a much higher rate of wear and tear than in peacetime. The director of the St Petersburg cartridge factory commented that the intensity of production deprived him of the opportunity to carry out even minor repairs to equipment. He pointed out that capital productivity would decline in the medium term, unless steps were taken to replace machine tools, boilers and other equipment which had worn out. The inspector of government armouries, Lt. Gen. Bestuzhev-Riumin, agreed, noting that 'machine tools should normally be replaced every 10 or 15 years, and so each year about seven per cent of the stock should be replaced ... but at the St Petersburg Cartridge Works only four per cent of the stock was replaced and at Lugansk less than three per cent'. Unless

re-equipment took place after the war, he affirmed, labour productivity would inevitably decline.[25]

At some state enterprises, the government did take steps to invest in
new plant. The Department of Mines sank 2.7 million rubles (more
than three-quarters of its total allocation to the Urals ironworks) into
Motovilikha, whose stock of fixed capital increased by 50 per cent
between 1904 and 1907. The GAU projected a new cartridge factory, to
supplement the existing capacity at St Petersburg and Lugansk, and
the privately-owned Tula company. The Ministry of Finances accepted
the project, on condition that funds were found from the army's
existing budget. Finding this impossible, the GAU placed all three
factories on a three-shift system, and allocated 224,000 rubles for new
equipment. By this means, the Tula Cartridge Company, like Putilov,
drew upon government funds for new investment.[26]

The war did little to alter the balance between state and private
enterprise. When not ordering from abroad, the GAU for the most part
favoured state arsenals. As the war drew to a close, the government
embarked upon plans to expand the state sector. A special commission
concluded that 10 million rubles should be allocated towards the
construction of four new works, one each for explosives, powder,
cartridge and fuse production. In the event, the government allocated
little more than 2 million rubles, for a fuse works at Samara. Such
parsimony was a clear sign that financial pressures had already begun
to constrain military spending plans. The navy was slightly more
favourably disposed to private enterprise than the War Ministry, a
difference in attitude that time did nothing to diminish.[27]

As we shall see, the war caused the GAU to reassess the administration of the factories under its jurisdiction and to consider the benefits
of commercial management. In the short term, other issues demanded
prior consideration. Many factories badly needed fresh infusions of
capital, in order to re-equip. A fortunate handful had found the
resources, even in the midst of war, to invest in new plant. But, as the
war drew to a close, it became obvious that the defence departments
were in no position to make substantial and long-term commitments to
their domestic suppliers. In the difficult conditions after 1905, state
arsenals and dockyards vied for reduced and erratic orders. Even
though the state sector enjoyed a monopoly of many items, management could hardly remain satisfied with this state of affairs. The
private sector occupied a still more precarious position. Managers
realized that by investing in new plant during the war, they had stored
up problems for the future. Whether orders could be found to justify

these wartime outlays, let alone maintain employment levels, became an inescapable concern. However, during the second part of 1905 and 1906, it was the revolutionary movement that claimed their immediate attention.

Industrial production during the war

On the eve of the war, according to Kokovtsov, the economy had begun to recover from the depression of the preceding three years, but the war 'once again destroyed the restorative tendency in our industrial affairs'.[28] This view was endorsed subsequently by Soviet economists. Mendel'son concluded that 'the advantages that accrued to some sectors of industry from the increase in military orders did not disguise the general negative influence of the war on the economy'. But this is not entirely true. Total industrial output increased by around eight per cent in 1904, sustaining the improvement that had already begun in the previous year. It was to be expected that mining, metallurgy, engineering, basic chemicals and construction showed a marked improvement in output, which in 1904 was more than 12 per cent higher than the previous year. But the upturn was not confined to these branches of industry.[29]

Inevitably, the war boosted the fortunes of those sectors which supplied inputs to defence industry, as well as those directly involved in military production. Branches of industry associated with the war effort found themselves carried along in the wake of defence production. The engineering industry received orders for military goods, including locomotives and wagons. The prosperity of Russian rolling-stock producers, whose fortunes had begun to revive in 1903 (partly as a consequence of the new committee for the allocation of rail orders) continued throughout 1904 and was no less marked during 1905. However, the war did little to stimulate investment in industry or, for that matter, in railway track. Uncertainties on the St Petersburg stock exchange made it difficult for companies to raise capital. The State Bank discounted fewer commercial bills, and the general rise in interest rates discouraged industrial investment. The output of structural steel shapes and roofing iron declined slightly in 1904 (and again in 1905), confirming the picture of stagnation in industrial investment.[30]

Other branches of industry managed a modest increase in output. Again, the war effort provided fresh opportunities. A survey of the textile trade in 1905 revealed that many firms, especially in Russian Poland, had been forced to reduce their labour force, because of the general tightening of credit and because of a reduction in the supply of cotton from central Asia. But flax-processing firms, which supplied the armed forces with cloth, performed relatively well. It is also difficult to accept the view that 'the increased production of manufactured goods for the army was balanced by the reduced purchasing power of the peasant market'. A record harvest in 1904, together with transfer payments made by the army to peasant conscripts, probably served to maintain rural purchasing power, and thus to prevent a downturn in civilian production. Nevertheless, the prospects for industry in general were hardly very favourable; and they were to get much worse during the following three years.[31]

Government, businessmen and labour in 1905: workers' demands, market uncertainties and employers' organization

The revolution of 1905 shook Russian employers, changed their habits of thought and impelled them to develop new forms of action. But it should not be thought that the outbreak of widespread labour protest in January 1905 disturbed an otherwise tranquil world of work. The wave of strikes in the Russian textile industry during the summer of 1896 still remained fresh in the minds of employers and workers. In 1901, workers at the main shipyard in St Petersburg had gone on strike.[32] Nor did labour activism alone create uncertainty in Russian factories. The delicate state of industrial relations in Russia was also liable to be thrown into confusion by government action. Throughout 1901 and 1902, the tsarist police and the Ministry of the Interior actively promoted trade union organization among workers in cities such as Moscow and Minsk. This interventionist programme ('police socialism') horrified Russian industrialists, not least because the officials involved could ultimately be called to account only by the Tsar. In Moscow, where the movement made considerable headway, textile magnates expressed their disgust with the experiment. Any means of curbing the arbitrary intervention of the bureaucracy in the workplace would enjoy the wholehearted support of the employers. Hence the efflorescence of liberalism amongst many businessmen on the eve of the 1905 revolution. In addition, the working-class struggle for political reform that gathered momentum before 1905 served a useful purpose for Russian industrialists: it diverted attention from workers' economic grievances and it challenged the unfettered powers of tsarist officialdom over factory industry.[33]

Nevertheless, nothing in the previous history of the Russian labour movement prepared employers for what followed in 1905. At the beginning of the year, businessmen in St Petersburg were driven to a state of complete panic by the vehemence and extent of labour protest in the capital, where around 160,000 workers walked out in the immediate aftermath of the Bloody Sunday massacre. It fell to the Minister of Finances to spell out the government's position. At a meeting with industrialists on 24 January 1905, Kokovtsov made plain that the government held them accountable for the outpouring of labour unrest. Strikes would end when employers made improvements in the material living conditions of their workforce. Kokovtsov's attitude appalled the industrialists. Coming so soon after the experiment with police socialism, this abdication of responsibility by government stuck in the throat of employers. They were goaded by the government's unwillingness to accept any responsibility for the outbreak of revolution into entering the political arena directly for the first time.[34]

The aftermath of Bloody Sunday signalled an important change of mood amongst employers. Of course, there had been petitions to the government and meetings with ministers in earlier years, but the terms on which these took place were dictated by tsarist officialdom. By contrast, the events of early 1905 conferred on businessmen a new degree of confidence, stimulated by government insouciance, no less than by the opportunities created by revelations of the political and military leadership's incompetence in the conduct of the war effort in the Far East. It was no accident that war provided the background to this tentative and (some argued) overdue intervention in politics.[35]

The first signs of employer activism came in the spring of 1905, when several industrial associations expressed the view that the prevailing unrest could only be curbed by political reform. In March, a group of industrial magnates met in private to discuss the need for a unified body that could advance the claims of industry in the face of labour protest and the frosty reception given by government. All major industrial regions were represented. They agreed on the need for a permanent representative organization. Discussion did not advance far before the project was overtaken by events, in particular by the Tsar's declared willingness to entertain a consultative assembly. In the tense spring of 1905, many industrialists were attracted by the idea of direct involvement in politics. What better way to act upon their widespread conviction that harmony in industrial relations could best be served by reform of the 'circumstances outside of industrial life', rather than by material concessions wrung from employers?[36]

The outbreak of revolution in 1905 forced Russian employers to confront the prevailing system of industrial relations. Broadly speaking, they disliked the idea of collective representation for workers, holding to the idea that an individual worker entered into a private contract with an employer. However, employers feared still more the likelihood that in the absence of such concessions the regime would step up its arbitrary interference in the internal affairs of the enterprise. Reform of the system of industrial relations was preferable to bureaucratic intervention. This position was by no means universally adopted. The Moscow Bourse Committee vigorously opposed the suggestion made by the municipal duma that peaceful strikes and trade unions be legalized.[37]

The struggle for immediate material improvements, however, dominated all other issues in the workplace at the start of the year. The strength of the strike movement in January and February forced employers to make concessions to workers over wages and hours. But this conciliatory response left a sour taste in the mouth of management. No sooner had they made concessions but employers found reasons for holding the line against further improvements. Some employers dug in their heels at the outset. The prevailing reluctance to concede a reduction in hours was especially marked in the central industrial region. The Moscow Bourse Committee formed a commission on the labour question, headed by the textile factory owner S. I. Chetverikov, which took a hard line. Goujon, the outspoken owner of the Moscow Metal Company, complained that he would go out of business if hours fell below ten and a half. Other employers shared his opinion. In the south Russian iron and steel industry, the employers' organization issued a statement in support of the status quo, remarking that 'private enterprises are designed to yield some returns, however small, on the capital invested in them'.[38]

The strike movement abated during the late spring and summer of 1905, although there were isolated exceptions. Russian managers drew scant comfort from this state of affairs. Workers had begun to establish new craft unions, which organized fresh protests. The strike wave intensified during the autumn, culminating in a general strike. Many employers responded by taking a harder line than they had done six months before. However, in several sectors of Russian industry, notably engineering, workers did extract some concessions from their employers. As if labour activism was not enough, by the end of 1905, the government was on the verge of legalizing trade unions. This imminent concession to labour served to remind industrialists of the need to give a clearer voice to their own collective interests.[39]

In common with all shades of liberal opinion, many industrialists wanted an assembly that could serve as a conduit between organized interest groups and the government. Some business leaders hoped for nothing more than a consultative assembly, without legislative powers. Others took a more radical line, advocating a parliamentary body, elected on the four-tail suffrage. But the creation of a parliamentary chamber threatened to create as many problems as it solved. Employers calculated that industry would be under-represented in any assembly and that any economic reforms would be correspondingly one-sided. These fears did not lack foundation. An electoral system based on *sosloviia* (estates), as in local government, seemed bound to satisfy the claims of landowners and the urban propertied classes. Industry had much less likelihood of obtaining a voice commensurate with its economic significance. Nor did the existing institutions of state offer any comfort. No men with a background of full-time activity in industry sat on the State Council.[40] Finally, business leaders rapidly discovered that the most dynamic and best organized political party on the scene in the middle of 1905, the Constitutional Democratic Party (Cadets) formulated an economic programme that included the recognition of workers' right to an eight-hour day. For these reasons business leaders embarked on an experiment in parliamentary politics. It soon became clear that it was easier to identify a need for action than to unite the disparate forces of private enterprise.

Discussions between industrialists during the course of 1905 revealed a fundamental lack of agreement over the nature and function of any parliamentary assembly that the Tsar might concede. Broadly speaking, the Moscow Bourse Committee (led by V. A. Naidenov) stuck close to the project favoured by the new Minister of the Interior, A. G. Bulygin, which envisaged a consultative assembly without any legislative authority. A younger generation of businessmen advocated a parliamentary assembly with legislative powers. They included the main figures in the textile industry. Some older men, too, espoused the cause of radical reform; Chetverikov, a scion of an old Moscow merchant family, advocated radical measures in order to secure a genuine legislature, including refusal to pay taxes and promote government loans. But discussions during the summer about political reform were nipped in the bud, when Naidenov invited the governor of Moscow to close down a conference of trade and industry that had gone too far for his liking.[41]

The October Manifesto altered the situation, not least by making Naidenov and his ilk appear faintly ridiculous. Several political parties representing businessmen appeared on the scene, albeit without making a dramatic impact on the overall development of politics. They included the Trade and Industry Party, formed in Moscow, and two parties in St Petersburg, the All-Russian Union of Trade and Industry (which recruited among small businessmen and merchants) and the Progressive Economic Party. The initiative for the latter came from businessmen in the iron and steel and engineering industries, disillusioned at the failure of other business leaders to forge a united front in support of parliamentary government and to stem the tide of revolution. Without adequate organization and publicity on their behalf, industrialists feared that the government would make too many concessions to the radical movement. But this infant political party failed to attract support even from those quarters where it might have expected to do so. Major business figures in the capital poured scorn on the idea of a separate political party, which could all too easily be seen as the plaything of plutocracy.[42]

In Moscow, business leaders set aside their differences to campaign for the 'realization of the new principles proclaimed in the October Manifesto' and for the restoration of law and order. The economic programme of the Trade and Industry Party contained obligatory references to the need for continued tariff protection, and for firm resistance to the eight-hour day. This party alone managed any kind of electoral success; the others disintegrated by the time the First Duma convened. At the polls, the middle-class urban professionals voted for the Cadets; the much more numerous class of peasant traders supported peasant candidates. Business activists eventually threw in their lot with the Octobrists, a tacit admission that organized party-political activity on behalf of industry had reached a dead-end.[43]

The weakness of this political strategy lay in its assumption that Russian businessmen could unite around a common business platform. But Russian merchants and industrialists could not even agree on the core content of a business party. In the wake of these abortive attempts to form a political party capable of articulating their interests in parliament, Russian industrialists turned once more to the creation of a pressure group that would lobby the government. Their motive remained the same as before, namely to convince the regime of the validity of the claims of industry. But industrialists had to adjust to the new situation brought about by the establishment of the Duma, dominated by largely hostile interests. Only a powerful union of industrialists might counter the unsympathetic forces represented in parliament. However, the experience of 1905 demonstrated beyond all doubt that no single organization could hope to speak on behalf of the divergent business interests of the country.[44]

The problems associated with the formation of a national body came to the fore in early 1906. Leaders of the permanent advisory office of ironmasters in St Petersburg convened a congress of 'trade and industrial establishments' in the capital, in order to defend the interests of heavy industry. Over one hundred delegates attended and heard a report about the need for unity in defence of industry, irrespective of the political convictions of its representatives. More controversial was the question of the relationship between member firms, their existing associations and the new all-Russian organization. M. F. Norpe, a leading steel magnate, spoke in favour of an organization that would empower a central executive committee to act on members' behalf between meetings of the congress. This proposal evoked a sharp response from a spokesman for the Moscow Bourse Committee, who argued in favour of maximum autonomy for member associations, lest Moscow forfeit its preeminence to the 'periphery'. Representatives from the Baltic region and from Poland also expressed reservations. Russia's beleaguered businessmen, it appeared, stood on the verge of another spectacular failure.[45]

The economic programmes of the various business parties reveal something of the extent to which uncertainties about the Russian market had seized hold of Russian employers. Curiously, Kokovtsov's argument in favour of concessions in 1905 failed to evoke the obvious response from employers, namely that the industrial depression tied their hands. However, during the course of the year employers' organizations began to seize the opportunity to shift responsibility on to government, by demanding a substantial injection of funds in industry. They supported calls for a reduction in the burden of taxation on consumers, on the grounds that 'the chief brake on the development of Russian industry is the absence of a domestic market, as a result of the starvation of the peasant masses'. Several of the short-lived business parties campaigned on a platform of economic expansionism. The manifesto of the Trade and Industry Party included a proposal for investment in a programme for the development of Russia's abundant natural resources. The Progressive Economic Party urged the government to release funds for the expansion of the railway network and the mercantile marine. Other proposals, such as those for improved credit for industrial clients, reduced subsidies for state-owned industry and protection for the engineering industry anticipated many of the demands that would be made by industrial pressure groups each year until the outbreak of war in 1914.

This kind of initiative held little interest for the politicians who succeeded where the business parties failed. The elections to the First Duma gave a majority of seats to radicals and left liberals, whose main concern was to enact a land reform. The plight of industry came well down the agenda. There were some exceptions in this unsympathetic assembly, notably Peter Struve, who spoke in support of a more active budgetary policy than that favoured by Kokovtsov. But the majority of new parliamentarians regarded industry with disdain and capitalists as self-seeking individuals.[46]

Revolution and the defence sector

The revolution impinged upon the capabilities of the Russian defence sector in dramatic fashion. Hard on the heels of the fall of Port Arthur in December 1904, a wave of strikes in St Petersburg in the aftermath of Bloody Sunday (9 January 1905) threatened to disrupt defence industry. Workers in the giant machine-building and armaments factories took the lead in labour protest and political radicalism. But the revolution entailed other consequences for the defence sector. Strikes of railway workers and dockers interrupted military supplies destined for the Far East; the Tsar responded with a decree militarizing the railways.[47] Troops were diverted from the war in order to deal with unrest in the chief urban centres of European Russia. During the later part of 1905 and throughout 1906, numerous contingents of the armed forces refused to obey orders. Little was done to remedy the outstanding grievances of soldiers and sailors, whose sense of outrage over poor conditions, low pay and the indignities they suffered at the hands of their superiors matched in intensity the feelings that provoked workers into action. Nor were they appeased by the signature of the peace treaty with Japan in August. Feeling that the regime had let them down, by failing to organize the prompt and efficient withdrawal of troops from the Far East, ordinary soldiers mutinied on a massive scale. In October, troops on the naval base of Kronstadt refused to obey orders, demanding a range of civil liberties and improved living conditions. Only when the Tsar managed to reassert his authority over the nationwide popular movement did the troops begin to fall into line. Even then, however, a question-mark hung over the underlying reliability of the armed forces.[48]

In the defence industry, the year began unpromisingly. Close to the capital, at the Izhora and Sestroretsk arsenals, workers walked out on 10 January, in support of the strike at the giant Putilov plant. Workers at the Obukhov, Baltic and Galernyi shipyards followed suit. Many of the claims lodged by workers reflected a common desire for a shorter working day. Petitions presented to management at Sestroretsk and Izhora called specifically for an eight-hour day. Workers demanded a guaranteed minimum daily wage; at Sestroretsk, where piece-rates for the manufacture of rifles (*vintovki*) had been reduced from 8.26 rubles in 1895 to 6.20 rubles by 1901, workers called for the restoration of the old rate for the job. Demands for better rates of pay were coupled with a demand for pensions for employees who retired after more than twenty-five years' service. Other improvements sought included the right to better medical provision, an indication that the engagement of a factory doctor did not guarantee either decent treatment or medical facilities; the right to choose whether or not to belong to savings funds instituted at the factory and to control such funds; and the abolition of fines levied on workers for defective work, where workers themselves were not to blame.[49]

Issues of job control were also sometimes at stake. At Sestroretsk, management had begun to employ semi-skilled labour and to downgrade the status of skilled workers. Craft workers called for the employment of additional numbers of unskilled men, 'so that skilled craftsmen aren't ordered about by foremen and storeroom supervisors [*kladovshchiki*]'. More widespread still was the desire of workers to reassert their dignity in the face of unsympathetic or tyrannical supervisors. Workers' complaints about their harassment at the hands of foremen were a constant refrain of the strike movement, and petitions frequently called for the dismissal of individual supervisors who had treated workers offensively. Finally, workers demanded guarantees of no victimization.[50]

At first, managers tried to browbeat their workforce into submission, appealing to workers' sense of patriotism. The plant manager at Obukhov reminded them of the war currently being waged against Japan. His opposite number at Izhora urged workers to return to work, 'which is now absolutely essential for the good of the country in its hard struggle against the insolent Asiatic [*s derzkim aziatom*]'. Kokovtsov reinforced the point, adding that 'evil-minded men in causing this unrest have not held back, in view of the problems our nation is facing at this difficult time of war'. They all received short shrift, with a reminder (from the men at Obukhov) that workers themselves were engaged in a bitter and potentially bloody confrontation: 'it's a waste of time to talk about the war with Japan at this historic moment, with people who are not completely conscious of our struggle. We have taken the decision to fight till the last drop of our blood'.[51]

Faced with an impressive degree of solidarity, managers in the state sector offered significant concessions. The manager of the Sestroretsk arsenal, N. G. Dmitriev-Baitsurov, adopted a markedly conciliatory tone. At a meeting in January with a delegation of workers, he resolved some of the issues raised during the strike to the satisfaction of workers' representatives. He agreed to increase daily wage rates (they were last increased in 1891!), to restore the rate paid per rifle, to pay overtime at time and a half, and to impose a minimum wage of one ruble for machine-tool operators and 1.50 rubles for turners. In justification of these steps, Dmitriev-Baitsurov informed the Main Artillery Administration (GAU) that workers had been badly hit by the recession after 1901 and by the rising cost of living during 1904. Commenting on the demand for pension rights, Dmitriev-Baitsurov pointed out that the War Ministry had been considering this question for 30 years and had yet to come up with a scheme similar to that operated by the Department of Mines. He stressed that a proper pension scheme would allow managers to release workers whose infirmity made them a liability: at present, pensionable workers 'are kept on because their position would otherwise be helpless'.[52]

The manager of the Izhora arsenal, General Gross, similarly pursued a conciliatory line. Gross ordered foremen to drop the use of the familiar *ty* form of address, a patronizing style deeply resented by Russian workers. He promised that skilled craftsmen would be paid on a regular basis: workers constantly complained at the erratic payment of wages. Workers who left of their own accord would in future no longer have to wait three months before being taken on again. The management also increased wages and offered no objection to the convocation of meetings of workers' delegates. This was enough to cool the temper of the workforce for the time being. A similar pattern – strikes, followed by a management climbdown – was repeated at Obukhov and at the St Petersburg Cartridge Works.[53]

These concessions ensured that the armaments industry did not come to a standstill for more than a few days in January. There were fresh outbreaks of protest during the following month: at Sestroretsk and elsewhere, workers went on strike when the authorities rejected the delegates chosen by workers for the newly-formed Shidlovskii commission. But these stoppages were an exception rather than the rule. In any case, dramatic moves by the Main Artillery Administration and the Admiralty offered a significant additional concession to workers. In April, the GAU instituted a nine-hour day at all factories under its jurisdiction. The Admiralty did likewise in the following month, for most workers in its shipyards. In the armaments industry, the message was clear: prolonged interruptions to production could not be tolerated, and were best resolved by negotiation rather than outright confrontation.[54]

The statement issued by the authorities at the Perm arsenal at Motovilikha in the Urals at the end of May 1905 gives an insight into the mind of factory management. Workers went on strike on 25 May. The director of the plant complex, P. P. Boklevskii noted that his willingness to make limited concessions showed 'our readiness to respond to sensible and feasible demands made by workers'. He went on to say that a stoppage at the works

> will have disastrous consequences ... when I sought additional contracts for the Urals ironworks from the Admiralty and army, they warned me that if I offered no guarantees that urgent contracts would be completed on time, then they intended to place orders with overseas suppliers. The defence of the realm would compel them to resort to this unwelcome step; and the factory would have to close. For this reason I ask all workers, both in their own interests and those of the state to halt the strike and to commence work without delay.

Workers seem to have heeded this appeal; news reached the capital that the Perm plant re-opened towards the end of May.[55]

The strike movement flared up intermittently throughout 1905. Workers in the 'hot metal' shops administered by the Admiralty demanded that their shift be reduced from 12 to nine hours, in line with other groups of workers. The management was still prepared to offer modest concessions. In June, workers organized demonstrations, in protest at the government decision to call up reservists. Workers at Sestroretsk denounced the mobilization and went on strike. Some factories passed resolutions in support of the Potemkin mutineers. In July, workers at Motovilikha struck again, in protest at the arrest of Social Democrat militants. This time the management took a harder line, calling in Cossacks to restore order, resulting in the death of one worker. A third strike during September was caused by the failure of management to honour an agreement reached in July. Workers presented a long list of fresh demands. They telegrammed Kokovtsov, complaining about the embezzlement of savings funds by management. But many workers seem to have tired of strike action. Reports in

December 1905 spoke of a militant minority which supported the SR
party, but concluded that 'the more solid family workers did not
support them'. The presence of Cossack troops led to confrontation
and further casualties at Perm, much to the dismay of officials in the
local Department of Mines.[56]

In St Petersburg and Perm, there was none of the extensive blood-
shed that occurred towards the end of the year in Moscow and Nizhnii
Novgorod, in which workers in the defence industry were not
involved. In St Petersburg, the atmosphere remained subdued,
because of the change in workers' bargaining power caused by the end
of the war. At Izhora, Gross put the workforce on a four-day week in
September, blaming a lack of orders in all sections, except in the
armour-plate shop. In December, he closed down the works completely. When the plant reopened in the following month, it was with
a much depleted and demoralized labour force. At Obukhov, the
management was sufficiently confident of the hold it exerted over the
workforce, that it laid on a steamship to convey elected delegates to
the newly-formed St Petersburg Soviet.[57]

Some enterprises in the state sector escaped disruption almost
entirely. The local cell of the Social Democrats complained that
workers at the Tula arsenal were completely apathetic. An appeal in
February 1905 to mobilize behind the clarion call for a constituent
assembly fell on deaf ears. Following the defeat of Russian naval forces
in the Far East, local party activists renewed the appeal in June: 'all the
failures of our armaments, the unemployment, hunger and poverty of
the people – all this clearly shows the incapacity of the tsarist government ... are you satisfied with this slave-like silence?'. Their rhetoric
evoked no discernible response. Workers at the Tula arsenal, supported as they were by plots of land adjacent to the factory, did not
conform to the classic model of a property-less proletariat. Yet their
comrades at Sestroretsk and Perm also had this 'bourgeois' attribute,
and it did not prevent them from engaging in militant protest. This
explanation, therefore, is difficult to accept. More important was the
proximity of Sestroretsk to St Petersburg, with its dense concentration
of metalworkers. Meanwhile, at Perm and Izhevsk the Socialist Revolutionary Party made a deliberate effort to appeal to contingents of
peasant-workers, by emphasizing the relevance of its programme for
the socialization of land.[58]

The revolution of 1905 had a similar impact on the private sector.
The involvement of workers at the Putilov plant is well enough known
not to require further comment. Workers at the huge Sormovo

machine-building complex in Nizhnii Novgorod followed suit, in support of higher wages, shorter hours and improved work conditions. Their elected spokesmen negotiated with the plant manager, A. P. Meshcherskii. Much of the plant lay at a standstill by the beginning of February: strikes closed the entire shipbuilding section during the first week. Meshcherskii found himself in a difficult position. The local governor held him responsible for the maintenance of 'order' in the factory. He obtained the approval of company directors for a package of concessions, including a guaranteed minimum rate for unskilled workers and a ten per cent wage increase for all workers. As at the government arsenals, these concessions persuaded workers to call off the strike.[59]

Strikers at the privately owned shipyards at Nikolaev on the Black Sea and Lange in the Baltic confronted managers with a range of demands, most of them familiar from the petitions drafted by workers in government yards. Prompt action by the owners of Lange, who called in troops as soon as news reached Riga of the massacre in St Petersburg, forestalled mass demonstrations by workers in support of their demands. At Nikolaev, much to the consternation of some workers, the petition included calls for basic civil liberties, such as freedom of speech, press and assembly, and the right to strike (included with these fundamental claims was a demand that management 'pay no attention to a person's eyes when taking him on'). Notwithstanding the use of troops to deter protests, management at both shipyards appear to have adopted a conciliatory stance. The Social Democrat press pointed out subsequently that 'the management at Lange "dismissed" all foremen and even engineers. But none of them tried to look for another job, because they knew that in a few days' time the director would yield to the wishes of workers and that they would take up their positions once again'.[60]

Workers at the privately owned Tula Cartridge factory displayed considerably more militancy than their counterparts at the Tula arsenal. A petition to management, presented on 22 January, evoked the same kind of conciliatory response seen elsewhere. Hours of work were reduced; management adopted a minimum daily wage, offered a day off in lieu of any overtime worked on Sundays, and even agreed to a holiday on May 1 (in place of 21 November). Promises were made to improve the factory premises and to find alternative means of protecting property than the use of degrading body searches of workers as they left the factory.[61]

The rest of the year witnessed further sporadic outbreaks of protest.

The call-up of workers in St Petersburg in the summer prompted protest strikes at Putilov and the Nevskii shipyards. In July, workers at the Tula Cartridge factory again went on strike; this time the management behaved in a much less conciliatory fashion, arranging a lockout and dismissing 141 ringleaders and others deemed unsuitable for re-employment by virtue of 'physical shortcomings'. At Sormovo, labour activism culminated during December in a bloody confrontation between workers and Cossack troops in the factory environs. The Cossacks took control of the plant until early the following year. The company wrote to the Main Artillery Administration, seeking a postponement of the date for the delivery of shrapnel. After a brief investigation of the firm's affairs, the GAU sharply rebuked the company for having taken on the order in the first place, when (according to the report) it lacked suitable equipment and specialists. However, the GAU authorities accepted the company's view that the strike had caused unavoidable delay, and Sormovo escaped financial penalty.[62]

Other firms adopted similar tactics in similar circumstances. Putilov, for instance, had taken on an order for howitzers and shell in December 1904, which were due to be delivered no later than August 1905. Putilov had the dubious distinction of being particularly strike-prone during January and February 1905: the strike movement had been launched and sustained by workers from this factory. In April, the company asked for two month's grace. At the end of the year the weapons had still not materialized; Putilov asked for a further delay of eight months, blaming strikes, demonstrations and high labour turnover for the disruption. The GAU imposed a modest financial penalty, apparently unwilling to inflict too much damage on the most prized enterprise in the private sector.[63]

The relatively brief duration of work stoppages in the armaments industry during 1905 nevertheless took its toll on military production and threatened output schedules for the foreseeable future. At state arsenals, production increased during 1905, but completion rates were down on the previous year. Fewer than three-quarters of orders for rifles from the state arsenals were completed during 1905, compared to a 100 per cent completion rate in the previous year. The fact that production was not disrupted to a greater extent reflected the readiness of management to make significant concessions.[64]

Managers were unlikely to let matters rest there, especially when the shock waves of war began to diminish. The extent of the gains made by workers embarrassed factory executives, threatening as they did the profitability of the enterprise and exposing the fragility of managers' hold over the workforce. The financial consequences of these concessions were not uniform throughout the defence industry. At the Zlatoust ironworks, managers conceded wage increases of around one-third. The plant suffered drastic financial losses as production costs rose; here, as elsewhere in the state sector, management was unable to recoup these losses by increasing contract prices. Privately owned firms stood a better chance of making good the losses they incurred during the revolution, either by forming agreements between themselves to force up prices or by instituting changes in the organization of work, with the aim of boosting labour productivity.[65]

Workers in defence industry gained considerable ground during 1905. Wages rose and hours fell, in the private as well as the state sector. These concessions reflected months of agitation by organized groups of workers, taking advantage of their bargaining power. The specific characteristics of the defence industry and the international situation help to account for these dramatic gains. Workers derived strength from the geographical concentration of the armaments industry: apart from Putilov, in the south-west, and the Baltic and New Admiralty yards, St Petersburg was home to Nevskii, Obukhov, and a private powder works on the Schlüsselburg side, and to St Petersburg Metal, Phoenix and Lessner on the Vyborg side. Factory elders from these districts kept in constant touch during the revolution; meanwhile, delegates from the nearby arsenals at Izhora and Sestroretsk moved in and out of the capital. But, labour activism apart, the working class stood to benefit from the nervous mood of managers, who knew that prolonged stoppages would threaten current output and jeopardize negotiations for new contracts.[66]

Retrenchment: the government perspective

As the immediate consequences of war and revolution died down, the tsarist regime was forced to confront their economic and military impact. The magnitude of the military losses sustained by Russia immediately prompted the defence establishment to prepare ambitious proposals that would repair the damage inflicted by the Japanese and modernize the armed forces. Whether the resources could – and even should – be found to finance rearmament was another matter entirely. Other government departments submitted competing claims for funding in the aftermath of revolution. Meanwhile, the government had to settle the bill for war. Thus, the financial legacy of war and revolution dominated government economic policy at the end of 1905 and throughout 1906, relegating the question of rearmament to a more modest place on the political agenda.

The immediate expenses associated with the war amounted to 2,350 million rubles, equivalent to the total state budget in a single year. This impressive sum far exceeded government estimates of the costs of the campaign. The costs of demobilization, and other outlays associated with the end of the war, added 700 million rubles to the budget for 1906 alone. More than half of total war spending had been met by borrowing, the remainder by note issues. Only minor adjustments were made during the war to the prevailing rates of taxation. The revolution intensified the financial crisis brought about by the war. Russian bullion reserves began to fall during the autumn of 1905, as gold flowed out of the country and the tsar's citizens demanded payment in gold from their accounts: savings banks' deposits alone fell by 13 per cent during the last quarter of the year. Ministers anguished daily over the question of convertibility, hoping to maintain the illusion of the gold standard by obtaining emergency infusions of foreign aid. During the winter of 1905, the government relaxed the rules on the issue of credit notes, which had to correspond to a prescribed gold reserve. The amount of paper currency in circulation increased as the months passed, a barometer of the political and economic crisis. In December 1905, Kokovtsov travelled to Paris to reassure the French about Russia's underlying political stability and credit-worthiness, and to seek a new loan to deal with the crisis. After lengthy delays, made all the more difficult to stomach because the imminent convocation of the Duma implied a dilution of his budgetary supremacy, Kokovtsov negotiated a loan in April 1906 for 2,250 million francs, or 705 million rubles.[67]

Russia's success owed much to the 'moral support' promised the French in their dispute with Germany over Morocco. French creditors had little choice but to prop up the faltering regime: the alternative was to see the value of their securities plummet still further, as happened during the peak of the revolution. But the tsarist government could hardly count indefinitely on such self-interested acts of French generosity. Serious doubts remained about Russia's credit worthiness. The government's freedom of manoeuvre was also limited by the stipulation attached to the loan, whereby Russia had to obtain French approval for any further foreign borrowing during the next two years.[68]

Throughout 1906 the financial constraints on the tsarist regime continued to tighten. Annual payments on the state debt had trebled since the turn of the century. The budget estimates for 1906 revealed a projected deficit of 481 million rubles; on top of this, the government had to find 330 million to cover the outstanding deficit in 1905 and to meet payments on the loans floated in that year. The government drew upon the sums made available step by step under the terms of the April loan. Kokovtsov continued to remind his cabinet colleagues of the need to prune their spending estimates, in order to restore some semblance of financial normality. Things became worse rather than better during 1906, because of the unavoidable follow-up costs brought about by the war: the government approved expenditure on emergency food relief and made further payments to Japan, on behalf of former Russian prisoners-of-war. These measures, together with the costs of containing civil unrest, added 155 million rubles to the over-stretched budget and could only exacerbate Russia's precarious financial position.[69]

The Russian government had little option but to inaugurate a programme of retrenchment. At the end of 1905, the Finance Committee and the State Council warned the defence departments that their spending plans would be curtailed 'until the financial position of the country improves'. Kokovtsov continued to reiterate this message. In September 1906, he told Stolypin to use his influence to stop the 'irresistible torrent of fresh claims for funds' from the War Ministry. Anticipating one possible response, Kokovtsov pointed out that the government could not find additional revenue: the country was already suffering from a second poor harvest in succession, income from redemption payments had ceased and receipts from private railway lines had fallen. More revealing were Kokovtsov's incursions into the realm of diplomacy, in the course of which he disputed the War Ministry's contention that Russia should counter Japanese imperialism in the Far East. He concluded ominously that Russia must give priority to financial and economic recovery, which alone would 'create a proper foundation for military strength'.[70]

Before the new policy of retrenchment triumphed, battles had to be fought and old scores settled. Out of office since April 1906, Witte proved a jaundiced and fickle observer of the economic calamity that Kokovtsov had inherited. Certainly, Witte had more cause than most to bemoan the consequences of war and revolution. However unjust the verdict, in view of the shared responsibility for the failures of Russian diplomacy, Witte's enemies, such as Schwanebach, could easily pin the blame on him for Russia's abortive far eastern adventure.

His reputation never recovered. What political trust had once existed between the Tsar and his former Minister of Finances evaporated, largely because of the role Witte played in persuading Nicholas II to issue the October Manifesto, a move the Tsar rapidly came to regret. Bereft of influence, Witte did little more than issue statements of self-justification and advice to his successor. The main thrust of his argument was that the war and revolutionary upheavals undid what he had achieved during the preceding decade. The events of 1904–5, Witte maintained, destroyed the integrity of the currency which had been established with such difficulty. They had brought about an otherwise avoidable increase in taxation (sic) and in the national debt. The priority now was to re-establish monetary discipline, by restoring the convertibility of the ruble, as a precondition of attracting private foreign investment. At the same time, Witte believed that the government would find it difficult to avoid making fresh commitments: 'the war will require huge outlays on the creation of a new fleet, the repair of the army and the healing of many other wounds which the body of Russia sustained as a result of the war'. Witte doubtless anticipated that his successor would find it impossible to reconcile these priorities.[71]

Kokovtsov agreed with Witte, that there were no grounds for complacency in these troubled times. Having concluded a loan with the French, Kokovtsov was determined to prevent a repetition of the humiliation to which he had been subjected during the winter of 1905, when he went cap in hand to Paris. He assured the French that Russia had no intention of seeking further foreign loans. His main target in the medium term was to ensure that Russia would be in a position to repay the creditors who had kept faith with the tsarist empire during the dark days of war and revolution.[72]

However, Kokovtsov and Witte parted company over the strategy to be pursued in the longer term. In February 1907, Kokovtsov set up a series of private meetings with his predecessor, to consider the financial position of Russia in the aftermath of the Russo-Japanese War. Witte argued in favour of a rapid reduction in credit notes, which had increased from 578 million to 1,170 million rubles by October 1905, and for the swift restoration of the gold-backed currency. He recommended that Russia pursue all means possible to attract a continued inflow of foreign funds for developmental purposes, rather than merely to prop up the gold standard. Kokovtsov disagreed strongly, both on matters of detail and substance, maintaining that the revolution had not been crushed completely and that developmental measures were therefore premature. In his memoirs, he argues that war and revolution made it impossible to think of any 'constructive economic policy'. The government had as its main task to settle Russia's obligations with its creditors, by building up the gold reserves. Only when the economic and political situation had improved would he be willing to countenance an increase in the amount of gold in circulation and thus in the domestic money supply.[73]

With the restoration of peace abroad and the repression of revolution at home, Kokovtsov had the opportunity after 1906 to implement his policy. There was little sign that the recession was about to come to an end. Throughout 1906 and 1907 the banks reported weak demand for credit. On the brighter side, a deal Kokovtsov struck with the French in 1908 provided not only for 300 million rubles to discharge Russia's obligations under the 1904 loan, but also to obtain a further 150 million rubles' worth of foreign currency, which boosted the 'free balance' (svobodnaia nalichnost') at the disposal of the government. Here lay the prospect of some relief from the constraints which shackled the Ministry of Finances in 1906 and 1907.[74]

The debates that took place during 1906 and 1907 revealed that the resources available to the government were strictly limited. The first claim on any new loan had to be Russia's outstanding obligations to its foreign creditors. There was only modest room for manoeuvre. In November 1906, the government inaugurated an ambitious programme for agrarian modernization. Russia's ailing industrial sector could not call on state support in the midst of these momentous changes. No less significant were the implications for foreign and defence policy of Russia's delicate financial health. The constant reminders of financial decrepitude reinforced the message that diplomacy and defence would be driven by financial policy, rather than the other way round.[75]

Rearmament programmes, 1906–07

The debate about Russian rearmament took place in painful circumstances. Russia's international standing had fallen to its lowest ebb for fifty years. Financial resources were extremely limited. Russian defence chiefs lost no time in seeking to make good the losses incurred during the Russo-Japanese War. Inevitably, disagreements arose over the questions of when and how to repair the damage inflicted by the enemy. There were other, broader dimensions to the question of rearmament. Russia had to bear in mind its treaty obligations to

France. More important still, the tsarist regime hoped to keep pace with the concurrent expansion in the military – and especially the naval – strength of other European powers. In 1906, Britain launched the first dreadnought, which changed the face of naval strategy and rearmament. Germany followed suit in 1907. By 1908, the Anglo-German naval race was in full swing.

As they licked their wounds after the Japanese victory in 1905, Russian military leaders had other things on their mind than the prospect of a naval arms race. The naval engagement at Tsushima ended with the destruction or capture of virtually the entire fleet that had been dispatched to the Far East in 1904. Losses of capital and auxiliary vessels – a total of sixty-nine ships – amounted to 230 million rubles, more than twice the annual budget for the navy as a whole and certainly more than half the capital value of the imperial fleet in 1904.[76] The stock of weaponry and other army equipment was also drastically depleted. And yet the physical destruction of the ships and weaponry in 1904–5 should be kept in proportion. Much of the existing military capital stock needed replacement in any event. A group of young officers in a new Naval General Staff expressed this view in an anonymous memorandum: 'even if our battleships had not been sunk, but had remained in our hands, we should in any case have had to rebuild our fleet. We have lost precisely those vessels that were no longer fit to serve in battle, as recent experience has demonstrated: we have lost what we no longer needed'. A leading economist endorsed this sentiment, adding that many of the lost vessels served no other purpose than to maintain Russian admirals in the style to which they had been accustomed. Seizing the opportunity created by defeat, the young Turks in the General Staff maintained that the navy could now acquire a wide range of modern vessels, including dreadnought-type battleships, armoured cruisers and submarines, in order to keep abreast of other European navies. Modernization, rather than mere replacement, was the watchword.[77]

However, the need for ships that embodied state-of-the-art technology could only inflate the projected cost of rearmament. Modern ships had to travel at faster speed, but at the same time to carry more powerful naval armaments. They also had more resilient armour-plate. These improvements in military shipbuilding did not come cheap. Between 1906 and 1908 the Admiralty fought a running battle with the Ministry of Finances over the scale and purpose of naval rearmament. The Anglo-German naval race leant greater urgency to Russian naval preparations, and at the same time raised the stakes of the game.

The Admiralty's intention to restore the losses sustained at Tsushima first became apparent in the summer of 1906. The Minister, A. A. Birilev, resolved that the navy should be supplied with two new battleships without delay. With this in mind, he approached Kokovtsov, to seek his agreement to the expenditure of 42 million rubles during the next three or four years. This proposal reached the Council of Ministers in October 1906. Somewhat lamely, Birilev acknowledged that this could only be a stopgap measure: the formulation of a comprehensive shipbuilding programme would have to wait upon decisions taken by other major naval powers. Nevertheless, Birilev asserted that the navy urgently needed to replace some of the vessels lost in the Far East, in order to sustain the capacity to wage war at sea. The Minister coupled this point with remarks about the employment consequence of shipbuilding: 'a question-mark hangs over the livelihood of a hundred thousand people, who will be left to starve if shipbuilding work ceases'. The need to embark promptly upon construction of vessels was of general political significance. No doubt, Birilev's appeal was carefully designed to win over the uncommitted members of the cabinet, who had recent and painful experience of working-class unrest in urban Russia.[78]

Kokovtsov instantly objected to this proposal, on the grounds that the available resources did not permit even short-term measures of this kind. In a caustic, and typically inelegant rejoinder, he remarked that 'in view of the numerous misfortunes and evils represented by the sum of agrarian and industrial disturbances, and the destruction of the normal order in the lives of the entire people, it is impossible to attribute especial significance to the consequences that might follow from the unemployment of a few thousand factory workers'. But Kokovtsov's main argument against the scheme was that it formed no part of any overall plan of naval strategy. This view, which was shared by a majority in the Council of Ministers, also prevailed in the newly-formed Council for State Defence (Sovet gosudarstvennoi oborony, hereafter SGO), which considered the Navy Ministry scheme in the following month. The SGO, under the chairmanship of a Grand Duke who had no time for Birilev and who hoped to weaken the power of his ministry, saw little merit in a scheme which provided for two new battleships, but which offered no satisfactory plan for the defence of the Baltic littoral. Birilev was forced to admit defeat, and he resigned at the end of the year.[79]

In these circumstances, the navy chiefs had no option but to rethink their plan of campaign. Following the injunctions of the SGO, the

Admiralty formulated a more ambitious and coherent programme of naval rearmament. The eventual realization of the new programme owed much to the close personal interest that Nicholas II maintained in naval matters. The Tsar recognized that the dreadnought spelled the end of the traditional battleship. The largest Russia ship of the line had merely four 12-inch guns, compared to ten on the new dreadnoughts. The dreadnought had advantages of speed and manoeuvrability, as well as firepower. Nicholas pressed for its incorporation into the Russian navy. The intellectual justification for his wishes was supplied by the Foreign Minister, A. P. Izvol'skii, who urged that Russia respond to the naval programmes under way in Britain and Germany: 'Russia needs a battleship fleet, irrespective of concerns about the defence of our shores … we need to play a full part in the resolution of impending international questions, from which Russia cannot be absent'. The government believed that the possession of a powerful fleet would make Russia a valuable partner in any future alliance and enable it to act as arbitrator between the two largest naval powers, Britain and Germany. As Stolypin put it, 'the fleet is a lever for the expression of the right to express a voice in resolving world affairs'.[80]

The Tsar instructed officials in the Naval General Staff to draft a range of schemes for naval rearmament. Four variants were hurriedly produced. The most ambitious scheme envisaged four new squadrons, two for the Far Eastern fleet and one each for the Baltic and Black Sea fleets, at a total cost of 5,000 million rubles. Knowing full well that this level of rearmament went completely beyond the resources of the tsarist state, Admiralty officials agreed a 'minimum' programme. The new minister, I. M. Dikov, returned to the SGO in the spring of 1907, this time with a comprehensive ten-year programme of construction, costed at 870 million rubles. The rationale behind the programme was the need to defend the sea approach to Finland and the Baltic coast and to create a modern, mobile fleet for action in foreign waters. The cornerstone of the programme was the construction of a fleet of 180 destroyers and 120 submarines to defend the north-west seaboard which, everyone agreed, was extremely vulnerable to attack by land and sea. Apart from a new squadron for the Baltic fleet, the programme entailed the repair and re-equipment of vessels in the Black Sea, together with the provision of new cruisers to patrol the entrance to the Straits. A further assumption behind the programme was that ships would be dispatched to the Far East, if circumstances required: there was simply no money for a new fleet in the Pacific. By contemporary standards this so-called 'small shipbuilding programme' entailed the expenditure of enormous sums: 738 million rubles on vessels for the Baltic Sea and 132 million rubles for the Black Sea fleet. The cost reflected not only the number of vessels to be built, but also the advances that had been made in European naval technology during the previous decade. With the emergence of new types of cruiser and destroyer, as well as the construction of the dreadnought by Britain and Germany, the Russian authorities took the decision to replace the vessels lost at Tsushima by much more powerful and heavily-armed ships.[81]

The SGO sympathized with the need to improve the defence of the Baltic coast. Such a strategy would not only safeguard the Russian capital, but would also force the enemy to fight on land further west. But members of the SGO rejected any scheme for an offensive fleet, intended to operate further afield. The SGO was motivated largely by the need to reconcile the competing claims of the two armed services. In view of the prevailing financial constraints, its members decided to curb the grandiose scheme for an entirely new ocean-going force. However, the Tsar refused to accept this verdict and insisted on a naval programme that incorporated battleships. The point of view expressed by Izvol'skii accorded with his own preference for a battle-ship fleet. A compromise of sorts was hammered out in cabinet. Kokovtsov continued to paint a gloomy picture of the country's financial position, Dikov eventually obtained the approval of his colleagues for the expenditure of 31 million rubles annually over the next four years on the small shipbuilding programme, giving priority to battleships, submarines and torpedo boats (plans that absorbed the ongoing 1904 shipbuilding programme). The government made the proviso that 'the release of these credits may only be allowed in accordance with established procedures for the estimates, through parliamentary channels'. Thus, financial constraints continued to dictate a modest level of expenditure.[82]

Throughout 1906 and 1907, the navy continued to make the running. Support for an ambitious programme of naval rearmament came from organized groups beyond the corridors of government. These groups did not always agree on the type of naval programme best suited to Russia's needs. Agrarian interests demanded the creation of a powerful fleet that would protect the passage of grain exports from the Black Sea ports to the Mediterranean and to western Europe. They tapped a deep well of rhetoric in the defence establishment about the need for Russia to secure freedom of action on its southern frontier and to protect the interests of 'fledgling Balkan states' in the face of the Turkish threat. On the other hand, Russian industrialists in the central industrial region and in the north-west were more concerned with the defence of the Baltic coast and the approach to St Petersburg and other ports, which handled coal and raw materials imports.[83]

These disagreements could not easily be reconciled. They were masked, at least in part, by new pressure-groups that called for the creation of a strong imperial fleet. The most active such groups were the 'League for the renewal of the fleet' and the 'Russian naval union', both of them connected with the Admiralty and the Naval General Staff. Iu. V. Rummel', spokesman for the League, published a book extolling the virtues of a strong fleet, 'as a means of defence and international politics'. However, even he acknowledged that current financial circumstances obliged Russia to set its sights more modestly, on the defence of the Baltic littoral. Only when state finances improved could Russia assert its interests further afield.[84]

The army, too, drafted highly ambitious plans for the replacement and modernization of armaments. Here, the newly constituted General Staff was the driving force. In December 1906, its military planners placed before Rödiger, the new Minister of War, detailed proposals for the immediate expenditure of 2,134 million rubles, in order to reorganize and re-equip the armed forces. Nearly 600 million rubles were earmarked for work on fortresses and railways. The Main Artillery Administration drew up a list of its requirements, at a cost of 900 million rubles. An additional 144 million rubles would be needed for annual maintenance, repair and replacement of armaments.[85]

These projections show how the lion's share of armaments outlays would be consumed in the provision of new fortress artillery. The only unusual feature was the proposal to reorganize field artillery into six-gun batteries, replacing the eight-gun batteries, a measure that took several years to reach fruition.[86]

Rödiger had the thankless task of assessing these proposals, before they went to the Council of Ministers. He recognized that the size of the programme 'precludes any chance of financial support'. Hard-nosed realism compelled him to whittle down the estimates from 2,134 million rubles to 425 million rubles, cutting the estimated annual outlays by half. This still left significant sums for reorganization and equipment. Rödiger's revised plans would establish new machine-gun units (each infantry regiment and cavalry division was to be equipped with five 8-gun batteries), seventy-four howitzer batteries, improved rapid-firing artillery, in addition to new fortress artillery. The programme

Table 2.2. *Projected expenditure on ground-based armaments, 1906 (million rubles)*

	Immediate	Recurrent (per annum)
Field artillery[1]	112.91	30.14
Fortress artillery	704.47	7.64
Training[2]	1.63	1.72
Production facilities[3]	42.44	1.23
Other expenses[4]	34.34	1.34

Note: [1] 17 3″-gun batteries, 90 mortar batteries (122mm howitzers), 31 field batteries (6″ howitzers), plus costs of reorganizing field artillery into six-gun batteries.
[2] Two new artillery schools; fortress artillery school etc.
[3] New powder, melinite and fuse factories; expansion of existing artillery works.
[4] Re-equipment of 13 mountain and 7 mortar batteries with rapid-fire pieces; production of 100,000 rifles for reserve.
Source: E. Z. Barsukov, *Podgotovka Rossii k mirovoi voine v artilleriiskom otnoshenii*, Moscow-Leningrad, 1926, pp. 54–5.

would enable the armed forces to make good the weaponry and ammunition they had lost during the Russo-Japanese War. Overall, however, the programme was conservative: Rödiger abandoned the proposed reorganization of field artillery and reserved pride of place for fortress artillery.[87]

Like his naval counterpart, Rödiger faced strong opposition to these proposals from civilian members of the Council of Ministers. Kokovtsov not only raised the question of Russia's financial weakness, but also drew attention to alleged deficiencies in Rödiger's proposals. According to the Minister of Finances, 'a general plan for the reorganization of our armed forces still does not exist. The proposals of the War Minister do not accord with the principles of the Chief of the General Staff, and the war department has not based its demands on any verifiable basis'. Kokovtsov knew full well that the War Ministry and the General Staff had begun to talk about the need for reorganization of the armed forces, but that internal disagreements about its scale and scope delayed progress. To that extent, his argument was a valid one.[88]

More powerful forces undermined the War Ministry's plans. The Tsar's personal commitment to naval rearmament represented the most serious threat to their realization. Rödiger held back from approaching Nicholas, believing it necessary to discover first the opinions of his cabinet colleagues. But any such approach to the Tsar, in an attempt to assert the claims of the army, would have made little impact. Nicholas was deaf even to the pleadings of close advisers, including his uncle, Grand Duke Nicholas, who stressed that the army deserved no less sympathy and attention than did the navy. This lobbying was to no avail.[89]

The army's draft plans thus came up against the rival set of proposals from the navy. Attempts were made to reconcile the two programmes, notably in the Council for State Defence. The SGO had been established to provide precisely the kind of overview of defence preparations that was now imperative. Chaired by Grand Duke Nicholas, it brought together the two defence ministers, the chief of the General Staff and his naval counterpart, and the various grand-ducal inspectors of artillery and other branches of the armed forces. The SGO considered the rearmament programmes at a meeting in October 1906, but rejected them on the grounds that they did not constitute an overall programme of defence. Not even the Tsar could argue with this conclusion.[90]

The defence departments continued to prepare programmes independently. In truth, the defence ministries had to make the most of the limited resources available to them, and these limitations, with the consequent inter-departmental tussle for funds, probably did more than traditional service rivalries to hinder genuine collaboration over strategy and defence preparations. The climate for the realization of substantial rearmament programmes in 1906–7 was not propitious. Kokovtsov enjoyed considerable leverage, and argued that the need for retrenchment outweighed the demand for large-scale rearmament. Defence ministers could do little but wait for the Treasury to relax the purse-strings, unless and until the international situation offered them the opportunity to regain their bargaining power.

The critique of defence industry and the campaign for reform

The years of war and revolution witnessed important initiatives and changes in the sphere of defence industry and military procurement, as in many other areas of Russian political life. Prior to 1905, the tsarist bureaucracy had not been subject to any kind of parliamentary scrutiny. Nor could taxpayers hold the management of state armouries and shipyards accountable for their decision. The only civilian check upon the use of funds, and upon the extent to which procurement targets were met, rested with the office of the State Auditor. Other than this, defence production and military procurement remained shrouded in mystery, their secrets known only to the officials concerned.

The creation of the Duma transformed this state of affairs. The defence budget, or at least part of it, now became subject to parliamentary scrutiny. Major items of expenditure were brought before the Duma for parliamentary approval (see next chapter). Given these budgetary powers, parliamentary representatives were now in a position to demand administrative changes from the defence ministries, as a condition of the release of funds. In due course, the Duma would insist upon the reform of management practices at state-owned enterprises. Its field of competence would also extend into the realm of defence procurement, where parliamentary representatives saw scope for improved planning.

The war against Japan led initially to the reassessment of management at the GAU factories. Other state enterprises soon fell under the spotlight. The author of a critical article in *Artilleriiskii zhurnal* argued that the way forward lay in administrative reform, allowing management much greater autonomy: 'the armouries and other state enterprises demand radical renewal, and in this respect the GAU might follow the example of the Admiralty, which is placing its factories on a commercial basis. The idealism that is evident in the actions and service of the staff at the GAU factories is contradicted by the lack of confidence in their activity that is expressed in the widespread and multifarious supervision that fetters and destroys all initiative'. In the short term, however, this voice went unheard, not least because the Duma had to deal with an extensive agenda. Faced with the complexities of land reform and the nationality question, the administration of government armouries assumed less urgency. In addition, critics of the status quo faced formidable resistance from officials in the GAU. It was more difficult for the Admiralty to stand in the way of demands for reform, largely because of the unparalleled disaster that had befallen the fleet, but also because two state dockyards had until recently functioned as commercial enterprises.[91]

The Urals ironworks rather than government armouries were the first sector of defence production to feel the impact of reform. These enterprises had always stood on the margin of the armament industry. The new Ministry of Trade and Industry had neither power nor inclination to block reform initiatives. No other government officials were willing to justify existing procedures. The renowned ordnance factory at Motovilikha was the first in the firing line. Despite its favourable location and other advantages, such as a recently-concluded technical agreement with Krupp, the government expressed grave doubts about the current management of the Perm works. An inability to generate additional custom gave particular cause for concern, especially in the light of recent investment in new plant. Between 1904 and 1907, the government had sunk 2.7 million rubles into the factory, more than three-quarters of all allocations to the Urals ironworks. The value of fixed capital at Motovilikha increased by more than 50 per cent. Meanwhile, the modest volume of work it received meant that this new plant remained idle, and was simultaneously depreciating. But the government flunked the opportunity to embark on a serious assault on production costs, in order to restore the competitive position of Motovilikha. Instead, a less difficult route was advocated to deal with the short-term deficit. Officials at the Ministry of Trade and Industry recommended a 25 per cent increase in the price charged for artillery and shell, justifying this measure on the grounds that the War Ministry paid Perm only three-quarters of the price charged by Putilov. They also conceded that unused assets must be sold. However, the government decided not to follow the recommendations on prices, because the function of Perm, like other state enterprises, was to 'regulate' prices, not to approximate prices charged by the commercial sector.[92]

This uncompromising refusal to endorse an increase in prices and reluctance to embark upon administrative reform left the financial position of the Urals ironworks in a perilous position. The plant at Motovilikha regularly failed to make a profit on its operations, making a loss of 2.51 million rubles in 1907, on a turnover of 3.70 million rubles. Losses would have been greater still, had management been required to allow for depreciation. Management shifted part of the blame for increased production costs on to the labour force. Costs doubled between 1905 and 1907, partly as a result of concessions extracted from management by striking workers. Other ironworks had a similar tale to tell. But this did not tell the whole story. Zlatoust supplied 3-inch shrapnel to the Ministry of War; at a price of 7.35 rubles this was more than two-fifths higher than the price charged by the Izhevsk works, also in the state sector. Other factories were not immune from the pressures generated by revolutionary ferment, but they nevertheless managed to avoid the kind of financial disaster that loomed at the Urals ironworks, where losses increased by 132 per cent between 1904 and 1906.[93]

Table 2.3. *Performance of Perm Cannon Works, Motovilikha, 1905–1907*

	Work completed	Work in arrears	Col.2 ÷ col.1
	(million rubles)		
1905	2.85	1.39	0.49
1906	4.10	5.47	1.33
1907	3.70	6.33	1.71

Source: Vsepoddaneishii otchet gosudarstvennogo kontrolera za 1908, St Petersburg, 1909, p. 141.

Other, more systemic reasons accounted for the high costs of production. These included the predominantly casual attitude towards materials and equipment that characterized management practice throughout the Urals iron and steel industry. A report commissioned in late 1906 by the Ministry of Trade and Industry made an unfavourable comparison between the arrangements at Perm and at enterprises in the private sector. Its author, Professor V. I. Lipin, observed that the director of a private firm would either monitor personally the progress of work or delegate this task to a qualified engineer, who was required to report back. No supervisor in the private sector would tolerate shoddy work, and both he and the workers were rewarded for their performance: 'the engineer and the craftsman alike have a vested interest in the success of production, receiving a bonus for work that is actually passed as fit, not just for work that has been completed'. Engineers at Motovilikha spent little time on the factory floor. Without the incentive to supervise work properly, quality inevitably suffered. A high proportion of output at Perm failed to meet quality norms. In 1907, 22 per cent of production was rejected. This poor attention to quality control did not exhaust the problems identified. Overhead costs remained high, because each shop maintained its own complement of carpenters, smiths and other ancillary staff; and each shop devised separate arrangements for the supply of materials. Motovilikha had a notorious reputation for failing to complete its contracts on time. Delays might have been pardonable during 1905, but there were persistent complaints about its inability to complete work on time, even when the situation had returned to normal.[94]

Clearly, more drastic action was required. Evidence presented to the Duma in the winter of 1906–7 gave its members the kind of information needed to justify a radical overhaul of procedures. The government finally yielded to parliamentary pressure and embarked on the reorganization of the Urals ironworks. As we shall see, ministers even contemplated the sale of ironworks to the private sector.

Procurement procedures also came under attack in the aftermath of the war and revolution. It was widely held that the chaos evident during the Russo-Japanese War necessitated a fundamental reassessment. This consideration certainly shaped attitudes within the Duma, whose members caught the public mood. Popular consciousness of failure in the Far East extended into liberal newspapers. A well-informed economist lambasted the Treasury which he likened to a 'private purse'. Government departments too readily concluded contracts without paying sufficient attention to the standing of the supplier. Sometimes, no price was agreed in advance. Meanwhile, unscrupulous contractors pocketed the advance and absconded.[95]

Russian industrialists also seized the opportunity to state the case for reform of the system of procurement. Their spokesmen pleaded for government departments, especially defence ministries, to allocate orders in a more rational fashion, and not in the haphazard and unplanned manner that was their custom. M. A. Tokarskii, representing entrepreneurs in the north-west argued that 'Russian factories and enterprises producing supplies for the army and navy own specialized and very costly equipment. Orders from these departments arrive sporadically. As a result, enterprises can never allocate work in a normal tempo and production, as well as the amortization of equipment is very much more expensive than if orders were given taking into account the full and regular utilization of all equipment in the enterprise'.[96]

These complaints resurfaced time and again until the outbreak of war in 1914. The tsarist government eventually acceded to this chorus of criticism, by instituting a series of senatorial investigations, whose devastating findings provided further testimony of the need for reform. At the same time, a new and more jaundiced generation of military officials joined in the chorus of complaint. Pressure for reform derived from within the defence departments, as well as from without.

Stolypin gave something of a lead in the drive to reform existing defence procedures. Two measures, in particular, assured government critics in the Duma of his seriousness of purpose. The first was the creation of a new post of deputy Navy Minister, with specific responsibility for the performance of state dockyards. The holder of the post chaired the Navy Technical Committee and the revamped Main Administration for Shipbuilding and Supply (GUKS). This measure established a degree of control over the activities of naval planners, and offered an opportunity to coordinate technical and economic aspects of military shipbuilding. Secondly, Stolypin created a Naval General Staff, charged amongst other things with the preparation of estimates of Russian and foreign naval capabilities. Unlike its counterpart in the army, the Naval General Staff was subordinated to the ministry. Such were the administrative arrangements with which the Admiralty embarked on the complex tasks of naval rearmament.[97]

The re-emergence of depression in the basic industries, 1905–1907: corporate agony and corporate response

The tribulations of the industrial economy during 1905 manifested themselves in a decline in total industrial production (see table 2.4). Few sectors of the industrial economy escaped the downturn. Mining and ferrous metallurgy and the entire range of consumer goods industries all suffered. Only the continued increase in machine-building output offered a glimmer of hope in the otherwise depressed market for manufactured goods. The following two years witnessed a modest improvement, both in capital and consumer goods. However, a close inspection of the data reveals a sharp decline in the output of metallurgy and machine-building during 1906. The following year brought a brief reversal of fortune. But this proved short-lived, and in 1908 these key sectors again suffered a drop in output. In that year, iron and steel production was actually lower than it had been a decade earlier. Nor did the engineering industry give any better prospect of recovery. The key capital goods sectors remained firmly in the doldrums.

In order to understand what gave rise to these short-term fluctuations in industrial production, we need to remind ourselves of the consequences of the 1905 revolution. The strike movement had a catastrophic effect on the oil industry and, to a lesser extent, coal mining. Prolonged political uncertainty in 1905–6 badly affected the level of activity in construction and metallurgy, by discouraging industrial investment. Nor could industry expect any relief from investment in the transport sector. By 1906, therefore, the writing was on the wall for many branches of heavy industry that had managed to escape the worst ravages of the recession at the turn of the century. Firms producing rolling-stock were particularly badly affected; Briansk, for example, dismissed 2,600 workers during 1906 and 1907. Specialist arms suppliers inevitably suffered. Nor did firms with a broader base

Table 2.4. *Gross industrial production, 1896–1910*
(1896 = 100)

	All industry	Group A	Group B	Iron & steel	Metalworking and machine-building
1896	100.0	100.0	100.0	100.0	100.0
1897	109.7	113.2	108.0	116.9	115.2
1898	116.5	129.2	110.2	136.2	134.3
1899	121.6	140.2	112.3	147.4	132.3
1900	127.2	153.2	114.3	176.8	132.4
1901	132.0	148.7	123.7	153.2	147.9
1902	132.2	137.5	129.6	129.7	136.1
1903	140.8	144.5	138.9	122.9	145.7
1904	151.8	162.5	146.5	141.9	151.8
1905	146.8	162.6	139.0	131.4	163.1
1906	159.4	168.3	155.0	116.7	155.7
1907	177.3	185.8	173.0	143.2	161.7
1908	177.1	172.3	179.5	135.0	144.4
1909	183.2	185.5	182.0	143.4	149.6
1910	209.7	199.4	214.9	153.5	162.2

Note: Group A comprises coal and coke, oil, other mining, ferrous and non-ferrous metallurgy, metalworking and machine-building, construction materials (excluding ceramics), sawn timber and veneer products, basic chemicals and varnish. Group B includes ceramics, paper, woodworking, rubber, perfume, matches, textiles, animal products, food, drink and tobacco.
Source: V. I. Bovykin, *Formirovanie finansovogo kapitala v Rossii*, Moscow, 1984, pp. 22, 31.

escape: at Putilov, the labour force fell from a peak of 10,600 at the end of 1906 to 7,200 in 1908. The setback to investment activity continued to make itself felt as well.[98]

The decline in ferrous metallurgy during 1906 was matched by a decline in output in metal working and machine-building. During 1907, coal, oil and steel registered a slight improvement in output, but this did not extend to the engineering trades. In any case, this partial recovery proved shortlived. In the following year, mining, metallurgy and machine-building moved back into recession, from which there seemed no escape. A report in 1908, on the iron and steel trades and the engineering industry, warned that 'the outlook for the near future gives no grounds for expecting a speedy recovery'.[99]

The fortunes of consumer goods industries followed a somewhat different path, but any improvement had only a modest impact on the general level of industrial production. After a poor showing during 1905, a sharp upturn in the output of consumer goods took place in 1906, in contrast to the rather feeble increase in output in capital goods industries. One factor at work was an increase in consumer purchasing power, brought about by the wage increases conceded by employers during the 1905–6 conflicts with labour. This upturn continued during 1907, but it was not sustained. By 1908, the outlook seemed no brighter for consumer goods industries than in other sectors of the industrial economy.[100]

The chief cause of the problems that beset heavy industry was the continued stagnation in investment. No relief could be expected from government quarters. Private investment showed a flicker of activity, but nothing more. On average, between 1903 and 1909, sixty-five new joint-stock companies were founded, but these ventures were only half the size of those established during the boom years of the 1890s. It remained difficult to interest investors in the market for industrial securities; they preferred to place their funds in government securities.[101]

In such unpropitious circumstances, industrialists persisted with the defensive strategy they had adopted at the turn of the century. They continued to seek salvation in devices aimed at minimizing inter-firm rivalry. However, the recently established syndicates did not magically transform the fortunes of Russia's hard-pressed iron and steel industry. Partly, this reflected disagreements within Prodamet, whose member firms differed in terms of their steelmaking technologies, labour productivity and the extent of vertical integration. This made it difficult to agree on contract prices and necessitated tortuous deals to compensate firms which felt they had a grievance. Over the short term, furthermore, the syndicate deliberately kept prices down in regional markets where it competed with outsiders, including members of a rival syndicate of iron producers in the Urals, Krovlia. In the depressed conditions of 1906, the energies that had gone into the formation of Prodamet hardly appeared to have yielded lasting benefit to its participants.[102]

By 1907, the direct intervention of government in the market for railway products had already begun to strain the relationship between firms in the iron and steel industry. Some participants wanted to increase their share of orders, whilst other major producers (Russian Providence and Makeevka Steel) resented being left in the cold. The decision by Prodamet to syndicate the production of rails in 1909 undoubtedly reflected pressure from these companies, which stood to benefit from a private arrangement. In agreeing to syndicate rails, the southern magnates must also have hoped to drive out Urals factories from the market.[103]

The government continued to support the committee for the allocation of rails. Russian ministers abandoned the principle that government orders could only be sanctioned after an auction had taken place. Instead, they acknowledged that orders, backed by appropriate credits, could be placed directly with steel producers. By establishing that it had a direct responsibility for the financial viability of private enterprise and the maintenance of a basic level of capacity in the steel industry, the government set an important precedent.[104]

However, the tsarist government by no means acceded to every wish of Russian iron and steel producers. The reluctance of the government to approve the formation of a giant steel trust is a case in point. A scheme originated during 1907, at a time when the iron and steel industry remained in the throes of depression (according to one observer, 'an extremely strong steel industry has been propagated too early in comparison with existing demand'). An anonymous French financier commented that several iron and steel factories 'have long dreamed of killing off their weaker competitors one by one'. At the end of 1907, the Russo-Belgian Company and South Russian Dnieper announced plans for a trust, which would have controlled around half of pig iron output and three-quarters of rail production. The trust proposed to close down smaller enterprises and pay off their shareholders; it would thus be in a position to exploit remaining capacity to the full. The proposals were enthusiastically supported by the BUP and the Société Générale, which had interests in Makeevka, Russian Providence and Ural-Volga, three of the weaker firms in the industry, whose shareholders stood to benefit from the package.[105]

The government refused to sanction the project. A concerted campaign of opposition to the trust was orchestrated by iron producers in the Urals. Representatives of consumer interests, such as the zemstvos, large landowners and Moscow manufacturers, fearful of the consequences for iron and steel prices, also mobilized themselves in opposition to the trust. In April 1908, the forum for opposition shifted from the financial pages of newspapers to the Duma, where Octobrist deputies mounted a vigorous campaign against the project. They presented Stolypin with a memorandum, signed by 106 deputies. Supporters of the trust fought a rearguard action in an attempt to keep the project afloat. The leading business journal made the point that it would improve the confidence of foreign investors in the Russian economy, at a time when their patience was being sorely tried. Stolypin did not share this view. The government, as a consumer of iron and steel – and at a time of fiscal stringency – was uncomfortable with yet another attempt by industrialists to impose control over the market.[106]

In some ways, it was remarkable that the Russian government went as far as it did in helping Russian businessmen. The institutions of government were not devised with business interests in mind. On the face of it, the formation of a Ministry of Trade and Industry in 1905 improved the access of industrial associations to government. The first incumbent, V. I. Timiriazev, who held office for two brief spells (in 1905–6 and 1909) sympathized with private enterprise. Between December 1906 and March 1907, he had actually been chairman of the Confederation of Trade and Industry: the suggestion, put about by Witte and others, that he was merely a 'chinovnik type' is unfair. Indeed, Timiriazev was berated in some official circles for maintaining too close a link with private enterprise. Some of his more imaginative proposals derived from his belief in the necessity to work more closely with private businessmen. But this philosophy aroused the ire of his traditionally minded colleagues in government. Timiriazev went so far as to entertain the formation of advisory councils within his depart-ment, on which the Confederation of Trade and Industry, the Associ-ation of Bourse Committees and civil servants would be represented. But this potential breakthrough in tsarist administration collapsed when he resigned. His successors, I. P. Shipov and S. I. Timashev, although sympathetic to private industry, lacked the same radical political vision. They both enjoyed the reputation of being indepen-dent of business, indeed on taking office Shipov boasted of his ignor-ance of trade and industry. He antagonized merchants and entre-preneurs in Moscow and St Petersburg alike. Timashev's background was in the Ministry of Finances; he, too, had no ties with business-men.[107]

The new ministry enjoyed much less status and power than other government departments, and this constituted the greatest stumbling-block to the success of entrepreneurs in influencing government industrial policy. The powerful Ministry of Finances not only deter-mined fiscal policy, but also controlled railway freight rates, much against the wishes of the new ministry. Within the Council of Minis-ters, the Ministry of Trade and Industry had a relatively humble place. For these reasons, Russian industrialists continued to labour under a disadvantage.[108]

Conclusion

Market uncertainties continued to dog manufacturing industry in the aftermath of war and revolution. Demand for manufactured goods remained depressed during the second half of 1905 and throughout the following two years. The domestic market for capital goods showed no signs of improvement, partly because of government retrenchment and partly because of the loss of confidence amongst private investors. Government orders for military products dwindled once peace had been concluded with Japan. Prospects for a revival of demand looked bleak. Neither investment nor consumer spending offered any relief. The financial markets displayed a worrying and persistent lack of confidence. The besetting uncertainties of 1905 – the working-class movement, the vexatious behaviour of government, the condition of the financial markets – began to drive Russian businessmen into new modes of thinking, in which political activity became an option for the first time. None the less, they were hamstrung by their ingrained subservience to the tsarist regime and by deep-seated divisions, which prevented them from becoming an organized business elite and developing into a coherent political movement. Moreover, the continued recession deprived them of the capacity to act decisively.

A hectic period of business agitation and organization, set against the background of massive labour protest, yielded a modest outcome. For a brief moment, Russian industrialists became embroiled in political life, as activists in the fledgling political parties or the resurgent municipal dumas and, more often, as passive supporters of the Octobrists or the short-lived business parties. But this flirtation with parliamentary politics was both uncongenial and unrewarding to the majority of industrialists. Business parties enjoyed a tenuous and ultimately brief existence. No sooner had these parties appeared on the scene but businessmen began to divide over questions of strategy. The All-Russian Union of Trade and Industry vigorously opposed the creation of industrial syndicates and supported free trade. The Progressive Economic Party argued in favour of government subsidy to private enterprise. It was impossible to reconcile these divergent views of the role of government and the market. The overall impression created by the events of 1905–6 is one of division, giving rise to business weakness, rather than to strength.

Those employers attracted by the idea of a parliamentary form of government found that in any case it offered no solution to their immediate economic woes. The volatile mood amongst Russian workers, which was manifested in widespread stoppages of work during 1905, did not abate in the following year. If business leaders believed that political reform would provide some relief from their economic troubles, they were quickly disabused of this notion. The tentative liberalization of the political system did not resolve the economic issues. Instead, it brought to the fore social groups which either (as in the First and Second Dumas) had little respect for private property or (as in the Third Duma) equated business with specu-lation.[109]

Russian industrialists, like Russian industry, thus presented a sorry picture. Set alongside government and the organized working class, they were weak, divided and lacking in direction. Alfred Rieber points out that some entrepreneurs, particularly in Moscow, still conceived of 'salvation in some form of political alliance'.[110] Industrialists elsewhere, notably in St Petersburg and south Russia, believed that the road to corporate power and commercial profitability lay through economic organization and not through dubious political experimentation. But it was difficult to translate beliefs into benefits. The newly formed syndi-cates in the basic industries, especially iron and steel, struggled to improve the economic performance of their members throughout the difficult years of war and revolution.

Having failed to engage in purposeful political activity to a sig-nificant extent, business leaders concentrated instead on the creation of pressure groups, which would represent the interests of industry before the government. Two developments proved significant here: the formation of a congress of representatives of trade and industry and the establishment of a separate Ministry of Trade and Industry. Industrialists now had an identifiable department of government which they could lobby.

So far as the private arms trade was concerned, the revolution instilled in businessmen the desire to recover the gains conceded to workers during 1905. These concessions made sound business sense at the beginning of the year (the war was still in full swing), just as they did to the management of state armouries and dockyards. As the year came to an end, however, business strategy began to take on a differ-ent complexion. The revolution and the inescapable depression encouraged a change of tactic on the part of firms that had hitherto dabbled in armaments production. They began to embark on a course which would transform their current status as participants in a depressed and incoherent industry. In due course, firms in the Russian engineering industry would become a more assertive and potentially more powerful force, with a greater awareness of their potential and corporate identity. The arms trade ultimately became part of the new entrepreneurial elite. In 1907, the opportunity to display entrepreneurial energy and flex managerial muscles was scarcely in evidence. Rearmament would provide just such an opportunity.

Part II

Rearmament and industrial ambition

MARCELLUS: 'Good now, sit down, and tell me, he that knows
   Why this same strict and most observant watch
   So nightly toils the subject of the land;
   And why such daily cast of brazen cannon,
   And foreign mart for implement of war;
   Why such impress of shipwrights, whose sore task
   Does not divide the Sunday from the week;
   What might be toward, that this sweaty haste
   Doth make the night joint-labourer with the day;
   Who is't that can inform me?'

(*Hamlet*, Act I, Scene 1)

3   The defence burden, 1907–1914

Introduction: the economics and politics of Russian rearmament, 1907–1914

The war against Japan and the revolutionary assault on tsarist government left no political institutions unscathed and few shibboleths intact. The war and revolution – a 'moment of truth', in the words of Teodor Shanin – had exposed the hollowness of Russian imperial pretensions and underscored the vulnerability of the old regime to popular protest. Military catastrophe might have been expected to induce a prolonged diplomatic retreat. Other things being equal, defeat should have occasioned a distaste and certainly a retreat from anything resembling an active foreign policy. But things were not equal. It is true that leading officials within the old regime counselled moderation in foreign policy. The Ministry of Finances tried to rally support for a policy of restraint in government spending after 1905, which would have restricted the freedom of manoeuvre of the defence departments. But countervailing forces were at work to undermine this policy. France urged its ally to rebuild the Russian army, lest the pressure on Germany diminish. Within the imperial corridors of power, fresh initiatives were also being demanded. A new generation of naval officers seized the opportunity to formulate an ambitious programme for the Russian fleet. Crucially, the Tsar lent his support, backed by advisers who invoked the image of Peter the Great in the cause of naval rearmament. By 1910–12, Russia was committed to the creation of a powerful and modern fleet in the Baltic and the Black Sea. Costly projects to re-equip fortresses on the frontier with Germany, as well as to acquire new weaponry, inflated the defence budget still further.[1]

Thus, Russia had committed itself fully to the arms race by 1913, with unambiguous consequences for military expenditure. Russia's active

117

participation was in part dictated by international pressures, first and foremost by the need to placate France. But rearmament also reflected the momentum of internal politics, notably the revival of the Tsar's power to affect decision-making. Government ministers argued in private that Russia had become embroiled in a costly war against Japan, as a result of the triumph of a court clique over the cabinet. Rearmament helped to signal the eclipse of the 'united government' that had been carefully assembled in the aftermath of the Russo-Japanese War. An increased level of defence expenditure was the inevitable result of these twin pressures, from the French military and from the imperial household. But it also derived from the peculiarities of rearmament, which entailed the acquisition of costly modern military vessels. For these reasons, the rapid rate of increase in defence spending cannot be reduced either to an 'arms race model' or to a 'bureaucratic model'. Technological imperatives combined with these considerations to drive the Russian defence budget relentlessly upwards.[2]

The budgetary consequences of rearmament impinged directly upon domestic politics. In the first place, rearmament opened up the possibility of parliamentary involvement in the sphere of defence and foreign policy, responsibilities which the Tsar and his immediate entourage jealously guarded for themselves. Given the sums involved, the Tsar could not hope to achieve his goals completely without parliamentary assent, devoutly though he might have wished to do so. Astute politicians and military leaders took a different line, realizing that they could win over the Duma, and thereby ally themselves with 'public opinion', in support of costly armament programmes. A related development saw important questions of industrial administration brought to the fore by the scale of rearmament.

The armament drive thus broached issues of political and economic power. The commitment of resources to the armament industry formed the backdrop to a struggle between two forms of ownership, one based upon the autonomy of the profit-seeking entrepreneur, the other a closely regulated and integral element of the fiscal system. To remain committed to an unreformed state sector was to expose oneself to charges of financial profligacy. Once again, the new parliament could not be discounted. Duma deputies demanded that the government relinquish its close supervision of such enterprises and place them instead on a commercial footing, making each enterprise responsible for its own financial performance.

The political transformation wrought by the events of 1905 thus brought defence issues under the spotlight of parliamentary scrutiny for the first time. Strictly speaking, the Fundamental Laws (April 1906) gave the new Duma no right to comment upon or influence the course of foreign and defence policy. However, major items of government expenditure were brought before the Duma for its approval, including the burgeoning naval estimates. The Duma did more than just concern itself with financial irregularities within the defence ministries; its members insisted, as a condition of approving the estimates, upon the reform of defence management and administration.

If rearmament burdened the tsarist regime with the rising expectations of parliamentary representatives, what kind of burden did the defence effort as a whole entail for Russian consumers and producers? Russian peasants contributed taxes to pay for rearmament and sent their young men to serve in the infantry. The two kinds of sacrifice were closely correlated, in so far as the increased size of Russian land forces helped to determine increased levels of defence spending. Russian villagers might have been hard pressed to make the connection. But they may have begun to question the tsarist defence effort when it impinged directly on their lives. The mobilization of rural conscripts (in 1904 and, again, in 1914), the use of troops for internal pacification (in 1905–7) and the recurrent presence of troops in rural billets or on military manoeuvres perhaps caused the Russian peasantry to reflect on the meaning of vigilance and the costs of defence. One thing was certain: those who sought to increase the burden of defence were unable to justify rearmament in terms of the material benefits it yielded the Russian consumer. No one could pretend that Russia required a navy to protect food imports. The integrity of the Russian loaf did not hinge upon food imports, as it did in Britain or Germany.[3] But vigorous rearmament might be justified more readily so far as food producers and manufacturing industry were concerned. A strong navy in the Black Sea would protect the grain export trade; its equivalent in the Baltic could protect imports of coal and miscellaneous industrial inputs. The depressed metalworking and machine-building trades could cash in on the arms race. Why should these myriad interest groups not be harnessed to the chariot of rearmament? The bulk of the population, meanwhile, had to be content with the rhetoric of pan-slavism, which alone served to justify the defence burden. But, in this troubled society, rhetoric provided a fragile foundation for rearmament.

Foreign policy, 1907–1914

If the central plank in Russian foreign policy during the 1890s had been the alliance with France, the corresponding element in foreign policy after 1905 became the diplomatic understanding with both France and Britain. The French had lent indispensable financial support during the Russo-Japanese War and revolutionary upheaval in 1905. The British, whose relations with Russia reached their nadir in 1904, at the time of the Dogger Bank Incident, were prepared to listen to Russian overtures. An agreement between the two countries was finally sealed in 1907. The advantages to Russia of this understanding were considerable, not least because Britain could be expected to restrain its Japanese ally. Japan was still smarting after the treaty of Portsmouth, New Hampshire, which had yielded less advantageous terms than those to which, as victor, Japan felt entitled.[4]

The character of the Franco-Russian alliance was inevitably affected by the Russo-Japanese War, which had exposed Russian military vulnerability and financial weakness. A joint meeting of the French and Russian General Staffs in Paris – the first for five years – took place in April 1906, and it symbolized the shift that had taken place. A decade earlier, the French had hoped to convince Russia that troops should be concentrated on the border with Germany, but Paris had none the less eventually conceded Russian anxieties about Austria-Hungary, which was regarded in St Petersburg as no less serious a threat to Russian interests. The relationship between France and Russia now assumed a quite different complexion. Russia agreed to recognize that Germany constituted the chief threat. If and when German troops mobilized, the two partners would automatically and jointly respond. By contrast, any mobilization by Germany's allies, Austria-Hungary and Italy, would lead to preliminary joint discussions and, only if appropriate, to a mutual response. The French military took the opportunity to cross-examine their allies about Russian military preparations and defence capabilities. They expressed particular concern about the length of time it would take Russia to recover from the losses sustained in the Far East, and about the timetable drawn up in St Petersburg for the mobilization of Russian troops on the frontier with Germany. In addition, they sought assurances about the supply of uniforms, medical equipment and rolling-stock. Finally, to add to the humiliation, the French demanded to know the state of morale amongst Russian troops. Palitsyn, the new chief of the reorganized Russian General Staff, sought to reassure his French

opposite number that the Russian army was making a satisfactory
withdrawal from Manchuria and that the army would be back to
normal peacetime strength, disposition and stocks within the next
twelve months. But he was unable to reassure the French over the
question of troop mobilization, and he was silent about the morale of
Russian troops. Keen to press home a temporary advantage, the
French urged the construction of additional railway lines that could
accelerate the movement of troops from the Russian interior to the
German border.[5]

The tsarist government did not see the alliance with France as a
reason for behaving any more aggressively towards Germany and its
allies. Unfortunately, the German government pursued precisely
those policies that were calculated to arouse traditional pan-slavist
fury. More specifically, Germany undertook to defend the interests of
Austria-Hungary with still greater fervour than during the late nineteenth century. The key demonstration of German loyalty towards its
ally came in 1908, when Austria annexed the principalities of Bosnia
and Herzegovina, a course of action underwritten by Berlin. The
precipitate annexation of slav-populated lands by the Austrians
aroused widespread opposition in Russia. The Serbian government
expressed acute anxiety about Austrian behaviour. However, in the
face of the Austrian threat, namely that concerted Russian opposition
would be met by an invasion of Serbia, Russia capitulated. In March
1909, Germany demanded that Russia officially accept the Austrian
action and dissociate itself from Serbian resistance. Paul Miliukov, the
eminent historian and leader of the Cadet Party in the Third Russian
Duma, aptly likened the Russian response to events in Bosnia and
Herzegovina to a 'diplomatic Tsushima'. Yet the tsarist regime had
little choice but to respond in the way it did, as Austrian diplomats
knew full well. A military response by Russia, acting alone, was out of
the question. The Russian government had to acknowledge the unpalatable fact that France would not offer its ally the kind of support
that Germany was prepared to offer Austria-Hungary.[6]

Even diehard Russian admirers of imperial Germany were insulted
by German behaviour in 1908–9. But the Russian government continued to exercise diplomatic restraint, the logical outcome of military
and economic weakness. It did not follow that Russia would remain
permanently weak, or inferior to its European neighbours. The Prime
Minister, P. A. Stolypin, acknowledged that 'any policy at the present
time, other than a strictly defensive policy, would be the frenzied
action of an abnormal government'. However, he also noted that 'in a

few years' time, when all is calm at home, Russia will once more speak with her old authority' (*zagovorit prezhnim iazykom*).[7] Until such time as Russia recovered the poise of which Stolypin spoke, it had two choices: either the government could acknowledge the superiority of Germany and come to some understanding with Berlin, at the likely expense of the alliance with France; or Russia could strengthen its ties with France and Britain, in the hope that any further increase in the influence of Austria-Hungary in the Balkans could be stifled. The first choice had much to recommend it. At the very least, it would provide a breathing-space, and a useful opportunity to remind France that the alliance should not be taken for granted. On the other hand, such a move would undo the results of many years of Franco-Russian diplomacy. The second choice entailed a logical extension of existing commitments, even if it hardly constituted a reliable insurance policy, so far as the Balkans were concerned.

In Persia and the Far East, Russia had less to worry about. The tsarist regime reached an accord with Britain in 1907, which recognized that both countries had interests to protect in Persia, Russia in the northern half and Britain in the southern zone. This cleared the way for a significant improvement in Anglo-Russian relations, even if it did little at present to stem the encroachment of German economic interests in the region. Russian military aims in the Far East were deliberately low-key. The General Staff noted that 'the political result of the war has made it necessary to confine ourselves to the comparatively modest task of preserving the inviolability of our possessions in the Far East', that is the defence of the Chinese Eastern Railway.[8] To this end, Russia maintained 64,000 troops in eastern Siberia and the Amur province, mostly located in fortresses. They were equipped with 796 field guns, 72 howitzers and around 200 machine-guns. Resources did not permit any addition to this modest complement. Similarly, Russia displayed a minimal naval presence in the Pacific: one first-class and one second-class cruiser, together with a handful of torpedo-boat destroyers and submarines, had to suffice. Kokovtsov was properly dismissive of the Russian naval presence in the Far East: 'none of the submarines meets the requirements of modern defence and none can venture far from its base. The situation is no better so far as the destroyers are concerned. All twenty belong to the old type – small, slow and poorly equipped with armaments'. He drew attention to a shortfall of around 50 per cent in the number of officers and 30 per cent in the number of ratings. But his analysis of Russian financial weakness left no room for improvement.[9]

[handwritten annotation at top: 1913: Tsarist concern about German designs on the Straits]

This lamentable chronicle of Russian weakness explains Russian willingness to conclude an agreement with Japan. The rapprochement took place with remarkable speed. On the Japanese side, too, an understanding with Russia had much to commend it. Japan needed to raise a loan in France, and its chances of doing so would be improved if Japan could demonstrate a readiness to deal with France's main ally. The rapprochement took a tangible form in 1907: Russia recognized a Japanese sphere of influence in southern Manchuria, whilst Japan acknowledged Russian rights in the north. This agreement was further strengthened three years later, by which time Russian military preparations had failed to show much improvement. Significantly, Japan had embarked on a programme of rearmament after 1909. The military share of the Japanese defence budget rose from 24 per cent, in 1906, to 40 per cent in 1911. Funds were allocated to the modernization of artillery and rifles, the construction of new naval bases in Korea and the acquisition of four dreadnoughts. By 1910, the Japanese fleet was twice as large as it had been in 1904. But the Japanese military did not have its sights set on Russia; rather, rearmament was designed to keep pace with the concurrent military preparations of the USA. By 1911, rearmament was in full swing, in the Far East, as well as in Europe, although for the moment Russia fell out of the race for supremacy in the Pacific.[10]

Until Russian rearmament had been completed, the tsarist regime was in no position to pursue an active policy in the Balkans, in support of the slav population. The relatively harmonious relations between Russia and Germany between 1910 and 1912 reflected this unpalatable truth. However, there were limits to this policy of enforced appeasement. The tsarist regime was prepared to support Russia's clients in the Balkans. Russia disliked the thought that other powers could take advantage of Ottoman weakness in order to gain control of the Straits. Yet, by 1913, there was increasing evidence to suggest that this was precisely what Germany intended.[11] By 1914, fortified by evidence, as it believed, of Germany's determination to control the Straits of Constantinople, the tsarist government was prepared to fight. But was Russia sufficiently powerful militarily to resist German and Austrian pressure, as it had singularly failed to do in 1909?

The dangers inherent in a policy of confrontation were articulated on the eve of the war by former Minister of the Interior P. N. Durnovo. In a famous memorandum, prepared for Nicholas II in February 1914, Durnovo began by pointing out that war would be the inevitable outcome of Anglo-German rivalry: 'the interests of these two powers are far too incompatible and their simultaneous existence as world powers will sooner or later prove impossible'. A war between the two powers would rapidly develop into a European conflict. In such a conflict, he argued, the main burden of fighting Germany would fall on Russia, because France was too deficient in military manpower to play its part. But the war would have serious internal political consequences for Russia, for example, by encouraging nationalist uprisings in Poland and in central Asia, against the central government. Neighbouring states, such as Persia and Afghanistan, might be tempted to exploit Russian preoccupations in central Europe.

In these circumstances, according to Durnovo, it made sense to come to an understanding with the German Reich. The advantage of such a policy should have been clear long ago: Germany and its ally had stood to one side during the Russo-Japanese War, when it would have been all too easy for them to exploit Russia's embarrassments in the Far East. Instead, foreign policy had taken a different turn, and the Russian government had drawn closer to the Reich's arch enemy, thereby entailing 'the rupture of neighbourly, if not friendly relations with Germany'. A rapprochement would serve to convince Berlin that Russia had no fundamental quarrel with Germany: 'the vital interests of Germany and Russia do not conflict'. Russia had nothing to gain from the seizure of German territory. Durnovo also argued that it was in Russia's interests to maintain favourable commercial relations with Germany. This was a contentious point: the trade treaty of 1904 gave several advantages to German exporters, while continuing, by means of the tariff, to deny Russian agricultural producers equivalent access to the German market. Russian exporters hoped for a revision of the treaty in their favour. Durnovo made the reasonable point that any concessions by Germany would obviously depend upon a prior political understanding, and would be prevented by the rapprochement with Britain. A Russo-German understanding would bring economic and social benefits: 'the British and French .. live in their own countries, removing from Russia the profits produced by their enterprises, down to the last kopek. The German investors, on the contrary, live in Russia for long periods and not infrequently settle down permanently'. Finally, the political system of imperial Germany made it the logical diplomatic partner of the tsarist state: 'it should not be forgotten that Russia and Germany are the representatives of the conservative principle in the civilized world, as opposed to the democratic principle, incarnated in England and, to an infinitely lesser degree, in France'. It made little sense to engage Germany in a war, when both victor and vanquished would likely fall victim to social revolution.[12]

However, this arch-conservative did not represent educated public opinion in Russia at large, which was prepared to countenance a war with Germany, if this was the price that had to be paid for a settlement of the slav question. Although pan-slavism in Russia was neither coherent nor well-organized, 'the cumulative effect of repeated frustrations helped to spread the fatalistic feeling that only a war could resolve the series of humiliations that Russia had suffered'.[13] The tsarist government was prepared to become embroiled in war, because it could no longer tolerate Austrian behaviour towards Serbia and because it could now count on the unwavering support of France. But would the Russian armed forces be equal to the task? The answer to this question depended in large part on the content and realization of the programmes of rearmament that had been drafted since 1906.

Defence planning and rearmament programmes, 1907–14

Defence policy in the interwar years was the product of conflicting priorities, departmental rivalries and budgetary constraints. Separately, these problems were neither new nor insoluble. But when they coincided, as they did after 1905, the enormity of the tasks confronting the architects of defence policy assumed unprecedented proportions. For a brief time, it appeared possible that newly created institutions would provide the kind of strategic overview and coherent planning that was required, particularly when resources were limited. But these hopes were quickly dashed. And when Russia's financial position improved, as it did by 1909–10, and the competing rearmament plans jostled for attention, there was no mechanism in place to ensure that funds were spent in accordance with an overall strategic plan.

In the short term, it had to be decided whether Russian defence priorities lay in Asia or Europe. Both theatres of operations could mobilize plenty of advocates on their behalf. The war against Japan bequeathed a legacy of suspicion between the two adversaries, leading some strategists to press for a renewed commitment of forces to the Far East. Russian military planners also dwelled upon the need to counter British domination in southern Persia; even after the agreement had been signed with Britain in 1907, Russia still felt it necessary to plan for the defence of its interests in the Near East. In other quarters, the emphasis switched to Russia's western frontier and to the need to

M Transport advocates more RR & on RFC
(1908)
126   **Rearmament and industrial ambition**

prepare for a potential conflict with Germany. This involved more than an increase in the strength of the army: the Baltic fleet had to be strengthened, if the north-west coast were to be defended against the threat from Germany. In the immediate aftermath of the Russo-Japanese War, the traditional Russian preoccupation with the Balkans diminished. But Austrian action in Bosnia in 1908 compelled strategists to restate Russia's longstanding interests in south-eastern Europe. Finally, the imminent expansion of the Turkish fleet, news of which reached the Russian government in the spring of 1909, served to complicate matters still further, by demanding a Russian response in the Black Sea.[14]

However, it was one thing to identify these diverse strategic interests; reconciling them was quite another. In practice, the tense situation in the Balkans, as well as Turkish naval rearmament, called for a strong imperial fleet in the Black Sea. But those who spoke in favour of this option faced the wrath of naval spokesmen who insisted on the primacy of the Baltic fleet, or even the Far Eastern fleet. The defence of the frontier with Germany, similarly, posed difficult choices: there could be no question of maintaining a substantial presence in the Far East or the Near East, if Russia wished to offer a serious challenge to German military power on the European mainland. As if the reconciliation of these alternative conceptions of defence were not enough, Russia's military planners operated against the background of spending constraints. Kokovtsov's looming presence hardly made it any easier to engage in defence planning, and he was always ready to exploit differences of opinion within rival services, in order to fend off their ambitious claims for funds.

The task of providing a grand overall design for Russian rearmament fell to the Council for State Defence (SGO). It did not enjoy any conspicuous long-term success. Admittedly, the SGO took some cautious and well-considered steps. For example, it inspired a secret initiative early in 1908, to identify appropriate measures that might be taken by all sections of government, including civilian ministries, in order to improve the defence of the realm. Even the Ministry of Education and the Holy Synod were asked to indicate possible projects for state defence that might come under their aegis. The sums involved were enormous – not surprisingly, given the open-ended nature of the exercise. The transport ministry outlined a programme for the extension of railway lines in the Far East and the construction of a second track along the length of the trans-Siberian, that would cost more than 500 million rubles. But these plans were always likely to be frustrated by the evident shortage of resources, and the element of fantasy merely served to underline the ineffectiveness of the body which inspired them.[15]

In some quarters, the very magnitude of the strategic tasks that confronted Russia served as a justification for a modest defence policy. In a paper prepared for the General Staff in December 1908, General Alekseev, currently chief of staff of the Kiev military district, set out the arguments in favour of caution. Russia's potential enemies included Romania and Sweden, in addition to Austria-Hungary and Germany, both of which had recently strengthened their position in the Balkans and Turkey. Japan had embarked on a programme to rearm. Neither Russia's grip on the Caucasus nor on Finland could be considered secure. In this unfavourable climate, Russia had to concentrate on the defence of St Petersburg and on the security of its western frontier. This meant that measures should be taken to strengthen Kronstadt and Reval; and that Russia should be prepared to abandon Poland, lest Russian troops be cut off by a joint attack by Germany and Austria-Hungary. Here was a programme that attempted to define strategic priorities and to reconcile them with resource constraints. It was difficult to argue that Alekseev's programme lacked internal consistency. But it was always vulnerable to attack from those who supported an offensive strategy, such as could be embodied in a strong Russian fleet.[16]

Whatever the boldness of individual initiatives, the SGO failed to generate a comprehensive defence programme. Criticism along these lines surfaced in the Duma, during a debate on the defence budget in 1908, when Koliubakin, a Cadet deputy from St Petersburg, pointed to the lack of an overall strategic plan and thus to the absence of any proper coordination between the defence departments. The SGO made an easy target, with its lack of experienced administrative staff, its preponderance of Grand Dukes and its elevated position, making it unaccountable to the Duma. When, at the end of 1908, the Tsar abruptly disbanded it, few tears were shed.[17]

With or without the Council for State Defence, Russia's defence ministries continued to prepare programmes independently. Until 1910, they had to make the most of the limited resources available to them. These financial limitations, with the consequent inter-departmental tussle for funds, probably did more than traditional service rivalries to hinder genuine collaboration over strategy and defence preparations. The climate for the realization of substantial rearmament programmes in 1907 and during much of 1908 was simply not propitious. Kokovtsov argued that the international situation was more stable than it had been in 1906, when the military first projected highly ambitious rearmament schemes. Rearmament, therefore, did not deserve high priority.[18] But, by 1910, circumstances had changed: rearmament moved to the top of the agenda, because of the aforementioned changes in the international scene, a shift in the relative political fortunes of the defence and finance departments, and broad parliamentary backing for rearmament.

The capacity of the Russian army to carry out the tasks assigned it between the wars depended, as before, upon the number of men in uniform, their training and morale, and the supply of food, uniforms and weapons. The disposition and organization of troops also preoccupied military planners. Because so many resources and so much attention were devoted to military administration, recruitment and troop disposition, these subjects require more than a bare mention. We shall then focus upon the question of armaments, to which (at least until 1913) relatively few resources were devoted.

Russia maintained a substantial military bureaucracy. The experience of the Russo-Japanese War convinced Nicholas II of the need to expand the agencies responsible for defence planning and military supply. With the end of hostilities, in June 1905, the War Ministry lost its old, and by now defunct Staff Office. In its place, the Tsar instituted a new General Staff. As in Germany, the General Staff operated independently of the War Ministry; and the chief of staff reported directly to the Tsar. In addition, inspectors-general of artillery, cavalry, infantry and engineering enjoyed the right of direct access to the Tsar for the first time. However, these changes failed to clarify the demarcation between the holders of these posts, on the one hand, and the new General Staff and Minister of War, on the other. To compound the problem still further, the SGO also intervened in the task of military planning until its sudden abolition. In his memoirs, Sukhomlinov describes these arrangements as a Tower of Babel: Russia lacked a single forum in which the various voices could ultimately be encouraged to sing the same tune.[19]

This administrative proliferation generated bureaucratic rivalries and in-fighting, which the Tsar did nothing to discourage. Typically, a plan of defensive measures worked out by Chief of Staff F. F. Palitsyn in August 1908 aroused opposition, both within the General Staff and the War Ministry. His opponents objected to Palitsyn's proposals to redeploy troops along the western border, along the line of the Niemen, Bug and Dniester rivers, with a second line of defence 200km.

further east, rather than their concentration in the north-west, where they were vulnerable to a two-pronged attack through east Prussia and Galicia. To cite another example, Minister of War Rödiger's insistence on the re-equipment of infantry clashed with the SGO's insistence upon the refurbishment and restocking of fortresses. At issue here were irreconcilable differences between those who espoused a mobile and flexible conception of future engagements in the field, and those who adhered to the orthodox view of static, positional war.[20]

No obvious military interests were served by the kind of administrative confusion described above. Instead, it played into the hands of the Minister of Finances. Time and again, Kokovtsov adopted a simple tactic: no funds could be released until the army chiefs had drawn up a clear and coherent programme. The multitude of different bodies could never generate this unity of purpose. All that they achieved was a plethora of proposals, most of them involving substantial expenditure. Eventually, in November 1908, the Tsar returned the General Staff to the War Ministry and abolished the SGO. Having long complained about the 'absolute chaos' in defence planning, Rödiger found himself unable to take advantage of the new arrangements. Early in 1909, he was forced out of office, the victim of a right-wing campaign that attacked him for supporting Guchkov's withering assessment of the capacity of the top army commanders. The demands of office had also taken their toll; Rödiger appears to have been completely exhausted by the time his tenure of the War Ministry came to an abrupt end.[21]

Rödiger was succeeded by V. A. Sukhomlinov, who enjoyed much greater authority and broader responsibilities than his ill-fated predecessor. Now that the General Staff fell within his jurisdiction, the new minister could oversee army supply, military intelligence and topography, mobilization planning and military transport, in addition to personnel and procurement. But the restoration of a degree of departmental unity in the War Ministry under Sukhomlinov did not immediately signify a political defeat for Kokovtsov. On the contrary, the Minister of Finances ostensibly welcomed the new state of affairs, because it brought defence planning and spending back into the Council of Ministers. Given his domination of the cabinet, this was an important development.[22]

Notwithstanding his advocacy of retrenchment, even Kokovtsov could not overlook the basic question of army strength. The war against Japan had depleted the ranks of the Russian army and denuded it of reserves. On the eve of the war, the army stood at just over one million soldiers and just under 42,000 officers; but by the beginning of 1906, its strength had fallen to around 735,000 men and 29,360 officers. Steps were taken almost at once to increase the numbers of reserve troops, by accelerating the rate of conscription. The length of service in the infantry and field artillery detachments was reduced to three years; other men henceforth were to serve for four years. Two categories of reserve were created: one to back up field troops, the other, comprising older men, to support troops in the rear. By 1908, the army stood at 1.31 million men and 43,000 officers. Nor were these the only significant changes that affected personnel. Before he resigned, Rödiger encouraged older officers to retire and increased the rates of pay for lower ranks and officers; poor salaries meant that the shortfall of officers reached 60 per cent in some units.[23]

The tsarist government could hardly avoid measures such as these to restore the strength of the army. Other important initiatives proposed by the army came to grief, because of financial constraints. Even quite modest and sensible proposals came under the knife. For example, the Main Artillery Administration drafted plans in spring 1908 to stockpile raw materials, on the assumption that Russia might be blockaded for a prolonged period (plans for a two-year blockade required 28 million rubles, in order to secure the necessary materials). But this proposal failed to find favour with the Ministry of Finances, which eventually agreed to set aside a mere three million rubles, on condition that this sum be reallocated from funds already approved for the procurement of rifle cartridges.[24]

The primacy of Kokovtsov and the financial cutbacks upon which he insisted also affected the army's traditional commitment to fortresses on the border with Germany. Of course, doctrinal considerations also operated here, as Sukhomlinov found when he proposed to scrap some of the more decrepit structures. The new minister did not support the allocation of scarce resources to fortresses, believing that the funds could be better spent elsewhere: in his view, it made more sense to plan for a strategic retreat from Congress Poland, and to prepare for a counter-offensive launched from European Russia, than to tie up troops and artillery in fortresses, over whose defence there hung a question mark. However, the opportunity cost argument found no favour with the Tsar and his advisers. The French, too, baulked at the thought that Russia could allow Germany such an easy passage into Poland. Sukhomlinov had to moderate his radical views, and the programme he drew up in 1910 made ample provision for fortresses.[25]

Weapons and ammunition had been consumed, seized or destroyed during the war against Japan. Some emergency measures were taken to replenish stocks. In the medium term, military leaders developed more ambitious proposals. Rödiger advocated the adoption of more manoeuvrable field artillery and new machine-guns, with corresponding measures to train artillery and infantry officers in their use. The diplomatic crisis that erupted in the Balkans in 1908 offered the War Minister his first real opportunity to seize the initiative from Kokovtsov. In January, with the backing of the SGO, Rödiger requested 315 million rubles, in order to build up stocks of munitions that had been lost three years earlier (55 million rubles); to purchase additional machine-guns and field artillery (192 million rubles); and to build up Russian armed forces in the Far East (68 million rubles). The Council of Ministers agreed to support an approach to the Duma for all but 16 million rubles of this sum. Thus, three years after the end of the Russo-Japanese War, the army finally received the means to fund a modest rearmament programme. The acquisition of machine-guns and the creation of the appropriate troop units were an important product of this programme, indicating that the War Ministry did not always give priority to the defence and improvement of fortresses.[26] This represented an important breakthrough: for the first time since the Russo-Japanese War, the War Ministry had managed to get its way. No doubt, Kokovtsov hoped that the allocation of 300 million rubles would satisfy the appetite of the military. Certainly, Kokovtsov's subsequent behaviour, which did nothing to endear him to Sukhomlinov (he appears in Sukhomlinov's memoirs as 'the shallow Kokovtsov') indicates that he had lost none of his appetite for budgetary discipline.[27]

In Sukhomlinov's view, the Russian army suffered at least as much from deficiencies in organization, as it did from financial constraints. The improved disposition of available resources could reduce the gap between the performance of the Russian army and that of the armies of the Triple Alliance. Sukhomlinov noted that army battalions contained anything from four to 10 companies, regiments consisted of two to four battalions, artillery brigades might have from five to nine batteries, leading to varying strengths in artillery from one army division to another. One army corps had 16 battalions, another 68, with 56 and 168 artillery pieces between them. The Russian army was deficient in howitzers (fewer than six per army corps, whereas Germany had three times as many). Russia could afford also to organize its soldiers and reserves more effectively, which Sukhomlinov proposed to achieve by creating three regional groupings, such that each infantry regiment, artillery brigade and reserve contingent had a specific territorial identity.[28]

In reorganizing field artillery, Sukhomlinov replaced the less mobile eight-gun battery with a six-gun battery. This allowed him to create extra reserve artillery brigades, attached to each reserve division. Additional batteries of field howitzers (eighty-three in all, instead of just twenty-nine hitherto) strengthened the army still further. However, this programme was not realized without significant costs. Norman Stone points out that the measures entailed additional numbers of artillery officers, promotions and thus an increase in the salary bill. Nor did these measures do anything to lessen divisions within the army; indeed, they antagonized the 'patrician' element, which stood to lose out to the younger, upstart officers who controlled the new artillery batteries.[29]

Sukhomlinov also supported technical innovation in artillery. During his first year in office (1909–10), the General Staff introduced an updated 3-inch field gun and 122mm and 152mm howitzers, capable of inflicting greater damage on entrenched enemy positions. However, the decision to maintain the fortresses meant that most resources were allocated to heavy fortress artillery, rather than to field artillery. Under the 1910 programme, relatively few resources were devoted to heavy field artillery.[30]

Improvements in transport also claimed Sukhomlinov's attention. As with fortresses, more was at stake than military doctrine: large amounts of cash were required as well. In 1908, Palitsyn and Alekseev showed the way, by calling upon the army to examine all forms of communication (road, rail and river), in order to weld them into a single strategic framework. Their scheme foundered, partly because of a shortage of funds and partly because of opposition to the proposals from other elements within the General Staff. Sukhomlinov revived the issue, emphasizing the importance of troop mobility in wartime and thus the need to invest in railways and to integrate them into military plans. But the expansion of military railway building had to await the commitment of funds by the French.[31]

The extent to which the international and domestic political situation had changed within a year of Sukhomlinov's appointment was evident in the preparation of a comprehensive rearmament programme in February 1910. The plans envisaged an outlay of 715 million rubles over ten years. This huge expenditure included 373 million rubles for fortresses, 114 rubles for strategic railway lines and 81 million rubles for heavy field artillery. The continued emphasis on the role of the fortress is self-evident, although sums were assigned for coastal fortresses (Vladivostok, Kronstadt), as well as for those along the German border with Russian Poland. Sukhomlinov drew some comfort from the fact that funds were now released for the reorganization of the army, in particular the standardization of the size of troop units. The Duma approved the programme in April 1910. But his victory proved something of a Pyrrhic one. Sukhomlinov's main aim had been to improve the ratio of field artillery to infantry, but there was precious little space for this aspiration in the final programme. The needs of field artillery had come unstuck on the twin rocks of financial constraint and service opposition.[32]

In 1912, Sukhomlinov devoted all his energy to the formulation of a new and comprehensive programme for the reequipment and expansion of the ground forces. The two Balkan wars (1912–13) provided the War Minister with the justification he needed for this programme. Increases in the size of the German army gave a further impetus to Sukhomlinov's plans. In addition, plans were being prepared to expand the size of the French army by one-third, through an increase in the length of service from two to three years; the French would naturally expect a reciprocal effort from their Russian ally. According to the new programme, the needs of artillery would finally receive proper recognition. In March 1913, the Tsar approved the expenditure of 225 million rubles on armaments, including 181 million rubles on artillery. Four months later, Sukhomlinov secured still larger sums for a five-year programme, designed to increase the quantity and quality of field artillery.[33]

The final piece in the jigsaw of military planning slotted into place in 1913, when the Tsar approved a 'great army programme' and a programme of railway building on the western frontier. The Russian military had already come to accept the French view that an offensive against Germany should be mounted within 15 days of mobilization. The new initiatives were designed to give further expression to the planned offensive.[34]

The cornerstone of the 'great army programme' was an increase in the size of the Russian army by nearly 500,000 men and just under 11,800 officers, an increase in its peacetime strength of nearly 40 per cent and 28 per cent respectively. Infantry would benefit by the addition of 266,000 new men, artillery numbers would grow by 126,000, and the remaining recruits would swell the ranks of sappers and technical staff. This growth in numbers would be accompanied by

the much-discussed reorganization of the army, the purpose of which
was above all to reduce the time taken to mobilize forces effectively.
Most of the additional recruits would form new army units, whilst the
remainder would bring existing infantry units up to full strength. The
programme envisaged an increase in the strength of heavy-calibre
field artillery batteries. By the time it was completed, in 1917, the army
would have a total of 8,358 pieces of artillery, including 6,048 light
pieces, 666 mountain guns, 1,176 light howitzers, 312 42-line guns and
156 powerful 6-inch howitzers. Finally, the programme contained – for
the first time – a rationale and detailed provision for military aviation.
These combined measures cost 433 million rubles. The Tsar gave his
blessing to the programme in October 1913. Sukhomlinov immediately
began to draft new recruits, well in advance of Duma approval for the
release of funds, which eventually followed on 22 June 1914, twenty-
seven years to the day before the German invasion of the Soviet
Union.[35]

With the adoption of the 'great army programme', the Russian
General Staff brought to fruition its preparations for a European war.
The programme represented the culmination of the view that the
Russian General Staff should mobilize troops against Germany with all
possible speed, a view that was shared by the military leadership in
Russia as well as in France. The underlying aim of the programme was
to effect the rapid mobilization of Russian troops and thereby threaten
any German incursion into France with retaliatory action by Russia.
But this was no 'Blitzkrieg' strategy, designed to head off a political
and social crisis at home by means of speedy victory abroad. Rather, it
was a long overdue attempt to improve the mobilization of Russian
troops, the rapid deployment of infantry and artillery at the front and,
once in place, their manoeuvrability. Both the French and the Russian
military leadership were broadly happy with the outcome of their
military planning.[36]

Budgetary restrictions until 1910 dictated modest measures as
regards Russian land forces. The reorganization of army units, the
recruitment of additional troops, the provision of extra firepower –
these were hardly the stuff of which dreams of military grandeur were
made. They were, nevertheless, important measures in themselves.
Anything more than this, such as improved fortresses, heavier calibres
of field artillery and especially new railway lines required substantial
additional funding. The 1910 army programme did little to redress the
imbalance between the army and the navy. Only in 1913 did the 'great
army programme' begin to chart a different course. What altered the

situation was the evident deterioration in international relations, the
readiness of the Duma to grant additional credits for the army and the
fact that Sukhomlinov's political skills (as he jubilantly boasted)
proved more than a match for those of Kokovtsov. But until 1913,
Russian planners, like those elsewhere in Europe, had to accept that
the real growth in defence budgets would derive from the imperative
to create large navies.

If Russian military planners entertained any doubts about naval
rearmament, they were quickly dispelled by the private utterances of
tsarist officials. It became axiomatic in the Russian Foreign Office that
naval requirements should be accorded priority. A. P. Izvol'skii, the
Minister of Foreign Affairs (1906–10), let it be known that 'states which
neglect the reconstruction of the navy after it has been lost inevitably
become second-rate powers'. Even the Minister of War was forced to
acknowledge that 'the fleet was bequeathed us by Peter the Great'.[37]
Nicholas II had no wish to abandon this legacy, and his views ultimately settled matters in favour of the navy. It was largely because of
his personal intervention, in 1907, that the navy received funds to
begin work on the dreadnought programme. Nor could the Duma
conceive of a defence strategy in which the Russian navy played
merely a minor role: influential spokesmen, such as A. I. Zvegintsev,
the Octobrist deputy and chairman of the Duma defence commission,
adopted a pronounced pro-navy position in Duma defence debates.[38]
The problem was that Russian strategists had to decide what kind of
navy Russia needed and what it could afford. Broadly speaking, until
1910 navy planners concentrated upon needs of the Baltic fleet. The
deteriorating situation in the Balkans changed this assessment. The
challenge from Turkish rearmament and the commitment to the
freedom of Russian exports through the Straits urged on strategists to
articulate the interests of a strong Black Sea fleet. The new Navy
Minister, I. K. Grigorovich, as well as Izvol'skii's successor, S. D.
Sazonov, wished at the very least to see a Russian fleet in the Black Sea
that would not yield to the Turkish fleet in its size and capability. The
temporary closure of the Straits in October 1911 and again in April 1912
reinforced the view that Russia required a strong naval presence in the
Black Sea in order to assert the freedom of passage of grain exports to
western Europe. This viewpoint gained ground in 1911; by 1914, it had
triumphed.[39]

Until 1908, the navy had been obliged to draw up its rearmament
plans under the watchful eye of the Council for State Defence. With its
abolition, the navy possessed greater freedom of manoeuvre. In 1909,

naval chiefs drafted an ambitious scheme for rearmament. A new, ten-year shipbuilding programme envisaged the reconstruction and modernization of all three fleets, in the Black Sea, the Baltic and the Pacific. The scale of the proposals led to the establishment of a special inter-departmental commission in August, which proved to be yet another forum for tussles between the defence chiefs and the Ministry of Finances, as well as between the army and navy. At successive meetings of the commission, representatives from the Naval General Staff and the Navy Ministry indicated that their comprehensive programme of rearmament would cost a total of 1,090 million rubles. This drew an immediate response from Sukhomlinov and his General Staff officer, A. Z. Myshlaevskii, who complained that even this estimate overlooked the need for expenditures on the defence of the proposed new naval bases (at Reval, Nikolaev and Nikolaev-on-Amur) and on training new complements of officers and men. According to Sukhomlinov, the total cost was likely to be nearer 1,500 million rubles. It was impossible to contemplate spending such extravagant sums on one branch of defence. Other members of the commission reiterated the point that had been made three years earlier, namely that the priority was for the navy to defend the Baltic approaches in general and Kronstadt in particular. The claims of the Black Sea and Far Eastern fleets would have to wait. Grigorovich found himself under attack from other quarters as well. Stolypin, although acknowledging that 'Russia cannot limit itself to the creation of a torpedo-boat or submarine fleet', nevertheless wanted to know how the scheme could be reconciled with the need for a defensive strategy.[40]

Kokovtsov, typically, spoke at length, complaining that he had not been consulted in advance about the proposals, and implying that the Admiralty had attempted to preempt a collective decision on the country's future defence needs. In any case, he remarked sarcastically, what role was left for diplomacy, when all powers – the Triple Entente, Japan, Turkey, Romania and Sweden – were presupposed to be the enemies of Russia? Finally, Kokovtsov dwelled upon the opportunity costs of this level of defence spending. In the event, the commission agreed to consider the shipbuilding programme in conjunction with the projected reorganization and expansion of the army, resolving that 'the tasks of the navy must be set modestly, and unfailingly in accordance with the tasks of the armed forces'. This meant a defensive role for the Baltic and Far Eastern fleets and sufficient commitment to the Black Sea fleet to make it stronger than the Turkish fleet.[41]

This decision proved only a temporary setback to naval rearmament.

Five months later, at the beginning of 1910, the Navy Minister approached the Council of Ministers with a revised plan for the expenditure of 730 million rubles on the fleet. As in 1907, the bulk of the expenditure, some 641 million rubles, was to be assigned to the re-equipment and expansion of the Baltic fleet, including 502 million rubles for eight battleships, four armoured cruisers, four light cruisers, 18 destroyers and 12 submarines. Of the remainder, 56 million rubles would be allocated to the Black Sea fleet and 34 million rubles to the Pacific fleet. Taking into account the 33 million rubles that had already been approved for shipbuilding, in the 1908–09 estimates, Grigorovich requested just under 700 million rubles of new money. Once again, the Tsar's vision of a grand imperial fleet had been placed on the agenda.[42]

Kokovtsov, meanwhile, had not given up hope of curtailing these ambitious programmes. He held out before his cabinet colleagues the prospect of tax increases; and, as everyone knew, changes to the budget would inevitably involve the Duma indirectly in questions of state defence. It was a clever tactic. The Duma did hold up the estimates, by questioning the competence of officials in the Admiralty. Some members of the Duma decided to oppose the release of fresh credits, until further reforms had been made to the administration of the state dockyards. It appeared that Kokovtsov had succeeded in forcing a delay in naval rearmament. But further debate revealed that the Duma was prepared in principle to look kindly on the Admiralty's spending plans, provided they were recast. Duma spokesmen found fault with the overriding emphasis in the scheme upon the expansion of the Baltic fleet. Members urged that proportionately greater resources be devoted to the expansion of the Black Sea fleet, because of the export imperative and the growing threat posed by the Turkish fleet. The resulting difference of opinion between the 'northerners' in the Naval General Staff and the 'southerners' in parliament provided ample reason for the lack of progress in naval rearmament during 1910.[43]

By the spring of 1911, the navy felt confident enough to prepare a new programme of shipbuilding. This revived confidence may be attributed to the fact that some administrative reforms had been carried out to the satisfaction of the Duma. Under the new proposals, which formed a draft law on the imperial fleet, immediate priority would once again be given to the Baltic fleet. But over the next twenty-two years, the Baltic fleet was to be transformed by the addition of two active squadrons and one reserve. So far as the Black Sea was concerned, the intention was to create a fleet that would be at least half as strong again as those of other states which maintained navies in those waters. This was a clear attempt to meet parliamentary concern about the neglect of the Straits. The navy requested 513 million rubles, to implement the first part of the programme for the reconstruction of the Baltic fleet. When the plans came before the Council of Ministers, in December 1911, the estimated cost had risen to 760 million rubles. Eventually, the government agreed to approach the Duma for 162 million rubles, in order to strengthen the Black Sea fleet, whose needs had become particularly pressing, as a result of the growing Turkish naval presence, as well as to provide for more modern battleships, torpedo boats and submarines.[44]

(1912) During the following year, the navy returned with fresh plans for the Baltic fleet. Its officials came up with a so-called 'enhanced programme' (*usilennaia programma*), designed to create two new naval squadrons in the Baltic by 1919, together with a reserve squadron. The programme provided for eight battleships, four battle cruisers, eight light cruisers, thirty-six torpedo-boat destroyers and twelve submarines. The civilian ministers again objected to the cost and, in particular, to the lack of prior consultation. But there was no longer any question of delay. After discussion in the Council of Ministers, and (Summer with the enthusiastic support of the Tsar, the project went to the Duma 1914) in March. Three months later the Duma approved a bill for the expenditure of 421 million rubles on shipbuilding. Meanwhile, the > interests of the 'southerners' were not neglected. The 1911 shipbuilding programme had recognized the claims of the Black Sea fleet. Now, on the eve of the First World War, the government approved plans for additional vessels – one destroyer, two cruisers, eight torpedo boats and six submarines – to be built on the Black Sea, at a total cost of 110 million rubles.[45]

The result of this feverish activity was thus to inject substantial resources into naval rearmament, and particularly into the creation of a large battleship fleet in the Baltic, to which the bulk of resources was devoted. Naval rearmament represented a triumph for Grigorovich and the Naval General Staff. The intense pace of construction was reflected in the fact that the construction of new warships accounted for 55 per cent of the total naval budget by 1914, a far higher proportion than in other countries. This activity meant full order books for Russian shipyards. Advocates of the Russian fleet believed that Russia would soon have a fleet to rival that of Germany.[46]

The defence budget and fiscal policy, 1907–14

The armaments programmes outlined above led to pronounced changes in the size and composition of the central government budget. Total defence spending increased from 680 million rubles in 1907 to 961 million rubles in 1913 (see table 3.1). Reported defence expenditure increased at an average rate of just under 6 per cent per annum, well in excess of the rate of growth of the budget as a whole. Defence spending also grew faster than elsewhere in Europe. In Germany, Britain and France, defence expenditure barely increased at half the Russian rate. However, the exceptional rate of growth of Russian defence spending is to some extent deceptive, because it began from a low base in 1904–7: in 1903, the government had pegged the war budget at its current level for the next five years, continuing the practice adopted in 1899. Besides, as we shall see, the Russian defence departments secured less for their rubles than did their counterparts elsewhere. These considerations put the scale of the increase in defence expenditure into perspective.[47]

The growth of the Russian defence budget concealed a huge disparity between the two armed services. While ordinary spending by the War Ministry increased by just over six per cent between 1907 and 1913, the ordinary expenditure of the navy increased three times faster, at a rate of 18.6 per cent. Most of this growth was concentrated in the last three years of peacetime, and reflected the heavy costs of acquiring modern warships, provided for in the small shipbuilding programme.

The Ministry of Finances estimated that defence consumed between 33 and 36 per cent of the total budget for 1907, figures that were arrived at by attributing all extraordinary expenditure for that year to defence.[48] Adopting the same criteria, this proportion fell to 31 per cent in 1908 and to 28 per cent in 1909, where it remained in the following year. In 1911, it climbed back to 33 per cent. On the eve of the First World War, defence spending amounted to just over one-third of the total budget. The Duma broadly agreed with these estimates. The defence ministries tended, not surprisingly, to underestimate their share of the budget, putting it at no more than 25 per cent in 1908. But their method of calculation failed to take any account at all of extraordinary expenditure, and thus gave a no less misleading impression than did the Ministry of Finances. But all these figures need to be treated with caution. Some items, such as the expenses associated with conscription, were charged to other ministries. In addition, the costs of building and maintaining strategic highways and railways were

Table 3.1. *Government expenditure, 1900–1913 (million rubles)*

	War	Navy	Transport	Finances	Debt	Trade & Industry	Extraordinary[1]	Total[2]
1900	332	89	367	280	267	–	284	1,883
1901	335	93	389	308	227	–	209	1,874
1902	343	100	446	334	290	–	365	2,167
1903	351	114	456	366	289	–	225	2,108
1904	372	113	449	350	298	–	831	2,738
1905	378	117	449	339	307	–	1,280	3,205
1906	393	112	477	353	357	32	1,152	3,213
1907	406	88	508	429	374	32	387	2,583
1908	463	93	571	432	398	33	273	2,661
1909	473	92	551	460	395	39	156	2,607
1910	485	113	537	409	409	39	124	2,597
1911	498	121	543	403	399	42	310	2,846
1912	528	176	555	425	394	54	449	3,171
1913	581	245	641	482	424	65	289	3,383

[1] includes debt payments (842 million rubles, 1900–13), cost of Russo-Japanese War (2,595 million rubles), state railways (1,198 million rubles) and officially acknowledged rearmament expenditure (463 million rubles).
[2] includes the following ministries and departments, not itemized separately: Imperial household, Holy Synod, Interior, Justice, Foreign Affairs, Education, Agriculture, State Audit Office.
Source: P. A. Khromov, *Ekonomicheskoe razvitie Rossii v XIX–XX vekakh*, Moscow, 1950, pp. 524–9.

frequently assigned to the budget of the Ministry of Transport, or to the extraordinary account, where they attracted less international publicity and parliamentary scrutiny.[49]

Within the budget of the War Ministry, additional resources were found for military manoeuvres (2.8 million rubles in 1908, rising to 11.0 million rubles by 1913), as well as for pay, for the construction and maintenance of barracks and for military training and education. The sharp increase in appropriations in 1908 reflected improved pay, provisions and housing. These items, as well as fodder for the huge number of army horses, continued (as before) to absorb around half the total budget. Much of the subsequent increase in the army budget is explained by the growth in the numbers of men in uniform. The sums devoted to military hardware, such as artillery, small arms and ammunition, did increase in absolute terms: for instance, the Main

Artillery Administration reported in 1912 that the programme to re-equip the army with field and mountain artillery had been completed, and promptly redirected resources towards the repair of guns and the purchase of small arms. But these items never amounted to more than 15 per cent of the total. The most notable change occurred in construction, the other chief capital item. Expenditure on the modernization of fortresses loomed larger during the interwar period than it had prior to the Russo-Japanese War. The share of the military budget devoted to fortifications, barracks and other construction projects roughly doubled between 1907 and 1913, reaching ten per cent of the total. In 1914, it stood at 12 per cent.[50]

The rapid increase in naval expenditure was similarly accompanied by changes in the composition of the budget. In 1908, 43 per cent of the navy budget had been devoted to the construction, repair and armament of military vessels. Five years later, this proportion reached 62 per cent, representing 193 million rubles. The share of the naval budget earmarked for administration declined, helped by efficiency gains in the naval bureaucracy in St Petersburg. According to N. V. Savich, 'eminence grise' of the Octobrist party and deputy chairman of the Duma defence commission, this shift in the naval budget vindicated the campaign by its parliamentary critics to improve the efficiency of the ministry. Meanwhile, the costs of staying in the naval arms race were increasing year by year. Savich commented that only 35 per cent of the budget had been devoted to the construction of new vessels in 1908, whereas this proportion had risen to 55 per cent by 1914, well ahead of the other chief naval powers, Germany and Britain. This demonstrated that Russia had belatedly begun to catch them up.[51]

The tsarist regime spent between 12 and 15 per cent of its total military budget on weaponry of all kinds between 1904 and 1914. The proportion spent on military hardware amounted to at least 20 per cent, inclusive of military shipbuilding. By 1911–14, expenditure on hardware represented one quarter of all defence expenditure. To give a clearer idea of its impact on industry, one should take into account defence-related capital expenditure, that is construction and hardware. During the last full year of peace, the government spent 7 per cent of its total budget on capital items associated with the defence effort, more than three times as much as in 1907. This level of spending (diluted by some orders placed with foreign suppliers) implied a major boost to Russian manufacturing industry and the building trades.[52]

These increased levels of military expenditure testified to Kokovtsov's slackening hold over the Council of Ministers. Prior to 1911,

Kokovtsov urged that the military should continue to observe strict limits on spending, as had been agreed in 1899 and 1903. But the rapid growth in military appropriations demonstrated that his attempts to restrain the defence ministries met with diminishing chances of success. Bearing in mind, furthermore, that 'economic-operational expenditures' constituted a significant share of extraordinary spending after 1908, Kokovtsov's ultimate lack of success in curbing the appetite of the armed forces becomes still more conspicuous. Army chiefs were able to exploit the war scare in the Balkans during 1908, in order to persuade the government of the need to increase defence spending. The threat of war in central Europe in 1912–13 justified additional outlays on fortresses, railways and artillery. In the most striking demonstration of the new mood, the Russian navy extracted huge additional amounts, in connection with the grandiose shipbuilding programmes.[53]

In seeking to overcome the resistance of the Ministry of Finances to higher levels of defence expenditure, both services were able to count on the support of the Duma. There were dissenting voices, such as the Cadet doctor Andrei Shingarev, who had been thrust into the limelight after the publication of his book, *The Dying Village*. Shingarev was a thorn in the flesh of the government and constantly criticized the defence estimates, for reasons that will be examined presently. But the Cadets and parties to the left formed a minority in the Third Duma, which was dominated by the Octobrist Party. The Octobrists provided the chairman of the Duma budget committee (Mikhail Alekseenko) and its defence commission (Alexander Zvegintsev), as well as the most vocal speakers on defence issues, Alexander Guchkov and Nikanor Savich.[54] The Third Duma provided a valuable ally for the Ministry of War during the Sukhomlinov era. The roots of this alliance are not difficult to detect. Reforming elements within the War Ministry counted upon the Duma to support administrative changes, in order to reduce the influence of Grand Dukes in their capacity as inspectors of artillery, engineering and so on. The Duma also endorsed the shipbuilding programmes, particularly when it had secured reforms at the Admiralty. The Minister appointed in 1911, I. K. Grigorovich, became adept at fostering cooperation between the Duma majority and his officials.[55]

Nevertheless, it would be misleading to suggest that the growth of the defence budget reflected significant initiatives on the part of the Russian parliament, given that the prevailing political system allowed limited room for manoeuvre. The law of 8 March 1906 carefully circumscribed the Duma's budgetary powers; in effect, it ensured that the Duma could neither initiate nor amend the budget estimates, but only approve or reject them as they stood. In practice, the right of rejection did not amount to much, in so far as the previous year's appropriation remained in force, should the Duma reject the estimates. The estimates presented by the War Ministry, in particular, were 'armour-plated', for the simple reason that its budget already provided a firm base. Parliamentarians complained that they could effectively scrutinize only 13 per cent of the army's budget, namely that part pertaining to new appropriations, a degree of impotence matched only in respect of the Holy Synod. By contrast, the navy estimates, like those for the ministries of Finances, Trade and Industry, and Transport, were exposed to greater *glasnost*, because the Admiralty constantly sought new appropriations. But, in the drama of naval rearmament and finance, the Duma played second fiddle to the Admiralty, particularly after the advent of Grigorovich. Further appropriations went through without a murmur of dissent; the final sessions of the Third Duma and those of the Fourth were notable only for the absence of parliamentary debate. On set-piece occasions, such as accompanied the approval of the small shipbuilding programme in 1912, government ministers and naval chiefs paraded before the Duma. But to pretend that the finance of Russian rearmament involved a partnership between government and parliament was pure fiction.[56]

How did the Ministry of War and the Admiralty manage the budgets at their disposal? Here, the Duma did manage to make its voice heard, largely by drawing upon the deep well of discontent that had been created during the Russo-Japanese War. Parliamentary representatives maintained that accounting procedures in both departments left a great deal to be desired. The Third Duma regarded officials in the defence ministries as incompetent and even corrupt men, who had been tarred with the brush of defeat in 1904–5. Even honest officials were thought to betray a casual approach to the management of the colossal sums at their disposal.

The charge most frequently levelled against the defence ministries, at least until 1911, was that they failed to spend sums that had been earmarked for specific purposes. Critics also accused defence officials of indulging in exaggerated estimates of cost, in order to build up a reserve of funds. These phenomena served as the pretext for reducing the claims of the defence ministries on the budget prior to 1910–11. Kokovtsov himself joined in the chorus of complaint, observing that 'the appropriation of credits ran far ahead of the realization of the projects' for which funds had been assigned.[57] To some extent at least, this mismanagement could be attributed to the behaviour of government contractors. Some offered their services, without being sufficiently prepared to handle contracts. By the time their irresponsibility dawned on officials, the funds had already been committed. Suppliers themselves told a different tale, of the reluctance of defence officials to commit adequate funds, such as would enable them to embark on projects with confidence. There was an element of truth in this accusation. Defence departments tended to operate rigid accounting procedures; once funds had been assigned to a given project, officials were reluctant to reassign them to another during the current financial year. In other words, the critics had got hold of the wrong end of the stick. Far from being too lax, accounting procedures were – if anything – too strict. Greater flexibility in the allocation of funds might have smoothed the relationship between customer and supplier, as well as have improved the speed with which contracts were completed.[58]

By 1911–13, criticism still centred upon financial mismanagement, but the focus had shifted. Hitherto, officials had normally been accused of a reluctance or inability to use the appropriations that had been approved. Now, their critics observed a tendency for the service ministries to overrun the approved estimates. Typical of such complaints were those delivered by Shingarev, during the debate on the 1911 budget. He accused the Admiralty of maintaining wholly unsuitable vessels as a reserve, of failing to speed up the time taken to repair vessels and of spending disproportionate amounts on administration. The Russian navy failed to exercise sufficient budgetary discipline and permitted spending on these and other items to spiral out of control. Some historians have confirmed his unfavourable verdict on naval administration, but without examining the operative factors, over most of which the ministry had no control.[59]

Shingarev and his fellow critics had a valid point. Officials in the two service ministries lacked skills in budget management, although it is by no means certain that they were any more deficient in this respect than their counterparts elsewhere in Europe. They received no proper training. They were poorly paid – hence the frequent charges that they had accepted bribes – and the career structure provided few incentives to develop better skills. Sukhomlinov and Grigorovich recognized this fact, but the hesitant steps taken to remedy the problem had little effect before war broke out.[60]

The management of defence budgets, at a time of rampant rearmament, inevitably subjected even the most assiduous officials to great strain. It should be emphasized that the difficulties they faced were not normally of their own making. The structure of the defence industry and the technology involved in modern armaments conspired to frustrate attempts in the defence ministries to make their budgets stretch further, and even to maintain a reasonable control over spending. The main business of officials in the Admiralty was to draw up and monitor contracts with suppliers of finished goods. But, in practice, the number of suppliers was limited by the nature of naval technology, which only a small number of firms possessed. These considerations had a direct bearing on costs, because any attempt to keep them down was undermined by the oligopolistic character of the industry and by the complex and costly nature of the technology embodied in modern naval vessels. Thus, any attempt to stretch the resources of the Admiralty came up against obstacles which no government official, however competent, could easily surmount.

The War Ministry found itself in a somewhat different position. It had responsibility for different branches of the armed forces, such as artillery and general military stores. Generally speaking, the War Ministry dealt with a larger range of suppliers than did the Navy; the question of having to cope with the cost implications of advanced technology arose less frequently. But here, too, complaints arose about the tendency of suppliers to collude, in order to force up prices. Some officials connived at this practice and were rewarded for their discretion. This made the job of even the most scrupulous and honest official more difficult.[61]

One other objective difficulty should be mentioned. The prewar inflation in materials prices was reflected in the charges passed on to government departments. This posed an acute problem, particularly where the construction of fortresses and port installations was concerned. It was also reflected in the cost of shipbuilding. Government officials blamed Prodamet and looked further afield for supplies of iron and steel. But, as we shall see, the inflation reflected the general buoyancy of the prewar economy and the claims being made on available capacity, rather than the activities of Prodamet. Wherever the responsibility lay, however, the pre-war inflation compounded the problem of budgetary planning.

A detailed breakdown of the defence budgets reveals the combined impact of these various factors. Tables 3.2 and 3.3 show the extent of the discrepancy between estimated and actual outlays on military goods and facilities. The figures do not suggest that the service ministries were becoming any more adept at bringing outlays and estimates into line.

Table 3.2. *The army budget: estimates and outlays, 1907–1913 (million rubles)*

	Weapons			Construction		
	estimate	outlay	% difference	estimate	outlay	% difference
1907	36.5	35.1	− 3.8	18.1	20.8	+ 14.7
1908	37.5	35.3	− 6.1	17.0	20.2	+ 18.9
1909	34.2	36.9	+ 7.8	21.4	21.4	0
1910	36.7	39.4	+ 7.5	34.0	36.0	+ 5.9
1911	33.7	37.1	+ 10.4	32.8	35.2	+ 7.4
1912	28.9	30.6	+ 6.1	33.4	42.7	+ 28.0
1913	35.4	35.4	0	59.2	60.3	+ 1.9

Source: *Proekt gosudarstvennoi rospisi dokhodov i raskhodov na (1908 .. 1915)*, 5 vols., St Petersburg/Petrograd, 1908–15.

Table 3.3. *The navy budget: estimates and outlays, 1907–1913 (million rubles)*

	Shipbuilding			Military ports		
	estimate	outlay	% difference	estimate	outlay	% difference
1907	25.4	34.8	+ 36.6	8.3	8.3	0
1908	27.2	31.3	+ 15.1	12.8	9.5	− 25.5
1909	21.6	24.6	+ 13.9	9.6	9.6	0
1910	29.5	26.2	− 11.4	9.5	13.5	+ 42.9
1911	43.4	55.3	+ 27.6	11.5	11.9	+ 3.3
1912	70.3	75.2	+ 6.9	13.1	18.3	+ 39.4
1913	103.1	108.1	+ 4.9	28.9	39.1	+ 35.6

Source: as table 3.2.

The continual overrun in the budget for weapons between 1909 and 1912 suggests a failure to prevent suppliers from passing on price rises. This was even more marked in the construction budget, which set funds aside for fortresses and ports. Estimates for the creation and modernization of ports proved particularly hazardous, reflecting the impact of inflation in construction materials. Demand from the military, combined with industrial and (later) railway investment, forced up the price of brick, cement and timber. The picture revealed by the naval budget is somewhat more complex. Here, too, actual outlays tended to overrun estimates, except in 1910. Thus, the army normally exercised a greater degree of control than the navy. But this was only to be expected, given the more complicated questions of technology with which officials in the Admiralty had to deal. Besides, the navy demonstrated a remarkable improvement in its ability to predict likely expenditure on vessels, although not on port construction projects (compare the divergence between estimates and outlays in 1913, when the budget was three to five times greater, with that in 1907–10). To this extent, we can endorse the views of the erstwhile critics of the ministry, who on the eve of war conceded that its officials performed creditably, at a time when the demands being made upon the Admiralty had increased enormously.[62]

How did the tsarist regime finance this growth in defence spending? One means at the disposal of the government was to reallocate resources. This strategy could clearly only work if those in charge of high spending departments – transport was the obvious case in point – could be persuaded to moderate their own claims for funds. In public, Kokovtsov preferred instead to emphasize the growth in ordinary receipts, which increased the government's room for manoeuvre. Finally, the government drew upon the so-called 'free balance' (*svobodnaia nalichnost'*) to obtain funds for rearmament, particularly after 1910. In Kokovtsov's view, the growth of these reserves reflected the care with which the Treasury had husbanded resources in the difficult years after the war against Japan. His critics countered that the fund was healthy, only by virtue of the French loan in 1909.

In the first instance, Kokovtsov hoped to curb the appetite of all his cabinet colleagues. Although, in his memoirs, he took care to explain that he never opposed reasonable demands, Kokovtsov vigorously opposed grandiose and (as he maintained) unjustified plans for rearmament. In 1909, he argued that the budget could not sustain the levels of expenditure anticipated by the military: 'the yearly increase in receipts, interrupted occasionally in years of poor harvests and sharp economic depression, is hardly sufficient to satisfy the inescapable increase in the most urgent state needs', amongst which he did not number rearmament proposals. To approve these programmes would, he argued, require a thorough reorganization of the budget and the introduction of new taxes that would invite the Duma to intervene indirectly in rearmament. Like Bethmann Hollweg in Germany, Kokovtsov consistently sought to restrain armament expenditure, and

Duchen an RR continche
1905-13
148   Rearmament and industrial ambition

for much the same reasons: to uphold 'sound finance' and to avoid unwelcome parliamentary interference.[63]

Kokovtsov pursued other cabinet colleagues no less vigorously. In some he found willing accomplices: when it became apparent that he could hold out against the defence departments only with great difficulty, it helped to have figures in the cabinet who could yield more readily to his axe. Foremost among them was S. V. Rukhlov, appointed Minister of Transport in January 1909. Rukhlov assumed responsibility for one of the largest departmental budgets, and rapidly proved a willing victim of budget cuts. Indeed, he took office after his predecessor had been defeated over a proposal to spend 916 million rubles on improvements to the railway network. Rukhlov believed that the railway network had become a milch-cow for private industrialists, who received large and lucrative government orders for rails and rolling-stock. This was not a view that Kokovtsov shared, but it suited his purposes admirably. In the words of Timashev, 'Rukhlov regarded industry with the utmost hostility, counting its leading representatives as people who were harmful from the point of view of the overall interests of the country'. Contracts should be pared to the minimum, as a matter of principle. For this reason, Rukhlov happily acquiesced in pruning the railway budget. The construction of new lines declined and orders for rolling-stock were cut back. In the quinquennium 1909–13 the annual average addition to the railway track barely reached 850km, one-third of the rate of construction in 1899–1903. Only in 1913 did total expenditure on the construction and operation of the railway system exceed the peak it reached in 1908.[64]

The policy of retrenchment was less easy to enforce elsewhere. The energetic and capable Minister of Agriculture, A. V. Krivoshein, who entered office in May 1908, formulated ambitious plans for the reorganization of land tenure and more extensive provision of credit to agricultural producers. Amongst other things, he proposed an increase in the lending powers of the Peasants' Land Bank. This scheme entailed the issue of securities on behalf of the Bank, and Kokovtsov opposed it, on the grounds that it would endanger investment in industrial securities, and might eventually require the government to step in with additional funds to support the Bank. But Krivoshein could call upon the powerful figure of Stolypin to support the claims of agriculture. As a result, his budget climbed steadily from 58 million rubles in 1908 to 136 million rubles in 1913: considerably less than the staggering growth in the navy budget, but an impressive increase all the same.[65]

[handwritten annotation at top: Revenue increased sharply, thanks largely to vodka monopoly]

Unlike Kokovtsov, Stolypin displayed greater willingness to fund rearmament programmes by increases in taxation. But neither of them believed in the need for a fundamental change in the fiscal system. Stolpyin advocated a higher excise on the sale of vodka, to generate an additional 65 million rubles. Kokovtsov tinkered with tax rates. He introduced taxes on a wider range of consumer goods and increased existing tax rates. He projected an increase in the tobacco excise, the tax on cigarette papers, an increase in the stamp duty and a revision of the tax on immoveable property in towns. But he believed that these new rates would yield no more than 30 million rubles per annum, far short of the sums required to satisfy rearmament programmes. Any further increases in the price of vodka would, he believed, be self-defeating, because they would discourage consumption.[66]

Faced with the need to obtain additional sources of revenue, the tsarist government chose to consolidate the existing fiscal system, rather than to change it in any fundamental respect. The proportion of revenue derived from direct taxation in 1913 stood at eight per cent, much the same as before the Russo-Japanese War. The proportion of revenue from indirect taxes, mostly taxes on personal consumption, was around 21 per cent in 1913, the same as in 1904 (see table 3.4). Thus, no major structural changes took place before 1914. The most obvious fresh source of ordinary revenue would have been provided by an income tax, for long the subject of acrimonious and inconclusive debates in official circles. But a proposal by the Ministry of Finances to introduce an income tax in conjunction with reduced rates of tax on land and forests, eventually foundered on opposition from industrialists and from other government ministers, who expressed alarm at the possible impact of such a tax on industrial investment.[67]

In the event, significant growth in recurrent revenue (direct and indirect taxes) was achieved in the prewar years. Recurrent revenue doubled between 1900 and 1913. Receipts grew by 7.2 per cent between 1908 and 1913, compared to 4.7 per cent between 1900 and 1907. In absolute terms, the most important items were government monopolies and revenue from state assets.

In percentage terms, the fastest-growing source of revenue was gross income from state monopolies. The government obtained huge sums from the vodka monopoly. Introduced into four provinces in 1895 and progressively extended, by 1902 the vodka monopoly operated in the entire Empire. Increased sales, together with an increase in the excise in 1905 and 1908 yielded gross receipts of 900 million rubles in 1913; net receipts (after the deduction of administrative costs)

Table 3.4. *Government revenue, 1900–1913 (million rubles)*

	Direct taxes	Indirect taxes	Tolls & duties	State monopolies	State assets	Extraordinary items[1]	Total[2]
1900	132	505	89	329	474	33	1,737
1901	131	470	95	439	494	164	1,963
1902	133	429	101	546	524	202	2,107
1903	135	440	107	606	571	171	2,203
1904	135	419	104	614	572	385	2,403
1905	127	409	100	686	553	794	2,819
1906	163	494	113	777	603	1,084	3,356
1907	183	510	123	791	636	143	2,485
1908	194	526	137	794	648	201	2,619
1909	199	530	152	814	708	163	2,689
1910	216	593	170	866	797	24	2,805
1911	224	630	190	890	888	3	2,955
1912	243	650	199	943	938	2	3,108
1913	273	708	231	1,025	1,044	14	3,429

annual growth rate (1900–1913)

5.8%	2.7%	7.6%	9.1%	6.3%		

[1] mostly government borrowing
[2] includes redemption payments to Treasury, revenue from sale of assets etc.
Source: Khromov, *Ekonomicheskoe razvitie*, pp. 504–13.

amounted to around 664 million rubles. The government continued to rely on this source, notwithstanding the reservations expressed by Kokovtsov. Only in 1914, when Nicholas II dismissed Kokovtsov and replaced him with P. L. Bark, did the Tsar urge that alternative sources of revenue be found, principally by taxing unspecified economic activity.[68]

The main income-generating state asset was the railway network, which yielded 362 million rubles in gross receipts in 1900 and 814 million rubles in 1913, an average annual rate of growth of 6.4 per cent. But the railway system was managed in a notoriously inefficient fashion, and net receipts were always much smaller, perhaps only one-third of the gross figure. Granted, a marked improvement in the ratio of net to gross receipts took place after 1908. But this reflected increases in tariffs for freight and passenger traffic, rather than significant improvements in the performance of state railways.

Direct taxes, the receipts from which increased by 6.0 per cent between 1900 and 1913, included a tax on industrial activity. But the recession tended to restrict the potential for growth from direct taxes until 1910; thereafter, this component of the budget grew steadily, and the industrial tax yielded 150 million rubles in 1913. It took the form of levy (*osnovnoi promyslovyi nalog*) on all commercial and industrial enterprises, which were also required to pay for a licence to trade (*svidetel'-stvo*). A supplementary tax was levied on the net profits of joint-stock companies and their paid-up capital also attracted tax. Non-corporate enterprises had to pay the supplementary tax on profits, in addition to a tax to which they were all liable (the so-called *rasklad*, or apportioned tax). Finally, all industrial enterprises were also liable to local government taxes, levied by the zemstvos or by municipal authorities.[69]

The government justified its continued reliance on indirect taxes, on the grounds that they were easy to collect and hardly noticed by consumers. Such increases as took place between 1900 and 1908 derived from the growth in population in the Russian Empire, as well as from an increase in consumer spending per head. Even critics of the government acknowledged the favourable impact of a series of good harvests. They also pointed out that the 1905 revolution had redistributed income to consumers.[70]

The 'free balance' represented a final source of funds, whose great advantage, from the government's point of view, was that it escaped parliamentary scrutiny. This fund represented the Treasury's cash balances, money in transit between government departments and any excess of revenue over expenditure. From time to time, the fund was swelled by the proceeds of foreign loans. The Ministry of Finances drew upon it to cover any budget deficit that arose and to meet emergency requirements, such as famine relief. In practice, the free balance allowed the Ministry of Finances considerable freedom of manoeuvre, for example, to check any fall in the value of government securities held abroad, and to conclude fresh loans on more favourable terms than might otherwise have been afforded a hungry supplicant.[71]

Critics of the arrangement alleged that the accumulation of the free balance did not signify the underlying health of the economy, but rather the underlying growth of government debt. On the eve of the Russo-Japanese War the fund stood at 381 million rubles. The war considerably depleted the free balance, which (according to official figures) stood at just two million rubles in January 1909. By 1910, the balance had jumped to 107 million rubles. In 1911, it stood at 333 million rubles; the next year it climbed to 473 million rubles. By January 1913, the free balance had fallen to 433 million rubles, rather less than the figure ten years earlier.

Foreign loans ✓

On 1 January 1914, it stood at 514 million rubles. These increases were attributed to various causes, such as the profits on grain exports and an increase in the sales tax levied on alcohol. The fund was also swelled by the proceeds from the loan that Kokovtsov began to negotiate with French bankers towards the end of 1908.[72]

The Ministry of Finances made heavy raids upon the fund, to redeem Treasury notes, to expropriate the Warsaw-Vienna railway and to relieve victims of famine. But Kokovtsov also drew upon the free balance, in order to finance the construction of new ports and to help defray the costs of rearmament. By this means, in 1913, the government financed the increase in troop strength, a decision that required the immediate outlay of 346 million rubles.[73]

The growth in the free balance demonstrated that Kokovtsov had moderated his previous opposition to foreign borrowing. Hitherto, he justified his reluctance to negotiate fresh loans in unmistakably orthodox financial terms: 'the conclusion of loans, even for productive purposes, will all the same eventually have the same result as loans concluded simply to cover unproductive expenditures, that is the destruction of state credit and the financial situation of the country'. In 1908, however, against the background of the Bosnian crisis and with the pressure to improve the capabilities of the Russian army, he relented. Negotiations with the French were successfully concluded in January 1909.[74]

Political pressures, therefore, were sufficiently strong to resist fundamental change to government revenue. In the pursuit of a stable fiscal system, Kokovtsov enjoyed conspicuous success. He also avoided seeking further foreign credit after 1909. On the expenditure front, his policies succeeded, to the extent that he managed to restrain the defence departments – vigorously until 1908, somewhat less so between 1908 and 1911. When it became impossible to stem the tide of rearmament, the government derived additional resources for defence at the expense of other claimants, particularly transport, and from the revenue generated by rapid economic growth between 1908 and 1913. Having defeated most claims from the defence departments for extra funding until 1911, Kokovtsov was thereafter fighting a losing battle.

The economic impact of defence expenditure: the military burden and opportunity cost

The unprecedented extent and pace of the European arms race led contemporary economists to consider seriously for the first time the economic impact of defence spending. The initial requirement was to devise a method whereby the burden imposed by defence expenditure could be measured. A pioneer in this field was the American economist Alvin Johnson, who analyzed the defence spending of the great powers between 1875 and 1908, concluding that 'modern peace is unquestionably vastly more expensive than the wars of an earlier period'. In 1908, he put Russian defence expenditure at $1.77 per head, slightly above the figure for Austria. In Britain, he estimated the figure to be two and a half times greater, whilst France spent three times as much as Russia. Similar calculations were presented independently to the Duma in 1908. The disparity remained huge on the eve of the war: in 1913, France spent more than two and a half times as much per head of population, than did Russia. Germany spent twice as much; and in Great Britain the figure was three times greater than in Russia. However, this measure evidently minimized the extent of the burden in Russia, because the enormous sums committed to defence were spread over a large population (170 million people in 1913). From this point of view, but from this alone, Russia paid a small price for its military expansion.[75]

Calculations such as these painted a misleading picture, on at least two additional counts. First, Johnson failed to convey the fact that the economies of continental Europe grew in size during the late nineteenth century and the early twentieth. In the second place, he overlooked the extent to which economic growth opened up wide disparities in the level of economic development, making the defence burden relatively heavier for less developed countries. A more appropriate measure, not liable to the same criticisms, would have been to relate defence expenditure to national income. But this practice only became commonplace after the First World War, with the spread of interest in national accounts, although – exceptionally – a Duma deputy from Perm province attempted a rough calculation during a debate on the 1908 estimates.[76]

When defence expenditure is related to the capacity of the population to sustain it, the relative burden of defence spending in imperial Russia is magnified. Russian defence spending in 1913 exceeded that of its European rivals, according to a range of estimates. It was heavier than the corresponding burden in Britain, a country with the cross of Empire to bear.[77] Furthermore, if we deduct national income in kind, and express Russian defence spending as a proportion of monetized national income, the burden was almost twice as heavy as for the economically more developed countries. Table 3.5 brings together

Comparative defence burden

Table 3.5. *Defence/national income proportions in Europe, 1913/14* (per cent)

	Estimate A	Estimate B	Estimate C	Estimate D
Britain	3.1	3.4[1]	3.6	3.8
Germany	n.a.	4.6	3.5	3.6
Russia	4.8	6.3	5.8	4.1 (7.1)[2]
France	5.0	4.8	n.a.	3.9

[1] British Empire

[2] The figure in brackets is derived by subtracting consumption of farm products in kind from net national product, and expressing total defence spending as a percentage of this figure.

Sources: Estimate A, *Industrielle Mobilmachungen: Statistische Untersuchungen*, Hamburg, 1936, p. 24; estimate B (1914), Quincy Wright, *A Study of War*, Chicago, 1942, pp. 670–1; estimate C, G. Hardach, *The First World War, 1914–1918*, London, 1977, pp. 150–1; estimate D, UK and Germany taken from P. Flora, *State, Economy and Society in Western Europe, 1815–1975*, 2 vols., Frankfurt, 1983, vol. 1, pp. 382, 387, 442; the figure for France is taken from Niall Ferguson, 'Germany and the origins of the First World War: new perspectives', *Historical Journal*, 35, 1992, p. 751. Ferguson confirms Hardach's estimate for Germany. However, according to Peter Witt, the share in Germany was 4.6 per cent: see P. C. Witt, 'Reichsfinanzen und Rüstungspolitik, 1898–1914', in H. Schottelius and W. Deist, eds., *Marine und Marinepolitik im kaiserlichen Deutschland, 1871–1914*, Düsseldorf, 1972, p. 177. The estimate for Russia is derived from P. W. Gatrell, 'Industrial expansion in tsarist Russia, 1908–1914', *Economic History Review*, 35, 1982, p. 105, and P. R. Gregory, *Russian National Income, 1885–1913*, Cambridge, 1982, p. 57.

various estimates of defence spending as a proportion of national income.

In Russia, as elsewhere, the preferred method adopted by contemporary economists critical of the regime was to express defence spending in terms of its share of the budget. The results yielded estimates of between 25 and 30 per cent in Russia. The Polish banker and railway magnate Jan Bloch looked forward to a time, not far off, when no modern state could afford to sustain a high level of defence spending, simply because of the other claims on available resources. Anticipating Alvin Johnson, he wrote that 'every day, new needs arise and old needs are made clearer to the popular mind. These needs remain unsatisfied, though the burden of taxation continually grows. And the recognition of these evils by the people constitutes a serious danger for the state'.[78] In identifying this phenomenon, Bloch pin-pointed one of the key problems in Russia. Here, more than anywhere else in Europe, the defence budget was shrouded in secrecy. Even the creation of parliamentary institutions in 1906 did little to lift the veil. Russian economists and public figures were hampered by a lack of data; besides, the political system hardly allowed politicians to alert 'the people' to the magnitude of the burden.

When government ministers sought to justify defence spending, they argued in terms that would be familiar to modern economists, namely that defence was a public good. Witte provided a clear expo-sition of this concept in 1903, when asked to justify the increases in taxation that accompanied an increase in the defence estimates: 'the people bear the burden of military service and pay the greatest portion of the taxes, and in return they have the inestimable consciousness, which cannot be outweighed by any material benefits, that their relatives, property and the whole fatherland are protected against foreign foes'. As always happens with public debate on defence spend-ing, its advocates were given to vacuous utterances. Typical of the rhetoric is the grand statement that 'the state cannot avoid making great sacrifices for state defence'. Few people – few, that is, of those who were in a position to do so – bothered to ask why these sacrifices were 'unavoidable'.[79]

Apart from resorting to arguments of the public good type, the other frequently heard justification for defence spending is that it may mobilize idle assets, particularly in a underdeveloped society. Unfortu-nately, economists have reached no very definite conclusions about the capacity of defence spending to perform this task. In a closed economy, the increased aggregate demand implied by an increase in expenditure might raise expectations of higher profits and, in turn, stimulate new investment and employment opportunities, assuming that there are no constraints on the supply of capital and labour. In an open economy, on the other hand, an increase in the level of defence expenditure might simply increase the demand for imports of military goods, siphoning off scarce foreign exchange.[80]

From a developmental point of view, the wages and transfers paid to members of the Russian army forces added to aggregate demand. Had they not been conscripted, peasants were hardly likely to have earned high wages in the rural economy. Troops quartered in garri-sons or near towns revived local economic activity, especially with the progressive dismantling of the regimental economy. Now that troops no longer manufactured their own uniforms or grew their own food, their modest expenditures stimulated commercial transactions and increased national income. Finally, the massive outlays on rearmament played a major part in the rescue of heavy industry from a prolonged recession; it is difficult to see how recovery could have come about earlier in the absence of defence spending of this magnitude.

The growth in defence expenditure did imply a curtailment of spending on infrastructure, although it failed to halt the programme of land reform. But how much truth is there in the charge that increased defence appropriations deprived Russia of health care or educational facilities? On several occasions, parliamentary critics of the regime confronted Russian defence ministers with the language of opportunity cost. A radical deputy from Irkutsk intervened in 1908 to ask how many schools and factories had been sacrificed on the altar of militarism, whose bill he put at 10 billion rubles over the course of two decades. In a debate on the budget estimates for 1911, N. N. L'vov, a Progressist deputy from Saratov, accused the government and the Duma of giving priority to defence; meanwhile, the country 'is still hoping that in vain that its most elementary needs will be satisfied ... what will you show your constituents a year hence and what will you tell them to justify the way in which you have interpreted your duties to the country?' Kokovtsov, who had himself used the language of opportunity cost in cabinet rejected the charge that the cultural needs of the country had been forgotten ('more money is being spent on such development than on defence'). He concluded his parliamentary oration with the motto that 'progress and culture can be safe only when a country is not left unprotected before its neighbours'. This line was supported by conservative politicians, such as Durnovo, who appealed to the image of imperial grandeur: 'in my eyes, all so-called cultural needs retire into second place before the urgent necessities on which depend the very existence of Russia as a great power'.[81]

These questions were taken up much later by Arcadius Kahan, in a justly famous article on tsarist economic policies and Russian industrialization.[82] Kahan founded his critique of the tsarist budget on its unproductive components, implying a failure on the part of the government to devote resources to educational and welfare programmes. But what might the government have done in this respect? A good place to begin is to ask how much more the government would have needed to spend, in order to bring the education and health budgets closer to some defined optimum. On the eve of the First World War, both the zemstvos and the Ministry of Education called for the employment of extra teachers in order to provide universal primary schooling for children between the ages of eight and eleven, assuming a staff:pupil ratio of 1:50. A calculation in 1915 indicated that an additional 118,216 teachers were required (the existing complement was 186,859 teachers), that is a shortfall of more than 60 per cent. Other estimates, which built in assumptions about the drop-out rate amongst peasant pupils, suggested that the shortfall was much less, perhaps as low as 16 per cent or 36,670 teachers. Rules adopted in 1911 stipulated that the central government had to support each primary teacher to the extent of 390 rubles. Thus, salary costs alone would have added between 14.3 million and 46.1 million rubles to the total education budget, equivalent to between 10 and 32 per cent of the budget for 1913.[83]

Before attributing the failure to deploy these extra teachers to a lamentable lack of initiative on behalf of the government, it is worth considering the demand for primary education. Ben Eklof has shown that peasants were willing and able to make non-institutional provision for the education of their children, in so-called free schools (vol'nye skhkoly). Before the 1890s, these were the chief means by which peasants acquired the basic skills needed in order to deal with officials and other outsiders. Peasants had no time for any formal system that emphasized character formation and the virtues of imperial government and Orthodox religion. When the zemstvos jumped on the educational bandwagon after 1890, they too found ample resistance to their concept of primary education in the countryside. Peasants did not think of schooling as an opportunity for upward social mobility: 'they saw schools not as a springboard to future careers but as providing tools to help cope with a world increasingly crowded with documents and, in particular, to avoid being duped, cheated or misled in a hostile and treacherous environment'. These attitudes offered scant hope for the development of the skills that have been associated with 'social capabilities'. Education did not overcome the social distance between the world of the village and the 'modern' world beyond. Additional spending on rural education would not in itself have transformed deeply entrenched peasant attitudes. Russia undoubtedly needed a better educated workforce; but to spend money within the existing institutional framework was unlikely to have contributed to that end.[84]

What about health care? In 1900, there were no more than 10,000 midwives across the Empire, of whom only one-fifth were zemstvo employees. Midwives attended no more than two out of every hundred confinements in the countryside. If we assume that each midwife received a salary of 300 rubles, it would have cost an additional 30 million rubles annually to employ the extra 100,000 midwives needed in the villages. There was also a shortfall in the number of doctors, although the ratio of doctors to total population improved markedly between 1880 and 1910, from one per 58,000 to one per 28,000. The government aspired to a norm of one per 10,000. To employ the additional numbers of doctors at a salary of 500 rubles would have cost no more than 3 million rubles per annum (this, out of a zemstvo health budget in 1910 of 64 million rubles). Nor would it have cost enormous sums to invest in basic rural health care facilities.[85]

But the argument that the government abandoned villagers to their fate contains two questionable assumptions. One is that extra health spending would have yielded improvements in the crude death rate or in infant mortality. The other is that peasants would have availed themselves of the potential facilities. The first assumption is dubious; European demographic history suggests that such factors as higher nutritional standards, attributable in part to improved inter-regional trade, served to reduce mortality by increasing human resistance to infectious diseases. In this respect, given its commitment to railway construction, the government cannot be accused of getting it completely wrong. The second assumption is also of doubtful validity. Ethnographic and literary evidence, such as the poignant short stories written by Mikhail Bulgakov during his years as a zemstvo doctor in a remote Russian village, testifies to peasant mistrust and even outright hostility to institutionalized modern medicine. Women preferred the village *povitukha* (midwife) to her professional counterpart. Peasants presented themselves to the surgery only *in extremis*.[86]

For these reasons, we should hesitate before attaching too much blame to the tsarist government for a misallocation of resources. We have accounted for the high level of spending on defence and shown how an argument for even greater spending, rather than less, could be made. Furthermore, additional spending on education and health would not in itself have benefited society, in the absence of more fundamental changes in state institutions and social attitudes. A more sophisticated budgetary policy could have targetted particular groups or activities in order to maximize 'social capabilities', but this possibility was certainly not part of official discourse at the time.

What, finally, of the spatial impact of armaments expenditure? Studies in America showed that the post-1945 development of nuclear missiles and supersonic aircraft was associated with the relocation of defence industry to Texas and California.[87] This dramatic shift in the geography of production had no equivalent in pre-1914 Russia. It is true that the development of a modern shipbuilding industry stimulated investment and employment in the Baltic provinces, in Riga, Reval and Tallinn, and on the Black Sea littoral at Nikolaev. But, for the most part, the growth of the armaments industry tended to follow the existing location of industry, rather than to open up new locations. Enterprises in St Petersburg and the Urals tended to dominate weapons production, as they had done during the reign of Peter the Great. The regional economic consequences of defence spending, particularly for industry, formed no part of the tsarist agenda. Serious attention only began to be given to the subject after 1914, when it formed part of the debate about the relocation of defence industry to regions less exposed to attack across Russia's western frontiers.

Conclusion

A profound contradiction was embodied in Russian defence strategy before 1914. In large measure, these shortcomings reflected underlying and unresolved differences of conception between the army and navy. In the immediate aftermath of the war against Japan, attempts had been made to devise a strategic plan upon which both armed services collaborated. But the momentum was not sustained. As a result, by 1914 it was difficult to discern any coherent purpose in defence planning. The army leadership sought to provide Russia with the means to defend its borders from German or Austrian attack: hence the emphasis given to the maintenance of fortresses on the western border. The planned disposition of troops and military matériel also served to prepare Russia for an offensive against Germany, a policy with which the French saddled the Russian military leadership. But the re-equipment and reorganization of land forces left Russian troops poorly equipped with key armaments, in particular light field and heavy artillery. For its part, the Admiralty increasingly espoused the doctrine of an offensive fleet. The commitment of resources to the expansion of the Black Sea fleet, in particular, testified to the triumph of this conception.[88] The hugely expensive commitment to a national fleet, based upon modern battleships, pandered to the court's ideal of Russian imperial grandeur and to a more widespread vision of enhanced national esteem. The promised investment in railways and fortresses, designed to improve Russia's capacity to mobilize troops against Germany, shows that Russia did not just pay lip-service to the alliance with France. But Russia proceeded to devote huge sums to the imperial fleet; and this commitment of resources suggested that Russian nationalism triumphed over the objectives embodied in the Franco-Russian alliance.

Several forces were at work to determine the size and trend of the defence budget. First, the overall context of defence and foreign policy served to maintain the gathering momentum of defence spending. Russia was simply unable to choose between meeting its obligations as a great power and accepting second-rank status on the international stage. Its size and geographical location in Europe deprived Russia of the chance to live a quiet life in the backwaters of international politics. The leading players in the drama of national politics reinforced the high-profile position that Russia occupied. The Tsar, in particular, backed ambitious plans for naval expenditure. Sukhomlinov cleverly exploited war scares, in order to extract additional spending on the armed forces. The Duma supported and, on occasion, demanded an increase in spending on the army. Initially, its members adopted a more circumspect and critical attitude towards the navy. But, ultimately, the Duma accepted the bill for battleships. Finally, the new technology embodied in modern armaments and military vessels imposed inflation on the defence budget; this, together with the increase in army size, drove military spending relentlessly upwards in the five years before the outbreak of war.

Given the limited resources available in the aftermath of the Russo-Japanese War, the Ministry of Finances exercised its right to scrutinize spending plans. The Duma found it could exercise some influence, especially over the naval budget, in order to press for administrative reforms, designed to ensure that the Admiralty obtained value for money. Subsequently, the Duma – with its built-in majority – proved a willing ally of the old regime, in the pursuit of the arms race. Only a few liberal dissidents were opposed in principle to the expansion of military spending. But they did not confront the fundamental issue, namely that more radical changes in institutions and society were required, before the redirection of resources could have any lasting benefit. However, any influence the Duma once commanded over events quickly evaporated. The same applied to the role played by Kokovtsov. When the pressure for rearmament became unassailable, as it had by 1911, Kokovtsov was forced to admit defeat. Neither he nor the Duma any longer stood in the way of the military ambitions of tsarism.

4   The economics and politics of industrial recovery

Introduction: the transformation of market conditions in the basic industries, 1908–1914

Between 1908 and 1913, the output of large-scale industry in Russia grew at an average annual rate of more than 9 per cent (in current prices) and more than 7 per cent (in 1913 prices). These were impressive rates of growth, approximating to the rapid rate of growth of industrial production during the 1890s, and far in excess of the modest rates achieved between 1900 and 1907, when growth barely exceeded 1.5 per cent per annum.[1] All sources agree on the fact that industry performed impressively during the last peacetime quinquennium. However, the reasons for this renewed upsurge in industrial production have never been properly explored or resolved. In this chapter, the opportunity is taken to review the explanations and to sift through the evidence. The initial assumption is that, since the revival of growth coincided with Russian rearmament, some kind of relationship existed between the two phenomena. However, it is also possible that industrial growth and rearmament were unrelated, or (in the language of the statistician) 'autocorrelated'.

Contemporary observers failed to agree on the causes of prewar industrial growth in Russia. Some, like Ivan Ozerov and Finn-Enotaevskii, maintained that by 1910 the state had once again become a significant customer for manufactured goods, notably for rails, transport equipment and armaments. Tugan-Baranovskii took a similar line. However, none of these writers believed that state orders played the decisive role in fostering industrial recovery and expansion. Soviet economists and economic historians were divided over the mainsprings of industrial growth. Liashchenko argued that 'the boom of 1909–1913 was to a considerable degree the result of new expansion of railway building', although he went on to draw attention to the growth of urban consumption and of investment in agricultural equipment and farm buildings. But Iosif Gindin dismissed the suggestion that the boom had anything to do with railway construction, observing that railway construction during 1909–1913 was no greater than it had been since the slump in orders at the turn of the century. In Gindin's view, 'the growth in group A industries rested upon an extension of the capital stock of industry, significant additions to the urban infrastructure and some growth in the gentry economy'. L. A. Mendel'son attached prime importance to rural purchasing power: *'the most important factor* was the acceleration in the development of (agrarian) capitalism in Russia after the 1905 Revolution'. According to this interpretation, the growth of a rural bourgeoisie increased the volume of grain marketings and created a more buoyant source of demand for manufactured goods. This trend was further accentuated by the upturn in agricultural prices, including export prices.[2]

Amongst non-Soviet scholars, Alexander Gerschenkron came closest to espousing the views of Mendel'son. Gerschenkron maintained that the driving force behind the boom was domestic civilian demand, boosted by the Stolypin land reforms. The growth in consumer spending, according to Malcolm Falkus, also induced new investment in consumer goods industries. On the other hand, Olga Crisp, noting the increase in government spending on railways, shipbuilding and armaments, was reluctant to attribute overriding importance to consumer purchasing power.[3]

Russian businessmen were equally at a loss to interpret the changes taking place between 1908 and 1913. Obviously, they realized that industry was deep in the throes of recession in 1908; and they took a pessimistic view of the options open to them during the depth of the slump. Some spokesmen had a high opinion of the potential demand for manufactured goods that would be unleashed by the government's land reform programme. Nikolai Avdakov, the leading figure in the south Russian iron and steel industry, believed that the Stolypin reforms would eventually 'create a huge consumer market'. But even like-minded businessmen realized that this happy outcome lay a long way off. In the meantime, industry sought more direct forms of government intervention, in order to stimulate investment and output.[4]

Rearmament, and the boost it entailed in public expenditure, eventually offered Russian industrialists a way out of the recession. This is not the same as saying that entrepreneurs in iron and steel and engineering pinned their hopes on defence contracts, to the exclusion of all other opportunities. Such a strategy would have been risky and unrealistic, and businessmen did not embrace it. But, as they struggled to weather the storm, industrialists did believe that the government should be reminded of its responsibility to industry. How much leverage could they exercise in pursuit of this goal? The direct involvement of businessmen in the political process had been short-lived, and its practical consequences unremarkable. In 1908, during the depths of the recession, industrialists could but pin their hopes on officials in the new Ministry of Trade and Industry, anticipating a sympathetic hearing. But, even if some sections of government were prepared to examine the catalogue of poor financial performance, redundancies and foreign competition, this was a far cry from gaining a total victory over the combined forces of government, some of whose representatives looked askance at business practices and derisively upon business protestations. Merely to pinpoint the magnitude of the crisis demanded a massive publicity campaign. To develop a strategy, sufficient to compel the government to take the recession seriously, was still more difficult. To extract a promise of government action represented the supreme challenge. In the event, the tsarist government never developed a coherent industrial policy. Industrial recovery was a by-product of rearmament. So far as the old regime was concerned, the revival of industry occurred in a fit of absence of mind.[5]

The failure of the business lobby, 1907–8

The industrial recession provoked Russian industrialists into a flurry of activity, designed to bring their plight to the attention of government. This represented a change of tactic and a return to conventional lobbying of government ministers. In 1905–6, industrialists had flirted with political activity. By 1908, they had reverted to the exercise of such collective entrepreneurial voice as they could muster.

Throughout 1907 and 1908, business journals and newspapers were filled with articles bemoaning the lack of government aid to industry. The government could always retort that businessmen themselves had divergent views on the desirability and potential scope of government intervention. Certainly, the spokesmen of heavy industry never adopted a unified stance on such matters as tariff protection and railway freight rates, where government made an indirect impact on the conduct of business. Whatever the magnitude of their past disagreements, however, Russia's leading industrialists decided to sink their differences and to concentrate on the issue that united them, namely their conviction that the tsarist regime did not recognize or respond to their basic needs. The 32nd congress of the south Russian iron and steel industry, in November 1907, passed a resolution, urging the Confederation of Trade and Industry to request that the Minister of Trade and Industry convene a special conference on the crisis in the iron and steel and metalworking industries. The conference eventually took place in May 1908.[6]

This was probably the most important, and certainly the most prestigious business-government conference in pre-revolutionary Russia. The relevant government departments all sent representatives: the Ministry of Finances and the Admiralty each had three representatives, the State Auditor's Department and the Chief Administration of Land Reorganization and Agriculture both sent two spokesmen, whilst the ministries of Interior, War, Transport and Justice each had a single representative. The Ministry of Trade and Industry had the largest presence, with twelve representatives. The Duma was allocated 11 seats. Three experts, including the eminent former factory inspector I. I. Ianzhul', were also invited to attend, making a total of forty representatives from non-business interests. From the business side, the four leading banks took part, namely the Russian Bank for Foreign Trade, the International Bank, the Northern Bank, and the Azov-Don Bank. Ten seats were assigned to members of the Confederation of Trade and Industry, including such leading figures as N. S. Avdakov, E. L. Nobel, I. S. Kannegiser, Iu. V. Rummel' and S. I. Mikhin, and four to the Society of Factory Owners and Manufacturers. In addition, thirty-six representatives participated from industry. Among the major iron and steel producers Hartmann, Briansk, the Russo-Belgian Company, the Donets Company, South Russian Dnieper, Russian Providence, Nikopol-Mariupol, Taganrog, Kramatorsk, and the New Russia Ironworks were all represented. Most of these firms belonged to Prodamet. Also present were leading engineering firms, notably Putilov, the Russian Locomotive Company, Nevskii Shipbuilding, the Nikolaev Shipbuilding Company, Sormovo, and the Kolomna Engineering Company. Prominent among the voices for the engineering industry were the Confederation of Northern and Baltic Engineering Industry, and the Confederation of Agricultural Machine-building Industry. Sundry other groups, such as bourse committees, railway managers and the editor of *Vestnik finansov* took up the remaining places.[7]

A background paper, submitted by the Confederation of Trade and Industry to the New Minister of Trade and Industry, I. P. Shipov, sketched the position of the iron and steel industry in gloomy colours. Amongst world producers of iron and steel Russian producers were virtually alone in suffering a fall in demand for their products: only in Austria did industry find itself in a similar position. The background papers also made the point that the crisis had deepended since business representatives first petitioned for action, in the autumn of 1907. As evidence of their concern, the Confederation cited the reluctance of the Duma to approve funds for a significant expansion of the stock of locomotives and wagons, the continued fall in the rate of railway construction and the reduction in market demand occasioned by financial uncertainties. Between 1902 and 1906, only eighteen of Russia's fifty-three iron and steel companies had regularly paid dividends to their shareholders, while a further thirteen ventures made losses and issued dividend payments only intermittently. Thirteen other companies paid no dividends at all. Eight others were in the hands of the official receiver. Only one new firm came into existence during this period. In 1907, Russia's rolling mills produced at less than three-fifths of capacity. Factories producing iron and steel for the construction industry and the railways were even more badly affected by the slump.[8]

Most of the speakers agreed that heavy industry was in the throes of a deep depression, but disagreed about its magnitude and they certainly disagreed about the remedies that might be taken to deal with it. Several Duma delegates argued that industrialists themselves had to accept responsibility for the 'crisis of overproduction' and that they should not expect the government to bail them out. Pleas for greater government spending on the construction of state lines should be ignored. However, the Moscow entrepreneur Jules Goujon argued that the government could instead offer incentives to private companies to build more lines and to lease to the private sector those state lines where modernization of track and rolling-stock was urgently required. Without such concessions, it was thought unlikely that private railway companies would embark on a programme of construction. The government had drafted regulations in June 1905, whereby the state guaranteed payments on funded debt and private companies were allowed to suspend payments to shareholders during the construction of new lines, but these had not been implemented extensively. The government had extended concessions to private companies to build lines in the northern Don region and between Bakhmach (north-east of Kiev) and Odessa. But calculations of the volume of iron and steel likely to be consumed on these projects only served to emphasize how much more was needed. Given its present size, the private sector could not by itself rescue Russian industry from the doldrums.

Other speakers dwelled on the current uncertainty in the financial markets that deterred new investment. For example, municipal authorities had all but halted new projects for lack of funds. The Briansk Ironworks had accepted a contract from the municipality of Ekaterinoslav to build a water supply, but this was the exception that proved the rule: Briansk was willing to accept municipal bonds, in lieu of immediate settlement of its account. More generally, speakers argued that the government had an obligation to improve domestic household consumption of iron and steel. Everyone seemed to have an anecdote about the use of wood by peasant households and crafts-men, who simply lacked the resources to acquire iron.[9]

But the outcome of the 1908 conference was disappointing to the private sector. The government refused to commit itself to the expen-diture of additional funds on railway building or on other projects, such as the construction or modernization of ports. Nor did the government react sympathetically to the idea that it should devise some form of industrial credit to alleviate the decline in industrial investment. In a cabinet meeting, the government also resolved that it could show no special favour to private engineering producers, such as those in the armaments industry, since the 'interests of state defence' dictated that the military procurement agencies should be free to choose the most suitable supplier, whether from the state or private sector. The immediate outcome of the conference therefore offered little satisfaction to the private sector. Iron and steel producers left the conference, reflecting upon the fact that their limited influence imposed no necessity upon the tsarist government to accede to their demands. Perhaps they would enjoy greater success in pressing other claims?[10]

Business-government relations, 1908–14

With what degree of success were other, subsequent efforts of business pressure groups crowned? The most common complaint concerned the level of protection to domestic industry. Here, organized business had, in the past, registered some notable victories. The government acceded to a request from southern coal and iron producers for the imposition of tariff protection during the 1880s. The government also imposed tariffs on a wide range of engineering

products. In most instances concerning the iron and steel and engineering industries, the government continued after 1908 to afford
protection to domestic producers. But ministers adopted a selective
approach towards tariff protection. This meant that some industrial
producers were bound to be disappointed. In 1911, the government
agred to admit pig iron free of duty. In another instance of government flexibility, in 1908 and again in 1911, the association of agricultural equipment producers failed to persuade ministers to reverse
Witte's decision to admit certain categories of agricultural machinery
free of duty.[11]

Company law traditionally generated almost as much heat as did
the tariff. Russian industrialists complained that the legislation on
corporations was both anachronistic and obstructive. The formation of
a joint-stock company involved a laborious and time-consuming procedure, which required promoters to prepare a submission for the
Council of Ministers. Typical of government attitudes towards corporate affairs was its policy on industrial syndicates. The existing legislation on industrial combinations dated back to a statute of 1845, which
stipulated a hefty fine or imprisonment for merchants and industrialists who had combined to raise the price of food or other necessities, or
who cut prices, with the intention of driving other suppliers out of
business. New legislation was projected in 1903, but never promulgated. Although the government made it clear that it would adopt a
less draconian interpretation of the 1845 statute (indeed, it encouraged
the formation of Prodamet), industrialists remained unhappy about
the legal position. In 1910, a government commission of inquiry began
work under the chairmanship of P. I. Miller, deputy Minister of Trade
and Industry, to consider the law relating to syndicates and trusts.
Industrialists were not represented on the commission, but, in accordance with established practice, they submitted evidence to it. The
commission found that government could not prevent the formation
of syndicates, but that it had a duty to monitor their activities and
curtail any 'abuses', such as the 'unreasonable' inflation of prices. To
this end, the government should order goods from suppliers who
adhered to acceptable standards of behaviour and could, in extremis,
order goods from foreign suppliers. The commission did not make
further progress on this subject until the eve of the war.[12]

By 1913, the government began to adopt a more lenient attitude
towards the principle of industrial syndicates, even though, in practice, it did nothing to stifle public attacks on the iron and coal syndicates. Timashev, the Minister of Trade and Industry, and Kokovtsov

went so far as to argue that Russia's growing participation in the world trade in manufactures demanded that domestic industry become more 'organized'. This view corresponded closely to that expressed in the journal of the Confederation of Trade and Industry, which asserted that 'international competition demands strong organization of each sector of industry'. The final report of the commission, in 1914, stated that historical experience in Russia and western Europe indicated that syndicates tended to stabilize, rather than raise prices. The report concluded that government had sufficient powers to undermine any syndicate, by adjusting the tariff, manipulating freight rates or levying export duties. But any such action required careful consideration.[13]

Russian industrialists expressed relief at the findings of the commission. But their respite from public opprobrium was short-lived. In 1914, the overt hostility towards syndicates within some quarters of government reached a crescendo, and the government prepared to act against the two most powerful groups. Fortunately, from the entrepreneurs' perspective, the government adopted neither a tough nor a coherent approach. A faction within the Ministry of Transport gained a temporary ascendancy and began to play a more influential part in the formulation of industrial policy. It began by targeting the committee for the allocation of rail orders, which had been devised to protect the interests of the leading rail producers. By 1907, some officials began to have misgivings about its activities. A joint submission to the Council of Ministers by the ministers of Transport and Trade and Industry (two departments which did not always see eye to eye on matters of industrial policy) observed that the committee had undermined competition between suppliers. In addition, 'the profits that firms have received from their dealings with the state allow them to reduce the price of products sold on the market, below the limits tolerable to other enterprises'. The outsiders, they went on, were understandably unhappy with these arrangements. Ministers agreed that in the present depressed conditions the abolition of the committee was unthinkable. Four years later, however, when industry had recovered, S. V. Rukhlov, the Minister of Transport determined to dismantle the established clique of suppliers. In the event, Kokovtsov persuaded his colleagues to approve the continuation of the committee, 'not for economic reasons, but for reasons of state'. In other words Kokovtsov, in line with the views he had expressed about syndicates in general, defended the decision to preserve the oligopoly of rail and rolling-stock producers.[14]

Rukhlov then turned his attention to the coal syndicate, Produgol'.

Taking a leaf out of the book of the Miller commission, he decided to buy coal from firms which did not belong to the syndicate. The difficulty he faced in implementing this policy was illustrated by the inability of the outsiders – all of them smaller ventures – to deliver on time. Rukhlov was forced instead to import coal from western Europe. In 1914, his patience finally snapped. Taking advantage of Kokovtsov's departure from government, Rukhlov brought a prosecution against Produgol' and Prodamet, with the backing of the Minister of Justice. Only diplomatic intervention by the French and Belgian governments, seeking to protect their investments in the Russian coal and iron industries, brought the legal action to an abrupt end.[15]

The government's attachment to state enterprise stuck in the throats of industrialists no less than its periodic assaults on industrial organization. Representatives of private enterprise at the 1908 conference on the metalworking and machine-building industry urged the government to renounce state ownership of industrial assets. The tsarist government hardly appeared likely to follow this advice. Entrepreneurs, therefore, concentrated instead on the terms which informed government procurement of manufactured goods, such as railway equipment and rails for the state lines, and military goods. These regulations were denounced as unfair and unreasonable. The procedures for the procurement of manufactured goods were set out in detailed regulations, first introduced in 1887, and modified in 1900, the text of which ran to more than 100 pages. It was not, however, the mass of detail in itself which aroused the ire of industrialists. Rather, they complained that the government conferred specific advantages on state enterprises. For example, the government gave recurrent subsidies to state ironworks, dockyards and armouries which, as a result, supplied goods at lower prices. In effect, these subsidies were concealed, by virtue of the fact that the state factories were not required to provide for the depreciation of their assets and did not have to take their overhead costs into account when preparing their invoices. Other forms of concealed subsidy included the provision that state works need pay neither the industrial tax nor any insurance premiums. The issue of insurance was brought into sharp relief by a major fire at the Obukhov shipyards, which necessitated an emergency rescue package, which came out of Treasury funds. Russian businessmen wanted to change other aspects of procurement policy. They urged the government to ensure that only manufacturers, and not middlemen, were invited to tender at auctions. More important – and more controversial – was the proposal that the government relinquish its power to levy a financial penalty on private enterprises, in the event of delays caused by industrial action. The government refused to accede to this request, on the grounds that management had to accept its share of responsibility for order in the workplace.[16]

The slump in industrial production did prompt the government to address the issue of procurement. In November 1908, the Tsar approved the formation of an inter-ministerial commission under State Auditor P. A. Kharitonov, charged with the task of drafting fresh legislation on 'state procurements and economic operations'. The commission met between February 1909 and February 1911, against the background of inquiries being conducted by Neidhardt and Garin into the affairs of the defence industries. On the face of it, the position of the private sector might appear to have been weakened by the senatorial investigations, which uncovered evidence of fraud and corruption in the award of government military and other contracts. However, the business lobby mounted a clever rearguard action, conscious perhaps of the fact that the government now had every reason to look more favourably on private enterprise, offering as it did access to advanced foreign armaments technology. Business spokesmen even used the evidence of corruption, in order to press for legislative change. The journal of the Confederation of Trade and Industry argued that such practices as undisclosed payments to government officials could best be countered by reform of the procurements system. The unspoken assumption was that private entrepreneurs or their agents need not engage in underhand or fraudulent practices, once the unfair advantages conferred on foreign and state suppliers were removed. In November 1909, the Confederation of Trade and Industry drafted its own proposals, not only to protect domestic producers from foreign competition, but also 'to regulate the participation of state factories in concluding government procurements' and 'to monitor the allocation of orders from a commercial point of view'.

For its part, the Kharitonov commission sought to remove 'the conditions which prevent many people from taking part in the fulfilment of state orders' and, thereby, to encourage greater competition. Appropriately enough for a commission headed by the State Auditor, cost-cutting aims were not far from the surface. Kharitonov and his colleagues concluded that contracts made on the basis of open auctions (*torgi*) were most desirable. No potential supplier was thereby excluded and (it was somewhat optimistically asserted) the unscrupulous fixer and dealer had less room for manoeuvre. But, as the defence departments were to find, this policy was easier to preach than to practise.

The Kharitonov commission urged upon the government the need to preserve the position of Russian industry and to promote those branches of industry 'which, for one reason or another, do not at present exist in Russia'. In a yet more radical departure from current practice, Kharitonov also proposed the establishment of a 'council for state procurements', headed by the Ministry of Trade and Industry, with the participation on an equal footing of representatives from private industry and government. Despite various disagreements about the details, the commission finally sent a project to the Council of Ministers. Not surprisingly, objections from the major procuring ministries put paid to this initiative. Rukhlov, who never lost an opportunity to berate private entrepreneurship, believed that the Kharitonov commission had conceded too much ground to the private sector and (he perversely argued) had given a clear signal to domestic suppliers to increase their prices. The cabinet rejected the proposal, on the grounds that it limited the freedom of manoeuvre of the main government agencies.[17]

Industrialists took little comfort from government procurement practices during the slump. The Confederation of Trade and Industry maintained that the government had not done enough to ensure that orders were placed with domestic suppliers, bearing in mind 'the dire situation of the Russian engineering industry'.[18] The government took no direct responsibility for the consequences of industrial depression. No government official was prepared to let himself be steamrollered into offering tangible support for the private sector, particularly if this meant redirecting resources away from the state sector. Nevertheless, business opposition to state enterprise had been aroused and could not easily be dismissed. Armaments production and procurement would become the main battleground for the struggle between state and private enterprise.

The record of inter-ministerial division 'underlines the difficulty of arriving at any simple formula for the relationship between industry and government in Russia'.[19] These divisions were evident in other spheres of government industrial policy. Proposals to involve industrialists formally in the arrangements for procurement unleashed a stream of objections. Usually, the large spending departments were those most anxious to retain freedom of manoeuvre. However, the exercise of choice depended upon the ability of alternative suppliers to meet technical specifications, delivery dates and prices. The Ministry of Transport, seeking to obtain sources of coal from firms outside the coal syndicate, came unstuck and resorted to administrative measures against Produgol', a sure sign of ministerial powerlessness to use the economic weapon. Industrial recovery offered businessmen a chance to exert greater economic leverage and to pose a more serious challenge to state-owned enterprise.

Industrial development, 1908–1914

The public and private protestations and aspirations of Russian industrialists were played out against the background of pronounced changes in industrial output and industrial structure. Russian industry climbed out of the depths of the recession which it plumbed in 1907–8. On the eve of the First World War, output, investment, prices and profits all testified to rapid growth. In the basic industries, a range of additional demands upon mining and metallurgical enterprises strained their capacity to the utmost. Iron and steel firms, faced with higher charges for inputs, bought out their suppliers, in an attempt to secure iron ore on more advantageous terms. The strain on steel producers in turn caused customers to complain that a deliberate attempt was being made to starve them of supplies of metal, in order to force prices ever higher. In machine-building, established firms consolidated their status and new firms appeared on the scene, particularly in the developing branches of electrical engineering and shipbuilding. Here, too, a handful of large conglomerates again dominated the market. In some branches, however, domestic firms were unable to compete with imports.

The published data on industrial production tell a story of depression and recovery. The output of capital goods branches of industry ('group A', according to the conventional soviet classification) grew by 12.9 per cent per annum, whilst consumer goods industries ('group B') grew by 4.7 per cent. But the rapid growth in 'group A' industries took place from a low base. 'Group B' industries grew more slowly, but from a less depressed base (see table 4.1).

The growth of real output in heavy industry affected all sectors. An increase in demand from the railways and from industrial consumers underpinned the growth in sales of coal. Fresh investment in manufacturing industry signified a new level of confidence in the industrial economy. By 1911, and throughout the following three years, the installation of new plant in mining and manufacturing helped to maintain the momentum of industrial growth. Although the market for new equipment was shared with foreign suppliers, its growth afforded plenty of scope for Russian enterprise. Investment also breathed new life into the construction industry.[20]

Table 4.1. *Gross industrial production, 1908–1913 (million rubles)*

	Output (current prices)	Output (constant prices)	Group A (current prices)	Group B (current prices)	Group A (constant prices)	Group B (constant prices)
1908	4,351.4	4,678.9	1,394.2	2,957.2	1,499.1	3,179.8
1913	6,559.4	6,559.4	2,564.0	3,995.4	2,564.0	3,995.4

Source: Dinamika rossiiskoi i sovetskoi promyshlennosti za sorok let, Moscow, 3 vols., 1929–30, vol. 1, pp. 66–77, 106–7; vol. 2, pp. 176–7. The shares allocated to group A and B are derived from I. F. Gindin, *Russkie kommercheskie banki*, Moscow, 1948, p. 158. The relevant price index is taken from S. Bobrov, *Indeksy gosplana*, Moscow, 1925, p. 91.

The growth of output of consumer goods did not lag far behind. It was most marked in rubber, footwear, woollens, fats and some food-stuffs. Gindin was surely correct to identify the dynamism in these branches of industry with the growth in total urban consumption. However, the evidence on urban real incomes is quite sparse. Urbanization created pressure on available housing space, which even significant housebuilding did not alleviate; rents rose accordingly. The crucial element in consumption was not the increase in urban real income, which must have been modest, but rather the increase in the size of the urban population, which displayed different patterns of consumption than those of their rural counterparts.[21]

Data on industrial employment also testify to the pronounced recovery. Between 1908 and 1913, total numbers employed in large-scale industry increased by more than 29 per cent. Again, there is an evident disparity in the rate at which the two broad groups of industry absorbed labour. Employment in capital goods industry increased by 39 per cent, but in consumer goods the increase was a more modest 21 per cent. As can be seen in table 4.2, in the three years preceding the outbreak of war, employment in group A industries increased by 10 per cent per annum; group B only matched this rate of increase during the last full year of peace.

This increase in the size of the industrial labour force was accompanied by a modest reduction in the length of the working day. Total hours worked in industry probably increased by around 30 per cent between 1908 and 1913. This implies that labour productivity (output per man-hour) increased by around 10 per cent. But this increase was confined to group A industries. In group B industries, output per worker hardly increased at all.

Productivity increases in heavy industry helped to furnish improved profit levels. Along with credit from the major commercial banks, and with capital raised on the stock market, higher profits generated resources for investment. According to Strumilin, the total value of industrial assets (in large-scale and small-scale industry) increased from 2,861 million rubles in 1908 to 4,116 million in 1913. Most of this increase took place between 1911 and 1913. In these three years alone, the estimated value of capital assets increased by 27 per cent.[22] The climate of confidence was maintained by the mainly covert actions taken by the tsarist government. When, during the final quarter of 1912, international events undermined confidence, the government reactivated the stock market 'Red Cross', in order to maintain share

Table 4.2. *Industrial employment, 1900–1913 (1900 = 100)*

	Employment		Group A	Group B
	millions	Index		
1900	2.000	100	100	100
1901	2.100	105.0	104.1	105.8
1902	2.101	105.0	104.8	105.3
1903	2.081	104.1	100.7	107.3
1904	2.078	103.9	101.0	106.9
1905	2.094	104.7	101.8	108.1
1906	2.138	106.9	101.8	111.7
1907	2.211	110.6	106.2	114.6
1908	2.229	111.4	104.7	117.7
1909	2.279	113.9	108.3	119.2
1910	2.399	119.9	113.2	126.2
1911	2.556	127.8	125.7	129.8
1912	2.670	133.5	135.2	131.9
1913	2.882	144.1	145.9	142.4

Source: L. E. Mints, *Trudovye resursy SSSR*, Moscow, 1975, p. 40.

prices. The State Bank underpinned the resources and the lending capacity of the chief commercial banks, whose role as industrial creditors assumed greater importance with each passing year. The joint-stock banks, drawing upon Treasury funds, private deposits and foreign funds, committed resources to industry on a long-term basis, helping to reorganize enterprise and to finance new ventures. In the financial sector, too, reorganization took place, with foreign (especially French) participation: the powerful Russo-Asiatic Bank came into being in 1910, by the amalgamation of the Russo-Chinese and the Northern banks. By 1914, it accounted for 13 per cent of total liabilities of the commercial banks, followed by the International Bank (with 10 per cent), the Foreign Trade, Azov-Don and Trade-Industry banks, with around eight per cent of the market apiece. Each bank had its own network of clients. Much more than in 1890 or 1900, the decisions taken in the boardrooms of mining and manufacturing companies reflected the strategies and interests of leading commercial banks. Their functions assumed critical importance in the development of armaments and shipbuilding.[23]

Iron and steel: patterns of production, consumption and industrial organization

The iron and steel industry began its slow escape from recession during 1909. In 1908, total output of rolled iron and steel amounted to 2.42 million tons, ten per cent below the peak reached at the turn of the century. In the following year, output finally reached the 1900 figure (2.67 million tons), and in 1910 it stood at 3.02 million tons. Each subsequent year registered an increase in production, which peaked at 4.04 million tons in 1913. Leading producers proclaimed higher rates for the utilization of available capacity. In 1907, output of pig iron barely exceeded 55 per cent of potential capacity; the proportion was lower still in respect of construction materials and railway products. In the following year, one-third of all blast furnaces lay idle in south Russia. Three years later, in 1911, this figure had dropped to 13 per cent. The upturn was marked by other indicators, such as the behaviour of prices. In 1908, rolled steel sold at the factory gate for one ruble per pud; in the following year the price had climbed to 1.26 rubles. By 1913 the price stood 50 per cent higher than in 1908. Share prices also began to revive.[24]

What factors may be adduced to account for the growth in iron and steel consumption that underlay the increased utilization of available capacity and this revival in business confidence? The industry's product mix provides helpful clues. In 1908, the modest level of output of rails, beams and channels indicated a depressed level of investment in railway construction and in industry. Demand for iron and steel was maintained by agricultural machine-building, electrical goods and other light engineering products, rather than by heavy engineering. Household consumption remained reasonably buoyant, to judge from the behaviour of roofing iron, which serves as a reasonable proxy for domestic consumption. Government purchases of iron and steel were much lower in 1908 than at the turn of the century, accounting for less than 30 per cent of iron and steel consumption (by weight) in 1908, significantly below their 38 per cent share in 1900.[25]

Between 1911 and 1913, investment in railway construction recovered. The market was inundated with orders for rails and related items, such as axles and tires. Prodamet boasted orders for 850,000 tons of rails in 1913, compared to 500,000 tons a year earlier. In the last full year of peace, the output of rails accounted for 18 per cent of total steel production, compared to 12.5 per cent five years earlier. Production of sheet and strip metal also increased as a proportion of the total,

Table 4.3. *Iron and steel consumption, 1908*

Consumer	Volume (000 tons)	%	Value (million rubles)	%
State	868	29	133	24
Households	459	15	161	29
Other private purchase	770	26	176	31
Other[1]	901	30	90	16

[1] mostly semi-finished products

Source: N. N. Savvin, *K voprosu o potreblenii metalla i metallicheskikh izdelii v Rossii*, St Petersburg, 1913, p. 6.

reflecting a revival in industrial investment. Prodamet had orders for 442,000 tons of sheet in 1913, representing a 70 per cent increase on orders in the previous year. The growth in output of beams and channels also testified to the recovery in industrial investment. Anecdotal evidence suggests a surge in demand for iron and steel from manufacturers of agricultural implements and machinery. Meanwhile, household purchases – again, using roofing iron as a proxy – fell as a proportion of total output, from 12.6 per cent in 1908 to 9.7 per cent in 1913. Most noteworthy, according to the journal *Finansovoe obozrenie*, was the increase in iron and steel destined for the new shipbuilding programmes, the effects of which already began to be felt in 1911.[26]

The commission on the condition of the iron market provided confirmation of the pattern of consumption in 1913 and of the prospective demand in 1914. Demand from the state-owned railways for new construction amounted to 262,000 tons. The maintenance and replacement of existing lines required an additional 377,000 tons. Iron and steel needed for the manufacture of wagons and locomotives accounted for an extra 737,000 tons. Together with orders from the private sector, the railway's consumption of iron and steel amounted to 1.51 million tons. This level of consumption put all other sectors in the shade. Other government departments put their requirements as follows: 50,000 tons for state armouries; a further 50,000 tons for the Chief Quartermaster's Department (GIU); and between 82,000 and 165,000 tons for the immediate needs of the navy. Port construction undertaken by the Ministry of Trade and Industry accounted for a further 16,000 tons. As can be seen from table 4.4, demand in 1914 was projected to grow still further, as a result of new railway building.

Table 4.4. *Consumption of iron and steel, 1913–14 (000 tons)*

	1913	1914
State railways		
construction of lines	262	} 753
maintenance & repair	377	
locomotives	246	410
passenger wagons	246	262
freight wagons	262	377
Private lines (total)	131	262
State defence requirements:		
GAU arsenals and armouries	50	50
GIU	50	50
state shipyards	82	116–166[1]
Port construction	16	33–50
Agricultural machinery	164	197–213
Oil industry	98	131–147
Other metalworking and machine-building:		
St Petersburg[2]	n.a.	131
Moscow	n.a.	328
Poland	197	229
Baltic[3]	16	16–32
Odessa	49	49
Kolomna-Sormovo combine	n.a.	32

[1] Including 100–150,000 tons required in 1914 for large shipbuilding programme
[2] Not including Putilov and Nevskii factories
[3] Not including demand from newly-built shipyards
Source: TsGIA f.23, op.27, d.120, 11.6–7.

At around 1.6 million tons, government demand for iron and steel amounted to at least two-fifths of total consumption in 1913. The government expected to purchase around 2.1 million tons for its various programmes in the following year, or around half of all projected output. Part of the increase in consumption can be ascribed to the direct impact of government orders for military vessels on private and state shipyards. In addition, rearmament created a climate in which these yards and other factories invested in new plant, fuelling the expansion in ferrous metallurgy. At a conservative estimate, armaments absorbed around 10 per cent of total iron and steel output in the last year of peace. If we were to include railway construction, part of which reflected a commitment to strategic lines, the share of steel production allocated to defence would be much higher.

Much remains obscure in the iron and steel market on the eve of the First World War. According to one authority, writing in 1913, 'private consumption of metal, in the form of products for the needs of manufacturing industry, agriculture and direct mass consumption represents by volume and by value a highly important influence, and private consumption in Russia has no less influence on the growth of production than does railway construction and the state requirements for the army and navy'.[27] But it seems doubtful that the growth in production owed quite as much to household consumption as Savvin believed. Certainly, there is evidence of growth in private agricultural investment, which called forth a response from the iron and steel industry. Nor should the stimulus that came from factory building and the creation of new urban infrastructure be overlooked. Nevertheless, government demand on the eve of the war once more assumed the significance that it enjoyed at the turn of the century. Although the boom in iron and steel production between 1910 and 1913 seems to have been more broadly based than it was during the 1890s, the stimulus of government demand played the crucial role during the second phase of industrialization.

Against the background of this revival, the relationship between consumers and suppliers of iron and steel underwent a dramatic shift. No longer did the financial press carry articles complaining of excess capacity in the iron and steel industry. Instead, talk of under-investment and restrictions on output gained wide currency. The emotive term 'metal famine' became a familiar and recurrent theme in the four years before the First World War. It now fell to the consumer, rather than the producer, to demand government action. The government itself took a closer interest in the affairs of the iron and steel industry.

Complaints of a shortage of metal first surfaced in the north-west. In the chief industrial centres of St Petersburg and Riga, manufacturers demanded a reduction in the duty on imported pig iron. The government refused to act, on the grounds that the shortfall was small in size and temporary in character, being caused mainly by an outbreak of cholera in the Donbass. Supplies could be re-routed from state ironworks in the Urals. There was a degree of complacency in the government response, which overlooked more ominous trends at work in the market for iron and steel. In particular, leading producers in Ukraine began to retain pig iron, in order to convert it into rolled iron and steel, whose price had risen more rapidly than pig. Shortages intensified during the second half of 1910. Stocks of pig iron dwindled rapidly. Consumers in the central industrial region now began to complain of shortages. Few consumers expected the Urals ironworks to offer any relief. Against this background, the government permitted the import of 164,000 tons of pig iron at reduced rates of duty.[28]

The situation eased slightly, but by 1913 consumers of iron and steel once again petitioned the government to take action, in the face of delays and shortages. Conscious of its own interests in the matter, the government convened a commission to regulate the domestic iron market. Twenty officials, representing the ministries of the Interior, Navy, Finances, War, Trade and Industry, Transport, Agriculture and the State Auditor's office attended a conference in December 1913. Also present were 66 spokesmen for industry, including representatives of Prodamet, the Urals iron syndicate Krovlia, iron and steel federations and individual steel producers. Manufacturing industry was represented by various industrial associations, bourse committees, railway companies and engineering organizations, including Prodvagon and Prodparovoz, the two syndicates that administered sales of wagons and locomotives.[29]

The commission was chaired by V. P. Litvinov-Falinskii, director of the industrial division of the Ministry of Trade and Industry.[30] He began by reminding the audience of the differences between current circumstances and the conditions five and a half years previously. In 1908, industry had been in the depth of the slump, with firms reporting under-utilized capacity. Now, capacity was strained, metal was in short supply and prices were rising. The decision to import pig iron free of duty in 1911 'had had no effect on the iron and steel industry', a remark that immediately put producers on the defensive. The proceedings revealed the extent of the antagonism between suppliers and consumers. Consumers bemoaned the inflation in iron and steel prices and, especially, the delays in delivery, for which they held Prodamet responsible. Iron and steel producers pointed to the growth in output that had taken place in recent years and the projected growth in the medium term.

Iron and steel producers were justified in stating that pig iron output had increased, by close on 50 per cent between 1909 and 1912 (see table 4.5). However, the rate at which pig iron was marketed had increased by only 28 per cent, and sales had actually fallen in 1912. Thus, 'given the present high prices for iron and steel, factories prefer not to release pig iron on to the market, but instead to process it themselves into a more expensive product'. During the second half of

Table 4.5. *Production and sale of pig iron, 1908–1913 (million tons)*

	Output	Processed	Reserves (31 Dec.)	Sales
1908	2.80	n.a.	0.78	n.a.
1909	2.87	2.80	0.70	0.80
1910	3.04	3.08	0.46	0.92
1911	3.59	3.44	0.37	1.03
1912	4.20	3.99	0.44	1.02
1913	4.64	4.34	0.53	1.15

Sources: col. 1–3 *Obshchii obzor glavneishikh otraslei gornoi i gornozavodskoi promyshlennosti*, 2 vols., St Petersburg/Petrograd, 1913–1915, vol. 1, p. 33; *Statisticheskii ezhegodnik*, Petrograd, 1914, p. 192; col. 4 TsGIA f.23, op.27, d.120, 1.4; *Narodnoe khoziaistvo v 1915g.*, Petrograd, 1918, p. 289.

1912, producers accumulated large stocks of pig iron, giving rise to a sharp price increase, from 47 kopeks per pud in 1910 to 65 kopeks per pud in 1913.[31]

These trends revealed a significant change in the prevailing market conditions. In Russia, as in pre-war Germany, syndicalization never took a complete hold of the market. Where a gap existed, suppliers tended to 'overproduce'. The sale of crude ingots, billets and rails was subject to tight quotas. But no restriction applied where these products were required for a factory's own consumption. Iron and steel producers manufactured larger quantities of products where quotas were less rigorous (for example, they exported bar steel, wire, plate and forgings). As trade picked up, firms began to use less of their quota in crude iron and, instead, produced finished goods, with the higher value-added that they embodied. This behaviour accounts both for the rapid growth in output of iron and steel during the prewar quinquennium, notwithstanding the operation of Prodamet, and for complaints about the 'metal famine'.[32]

A similar trend, though less marked, operated in the market for iron and steel shapes. Between 1908 and 1913, the production of shapes, forgings, sheet and strip increased by more than two-thirds, but by 1913 a higher proportion of output was retained within the factory for processing. Correspondingly less iron and steel came on to the market. Sales of rolled iron and steel increased by 38 per cent between 1909 and 1912, whereas the volume of iron and steel retained and processed at the point of production increased by 75 per cent. Factories which sought more lucrative contracts tended to produce finished goods themselves, to a greater extent than hitherto. The industrial boom gave iron and steel producers the opportunity to obtain profitable work and recoup some of the losses they had sustained during the recession.[33]

However, more was at stake than the relative returns from the sale of pig iron and the production of iron and steel products. During this period, members of Prodamet sought to improve their bargaining position within the syndicate. By increasing their output of pig iron, which was not subject to quota restrictions, they could strengthen their claim for a larger share of the quotas for iron and steel when these next came up for renewal. Fierce battles over quotas took place during 1911 and 1912, resulting in victory for the powerful French-backed giants, the South Russian Dnieper Company, the Donets Steel Company at Druzhkovka, the Briansk Ironworks and the Russo-Belgian Company. Their behaviour undermines claims that the syndicate directly restricted output of pig iron. But it also shows something of the problems that faced the consumer.[34]

Promises and projections of increased output did not satisfy consumers of pig iron, especially spokesmen for the agricultural machinery and railway companies. They made loud complaints at Litvinov-Falinskii's commission. To their concern about rising prices, they added the charge that many iron and steel producers deliberately refused new orders. Prodamet made a stout defence of its policy: 'several consumers, in placing orders, do not reckon with the conditions of contemporary mass production, according to which our iron and steel industry is equipped; they place orders without sufficient planning and foresight (*planomernost'*), for small quantities and for shapes that are not available (*nekhodovye profilia*)'.[35] It argued that major consumers, such as the railways, could avoid this problem, if only they were willing to maintain stocks of iron and steel; but instead they kept coming back to their suppliers with petty orders. The Admiralty placed orders for as little as 200kg of steel at a time! Many consumers changed their specification each time they placed an order. For example, the North-West Railway ordered 2,750 tons of iron and steel in one twelve-month period, but spread this amount over 284 separate orders; the managers ordered an additional 750 tons, in more than 900 different specifications! This argument failed to mollify iron and steel consumers, who pointed out that what the syndicate regarded as petty orders were vital to the success of investment in railways and to the armament programmes. But railway executives and officials from the Ministry of Transport and Admiralty promised to try to rationalize their orders in future.[36]

One way of tackling the problem was to locate suppliers who did not belong to Prodamet. The Admiralty tried to pursue this tactic during 1912, when it began negotiations with the Kolomna works, whose Kulebaksk plant produced more steel than the parent company needed. Admiralty officials hoped to obtain steel for hulls and boilers at a lower price than Prodamet charged, although their main concern was to improve the speed at which the contracts could be completed. In the end, the managing director of Kolomna, A. P. Meshcherskii, was unable to comply with the terms of the contract, which went to Prodamet. However, the government extracted a promise that the syndicate would compensate the Admiralty for failing to meet the deadline, by guaranteeing to pay for imports.[37]

Evidently, the defence departments had a different set of priorities from those of the Ministry of Trade and Industry. Back in 1908, the Admiralty had planned to import non-ferrous metal on behalf of the Obukhov works. This proposition occasioned a stiff note from the Ministry of Trade and Industry: 'taking into account the general difficulties experienced by our metallurgical industry and the totally insufficient provision of work in the current year, the transfer to foreign suppliers of orders that could be handled in Russia is highly undesirable'.[38] The Artillery Administration and the Quartermaster's Department subsequently proposed to import 50,000 tons of iron, representing their entire requirements for a single year. The Admiralty asked that state yards be allowed to import up to one-quarter of their steel plate requirements, 8 per cent of steel forgings for turbines and rotors, 6 per cent of forgings for propellor shafts and 11 per cent for other items. These requests went against the spirit of the regulations agreed in 1907, which limited purchases from foreign suppliers to cases of extreme urgency or absolute necessity and, on this occasion, the military failed to get their way.[39]

In a remarkably sanguine conclusion to its deliberations, Litvinov-Falinskii's commission calculated that the worst of the crisis was over. There had been a clear shortfall in the supply of iron and steel in 1910 and 1911, but domestic production was able to satisfy demand in 1912 and promised to keep pace with the growth of demand in 1913 and 1914. None the less, in order to provide an additional safeguard, the government decided in July 1914 to permit the import of 330,000 tons of iron during the next eighteen months, indicating the importance the government attached to measures designed to overcome any supply bottlenecks. For all the talk in the press about the nefarious activities of Prodamet, the syndicate escaped with only a few bruises from this encounter with its customers.[40]

Output grew, therefore, but not rapidly enough to satisfy the claims of iron and steel consumers. The taut market conditions reflected the sudden and intense impact of government spending on the eve of the First World War. Government devised various strategies to improve its access to iron and steel supplies, but the magnitude of the task set by its officials posed problems for client and supplier alike.[41] Although their aggregate consumption was large, government departments tended to place frequent orders for small quantities of metal. Industrial consumers behaved in a similar erratic fashion. Many customers, particularly those involved in rearmament, placed orders for newer and more specialized kinds of steel, demands which might have been easier to accommodate had producers not been forced to work under such intense pressure.

To the charge that Prodamet forced up the price of iron and steel was added the accusation that its members failed to invest in additional capacity. This claim was repeated by Tsukernik, in his classic account of the syndicate.[42] He noted that the capacity of blast furnaces in south Russia averaged 426 cubic metres, whereas the norm for furnaces built elsewhere (in 1911–13) averaged 600 or even 700 cubic metres. But the comparison is a weak one: many of Russia's furnaces dated from the 1880s and 1890s and the recession – not the behaviour of Prodamet – made it difficult to conceive of investment in large, new furnaces. As the market improved, several large furnaces were built. Several firms (Donets-Iurevsk, Chaudoir of Ekaterinoslav, New Russia Ironworks, Briansk and Kramatorsk) planned to have new furnaces operating in 1914 or 1915. Tsukernik's argument is also undermined in other respects. He compared the daily output of furnaces in south Russia and the United States. In 1913, one-third of Russian furnaces had a capacity lower than 200 tons, whereas in America the corresponding proportion was only one-tenth. In America, one-third of all furnaces had a capacity in excess of 500 tons; no Russian furnace could match this size. But this comparison is also not very apt, because the American market was larger and more robust than the Russian. Tsukernik himself noted the progress that was made in expanding the size of furnaces in Russia. In 1895, the newest furnace boasted a capacity of around 160 tons of pig iron; by 1913, one-third of all Russian blast furnaces exceeded 270 tons capacity. Finally, Tsukernik observed that Russian factories used relatively more manual labour in auxiliary tasks, which elsewhere tended to be mechanized. But this practice simply reflected the relative abundance of cheap labour in the Ukraine; elsewhere, new plants did adopt mechanical means to lift and carry pig iron.[43]

In steel production, Tsukernik again accused the industry of lagging behind the United States in furnace capacity, and of failing to mechanize production, for example in loading the furnace. But he overlooked the construction of new steel works at the New Russia Ironworks and Nikopol-Mariupol in the years preceding the outbreak of war. Where rolling mills are concerned, Tsukernik was on somewhat stronger ground. Rolling mills retained old technology until 1909, but thereafter steam power was progressively replaced by electric power, first at Briansk and then at Taganrog and Makeevka. However, this innovation was less marked elsewhere. The factories that played the biggest role in Prodamet and had the highest profits were also the least well-equipped with electric power. The syndicate allowed the largest firms to reap profits, without the need for technical improvements. The others, in order to compete, could not afford to lag behind technologically. In short, the innovating firms tended to be the outsiders, rather than the stalwarts of Prodamet. But the suggestion that Prodamet hindered the adoption of new technology is, at best, a half-hearted one. Even Tsukernik admitted that progress did take place, conceding that the industry employed indigenous technical personnel to a greater extent than hitherto, a point made by John McKay in his authoritative study of foreign entrepreneurship.[44]

For all the rhetoric deployed in attacking Prodamet, in zemstvo boards, in the Duma and in some engineering circles, its critics missed the point. Whilst stories circulated of the damage inflicted by the syndicate on the industrial economy – stifling technical change and creating shortages of basic inputs – the iron and steel industry underwent profound structural changes. New combines came into being, exercising market power, by virtue of having integrated backwards, into coal and iron ore mining and, occasionally forwards, into metal-processing. By 1913, twelve iron and steelworks had acquired more than thirty iron ore mines. The three largest steel producers – Briansk (with five mines), South Russian Dnieper (two) and the Russo-Belgian Company (five) – produced around 300,000 tons of iron ore, equivalent to almost one-half of total output in the Krivoi Rog basin. Briansk cornered part of the market for coal; Makeevka Steel, South-Russian Dnieper, the New Russia Ironworks and the Russo-Belgian Company all expanded the output of coking coal from mines under their control.

The rise in the market price of iron ore (by around 25 per cent between 1908 and 1913), coal and pig iron gave a competitive advantage to enterprises which now had access to their own sources of supply. Backed by powerful French and Russian financial institutions, these combines could exercise enormous leverage.[45]

In the meantime, the difficulties that confronted consumers of iron and steel should not be laid at the door of Prodamet. The chief difficulties originated elsewhere and reflected the scale of aggregate demand on the eve of war. The syndicate simply provided a whipping-boy, a convenient focus for widespread anti-corporate sentiment. More profound changes – vertical integration, the creation of powerful metallurgical and machine-building combines – attracted much less attention. It was here, in the boardrooms of banks and industrial enterprises, rather than in government commissions or in parliament, that the revival and restructuring of the iron and steel industry were planned and carried out. The alarums and excursions over Prodamet were something of a sideshow.[46]

The engineering industry, 1908–1914: the civilian dimension

The upsurge in industrial production after 1908 was particularly marked in the engineering industry. The most reliable estimate implies that the gross output of all branches of machine-building increased from around 278 million rubles in 1908 to 478 million rubles in 1913, an increase of 72 per cent in 1913 prices. In the single year 1912–13, output probably increased by at least 25 per cent. These were impressive rates of growth.[47]

Much more difficult a task is to distinguish between the separate components of Russian machine-building, particularly in 1913 (in 1908 they can be derived from the industrial census). A set of estimates for machine-building output in 1913 appears in table 4.6.

It should be emphasized that only the figure for agricultural machinery commands complete confidence, although all the other estimates are the result of detailed reconstruction from several sources. Marked differences emerged in the performance of individual branches of engineering between 1908 and 1913. The output of transport equipment increased by 14 per cent and industrial equipment by 23 per cent. But the output of agricultural equipment and shipbuilding more than doubled, by 104 and 115 per cent respectively. The output of electrical equipment rose by a staggering 760 per cent.

The market for transport equipment, largely railway rolling-stock,

Table 4.6. *Gross output of machine-building, 1908–1913 (large-scale industry, million rubles, 1913 prices)*

	1908	1913
Industrial equipment	97.2 (34.9%)	c.120.0 (25.1%)
Transport equipment	87.7 (31.5%)	c.100.0 (20.9%)
Shipbuilding	54.0 (19.4%)	c.116.0 (24.2%)
Agricultural machinery	29.7 (10.7%)	60.5 (12.7%)
Electrical equipment	9.5 (3.4%)	81.6 (17.1%)
Total	278.1	478.0

Source: derived from *Dinamika rossiiskoi i sovetskoi promyshlennosti*, Moscow, 3 vols., 1929–30, vol. 2, pp. 128–41; vol. 3, pp. 10–11, 18–20, 52–79, 176. The equipment price deflator is taken from P. R. Gregory, *Russian National Income, 1885–1913*, Cambridge, 1982, table I.1 cols. C.1 and C.1.

remained depressed for much of this period. The output of wagons increased rapidly between 1910 and 1913, but the production of loco-motives failed to regain the volume reached in 1908. The industry never again operated at the level of output that had obtained during the first years of the century (see table 4.7). The Ministry of Transport pursued a policy of ruthless retrenchment throughout this period. State lines were instructed to increase the carrying capacity of their existing stock and to repair locomotives wherever possible. Orders from private companies failed to compensate for the decline in government purchases. The only bright spot in this otherwise gloomy predicament was that the market, limited though it was, remained in Russian hands. This sorry story is confirmed by the experience of individual factories. In 1900, at the peak in its fortunes, the Kharkov Locomotive company employed 3,491 workers. By 1908, the workforce had been slashed to just 936, a decline of two-thirds. Only in 1913 did the workforce regain its 1900 level. Workers were once more engaged on the manufacture of goods wagons; others built agricultural machinery. For much of the period, the locomotive shops here and elsewhere operated at around 20 and 25 per cent of capacity.[48]

This pattern of diversification was repeated at other factories. The beleaguered Nevskii shipyards concentrated on the manufacture of merchant and military vessels, helped by the funds that poured in from the State Bank. The Hartmann factory at Lugansk turned to the production of boilers and iron and steel forgings and castings, while

Table 4.7. *Output of rolling-stock, 1900–1913*

	Wagons	Locomotives
1900	n.a.	1,005
1901	25,627	1,225
1902	24,419	1,160
1903	21,049	922
1904	22,754	1,198
1905	27,054	1,157
1906	22,352	1,266
1907	15,506	823
1908	9,970	658
1909	6,389	525
1910	9,076	441
1911	8,878	433
1912	12,033	313
1913	20,492	609

Source: P. G. Ivanov, *Ocherk istorii i statistiki russkogo zavodskogo parovozostroeniia*, Petrograd, 1920, p. 4; D. P. Il'inskii and V. P. Ivanitskii, *Ocherk istorii russkoi parovozostroitel'noi i vagonostroitel'noi promyshlennosti*, Moscow, 1929, p. 100.

other firms manufactured a wide range of general engineering products. However, this did not extend to the production of vehicles, let alone aircraft. With the exception of the Russo-Baltic Engineering Company based in Reval, the manufacture of motorized vehicles and aircraft hardly existed in 1913, and even this enterprise was known more as an assembly works than as an independent producer of motor cars. As a consequence of these various changes, the share of transport equipment in total Russian machine-building production fell from around one-third to one-fifth between 1908 and 1913.[49]

The agricultural machine-building industry fared much better. The market grew, partly because of the improvement in cereal prices and partly because new territory was being brought under cultivation. Between 1908 and 1913, Russian producers began to manufacture harvesters and threshing equipment on a larger scale. No major new enterprises appeared on the scene; instead, production grew rapidly at the existing specialist suppliers, such as the subsidiary of International Harvester at Liubertsy (outside Moscow), and Helferrich-Sade of Kharkov. Production grew more rapidly than at the general engineering firms.

Russian producers were not able to meet domestic demand in its entirety, especially where more complex items of machinery were concerned. In aggregate terms imports still accounted for more than two-fifths of domestic consumption, slightly above the share in 1908. But in this period Russia reduced its dependence upon imports of ploughs, harvesters and threshing equipment. Only in the case of advanced agricultural equipment, such as steam traction engines (*lokomobili*), that were purchased by large landowners, did Russian firms fail to keep up with the growth of demand. Russian firms were hampered by the fact that the technically more sophisticated items of agricultural machinery were imported free of duty. But the industry did manage to obtain some concessions in 1912, such as subsidies for the production of *lokomobili* and steam threshing mills, tax relief for firms that competed in product markets with foreign firms, and favourable terms of credit.

Foreign penetration of the Russian market was not the only constraint on further growth of the industry. Arguably, the main difficulty that beset producers of agricultural machinery was the increased control over the market imposed by organized consumer interests. The zemstvos, major customers for farm tools and machines, agreed with each other about the price they were willing to pay for the product. Producers complained that their customers failed to settle their invoices promptly: Russian peasants, many of whom were organized into consumer cooperatives, asked for as much as three years' credit. This had serious consequences for the financial position of firms, twenty-five of whom were owed 38 million rubles by customers on the eve of the First World War. Attempts by producers to organize themselves, in order to improve their bargaining position and to maintain prices, never succeeded in this industry. Unlike those branches of manufacturing that supplied rails, roofing iron or locomotives, the agricultural machine-building industry was characterized by a heterogeneous product mix, which is why syndicates never emerged. In addition, the government agreed to protect the interests of consumers and never tolerated serious attempts to create a monopoly. As a result, the industry remained more competitive than other branches of engineering. Profits remained modest. Specialist suppliers did as best they could. The larger engineering firms did not regard this branch of their activity as particularly lucrative. Other activities, such as shipbuilding, offered better prospects.[50]

The manufacture of electro-technical equipment developed with remarkable rapidity, albeit from a low base. In 1903, domestic production was valued at no more than 12 million rubles. During the recession this figure is unlikely to have increased. But table 4.6 tells a story of dramatic growth between 1908 and 1913, when output grew almost nine-fold. By 1913, electrical engineering accounted for 17 per cent of total machine-building output, compared to less than 4 per cent five years earlier.

Foreign direct investment played a crucial role in the early stages of this branch of industry. German capital accounted for half the total investment in electrical engineering by 1913. Notable ventures included subsidiaries established by AEG in 1901 (in Kharkov and Riga), by Siemens-Schuckert in 1912–13 (in St Petersburg), and by Westinghouse (in Moscow, in 1898). In 1907, AEG came to an agreement with the General Electric Company, giving the German firm the right to exploit the Russian market. AEG and Siemens-Schuckert accounted for around three-quarters of total output.

The growth in market demand was met in part by imports, especially from Germany. Total imports of electrical goods, however, grew at less than half the rate of domestic production. As in other branches of the engineering industry, the degree to which imports penetrated the market for electrical goods varied from one kind of product to another. Generally speaking, Russia imported two-thirds of electrical goods. Virtually all valves, electrical fixtures (*armatura*) and switches were imported. On the other hand, a significant degree of import substitution had taken place in other products, and by 1913 most cable, batteries and low voltage equipment were produced domestically. Foreign investment also created the conditions for the early stages of import substitution in such products as turbines and high-voltage equipment. It is difficult to quantify the sources of domestic demand, but it seems clear that the expansion of the market for low-voltage equipment, such as telegraph and lighting, derived from government through its purchases for state railways, dockyards and the military.[51]

Industrial equipment is a more complex aggregate than any of the other branches of engineering, comprising such diverse products as boilers, pumps, sewing machines, textile machinery, food-processors, internal combustion engines and machine tools. This branch of the machine-building industry grew modestly between 1908 and 1913. Some sub-branches grew more rapidly than others. Domestic output of sewing machines, internal combustion engines and boilers grew steadily, as did the manufacture of lifting machinery. By 1913, domestic firms supplied 64 per cent of the rapidly growing market for sewing machines, 48 per cent for internal combustion engines and 79 per cent for boilers. Other branches were less impressive: domestic industry accounted for only 23 per cent of the large market for textile machinery and only 12 per cent for steam engines. Printing equipment was entirely foreign-made. On the other hand, the famous firm of Semenov in St Petersburg manufactured high quality cigarette and tobacco processing equipment, and had the market virtually to itself.

The modest revival of production of industrial equipment was reflected in the experience of individual enterprises. The slump at the turn of the century led Phoenix Engineering to make half its workforce redundant; by 1902, employment had fallen to just over 200. As the firm began to recover from the depression, employment increased to around 350 in 1910. The ensuing boom brought the total to 750 by 1913. Phoenix began to establish itself as a manufacturer of machine tools.[52]

In view of its crucial importance subsequently, during the First World War, the machine tool industry deserves special attention. This sector made little progress between 1900 and 1910. No new specialist firms came on the scene, nor did the existing specialist firms manage to expand their capacity. Most of the growth in output that took place between 1900 and 1910 appears to have been the result of 'in-house' production of machine tools. After 1910, however, machine tool production increased. Domestic output probably amounted to 1.5 million rubles in 1910 and 2.8 million rubles by 1912. Notwithstanding this growth, domestic production satisfied only one-third of total consumption, largely of simple lathes for turning metal and wood. Imports, predominantly from Germany, accounted for more advanced items, in particular pressing machines, turret lathes, and boring and planing tools. The import statistics, which are difficult to unravel, suggest that Russia imported machine tools to the value of 3.0 million rubles in 1910, 7.4 million in 1911, 8.0 million in 1912 and 12.7 million rubles in 1913. This gave imports around 70 per cent of the market.[53]

The expansion of the domestic machine tool industry was hampered by two constraints. The first of these was the limited size of the market, which did not extend beyond a few dozen engineering firms in the Baltic, St Petersburg, Moscow and Kharkov. Specialist producers supplied these enterprises with custom-built tools. The low level of demand imposed small production volumes, which kept prices high and reinforced the underdevelopment of the market. Besides, the largest engineering firms – Putilov, Kolomna Engineering, Briansk Ironworks – normally supplied their own requirements, which curtailed the market still further. The small market limited the scope for standardization. Even workshops in the same factory laid down different specifications for machine tools. The machine tool industry thus displayed in microcosm all the hallmarks of the machine-building industry as a whole, namely a lack of specialization and standardization, reflecting the varied tastes and traditions of individual factories.[54]

The government did not – indeed could not – alleviate this difficulty. Granted, the state ordered machine tools for state railway workshops, state ironworks, armouries and shipyards. But the level of demand was not very significant and the government, like most clients, tended to order small quantities of varied types of machine tool. The government, it argued, had no alternative but to order from foreign suppliers, who were technically more competent and more reliable.[55]

Problems of market demand were compounded by the structure of the Russian tariff. The 1903 tariff levied duty on machines according to value, affording greatest protection to the cheaper and least sophisticated items, such as heavy-duty milling, planing and drilling tools. More valuable items, such as modern milling and turret lathes, escaped relatively lightly. The tariff reinforced the existing differential between the cost of foreign and of domestic machine tools, and gave no incentive to Russian engineering firms to produce more sophisticated items. Those in favour of the all-round development of the Russian machine tool industry argued that the government should introduce a tariff that protected the producer of complex items and, in particular, deterred customers from importing parts for assembly in Russia.[56]

The Russian engineering industry contained several large and well-equipped firms, many of them having been in existence for at least half a century. A handful of firms made their entry after 1908 into branches of the industry where they were able to specialize, as, for example, in armaments and machine tools. But the outstanding names in the industry in 1913 had already been established by the 1890s or earlier: Putilov, Sormovo, Kolomna and Phoenix. These firms either began to specialize in armaments, or opted, as before, for a broad mix of engineering products. In both cases, the industrial boom stimulated an increase in investment. The capital stock of engineering factories increased from 98 million rubles in 1900 to 129 million in 1908 and 161 million rubles in 1911. At the well-established firms, however, the plant grew like coral, with newer shops superimposed upon existing, and technologically less modern areas of the plant. As a result, bottlenecks began to develop, because the factory could only function at the pace of its slowest part. The giant engineering firm Sormovo was a case in point. The assembly shop could handle up to 280 locomotives each year, but the rolling mill was equipped to produce steel for the equivalent of 130 units and the boiler shop for fewer than 100. Similar problems beset the manufacture and assembly of boilers at the Briansk Engineering plant.[57]

The market for engineering products in Russia remained small and fragmented. The industry produced a wide range of products, usually at the cheaper end of the market. Specialization entailed too many risks. An early student of the industry, V. I. Grinevetskii, blamed entrepreneurial deficiency for the lack of specialization, rather than the size of the market, but this does not seem to have been the main factor. In the most dynamic branches of machine-building, such as military shipbuilding, the expansion of opportunity called forth a dynamic entrepreneurial response. The limited market also discouraged standardization, as in the manufacture of rolling-stock, but the government did little to promote this process, allocating numerous orders in small quantities. In any case, this market contracted after 1907, barely recovering on the eve of the war. The capital required to build, equip and operate a machine-building plant also constrained the expansion of the industry: in particular, considerable amounts of working capital were needed, because of the low rate of turnover of production and the need for large stocks of fuel and raw materials. As if these difficulties were not enough, Russia suffered from a dearth of skilled workers and technical staff: compared to western Europe and the United States, the ratio of technical staff to workers on the shop-floor was distinctly unfavourable. Last, but not least, the structure of the Russian tariff no longer suited conditions in the industry. In 1903, the revision of the tariff did away with the imposition of duty according to the weight of machines, and imposed duties in accordance with their value, a system that afforded least protection to more complex and higher-value machines. The tariff also permitted the import of machine parts at a similar rate of duty to that imposed on completed machines. Rather than manufacture complete machines, especially of the more sophisticated kind, many engineering firms assembled machines from parts that had been imported from western Europe.[58]

The most dynamic branches of the engineering industry on the eve of the First World War stood in sharp contrast to one another. Agricultural equipment producers faced a growing, and potentially enormous mass market for their output. But this branch of the industry attracted few new entrants between 1905 and 1914. The shipbuilding industry, on the other hand, was built on the foundations of government contract work. In the years before 1914, as we shall see, it presented a dynamic picture, marked by rapid growth in output and employment, the formation of new enterprises and technological change. The contrast is evident in the differential growth of share capital. Between December 1911 and December 1913, the subscribed capital of engineering firms virtually doubled; but the sharpest increase was reserved for firms in receipt of government orders, particularly armaments. Their proportion of total share capital increased from 32 per cent to 45 per cent. In this sector, more than in any other branch of Russian industry at this time, with the possible exception of electrical engineering, capital investment, research and development assumed prime importance. By the same token, it was here that foreign capital and expertise would have their greatest impact.[59]

Conclusion

The growth and fluctuations in demand for the products of the iron and steel and engineering industries corresponded closely with government spending programmes. The production of rails, axles and metal tires accounted for a substantial proportion of iron and steel output, around one-third in 1898 and one-fifth in 1912. The manufacture of rolling-stock accounted for one-third of engineering output in 1908. Most of this output was purchased on behalf of state lines. The inclusion of orders for iron and steel or finished products from other government departments, such as the Admiralty, increased still more the proportion of output consumed by government: total government demand accounted for around two-fifths of the products of the iron and steel industry in 1913. What kind of relationship between industrialists and government was implied in these statistics, and how did it manifest itself?

The government strove at all times to avoid the impression that it was merely a soft touch for private industry. There were plenty of government ministers, members of the State Council and other influential figures whose attitude to private enterprise remained lukewarm, if not hostile. During the 1890s, when the Ministry of Finances occupied a central role in economic policy, Witte – by virtue of his close ties with the Tsar, and by means of judicious handouts to the nobility – managed to head off these attacks, and to keep secret the extensive character of government aid to industry. But a less astute person at the helm of the Ministry, or a change in the circumstances under which it operated, could easily upset these policies.

The depression witnessed a cautious policy of relief to the struggling firms in heavy industry, especially in iron and steel. Under Witte, this assistance took a largely surreptitious form. Special subsidies were agreed; the government set up the committee for the allocation of rails and approved the statutes of Prodamet. However, Witte's opponents hounded him from office in 1903. The authority of the Ministry of Finances, weakened by Witte's departure, nose-dived. After the Russo-Japanese War, with the resources of the Treasury seriously depleted, the Ministry did not have the means to rescue industry from its profoundly depressed condition, even had the political will been there to do so.

Russian industrialists, for their part, organized themselves in defence of their economic interests. The Association of Southern Coal and Steel Producers, having taken a prominent part in the negotiations leading to the formation of Prodamet, continued to press the claims of ferrous metallurgy. No organization of equivalent power and influence existed in the engineering industry. A national confederation of firms in the engineering industry only gained adherents in 1916. Prior to that time, the most significant associations were the Confederation of Northern and Baltic Engineering Industry, formed in 1902, and the Confederation of Agricultural Machine-Building Industry, established in 1906. By 1913, these associations represented thirty-seven and fifty-three enterprises respectively, but their influence upon government was minimal. The associations periodically sent delegations to government departments, in order to lobby for changes in corporate law, the tariff or procurement policy.[60]

The formation of a new Ministry of Trade and Industry in 1905 went some way towards improving the access of industrial associations to government. Timiriazev was certainly sympathetic to private enterprise, and was berated in some circles for maintaining too close a link with private enterprise. However, the initiatives he launched came to an end with his resignation. His successors lacked the same radical political vision. The new ministry enjoyed less status and power than other government departments, and this constituted a stumbling-block to the success of entrepreneurs in influencing government industrial policy. The Ministry of Finances not only determined fiscal policy, but also managed to keep industrialists at arms' length. In these circumstances, industrialists appeared vulnerable and impotent.

Yet, for all the public lamentation about industrial crisis, the relationship between government and business underwent a subtle change between 1908 and 1914. The political weakness and the manifest shortcomings of industrial associations disguised the growth of a different kind of corporate power. Changing economic strength manifested itself in the emergence of powerful integrated steel and engineering combines. Granted, the increase in aggregate demand after 1910 created taut market conditions and put pressure on government to control the behaviour and organization of business enterprise. But many of the complaints emanated from quarters that could be ignored, such as the zemstvos, municipal authorities, and parliamentary speakers. The central government had fewer qualms about footing the bill for iron and steel and for capital ships, once it embarked on the cause of rearmament. And the major engineering firms reorganized themselves, in order to absorb the rising costs of industrial inputs.

The record of industrial growth, therefore, does not tell the whole story; indeed, the statistics of output can be quite misleading. With hindsight, it is evident that the basic industries grew rapidly between 1908 and 1913. Contemporary businessmen, closely involved in their own enterprises, obviously had a quite different perspective on output and investment from that adopted by later generations of economic historians. Only after 1910 did businessmen begin to contemplate their affairs with anything approaching optimism; and only in 1912 did they exude real confidence. For much of the period their prospects looked bleak. Order books and employment told a story of recession. Nor did government policy across a range of issues offer much succour. The efforts of businessmen in the capital goods industries to persuade government to take a more sympathetic view of their plight met with little success. In retrospect, then, rearmament and its associated demands did rescue the basic industries from the recession. But this was a fortuitous outcome; no-one in government regarded rearmament as a device to aid industrial recovery in the private sector. If anything, the orders generated by rearmament were expected to go to established enterprises in the state sector. More would be needed than protestations of corporate agony, however eloquent or sincerely held, if rearmament were to bring relief, as it eventually did, to Russia's hard-pressed businessmen.

5   The armaments industry: the search for identity and influence, 1908–1914

Introduction: the organization and reorganization of the armaments industry

The specific characteristics of defence industry, tsarist ideology and Russian economic backwardness impart a multiple fascination to the study of the armaments industry. Like any sovereign state, the tsarist regime had no choice but to concern itself with matters relating to the output of defence goods. These it preferred to entrust to government-owned arsenals, shipyards and ironworks. To leave the production of military goods to the commercial sector exposed the government to the whim of the entrepreneur, whose prime concern was with the survival of his business. If entrepreneurs colluded, then the government, being their sole customer, would be unable to enforce competition in the arms trade. In practice, the tsarist regime rarely needed to confront these issues prior to 1905. Whether the government could or should close off for good the opportunities for the private sector remained an intermittently articulated question of principle that was ultimately decided by the practical needs of rearmament.

Few entrepreneurs were brave or foolish enough to enter the 'arms bazaar'. The risks of entering this peculiar market required little emphasis. In the uncertain world of defence production, it made little sense to invest heavily in new plant or to recruit skilled workers, only to find that the government cut off their life-blood, whether by withdrawing orders altogether, by privileging the state sector or by importing arms. Even if private businessmen claimed and retained a modest share of the defence market, the government could complicate business plans, by adjusting or even abandoning its requirements. None the less, after 1905 the armaments option began to commend itself to established firms in the private sector. New entrants to the industry

197

also appeared on the scene. How this process came about, with what consequences for state enterprise, and whether the fears of state 'subordination' to capitalist entrepreneurs were realized, form the subject of this chapter and the next.

Armaments production had traditionally been dominated by state armouries and dockyards. Long familiarity with the task of weapons manufacture conferred on them the capacity to cope with the demands of military customers. Recent events, too, had demonstrated that the state enterprises played an indispensable part in the procurement process. During the 1890s, state-owned arsenals dealt effectively with the task of equipping the armed forces with modern rifles. Nor could government yards be faulted during the Russo-Japanese War, when they coped more than adequately with the tasks suddenly thrust upon them. It seemed prudent to continue to rely upon government enterprises in the future.

On the other hand, powerful arguments could be advanced in favour of a greater reliance upon private contractors. Many of the most important private firms enjoyed close links with foreign firms, by virtue of the patronage extended simultaneously by financial institutions in St Petersburg and Paris to Russian and west European arms producers. The tsarist government acknowledged that private enterprises had access to advanced foreign armaments technology. But could the government allow private entrepreneurs to dominate the armaments industry, with the attendant risk that private businessmen could dictate prices, technical specifications and other contract terms? Although it was as yet unclear how much leverage the arms trade possessed and in what ways it would seek to exercise that leverage, this risk was sufficiently great to convince the government of the need to retain a substantial portion of armaments-producing capacity in the hands of the state.

The tsarist government could not, however, ignore arguments in favour of reform of the state sector. Influential members of the Duma, by no means sympathetic towards private enterprise, argued that administrative reform of government armouries and shipyards made sound financial sense. Pressure for reform emanated also from Russian businessmen, who complained that they faced unfair competition on prices, because the losses incurred by state enterprises were offset by government subsidies. There was an element of truth in this claim: the state sector was obliged to keep prices low, in order that it could 'regulate' prices charged by the private sector. But the high costs of production that characterized state enterprises meant that losses were inevitable. Government subsidies to state-owned enterprises thus had the air of permanence about them.

Debates about the relative merits of state and private enterprise were played out against the background of genuine economic uncertainty. The crucial issue was investment, to which problems of recruiting and retaining labour took second place, until the eve of the war. The government had to consider what resources were available to finance the new investment that was badly needed, especially at the GAU factories. The situation was not promising, bearing in mind the policy of retrenchment to which the Ministry of Finances rigidly adhered. The reform of state dockyards meant that they were required to finance investment from their own resources. But would internally generated funds suffice? The replacement of capital at existing enterprises was not the only issue involved. The government also came under pressure to allocate funds for the construction of new enterprises in branches where current capacity was regarded as inadequate, particularly in fuses, explosives and cartridges. These proposals to expand the state sector generated additional criticism from the private sector. Capital investment in defence industry became the touchstone of attitudes and policy towards state and private enterprise.

The balance between the two forms of ownership began to shift after 1900. Between 1900 and 1913, the private sector doubled its share of the defence industry, in terms of employment, from 12 to 23 per cent. This shift was particularly marked between 1908 and 1913. It owed virtually everything to the spectacular programme of naval rearmament. In 1900, around one-third of the labour force in the military shipbuilding industry was employed in the private sector. In 1908, with the contraction in the workforce at state yards, the proportion rose to two-fifths. On the eve of the First World War it stood at just under three-fifths.[1] The shipbuilding programmes allowed existing private firms to obtain new contracts and to recruit new workers, and also inspired the creation of a handful of powerful new ventures. The attempt to fend off the interlopers' challenge would require managerial acumen, improved productivity and the exercise of political skills by those who administered state shipyards and arsenals. It is with these that we begin.

The management, finance and status of state enterprise, 1908–1914: government shipyards

As Russia embarked upon naval rearmament, it gradually dawned on the imperial regime that the dockyards in its possession were ill-equipped for the task. Each yard manifested its own amalgam of problems, which related chiefly to plant size, layout and capital equipment. The four yards in the Baltic had been built and equipped with smaller vessels in mind, not the enormous battleships around which the Tsar intended to build his fleet. The government also had to decide whether or not to invest in the construction of entirely new yards in the Black Sea, where the single state-owned facility had recently passed into private hands. Financial constraints made it doubtful that the government could sanction the construction of an entirely new state yard to handle the Black Sea shipbuilding programme.

The government intended to improve the potential of the state sector, enabling it to address the tasks of rearmament in a more professional fashion. But the measures taken did not always serve that purpose. In particular, the desire to make state shipyards financially independent of the Treasury conflicted with their pressing needs for new investment. Prior to 1908, the navy determined the level of financial support to the Izhora factory and the 'New Admiralty' yards in St Petersburg. The ministry assigned a budget, which specified the funds available and laid down strict conditions as to their use. As formerly privately owned yards, the Baltic and Obukhov dockyards already operated as self-financing enterprises. The distinction did not matter before 1908, because the level of activity at Russian shipyards remained modest. But it was a different matter after 1908, when rearmament began to gather pace and new investment became an urgent priority.

The government chose precisely this moment to extend the principle of self-finance to all shipyards under its jurisdiction. This decision followed criticism within the Duma about accounting practices in the state sector, and in particular the lack of a mechanism for monitoring production costs. With the adoption of the 1907 shipbuilding programme, the navy planned to order new vessels from state yards. But it became apparent that this decision would add around 15 per cent to the total cost of the programme. Shifting the burden of financial responsibility on to the shoulders of the state yards was an attempt to encourage them to reduce production costs, whilst at the same time drawing the teeth of parliamentary critics. The Admiralty had little choice but to accede to the demand for reform.[2]

The new regulations required all four shipyards to finance capital investment from internal resources, without recourse to the Treasury: 'no credits from the Naval Ministry for the maintenance and activity of the factories will be assigned. Their expenses will be covered from sums obtained from orders and from other internal sources and, in case of necessity, from the factories' reserve capital'. According to the new rules, the price agreed with the Main Administration for Shipbuilding and Supply (GUKS) embodied an allowance for profit, which was calculated as a percentage of the production cost. The regulations made no mention of the actual percentage allowable on each contract, stating merely that the profit should ensure that the procurement price did not exceed the price quoted by either private or foreign suppliers. By placing this ceiling on procurement prices, the government avoided a straightforward cost-plus contract for military vessels.[3]

How would the state shipyards operate under this new dispensation? In practice, government officials determined prices in accordance with an outdated assessment of profits required to finance capital investment. That is, officials took into account the technology in shipbuilding that existed at the turn of the century, on the assumption that the basic elements of production costs remained constant. How unrealistic was this assumption may be seen from the remarks made by plant managers at the end of 1911, by which time the financial position of state yards had become quite desperate. The Baltic and Admiralty yards reported that profits had plummeted by 40 per cent and 80 per cent respectively, and that reserves had been drastically depleted. Debts incurred before 1908 had a prior claim on profits: 'our profits, and the reserve and amortization funds have a purely accounting significance and do not represent cash in hand, because the question of debt has not been resolved and because the Baltic factory has been obliged to write off the debts outstanding from the Admiralty'.[4]

The new regulations came into force at a time when the condition of buildings and plant at government shipyards left a lot to be desired. At Obukhov, the water supply, generating plant and especially the steel mill appalled government inspectors. Other needs, not directly associated with shipbuilding, but no less important, also suffered from neglect. Obukhov lacked school and leisure facilities for workers and their families, whilst a newly-built canteen catered for 50 people, less than 2 per cent of the workforce. The Admiralty yards gave even greater cause for concern. An official report spoke of 'antiquated' capital equipment. Machine tools functioned at slow speed. Most alarmingly, 'a significant decline in orders took place, because the workshops of the New Admiralty were unable to compete with private producers'. The Admiralty appealed for an immediate injection of funds to finance reconstruction and investment in new equipment.

But the Minister of Finances and the State Auditor insisted that the dockyards should finance their own investment. After a fierce battle in the Council of Ministers at the end of 1909, the project collapsed.[5]

Even the most highly-regarded yards suffered under the new regime. At the Baltic yards, profits generated during the heady days of 1904 and 1905 enabled the management to accumulate a large reserve fund. By 1909, this stood at 2.5 million rubles. But the yard could not keep up with demands being made upon it. Advances on major contracts amounted to 30 million rubles, but this sum was earmarked for materials and other operating costs associated with the battleship-building programme. The factory did not have sufficient revenue to cover operating expenses on other contracts, let alone to accumulate additional reserves. A request for 18 million rubles from the Main Shipbuilding Administration got an unsympathetic and unhelpful hearing. Officials urged that the factory should use its reserves to cover any shortfall between receipts and outgoings, a suggestion that went quite against the spirit and letter of the regulations that had been introduced in 1907, which stipulated that the reserves were to be used for capital investment, not to cover operating expenses. The situation worsened during the following two years, because government departments failed to settle their invoices on time. By December 1911, the reserves had completely disappeared. An urgent request went out for the funds to acquire machine tools for the machine shop and foundry. Admiralty officials tried to avoid the injection of fresh funds from the budget, proposing instead to transfer funds from Izhora to the Baltic account. The directors of Izhora, not surprisingly, would have nothing to do with this proposition.[6]

If such a miserable fate befell even these well-managed yards, it is hardly surprising that the 'New Admiralty' yards, with a much poorer reputation, got into difficulties. Notwithstanding the increased volume of work and the growth in the value of gross output, the yards failed to increase profits, either in absolute terms or as a percentage of output (see table 5.1).

As the shipbuilding programme gathered momentum, Admiralty officials counterattacked. In a submission to the Duma in April 1912, Grigorovich pointed out that the revolution in shipbuilding techniques had left previous accounting assumptions and rules in tatters. Management could not function properly, unless the framework of shipbuilding costs was substantially revised. Rising costs reflected primarily changes in shipbuilding technology, as well as inflation in raw material prices and wages. State yards could not top up their

Table 5.1. *Profile of the 'New Admiralty' yards, 1908–1912*

	1908	1909	1910	1911	1912
Gross output (million rubles)	4.14	5.35	6.12	8.45	6.96
Profit[1]	4.9%	4.0%	2.3%	1.9%	n.a.

[1] Expressed as percentage of output
Sources: *TsGAVMF* f.401, op.6, d.37, 1.186; *Vsepoddaneishii otchet po morskomu ministerstvu za 1906–1909*, St Petersburg, 1910, p. 21; *ibid., za 1913*, p. 308.

reserve and amortization funds as the regulations required them to do, and it was unfair to pin the blame on managerial shortcomings.[7]

In fact, under the more liberal financial regime, management did initially exercise some flexibility in handling labour costs. Cuts in wages served as a crude yet effective means of making economies. The director of the Izhora works reported that he had reduced wages in 1909: 'if this were not done, the factory would lose work, and in view of the serious unemployment problem workers themselves have been prepared in their own interests, as well as those of the factory, to get more work and to receive modest wages, rather than to be laid off because of a lack of work'. At the Baltic yards, the average daily wage fell from 2.32 rubles in 1908 to 2.26 rubles in 1909. By 1911 wages had fallen to 2.04 rubles. However, there were limits to this strategy, and in 1912–13 – as the entire industry worked at fever pitch – wage rates once more picked up sharply. Other factors also eroded the capacity of management to keep production costs under control, notably increases in raw material prices.[8]

In principle, one solution to the financial difficulties described above would have been to increase the rate of profit allowed to the state yards. But to have done this would have raised procurement prices and thus have undermined the principle on which the state sector operated. An alternative course of action was to inject funds directly from the Treasury. Both devices involved a departure from the principles embodied in the 1908 regulations. The government ruled out the first solution, on the grounds that state factories should continue to keep their prices below those of the private sector. Only a few contracts – and with the Artillery Administration, rather than the body responsible for shipbuilding – were renegotiated.[9]

Predictably, the Ministry of Finances strongly opposed the second solution. The naval procurement administration (GUKS) had already approached the Admiralty in 1908 with a request for 21 million rubles, to finance capital reconstruction over a three-year period at the Obukhov, Izhora and Admiralty yards. The Navy Ministry whittled this proposal down to 15 million rubles, but kept intact a proposal for an additional nine million rubles, in connection for work on the new battleships. This proposal came before the Council of Ministers in September 1909. The State Auditor challenged it, on the grounds that state yards invariably 'frittered money away'. Kokovtsov objected as well, and the Council of Ministers turned down the requst.[10]

The financial problems described above eventually evoked a different response. First, factories used funds from current reserves, such as they were, in order to finance running repairs to capital equipment. Second, some emergency credits were transferred by the Ministry from other items to the state yards, in order to fund new investment. In 1912, the government released 6 million rubles, in order to purchase equipment for work on armoured cruisers. Third, the advances on the growing volume of orders allowed factories to settle some of their debts to private suppliers and to conclude contracts for new equipment. At the same time, management withheld payments to other factories within the state sector, and other claims within the state sector on state shipyards were written off. In effect, the financial problems faced by state yards were transferred to other state factories, such as Perm and Izhevsk, which supplied steel and other items to shipyards.[11]

The government eventually decided to opt for expansion. First to feel the benefit of greater generosity was Izhora, whose crucial importance as the sole source of armour-plate did not need to be emphasized. The navy estimated that a complete refit of Izhora would cost around 9 million rubles, to bring its armour-plate producing capacity up to 10,000 tons, five times larger than at present, and to instal a press with a 10,000-ton load. With these improvements, designed to enable the factory to produce stronger armour-plate for gun decks and turrets, it was hoped that Izhora would reach the technical level of Krupp. The programme of expansion did indeed yield impressive results. By 1913, the factory produced 14,000 tons of armour-plate, of a quality and at a price that compared favourably with foreign suppliers.[12]

The Navy Ministry also allocated ten million rubles to Obukhov for a programme spread over five years, designed to bring the yards 'into order'. This programme included the expansion of ordnance producing capacity. In 1912, Obukhov received a further 3.2 million rubles to fund the acquisition of equipment to build 14-inch naval guns. Overall, these investments increased the capital stock at Obukhov, from 27.4 million rubles in 1910/11 to 30.2 million in 1912/13. On the eve of the war, Obukhov was five times bigger than it had been twenty years earlier.[13]

The government also agreed to a major investment effort at the impoverished Admiralty yard. Orders poured in for work on two battleships and on armoured cruisers. Private shipbuilders, such as the newly created Noblessner, also subcontracted work to the yards. From the advances that accompanied these orders, management financed some modest capital investment. But most of the increased investment, for example to manufacture gun turrets, came directly from the government: more than seven million rubles in 1913 alone.[14]

The decision to inject fresh funds from government represented a vote of confidence in the state yards and a conscious decision to retain significant capacity in state hands. One touchstone of this policy is revealed by the government's response to privatization proposals. In the middle of 1912, the government learned that the Russian Ship-building Company (Russud) was interested in leasing the Admiralty yards. Russud cited as precedent the previously agreed lease of the old state yards at Nikolaev to the French-backed Nikolaev Company. But naval officials on the Shipbuilding Commission rejected the application and the precedent that had been cited: 'Nikolaev had only repair workshops, which were entirely unsuitable for the construction of large modern vessels. The Admiralty yards are in a quite different position. Here everything (wharves, rail transport and so forth) is already to hand'.[15] Soon after this decision, the newly-formed Franco-Russian Wharves brought forward a similar proposal, which the Commission also rejected, on the grounds that it would only benefit the private firm, which sought to improve its competitive position vis-à-vis Putilov. The Council of Ministers subsequently took up the proposal. The Ministry of Finances objected that the bidder was not a genuinely Russian-owned business. The Admiralty backed the scheme, on the grounds that funds were otherwise unavailable to modernize the Admiralty yards, which lacked proper engineering workshops and could only repair or build hulls. If the lease went ahead, the state would eventually have returned to it a modern and well-equipped shipyard, comparable to those owned by Putilov. But it should not be thought that the Navy Ministry had suddenly become converted to the principle of private enterprise. Rather, officials wanted to use the funds from the deal to finance the construction of a new state yards, equipped to produce gun turrets. The estimated cost of a new venture was put at 6.3 million rubles, which would be used to build and equip a state-owned rival to the powerful – and privately-owned – St Petersburg Metal Company. Persuaded by this argument, the government eventually approved the lease in July 1914.[16]

By 1911, the dispensation agreed three years earlier had virtually broken down under the financial pressures induced by the scale of naval rearmament. The Duma took advantage of the opportunity created by the financial embarrassment of the Admiralty to press for further administrative reforms. The government could not avoid – and the Duma could hardly refuse – the injection of additional funds in the form of new shipbuilding orders, which in turn generated advances that helped to reduce the desperate financial position of enterprises in 1911–12.[17]

The results of a quinquennium of government support for state shipbuilding are seen in the fact that the state yards received around 36 million rubles in government grants for new investment between 1908 and 1913. Some of the enterprises found additional funds from internal sources. The value of the capital stock at the state yards amounted to at least 140 million rubles at the beginning of January 1914. The shipyards accounted for at least a quarter of all state-owned fixed capital in industry. They employed thousands of workers. In terms of assets and labour force, they remained at the centre of the Russian shipbuilding industry.[18]

State arsenals and ironworks

The faith placed by the tsarist government in the state sector is further confirmed by decisions to finance the expansion and construction of enterprises under the jurisdiction of the Main Artillery Administration (GAU), as well as to retain significant capacity in the Urals iron and armaments complex. In the case of government arsenals, there was never any question of renouncing state control. The main issue concerned the degree of investment needed in order to maintain their productive potential. Their needs were generally held to be modest, given that the rearmament projects of the GAU lacked the scale and scope of the naval programmes. The Urals ironworks posed a different set of problems. Most of them were unglamorous, decrepit and consequently short of supporters within official circles. But they did maintain a huge labour force. What would a stricter financial regime imply for ironworks such at Votkinsk, Zlatoust or the huge

Table 5.2. *Employment at state armouries, 1890–1914*

	1890–1900	1902	1904–05	1908–09	1913–14
Armouries					
Izhevsk	8,000(a)	4,781	11,000(a)	6,684(b)	11,000(b)
Tula	7,035(d)[2]	3,759	n.a.	4,029(b)	7,000(b)
Sestroretsk	1,725(d)[2]	982	n.a.	1,460(b)	1,460(b)
Cartridge					
Lugansk	n.a.	974	n.a.	1,200(b)	2,490(b)
St Petersburg	n.a.	1,553	n.a.	n.a.	1,200(c)
Fuses					
St Petersburg					
Tube	n.a.	5,033	n.a.	n.a.	5,500(c)
Samara					
(est. 1910)	–	–	–	–	n.a.
Explosives					
Kazan	n.a.	1,529	n.a.	n.a.	n.a.
Okhtensk	n.a.	1,980	n.a.	n.a.	n.a.
Shostensk	n.a.	1,529	n.a.	n.a.	n.a.
Ordnance					
St Petersburg					
Ordnance	975(d)[2]	742	n.a.	800(b)	1,000(b)
Total[1]	n.a.	26,117	46,679[3]	31,734	47,400[4]

[1] Total includes employment at the three first-rank and three second-rank arsenals (St. Petersburg, Briansk, Kiev; Warsaw, Tbilisi, Khabarovsk), whose chief function was to repair ordnance and gun carriages, and to prime cartridges. The total also includes other GAU enterprises (various workshops, pharmaceuticals factory and firing range). Clerical workers are included in the total.
[2] 1900
[3] 1906
[4] 56,601 in 1914

Sources: (a) E. K. Germonius, 'Izhevskii oruzheinyi zavod i rol' kazennykh zavodov v dele oborony', *Russian Economist*, vol. 2, 1922, p. 2904; (b) *Fabrichno-zavodskie predpriatiia Rossiiskoi imperii*, St Petersburg, 1909; second edn., Petrograd, 1914; (c) E. E. Kruze, *Peterburgskie rabochie v 1912–1914 godakh*, Leningrad, 1961, pp. 72–3; (d) figures for 1900, from L. G. Beskrovnyi, *Armiia i flot v nachale XX veke*, Moscow, 1986, pp. 73, 87. 1902 data from N. M. Lisovskii, *Rabochie v voennom vedomstve*, St Petersburg, 1906, pp. 8–9. Total employment derived from War Ministry documentation, cited in G. K. Miftiev, 'Artilleriiskaia promyshlennost' Rossii v gody pervoi mirovoi voiny', kandidatskaia dissertatsiia, Leningrad, 1953, p. 100.

Table 5.3. *Estimated expenditure on machine tools by GAU, 1908–1914 (rubles)*

	Armouries	Powder	Fuse	Cartridge	Explosives	Total[1]
1908	58,400	218,600	15,500	49,000	18,800	360,300
1909	70,600	195,500	99,000	67,900	33,600	466,600
1910	115,100	259,900	44,800	36,100	65,700	521,000
1911	185,550	209,400	66,000	73,800	22,400	552,800
1912	224,650	248,600	64,400	110,630	44,750	693,100
1913	220,000	171,400	63,300	83,700	51,200	592,600
1914	138,350	291,400	44,600	58,000	37,000	569,400

[1] Excludes allocations to the arsenals listed in note to table 5.2 (in 1913 these amounted to a further 90,000 rubles).
Source: Smeta voennogo ministerstva po GAU, St Petersburg, annually, St Petersburg, 1908–13.

plant at Motovilikha? Should the government accept proposals to privatize some or all of the ironworks? In the end, these proposals came to naught. This left the state with more than a dozen lame ducks. Even fairly unambitious measures to rationalize capacity achieved only modest success. With the notable exception of Motovilikha, the state ironworks remained an albatross around the neck of the tsarist regime.

The armouries under the aegis of the GAU had reduced their capacity considerably in the aftermath of the war against Japan. But, from this depleted base, they grew rapidly in the years before the outbreak of the First World War (see table 5.2).

It remains to be established whether these enterprises were able to finance a corresponding increase in investment. The only means at our disposal to answer this question is provided by estimates of the resources secured by the GAU for the acquisition of machine tools. Table 5.3 implies that investment more than matched the increase in the labour force. In 1908, the total GAU budget for machine tools was equivalent to ten rubles per worker; in 1913 the corresponding figure was 12.5 rubles.[19]

As the figures suggest, the government made no attempt to insist that these enterprises operate on self-financing principles. Government armouries continued to be funded, as before, from the GAU budget. The results of budget expenditure at individual plants were often quite impressive. The cartridge works at Lugansk and St Petersburg were re-equipped, 'chiefly with the assistance of domestic engineering industry'. The GAU spent 600,000 rubles on new equipment for the Shostensk powder works in 1913, increasing its capacity by 50 per cent, to around 6,000 kg of explosives. Tula received generous assistance with an ambitious re-equipment programme, at the cost of running up colossal debts with the Treasury.[20]

In a further contrast with practice elsewhere in the state sector, the GAU advocated the construction of new enterprises, with some success. In 1909, officials brought forward two proposals, for the construction of an explosives factory and a fuse factory, both to be located in Samara. The total cost was put at more than 4 million rubles. Only the explosives factory attracted sufficient funding at first, although the project turned sour when construction costs rose, because of the inflation in the prices of cement, brick, timber and labour. By the end of 1910, when the fuse works received government approval, construction costs were already one-third over budget. When it was completed, in 1911, delays in the delivery of measuring instruments from St Petersburg held up production, as did the failure of the GAU to approve specifications for new fuses.[21]

It is difficult to assess the profitability of these enterprises. The issue failed to generate the same degree of heat in public discussions as did the financial condition of state shipyards, where the scale of investment sometimes beggared belief. Certainly, the dismal appraisals often made of the financial condition of government enterprises did not apply to the Izhevsk arsenal. Izhevsk made a profit from its steel-making capacity, which allowed management to keep control over the price of inputs and – by enabling Izhevsk to sell steel to other customers – subsidized the armoury.[22]

Another difference between practice at government armouries and state shipyards emerges in the choice of client. Managers of most GAU enterprises could not and did not rely exclusively on contract work for the army. Throughout the pre-1914 period, they accepted orders from other clients, permitting them to spread their overhead costs over a larger volume of output than would otherwise have been the case. For example, the three armouries had a combined capacity of 525,000 rifles in 1912, but produced a mere 37,000 in 1911 and no more than 47,000 rifles in the following year. Faced with this miserable volume of orders, managers chased and secured work on behalf of other government customers, such as the Ministry of the Interior and the Ministry of Agriculture. The armouries even acted as sub-contractors to private arms firms. The Tula armoury had orders worth 40,000 rubles from private clients.[23]

By contrast, against the background of rearmament, the proportion of work undertaken for the civilian market by Urals factories contracted. In 1911, virtually one-third of all output from the state ironworks was purchased by private customers. In the following year, this proportion dropped to one-quarter. In 1913, it fell to below one-fifth, mostly pig iron and steel ingots. The financial consequences of this shift did not always bode well. The ironworks sold their products at a high price during the so-called 'metal famine' of 1911–12. But what they gained on the swings, they lost on the roundabouts. The law forbade private customers to advance funds to state factories, which could only harm their cash flow. Hence, the financial problems of the Urals ironworks proved difficult to surmount.[24]

The continued lack of profitability made it difficult to find funds for investment programmes. Zlatoust, producing shell and rifles, regularly made a loss, because of its high overhead costs, resulting from the dispersed character of the plant and the consequent time and effort spent in moving goods from one point to another. The financial position of factories was not entirely a function of managerial incompetence. Managers had no control over the prices set by the procurement agencies, whose officials thereby helped to determine the fate of the ironworks. Some enterprises seemed preordained to make a loss. The Ministry of War paid only 3,150 rubles per cannon to Perm, whereas Putilov received 4,000 rubles. The Ministry of Transport, by contrast, paid Sormovo and Putilov only 22,500 rubles for locomotives, but paid 33–34,000 rubles for the locomotives it purchased from Votkinsk: even at this price, however, Votkinsk made a loss.[25]

The provision of capital to major enterprises remained a constant nightmare. The inflexible system operated by the Treasury meant that a factory that exhausted the funds available for one purpose might have to suspend operations, even though other credits had not been committed or spent in full. Management could not predict exactly the mix of products it intended to produce in a given year and, therefore, could never be certain of its precise input requirements. Other factories got round this problem by concentrating on a smaller and more uniform range of products. Zlatoust and Votkinsk, producing a wide range of products, constantly found themselves in financial difficulties.[26]

Management also complained that government departments delayed the settlement of invoices, compounding the problem of working capital. In 1912, the outstanding combined claims of the Urals ironworks reached 15 million rubles. A year later, the figure stood at 19

Table 5.4. *Total output and defence production, Urals ironworks, 1908–1914*

	Total (million rubles)	Shell production (%)	Total defence (%)
1908	12.76	32.3	n.a.
1909	13.65	36.7	n.a.
1910	17.17	41.9	47.4
1911	19.68	35.0	37.1
1912	20.40	44.1	48.8
1913	21.00	51.2[1]	56.3[1]
1914	25.00	58.2	63.8

[1] Interpolated figure
Sources: Col. 1 *Vsepoddaneishii otchet gosudarstvennogo kontrolera za 1908 ... za 1915*, St Petersburg, 1909–16; col. 2 derived from Miftiev, 'Artilleriiskaia promy-shlennost'', appendix 2; col. 3, shell and cannon output, from *Smeta gornogo departamenta na 1913; ibid., na 1914; ibid., na 1916*, St Petersburg, 1912–15.

million rubles, more than half of it due from the War Ministry. To this extent, the increase in government orders merely exacerbated their financial problems.[27]

In the face of parliamentary pressure, the state adopted a series of reforms, designed to address some of the besetting problems of the Urals ironworks. The Duma advocated the adoption of proper commercial accounting procedures, the recruitment of more highly-qualified technical personnel on a 'voluntary' basis, greater specialization of production, inter-enterprise cooperation in the allocation of orders, especially for shell, and the reduction of 'excessive' stocks of raw materials. Their purpose was to reduce the backlog of unfinished orders and to eliminate enterprise debt.[28]

These changes eventually reached the statute book in December 1910, and appear subsequently to have had the desired effect. Government inspectors made fewer complaints about the lack of attention given to the storage of raw materials and to the inadequate care of instruments and other equipment, complaints that had been regularly aired earlier in the century. But not all projected reforms were implemented: the production of shell continued to be dispersed, rather than concentrated at two or three enterprises, as the Duma proposed. Other reforms also proved difficult to implement in Russian conditions. The management of the Perm Cannon Works at Motovilikha endeavoured to ensure that supplies of raw materials did not exceed actual requirements for current production, but this was only feasible where factories were not isolated. In the Urals, of all places, it was vital to maintain adequate stocks, lest deliveries be interrupted.

The performance of Motovilikha gave grounds for cautious optimism. A substantial amount of money (nearly three million rubles) had been spent on the factory after 1907, in line with the recommendations of the Sol'skii commission. Output increased from 2.7 million rubles in 1908 to 4.9 million rubles in 1911; in the following year it reached 5.9 million rubles. By 1911–12, as a result of the reforms mentioned above, the Perm factory as a whole began to show a profit: a genuine profit, too, allowing for depreciation, and taking account of its tax liabilities. Although defective production (*brak*) remained a problem, and although the storage of materials left a lot to be desired, many of the criticisms that had previously been levelled at the factory now lost their force.[29]

Nevertheless, the government could not afford to be complacent. The production of artillery at Motovilikha showed a loss in 1912. According to the State Auditor, 'equipment is inadequate and most work (such as the manufacture of gun carriages) is done manually'. The main problem was the modest volume of orders, making it impossible for management to standardize production. Until such time as the factory was given additional orders, it would continue to be plagued by high unit costs. Other reports also adopted a critical tone. A confidential assessment made several sharp criticisms of the Perm works: the technology for the manufacture of large calibre shell was outmoded, and only the low cost of producing smaller shell allowed the factory to make a profit. In the artillery workshop, labour costs were low, but the productivity of capital left a lot to be desired.[30]

These criticisms gave a group of private businessmen an opportunity to claim the Perm plant for themselves. In 1912, Putilov and M. E. Verstraete (chairman and vice-chairman respectively of the Russo-Asiatic Bank), E. K. Grubbe (chairman of the Siberian Trade Bank) and Zurov (from the Russian Trade and Industry Bank) requested a lease of twenty years on Motovilikha. They pointed out that the Admiralty urgently needed 14-inch guns. Obukhov was capable of producing up to fifty guns each year, but the navy needed around eighty. The government would have to order the shortfall from foreign contractors, if steps were not taken to develop production facilities at Perm or elsewhere. Perm already had one large press (3,000 tons); with additional investment, it could produce 14-inch guns within six months. They concluded that private enterprise, with the involvement of French technical assistance, could complete the modernization programme quickly. By contrast, if matters were left in state hands, the enterprise would inevitably experience delays in the provision of the necessary credits.[31]

Strong objections were expressed by a shadowy group, called the 'Perm National Society'. Its members pointed out the strategic importance of the factory, located deep in the interior of Russia (the other main state-owned artillery works, at Obukhov, was located close to the western border of the Empire and relied upon imports of fuel and pig iron). In addition, only state ownership of Perm and Obukhov prevented the production of heavy artillery from becoming a private sector monopoly: negotiations were already under way between Putilov and Parviainen over the joint production of heavy artillery (see below), and the Perm proposal was clearly designed to neutralize a potential competitor from the state sector. The objectors also observed – perhaps disingenuously – that the new private consortium would import large numbers of foreign workers to the Perm works, threatening the livelihood of up to 6,000 workers. The most persuasive argument used against this proposal in the Council of Ministers was a familiar one: state ownership of the Perm works guaranteed that the government would not be wholly bound by the prices set by the private sector, in this instance for heavy artillery. This was a sensitive issue: the government believed that private monopolies had pushed up iron and steel prices, and was unwilling to see the same fate befall the armaments industry. It has been argued that the government did not object in principle to the greater involvement of private capital in defence industry, because it concurrently (November 1912) approved a projected artillery factory on the Volga, financed by a consortium headed by the International Bank. But this venture was quite different from the Motovilikha proposal, because the former involved an *addition* to capacity and posed no immediate threat to the Perm works. In the event, the Council of Ministers concluded that 'the removal of the Perm Cannon Works from state administration, and the transfer of responsibility to a private joint-stock company, must be seen as unwelcome and even harmful from the point of view of the proper supply of armaments to the army and navy, at the cheapest possible price'.[32]

The government continued, therefore, to keep faith with Motovilikha. In 1913, the Ministry of Trade and Industry requested more than 6 million rubles for the reconstruction of the factory, part of a proposed allocation of 11 million rubles for all state ironworks. The main purpose was to develop the manufacture of heavier calibres of artillery (viz. 14-inch and 16-inch), an area in which other European powers were investing heavily. The money was used to build a new Martins furnace, a massive new forging press (7,000 tons, more than twice as large as the existing press), a new artillery workshop, plus additional furnaces, cranes and other equipment. The programme of reconstruction began in June 1913, with the release of 4 million rubles. In April 1914, the government drew up plans to allocate a further 13 million rubles to Motovilikha.[33]

The implementation of this programme proved less straightforward. Russian factories could supply some of the equipment easily enough, but no Russian enterprise had the kind of experience needed to advise on the creation of a facility for the manufacture of heavy artillery. A previous technical agreement with Krupp, concluded in 1904, came to an end in 1913. But in any case this was for the manufacture of shell. It would be necessary to look elsewhere for the relevant assistance; we shall pick up this story later on.

As happened at government armouries, and (more reluctantly) at the state shipyards, the decision to support expansion in the Urals inevitably meant the commitment of government funds. The Duma approved new spending plans in 1912 and 1913, the opposition having been silenced by the reform proposals that had already been initiated. As a result of this expansion, the most important armaments suppliers, such as Motovilikha and Zlatoust, created additional munitions capacity on the eve of the war.

Investment, therefore, provided the key to the retention by the state of direct control over armaments manufacturing capacity. Without the injection of resources in new equipment to manufacture armour-plate, naval ordnance and heavy artillery, the government might as well have bade farewell to its attempts to influence the course of armaments production through its ownership of assets. However, the decision to invest in government dockyards, ironworks and arsenals was a belated one, giving private firms an opportunity to establish a foothold in the rapidly growing market. Government shipyards, in particular, struggled to replace worn-out assets; and, until 1911, they made no net addition to the capital stock. The financial difficulties under which they laboured until shortly before the war helped to open the door to the private sector.

The formation of a private arms industry: the search for collective identity

Russia possessed little in the way of a developed private armaments industry prior to 1910, a year that witnessed a wave of company creation and reorganization. Several private firms engaged in defence work, but they operated independently, on a modest scale, and without any conviction that defence contracts could yield long-term rewards. No Russian firm dominated the industry in the manner of European giants, such as Schneider, Vickers or Krupp. Russia lacked the equivalent of these specialist suppliers of armaments.[34] The relatively small size of the Russian market compelled engineering firms to engage in the manufacture of a broad range of products. Even firms that ostensibly concentrated upon armaments (such as the Tula Cartridge Company) maintained a diverse product mix. Putilov, one of the few Russian businesses (like the world-famous Krenholm Cotton mill) that enjoyed a reputation abroad, came closest to the image of a Russian Krupp. But Putilov did not specialize in armaments and offered a varied menu of products that included railway and other non-military products. The same applied to other leading engineering firms, none of whose directors remotely considered themselves before 1910 to be part of a nascent arms trade.

For years, leading engineering firms had regularly regaled an unsympathetic government with a sorry tale of empty order books and idle plant. Attacks on the privileged position of state enterprise fell on deaf ears. The government resolved to stand firm, on the grounds that procurement agencies should be free to choose the most suitable supplier, without privileging the private sector.[35] The rhetoric of industrialists failed to shift the government from its entrenched position. But all was not yet lost. In the very process of articulating their grievances, private entrepreneurs could appreciate how much they had in common with one another. To that extent, rhetoric played a vital role in the creation of identity amongst manufacturers in the capital goods industries. However, the government would not be moved by conference speeches. Private producers who recognized the potential scope of defence contracts would have to come up with a different strategy, if they were to survive.

By 1910, the battle for survival was over; two years later, defence producers positively glowed with confidence. Firms that had hitherto merely dabbled in armaments invested in new plant, took on additional workers and turned themselves into major defence contractors. Their ranks were swelled by several important newcomers. As a result of these developments, no less marked in military shipbuilding than in other branches of defence, private arms merchants shed their traditional sense of inferiority to government enterprise. By 1914, after a lengthy struggle to gain a foothold in the defence market, they were in a position to mount a powerful challenge to the entrenched state sector. The arms trade in Russia had come of age.

The creation of large and powerful armaments firms, often linked with one another, precipitated the kind of criticism of collusion and monopoly power that surfaced in western Europe at the time. In Russia, the criticism took on a sharper edge, because of the deep-rooted aversion in certain quarters of the political establishment to industrial enterprise in general, and to trusts in particular. The scene was set for a bitter struggle between those, on the one hand, who upheld traditional state-owned enterprise and those, on the other, who supported the newcomers in the private arms trade. This struggle was evenly balanced, so long as armaments technology stayed fairly static and government demand for armaments remained modest. But with the burgeoning demand for armaments and the revolution in armaments technology, the barriers to entry fell away. Opportunities arose for private firms to enter the market, backed by powerful financial institutions and foreign firms, with untrammelled access to capital and advanced armaments technology.

Rearmament, revival and reorganization

The initiative in forging a domestic privately-owned industry in armaments and shipbuilding rested with a new generation of dynamic entrepreneurs, with a background variously in government, banking and the engineering profession. Many of them left government service, in order to pursue a career in banking. It is difficult to uncover evidence of their personal opinions and aspirations. Unlike politicians, they tended to leave no track in the memoir literature. Unlike full-time officials, their deliberations do not figure in the public record. Many business archives, which might shed light on their ideology and policies, failed to survive the war and revolution. However, they did leave traces of themselves in the actions of the corporations they headed. One should beware of ascribing 'personality' to a joint-stock company, whose behaviour will reflect the influence of different factors and individuals. With this qualification in mind, however, it is possible to reconstruct something of the aims and strategies of leading entrepreneurs.

All of them were driven by a common goal, namely to establish a modern and internationally competitive industry. They were familiar with government bureaucracy, but at the same time maintained their distance from its more conservative elements. The most prominent member of this entrepreneurial core was Alexei Putilov, the forty-year old son of the founder of the company that bore his name. Putilov served in the Ministry of Finances between 1890 and 1905, a typical career pattern for business leaders in the arms trade. After he left government office, apparently because of right-wing complaints that he sympathized with 'the radicals', Putilov moved into the world of commercial banking, becoming director of the Russo-Chinese Bank. In 1908, he took control of the Putilov company. Other leading entrepreneurs emulated this career path. A. I. Vyshnegradskii, who became closely associated with the engineering conglomerate Kolomna-Sormovo, also had an eminent father, the former Minister of Finances. Vyshnegradskii had numerous contacts at home and abroad, having worked in the department responsible for negotiating foreign loans. Like Putilov, with whom he was closely associated, Vyshnegradskii joined the Russo-Chinese Bank in 1902, and served as managing director of the International Bank from 1906 until the revolution. The exotically-named K. K. Racouza-Soutschevsky, who (in 1904) became Schneider's permanent representative in Russia, had also served 'on special assignment' with the Ministry of Finances between 1892 and 1897, before leaving to join the Trade and Industry Bank. A. A. Davydov, whose varied interests included directorships of Siemens-Schuckert and the machine-builders Hartmann, worked for the Ministry of Finances from 1895 to 1897, before joining the International Bank. They were all protégés of Witte, which made them outsiders in the bureaucratic milieu dominated by Kokovtsov and determined them to make a mark in a different sphere.[36]

Other members of the arms trade entered the industry after receiving an education at the polytechnic schools in St Petersburg and Riga. These professional engineers included M. S. Plotnikov, associated with Lessner, and I. S. Kannegiser, the head of the giant shipyards at Nikolaev. Plotnikov's career took off when he joined the Loan and Discount Bank. He had a knack for making useful contacts in the Admiralty. One of its officials commented that 'he commanded such influence that – if I'm not mistaken – the ministry placed no contracts without his knowledge, if not his agreement'. Kannegiser was a close friend of the directors of the International Bank. Both men became leading lights in the machine-building industry during the First World War. Like Putilov and his associates, they had no sympathy for the privileges enjoyed by the state sector.[37]

A third group originated in the world of commercial banking. Foremost amongst this group were A. P. Meshcherskii, Iu. I. Ramseier, G. A. Bloch and Ia. I. Utin, all of whom used their expertise to reorganize engineering firms, such as Sormovo and Kolomna. Meshcherskii's meteoric rise made him virtually synonymous with the fortunes of Kolomna, whose assets and influence he jealously guarded, leading him to enter negotiations with the Bolsheviks after the October Revolution. Some of these bankers, such as S. S. Khrulev, who sat on the board of the Tula Cartridge Company, had a background in law. Unlike his colleagues, Khrulev also published specialist works on finance.[38]

These were the men responsible for a programme of corporate expansion in the nascent armament industry. They followed a simple basic strategy, which in the first instance involved raising new finance on the St Petersburg stock exchange, in order to modernize and expand the capacity of the parent firm. Coupled with the share flotation went a decision to acquire interests in businesses that were closely allied to armaments or shipbuilding, including steelworks and general engineering firms. Finally, they devised a package of financial and technical assistance from foreign firms, such as Schneider or Vickers, which raised their profile and gave them bargaining power *vis-à-vis* the state sector. All potential arms producers stood in great need of fresh funds to finance the programme of expansion that would take them into the first division. In addition to funds for capital investment, they also required an adequate supply of working capital, in view of the long lag between the receipt of a contract and final settlement of an invoice. These basic needs required that the leading joint-stock banks in St Petersburg involve themselves closely in the affairs of the armament industry.

By 1914, three basic groups stood out.[39] The first group was united under the umbrella of the newly-formed Russo-Asiatic Bank, largely a creation of the Banque de l'Union Parisienne. The Putilov Company (whose managing director, Alexei Ivanovich, was also in charge of the Russo-Asiatic Bank) stood to be the chief beneficiary. In 1911, the banking consortium put together a package on Putilov's behalf, increasing its share capital from 16 to 25 million rubles. Another favourite tactic adopted by the group was to acquire an existing venture and restructure it completely. Typical examples of financial

Table 5.5. *The Russian arms trade, 1908–1913: selected indicators*

Firm (date of incorporation)	1908 Capital[1] million rubles	Labour	Output million rubles	1913 Capital[1] million rubles	Labour	Output million rubles
Putilov (1873)	12.0	7,200	12.7	25.0	13,500[2]	23.9
Baranovskii (1912)	n.a.	150	–	5.0	800	4.5
Parviainen (1910)	n.a.	500	0.3	10.0	1,600	5.4
Sormovo (1894)	10.0	12,000	15.0	10.0+	11,000	20.0–22.0
Kolomna (1871)	10.0	10,200	15.0	15.0	12,000[3]	17.0
St Petersburg Metal (1857)	3.6	1,700	4.0	5.4	3,000	9.6
Tula Cartridge (1898)	6.0	1,300	4.97	9.0	6,500	12.0
Briansk[4] (1887)	24.2	4,165	9.0	35.3	8,166	22.8
Nikopol–Mariupol (1896)	6.6	1,890	5.64	15.4	3,000	9.58
Lessner (1898)	1.1	600	2.0	4.0	1,260	3.2
Phoenix (1868)	1.2	350	0.54	2.4	500	1.2
Schlüsselburg (1884)	3.6	1,200	–	4.5	1,970	3.0

[1] capital refers to share capital, and excludes reserves and obligation capital
[2] January 1914 (12,000 on 1 January 1913); excludes Putilov Wharves
[3] Excludes 4,000 employed at Kulebaksk steel mill
[4] Steel mill only + 1912
n.a. = not applicable; a dash indicates no data found
Sources: LGIA f.1314, op.1, d.66, 1.20 (Parviainen); S.B. Okun', ed., *Putilovets v trekh revoliutsiiakh*, Leningrad, 1933, pp. xvi, xxvi (Putilov); other data from *Fabrichno-zavodskie predpriiatiia*, 1909, second edition, Petrograd, 1914; and E. E. Kruze, *Petersburgskie rabochie v 1912–1914 godakh*, Leningrad, 1961, p. 41.

reorganization were Baranovskii and Parviainen. The first of these was a small venture, employing only 150 men in 1908. The Russo-Asiatic Bank, together with the BUP and Schneider, reconstructed Baranovskii as a joint-stock company, with a share capital of 5 million rubles. The St Petersburg firm of Parviainen, like Baranovskii, began life as a small unincorporated business (*tovarishchestvo*). Originally established by the Finnish businessman Otto Brunstrom in 1899, it took on a new identity as the Russian Shell and Munitions Company. In 1910, the new company was floated on the stock market, with a share capital of 10 million rubles. Two years later a fresh share issue, with the active participation of French institutions, took the capital to 18 million rubles. This recapitalization enabled Parviainen to enter the shipbuilding industry, although these plans were scrapped within a year (see below). The proceeds from the eventual sale of the wharves under construction at Reval went to finance expansion of the munitions plant in the capital.[40]

A second major group was organized around the International Bank. Racouza-Soutschevskii described this, somewhat misleadingly, as 'the Vickers group'. It comprised St Petersburg Metal, the Tula Cartridge Company, Sormovo, Kolomna Engineering and Nikopol-Mariupol. Lessner also 'fell within the sphere of influence of this group'. A well-established general engineering firm, whose expertise lay in the production of engines and boilers, Lessner entered the defence market for the first time. By 1912, its products included shell, mines and other munitions. The Loan and Discount Bank was also associated with this group, and took a controlling stake in Lessner. Its chairman, Iu I. Ramseier, sat on the board of Lessner, Phoenix, Kolomna and Sormovo. The consortium headed by the International Bank enabled the Tula Cartridge Company to raise new capital, increasing its nominal share capital to nine million rubles. Lessner's share capital increased from 1.65 million rubles in 1911 to 4.0 million rubles in 1913. By 1914, Lessner planned a new munitions factory on the Black Sea. This group also stood to gain in scope and power by the inclusion of the future Tsaritsyn works, currently under construction on behalf of Vickers.[41]

The International Bank was not just interested in adding to its portfolio of arms producers, but in forging productive links between them. Its acquisition of a controlling stake in iron and steelworks offered great potential. The Bank had interests in major engineering plants, such as Kolomna and Hartmann, and in steelworks, such as Nikopol-Mariupol. The Nikopol-Mariupol Mine and Steelworks had been established at the height of the iron and steel boom and had a rolling mill in Ekaterinoslav province, as well as iron-ore, coal and manganese workings in the same area. It is not difficult to see the advantages of bringing such a firm within the orbit of the group. By 1908, the labour force stood at just under 1,900 and output was valued at 5.64 million rubles. Between 1911 and 1913, the share capital was increased from 6.6 to 13.2 million rubles, making it second only to Putilov in terms of capital. Yet another share issue followed in 1913–14, taking the capital to 15.4 million rubles, a virtual trebling of capital in the space of three years. The labour force stood at 3,000, and output had risen to 9.58 million rubles. Having been a general iron and steelworks, Nikopol-Mariupol now began to concentrate on the production of armour-plate for the navy. A report to shareholders in 1914 indicated that the factory was replete with orders. The directors forecast an excellent dividend and announced plans to build a new factory in Ekaterinoslav.[42]

Having begun to supply shell to the Artillery Administration at the end of the nineteenth century, Sormovo played an important role during the Russo–Japanese War. The firm compensated for the decline of orders for transport equipment by manufacturing munitions on behalf of the GAU. At Kolomna, the AGM of shareholders in 1910 heard a report from the chairman to the effect that funds were needed to finance the installation of new sources of mechanical motive power (diesel engines) and to reorganize the locomotive shop. In 1910, the share capital was increased from 10 to 12 million rubles. In 1912, a further increase was approved, taking the nominal share capital to 15 million rubles.[43] Phoenix Engineering Company was smaller in size than other defence contractors, even than Baranovskii. The company conformed to the usual pattern of general engineering, with a range of products that included machine tools, hydraulic presses, shell, cartridges and torpedoes. Between 1908 and 1914, Phoenix expanded rapidly. Its share capital increased from 1.2 million to 2.4 million rubles. Significantly, the board took on a different complexion: Ramseier and Plotnikov joined the descendants of the original English founders on the board.[44]

The final enterprise in the group, St Petersburg Metal, maintained a diverse product mix, including pumps, boilers and heaters, presses and lifting equipment, turbines, gun and torpedo emplacements and shell. The support of the International Bank enabled the company to increase its capital to nine million rubles, and to begin the construction of a shipbuilding yard at Ust-Izhora, south-east of St Petersburg, on the Neva.[45]

A third group, organized around the Private Commercial Bank (*Chastnyi Kommercheskii Bank*), concentrated on military shipbuilding, developing a stake in Becker shipyards and the Franco-Russian Company. Its activities are considered in the following section.

This level of financial support, against the background of Russia's fervent entry into the arms race, yielded spectacular results for corporate participants. The first hallmark of their gathering strength was investment in new plant. Plans to expand capacity at Putilov were quickly realized. Between 1910 and 1913, Putilov constructed a new steel-making facility, equipped with 40-ton presses. Other sections of the factory were overhauled, and Putilov completed the electrification of the entire works. One-third of the capital raised through the 1911 share issue financed an extension of the firm's ordnance manufacturing capacity. Between 1912 and 1914, Putilov spent more than six million rubles on its artillery shop. At Baranovskii, where mechanical motive power doubled between 1908 and 1913, the directors drew up grand designs for expansion. They proposed to construct a completely new plant, to be built at Vladimir, for the manufacture of explosives and set aside eight million rubles for this project in the financial year 1913–14.[46]

Nor did the International Bank allow its clients to lag behind. At St Petersburg Metal, total mechanical horsepower more than doubled. Safeguarding its existing share of the civilian market, Kolomna continued to construct a new locomotive works and expanded the capacity of its rolling mill at Kulebaksk. The value of fixed capital at the engineering works increased from 11.6 to 15.4 million rubles between 1906 and 1913.[47]

Some companies offered products which they had already successfully sold to the government. Putilov continued to develop the capacity to manufacture heavier calibres of artillery, in collaboration with Schneider. Kolomna used its new capacity to supply shell and naval munitions, as well as steel to government enterprises, from its iron and steel works. Other firms entered the market by manufacturing a new product. Schneider was again instrumental in helping the newly-established Baranovskii company, by undertaking to share its patents for 34-second time fuses, in return for a percentage payment on any orders the Russian firm received. By February 1914, the firm had signed a contract to supply explosives to the War Ministry; the following month it agreed to supply the Admiralty with smokeless powder. Baranovskii thus became a genuine competitor to the long-established Schlüsselburg company, which had a much larger labour force, but had a lower capital:labour ratio.[48]

Where a private firm could offer neither a new product nor an enticing deal with a foreign firm, it had to resort to less subtle means to secure government contracts. The Tula Cartridge Company, in desperate straits in 1908, turned bribery into a regular business practice. GAU officials were induced to look favourably on the struggling firm. This crude strategy paid immediate dividends: by 1909, the Tula factory produced one-fifth of all cartridges. Four years later, the proportion was still rising.[49]

By the chief criteria of output, labour and capital, the arms trade was dominated by the enterprises that came under the umbrella of the Russo-Asiatic Bank. Between 1908 and 1913, the value of goods produced by Putilov nearly doubled, from under 13 million rubles to nearly 24 million rubles. The shift at Putilov towards armaments continued to gather momentum. In 1908, armaments accounted for around 30 per cent of production. Two years later, more than two-fifths of Putilov's production was destined for military use. By 1912, this proportion had risen to 46 per cent. In 1913, artillery alone accounted for two-fifths of total output. Specialist suppliers within the group, such as the Tula Cartridge Company, did equally well. The value of gross output increased even more rapidly than at Putilov, from five million rubles in 1908 to 12 million rubles by 1913. Output of munitions at Baranovskii amounted to 4.5 million rubles by 1913, well in excess of the state works at Tula, Sestroretsk and Izhevsk. By 1913, even a relative newcomer such as Parviainen was larger than many state works: on the eve of the war, Parviainen was handling orders worth more than 10 million rubles, mostly from the Admiralty and Ministry of War. But it was dwarfed by Putilov, which had contracts worth an astonishing 125 million rubles by January 1914.[50]

But how successfully did these firms utilize the resources at their disposal? The pattern of labour productivity is one criterion of success, and we can construct a crude measure of this variable, based upon the material presented in table 5.5. Important differences emerge between one firm and another. At Putilov, output per worker showed a barely perceptible increase, the growth in output being matched by an equally rapid increase in employment between 1908 and 1913. A slightly bigger increase took place at the firms associated with the International Bank, namely Phoenix, St Petersburg Metal, Briansk, Sormovo and Kolomna. But both armaments groups included very weak performers. Output per person fell sharply at the Tula Cartridge Company and at Lessner Engineering, two firms that shared the same date of incorporation. There is no simple explanation for this difference in outcome. The first-named was a specialist arms supplier, well-established in the field; the second developed a profile as a general engineering firm, making some attempt to specialize in armaments before 1914.

Nor was growth at breakneck speed without financial pitfalls. Putilov represented the most extreme example. Professor Girault has demonstrated that Putilov found itself in acute financial difficulties by the end of 1913, with total liabilities amounting to 16.52 million rubles and assets that were lower than those publicly stated. The situation failed to improve during the following year. The company reported profits of 2.87 million rubles in 1914, on a turnover of 26 million rubles, but this favourable account contrasted sharply with the reality: according to one analyst, Putilov managed to conceal losses of 1.14 million rubles in 1914. It is not difficult to see why the firm should have recorded a loss. A confidential report on the firm, prepared on behalf of the Banque de l'Union Parisienne, made a withering indictment of Putilov's financial position. Funds had been spent without proper accounting procedures having been followed. Management paid excessive dividends to its shareholders, instead of making adequate provision for the depreciation of assets. This last charge carried a serious connotation, in view of the fact that the physical fabric of the plant was reportedly 'decrepit'. Putilov resembled the colossus with feet of clay, absorbing huge amounts of capital in an inherently risky environment.[51]

Within the group assembled by the International Bank, Briansk – a relative newcomer to shell production – managed a profit of only 10 per cent, despite its participation (along with Sormovo) in informal agreements on shell prices. The company's modest rate of return was attributed to the inexperience of management and labour alike. By contrast, Sormovo generated profits of 80 per cent on its munitions contracts. However, these profits were not great in absolute terms, and other contracts did not prove so successful. The projected modernization of the plant required the outlay of more than five million rubles, but the financial position of the company made it impossible to contemplate finding such sums from internal resources. By 1912, the company had not paid a dividend for four of the last five years. In these circumstances, the directors looked around for a firm with which it could merge. They found a willing partner in Kolomna Engineering. Potential competition from the state sector, and the emergence of fresh competitors on the scene, made such inter-firm agreements and amalgamations the logical outcome of the hothouse environment of armament production.[52]

The links between Kolomna and Sormovo were designed initially to improve the companies' prospects in the market for steamships. The director of Sormovo, A. I. Lessing, proposed a merger between the two firms, in order to reconstruct the Volga merchant fleet. The scheme attracted strong support from the International Bank and the Loan and Discount Bank. The prime movers were Meshcherskii, Ramseier and Vyshnegradskii. By the middle of 1912, the two companies worked in tandem. A letter addressed to the GAU from the board of Sormovo requested that the Artillery Administration order machine-guns from Kolomna and the wheeled supports from Sormovo, 'in order to use the two factories in the most appropriate manner'. Overhead and administrative costs would be reduced. The projected rationalization of production would concentrate steel-making at Kulebaksk, the production of forgings, special steel and shell at Sormovo, reserving machine-building projects for the Kolomna plant. New investment would be financed by a share issue. In May 1913, a joint meeting of shareholders agreed to proceed on this basis. No formal merger took place: Russian law did not recognize mergers. None the less, the two companies cooperated closely over the completion of orders for the War Ministry. In 1913, the companies divided up an order for military transport ships, making Sormovo responsible for boilers and engines, and giving Kolomna the work on hulls and other items. By the end of the year, the two firms were in receipt of orders worth 78 million rubles.[53]

By 1913, the extent of inter-firm collaboration had become evident through the multiple directorships claimed by a small handful of St Petersburg financiers. The original core of entrepreneurs was swelled by other men who served on company boards. By 1913, the armament industry displayed a web of inter-locking directorships. Putilov himself sat on the board of three other companies with a defence-related profile. His close colleague, A. K. von Dreier – like Putilov, a former civil servant in the Ministry of Finances – held two other directorships in the defence industry, notably as vice-chairman of Nevskii Shipbuilding. K. K. Spahn also sat on the boards of two defence companies. K. M. Sokolovskii was associated with three other armament firms. The remaining members of the Putilov board, I. M. Peroni and L. A. Bischliager, also held office in other defence firms. Racouza served on the board of Putilov, Parviainen, the Russo-Baltic shipyards and the newly-formed Optical Company. These men seem to have collected directorships, as Moscow merchants collected impressionist paintings.[54]

They ruled over an industry that had grown frantically in the years before the outbreak of the First World War. Much of their activity had been devoted towards the reorganization of businesses into joint-stock companies. In association with the banks, which nominated many of them to company directorships in the first place, they raised new capital to finance investment in new buildings and equipment: this, rather than the plough-back of profits, represented the main source of funds. Only in one instance did private enterprise establish an entirely new corporate venture outside shipbuilding, an innovation made possible only by a massive commitment of foreign capital (p. 241).

Shipbuilding manifested most dramatically the process whereby the balance of power in defence production tilted towards private enterprise. The period between Tsushima and the outbreak of the First World War witnessed the creation of large and powerful private shipyards, which by 1913 employed more than 23,000 workers, three times as many as in 1908. As a result of this rapid increase in employment, the private sector overtook the state shipyards. On the eve of the First World War, private firms employed half as many workers again as did the state yards.

The small number of private shipbuilding firms reorganized themselves, raised fresh capital and modernized during this period. The most notable examples included the Nikolaev dockyards and the Becker yards. Even more significantly, several new firms entered the market: chief amongst these were the Russian Shipbuilding Company ('Russud' for short), the Russo-Baltic Company, Putilov Wharves, the Franco-Russian Company and the submarine specialist, Noblessner. New and old ventures alike shared a common goal, namely to exploit the growth in the size of the market for military vessels in Russia, whose most striking manifestation were the shipbuilding programmes adopted in 1907 and 1910–12. Unlike the emergent arms firms, which were obliged to retain an interest in non-military goods, as well as in small arms, artillery or ammunition, the shipbuilding firms specialized, either in the production of hulls, armour-plate, marine propulsion or in naval ordnance. The newcomers established a share of the market by offering the navy access to modern shipbuilding and weapons technology, which they derived by virtue of their close ties to foreign armaments firms.

Of the well-established companies, the Nevskii shipyards presented a curious case. The company had a chequered history, surviving the slump at the turn of the century only by virtue of a rescue package put together by the State Bank (in 1908, according to Kokovtsov, Nevskii was 'in effect a state enterprise'). After a further shaky period, which the Russo-Japanese War did nothing to alleviate, the company found itself with enormous debts, in excess of 20 million rubles. Cutting its losses, the government returned the company to the private sector. Nevskii had a lot to offer a private buyer, because the firm made high-quality torpedo-boat destroyers. On the other hand, Nevskii lacked the capacity to produce specialized forgings and castings for other shipyards. This had been the government's original intention, but the growing burden of debt made it impossible to realize.[55]

Table 5.6. *Russian military shipbuilding, 1908–1913: basic indicators*

Company (date of incorporation)	1908			1913		
	Capital (million rubles)	Labour	Output (million rubles)	Capital (million rubles)	Labour	Output (million rubles)
Nikolaev (1895, 1911)	26.3	2,150	4.96	7.0	5,600[1] 7,900[2]	8.16
Russud (1911)		n.a.		10.0	2,600 2,900[2]	–
Putilov Wharves (1912)		n.a.		–	2,400 3,700[2]	10.90
Russo-Baltic (1912)		n.a.		10.0[3]	2,600 3,000[2]	–
Franco-Russian Wharves (1911)	12.5	1,500	–	12.5	2,100	8.00
Crichton (1897)	–	800	–	–	1,000	–
Noblessner (1913)		n.a.		3.0	2,000 2,700[2]	–
Nevskii (1891)	8.54	3,500	6.20	10.0	3,500 5,500[2]	14.24
Becker (1909)[4]		n.a.		11.0	2,000	–
Lange & Son (1898)[4]	–	450	0.7		n.a.	

[1] monthly average for April to December 1913 [2] January 1914 [3] increased to 20.0 million in March 1914
[4] Becker, in receivership until 1911, merged with Lange & Son in 1912. n.a. indicates not applicable; a dash indicates no data found.
Sources: TsGAVMF f. 512, op. 1, d. 536, l. 7; *Fabrichno-zavodskie predpriiatiia*, 1909, second edn, Petrograd, 1914; *Finansovoe obozrenie*, 1914, 7, p. 9; E. E. Kruze, *Peterburgskie rabochie v 1912–1914 godakh*, Leningrad, 1961, p. 41; K. F. Shatsillo, 'Inostrannyi kapital i voenno-morskie programmy Rossii nakanune pervoi mirovoi voiny', *Istoricheskie zapiski*, 69, 1961, pp. 78–9, 93; and *Russkii imperializm i razvitie flota v 1906–1914gg.* Moscow, 1968, p. 240.

The sale of the Nevskii yards in 1911, to a consortium headed by the Russo-Asiatic Bank, released the government from a long, costly and almost fruitless association with the company. The new owners unveiled ambitious plans for corporate investment and modernization. The Russo-Asiatic Bank transferred the company's shares to its most famous client, the Putilov Company, which paid 6 million rubles for them in 1912. In the following year, Putilov and the Russo-Asiatic Bank began the long-overdue process of technical construction at Nevskii. A new share issue brought the nominal capital up to 10 million rubles. In what had already become a familiar tactic, the Bank brought in foreign expertise, in order to realize the longstanding plan to turn Nevskii in to a specialist supplier of iron and steel to other shipbuilders.[56]

The strategy pursued by the Russo-Asiatic Bank considerably strengthened the position occupied by Putilov in the private sector. The St Petersburg engineering giant began to build a shipbuilding facility in the capital in 1912, two years after its directors first discussed the possibility with the Russo-Asiatic Bank and with the German firm Blohm und Voss. In 1912, Putilov's shareholders approved the construction of wharves, costing a total of 14 million rubles. The government immediately placed an order for two light cruisers and eight torpedo boats. At the end of the year, the company formed a subsidiary, Putilov Wharves, under the management of Orbanovskii, a representative of Blohm und Voss. This association aroused fierce opposition in Paris. When, in 1913, Putilov approached the BUP for additional funding, the French extracted a promise that Schneider would be given equal treatment with the German firm in future orders for marine engines. With these deals in place, Putilov's position in the market for military vessels became secure: having invested 450,000 rubles in fixed capital during 1912, Putilov followed this up with 6.7 million rubles in 1913 and 4.4 million in 1914. With this level of investment, the firm held out the enticing prospect of import substitution in warship construction.[57]

This strategy was repeated elsewhere. In 1912, the Russo-Baltic Shipbuilding and Engineering Company made its debut, with a share capital of 10 million rubles. Once again, the Russo-Asiatic Bank took the lead: along with the Russian Trade and Industry Bank and the St Petersburg Private Commercial Bank, it held three-quarters of the shares. The initial share issue was soon found to be insufficient, and the banks issued an additional ten million rubles' worth of shares. As with Nevskii, the banks inaugurated a programme of vertical integration: the new firm supplied finished vessels and marine engines, but – its charter of incorporation boasted – intended also 'to process metals and forge finished goods, construct and operate hearths, Martins and electric furnaces'.[58]

The directors of the new company had their eyes on the wharves currently under construction at Reval, on behalf of Parviainen. The government had already awarded contracts for two cruisers and six torpedo boat destroyers. The proposed acquisition of these yards avoided the need to create new capacity. In May 1913, the sale went ahead, at a price of 7.1 million rubles, giving the Russo-Baltic Company the title to Parviainen's contracts with several French and German firms, notably Schneider, Vulkan and AEG. The directors also floated an ambitious proposal to acquire the Putilov Wharves, for which purpose they called for an increase in the share capital of Russo-Baltic to 35 million rubles. Had this plan gone ahead, the Russo-Baltic would have become the largest company in the entire defence industry. In the event, the plan went awry, not because the financial institutions baulked at the prospect of another huge capital issue, but because the government intervened. Ministers looked askance at the potential creation of such a large venture in private hands, rivalling the government presence in the Baltic shipbuilding industry.

The government need not have worried, because the firm's fortunes failed to live up to the original expectations. The Reval shipyards were still unfinished at the end of 1914, by which time the Russo-Baltic Company was in serious financial straits. Ambitious plans to build cruisers and destroyers had to be postponed. The firm suffered a devastating shortage of working capital. Eventually, a consortium of French and Russian banks agreed to issue fresh debt ('obligation capital') to the tune of 7.5 million rubles, against which they would extend fresh credit. These measures only exacerbated the company's underlying financial weakness. The Russo-Baltic venture finally came to grief during the First World War. In overcommitting itself, the company followed the fate that befell the Putilov arms giant.[59]

As in land-based armaments, new products offered new opportunities to the private sector. Submarine construction, which formed part of the shipbuilding programme adopted in 1912, was a case in point. Private enterprise entered the market, by creating a specialist supplier in 1913, under the name of Noblessner, with an initial share capital of three million rubles. Two main parties were involved in its creation, the Nobel industrial group and the Loan and Discount Bank. Plotnikov, the managing director of Lessner, who enjoyed close ties with

Grigorovich, took a leading part. Under the corporate plan, Nobless-ner subcontracted orders for finished vessels to members of the Nobel group: Nobel itself agreed to supply diesel engines, Lessner and 'Russian Whitehead' would supply torpedoes and cooling equipment and Atlas the shrapnel and feed heaters. Noblessner assumed respon-sibility for the manufacture of hulls. The group took two-thirds of the orders for submarines for the Baltic fleet, although it failed to make any inroads into the Black Sea market, which was cornered by the Baltic yards, Nikolaev and the Nevskii company. Other problems com-pounded this disappointment: the yards at Reval took an interminable time to complete and delays prevented the launch of a single sub-marine by Noblessner until 1915.[60]

On the Black Sea, the government allowed the private sector a free hand. The Nikolaev shipyards had already been in existence for almost two decades. A newcomer, the Russian Shipbuilding Company appeared on the scene in 1911. But both were essentially children of the prewar rearmament boom. The decision to build a Black Sea fleet entailed the construction of ships at Nikolaev or Sevastopol. Nikolaev commended itself as a good location for shipbuilding, having adequate deep-water facilities, well-equipped yards and good supplies of fuel and steel, which cost 15 or 20 per cent less than in St Petersburg and Reval. The Black Sea programme opened up a golden opportunity for the private sector. The existing state works had fallen into disrepair by the end of the nineteenth century, and in the straitened times after 1905 no one believed that it was feasible to construct a new state facility.[61]

The prospects for a successful private venture on the Black Sea did not look very bright in 1907. The expansion of capacity during the war against Japan had saddled the Nikolaev yards with a heavy burden of debt. The company remained in acute financial difficulty after 1906, because government orders had been slashed and no private contract work could compensate for this collapse in the market. The directors reported to shareholders in 1908 that 'the Russian government con-tinues to limit its orders to what is absolutely necessary. Those orders that have come our way have been rare and of little account ... With the reduction in the quantity of orders competition has correspond-ingly increased and prices have dropped.' The directors could report no improvement in the following year. The prices paid for commercial vessels did not cover costs. The only crumb of comfort was that 'the calm that has descended on Russia has allowed us (in 1909) to intro-duce changes into the organization of work, thanks to which significant economies of outlay on labour have already been achieved'. These included a decision to increase the hours worked at the ship- yard from nine to ten, thus restoring the status quo ante 1905.[62]

None the less, the financial position of the company left much to be desired. In 1908, it had been encumbered with fresh debt, when it acquired a neighbouring engineering company. The chairman of Nikolaev, I. S. Kannegiser justified the purchase on the grounds that it would give the firm access to a facility that supplied boilers and shell, and would reduce overhead costs, but the acquisition proved costly. By 1910, the board desperately sought to keep the company afloat, and even talked about re-launching Nikolaev as a producer of agricultural machinery or bridges. In the same year, approaches were made to the St Petersburg stock exchange, to have the company taken into receivership. Coincidentally, as the affairs of the company reached rock bottom, the Black Sea shipbuilding programme was launched.[63]

In July 1911, Nikolaev assumed a new existence as the Obshchestvo Nikolaevskikh Zavodov i Verfei. The reorganization took place as a result of a joint initiative by French and Russian banks. The underlying strength of the new company depended upon substantial financial support from French creditors and upon technical agreements struck with foreign firms, in particular with Vickers and Thorneycroft (see below). Throughout 1911 and 1912, the shipyards at Nikolaev hummed with activity, as the yards themselves were rebuilt, with new slipways, engineering workshops, a new power station, hydraulic presses and new shell, boiler and castings shops. At the AGM in January 1913, the company informed its shareholders that the factory was working round the clock to process orders for the government and for commer- cial customers. By the beginning of 1914 the company employed 6,700 men, more than twice as many as twelve months previously. During the second half of that year, the workforce stood at an astonishing 10,600. But gains in labour productivity seem to have disappeared; the yards swallowed up as much labour as possible, with the result that output per person in 1913 stood at virtually the same level as in 1908. The company reported very modest net profits: only 233,000 rubles in 1912–13 and 454,000 rubles in 1913–14. This was barely one per cent of total capital employed.[64]

No sooner had the Black Sea programme received official approval than Nikolaev found itself with a close rival for the new contracts. The Russian Shipbuilding Company was the creation of the International Bank, whose previous attempt to collaborate with Nikolaev had been

Table 5.7. *Nikolaev Shipbuilding Company, 1904/5–1913/14*

	Gross output (million rubles)	Labour force (annual average)
1904–05	6.66	2,717
1905–06	5.93	2,396
1906–07 ⎫ 1907–08 ⎭	8.43	2,144
1908–09	4.48	2,013
1909–10	n.a.	n.a.
1910–11	n.a.	1,800 (June 1911)
1911–12	n.a.	2,200 (December 1911)
1912–13	8.16	3,200 (December 1912)
1913–14	n.a.	6,700 (December 1913)
		8,180 (January–May 1914)
		10,600 (December 1914)

Source: TsGAVMF f. 512, op. 1, d. 1782, ll. 2–20b.; d. 285, l. 15; d. 536, ll. 7, 28, 58.

rebuffed. The company's backers intended that Russud should act as an assembly plant, with the various ship components being supplied by steel and engineering firms elsewhere in south Russia, all of them affiliated with the Bank. The directors anticipated that the government would favour Russud on patriotic grounds, because the company lacked the close ties with foreign capital that distinguished Nikolaev (Russud could point to nothing more than an innocuous technical agreement with John Brown). As a 'national' company, Russud hoped to trump the Nikolaev yards.[65]

The nationalist card played only a modest role in the decision of the tsarist government to place orders for battleships with Russud. More important a consideration was the hope that Russud would compete with its rival and keep prices down. This explains the alacrity with which the government placed an order for two battleships with Russud, even before the company had formally been constituted in 1911. The decision of the government came as a blow to the ambitions of Nikolaev (and, incidentally, makes nonsense of the argument that the French company had the Navy Ministry in its pocket). The International Bank brokered an agreement, giving rise to a new conglomerate. The Russo-Belgian steelworks supplied iron and steel, Nikopol-Mariupol supplied armour-plate and the Kharkov Locomotive Company agreed to deliver boilers. Kolomna undertook to supply special steel and diesel engines; gun turrets would be manufactured by the St Petersburg Metal Company.

Before long, however, the two shipbuilding rivals came together, forging a powerful private presence on the Black Sea. In 1912, the two companies decided to collaborate. The new arrangement commended itself to shareholders: Russud stood to gain from the turbine-manufacturing facilities at Nikolaev, whilst Nikolaev could call upon the financial resources of the International Bank. In a move calculated to appeal to the tsarist government, the International Bank bought out the French stake in Nikolaev. Soon after, in April 1913, under the watchful eye of the Bank's chairman, A. I. Vyshnegradskii, the two companies signed an agreement which committed them to act in common over the price and delivery date of cruisers. One year later, the two firms set up a joint technical office. But once again one should not exaggerate financial results: the alliance anticipated net profits of 2.7 million rubles in 1914–15, on a projected output of 30 million rubles. This was hardly excessive, and reflected the heavy costs of capital amortization.[66]

Nevertheless, the significance of the formation of two large and powerful shipbuilding companies in south Russia cannot be exaggerated. Their evolution demonstrates the crucial importance of financial backing from Russian banks and the technical assistance obtained through foreign armaments firms. This powerful combination created a modern, privately-owned shipbuilding industry on the Black Sea, just as it had done on the Baltic and in other sectors of the defence industry.

The new and the revived firms in the private sector could hardly expect government orders to drop into their lap. Tantalizing though the prospect might be of lucrative contracts, the government would inevitably drive a hard bargain, counting on the state sector and the plethora of new firms to create a competitive market. Nor would the award of a contract put an end to the problems that confronted defence firms. Having invested in new plant – the price to be paid, in order for the government to take them seriously – and having outlined ambitious schemes for expansion to sometimes sceptical shareholders, company directors had to keep their businesses afloat beyond the short term. They were haunted by the prospect that the government might ditch them, no sooner than they had entered the market. They had to strengthen their bargaining position in a competitive market. Hence, the moves taken by the major financial institutions in St Petersburg to encourage collusion between their clients, to foster joint technical agreements, to promote vertical integration and to propose more formal associations.

The groupings and joint ventures described above conferred on their members a sense of corporate identity and power, quite different from the conspicuous weakness and lack of confidence that characterized the defence producers who attended the conference on the iron and steel and engineering industry held in 1908, during the depths of the recession.

Did these links amounted to an incipient 'military-industrial complex' in late tsarist Russia? It is difficult to know what use, if any, entrepreneurs made of the contacts they had established during their previous time in government. Given the nature of the industry, secrecy tended to prevail, and when the veil was lifted momentarily, as it was during the senatorial investigations in 1909–11 (see chapter 6), they revealed dealings between minor officials and small businessmen, not the kind of contact between industrialists and government ministers or high-ranking civil servants that would testify to significant business-government links. The more important element in the private sector was the close association between entrepreneurs in the same industry, and between industrialists and financiers, rather than the links between industry and government. The development of inter-firm agreements and combines, such as the Kolomna-Sormovo group, testifies to the growth of corporate power, which was all too ready to exploit its access to capital and technology, in order to challenge and supplant the hitherto dominant state sector. As a crucial ingredient in this campaign, foreign assistance to the nascent Russian arms trade deserves separate consideration.

Foreign investment and technical assistance

Russian industrialization during the late nineteenth century drew heavily on foreign investment. The import of capital was accompanied by the provision of technical advice and managerial expertise. Many foreign businessmen demonstrated a long term commitment to the development of industrial enterprise, by reinvesting profits and training a new generation of Russian managers and workers. After 1905, however, direct investment increasingly gave way to passive portfolio investment by foreigners. In addition, Russian banks took upon themselves the responsibility for mobilizing funds, organizing enterprises and obtaining technical assistance. During the boom years of the 1890s, the engineering industry – including the nascent defence industry – had barely been touched by the invigorating hands of foreign capital; most of the inflow of funds was directed towards extractive industries, such as coal and oil, and metallurgy, rather than machine-building. It was a very different story during the pre-1914 boom. Foreign armaments firms expressed a keen interest in the Russian market. One evident reason for their discovery of Russia was the scale of the rearmament programmes upon which the tsarist government pinned so many hopes. Other considerations also loomed large. The tsarist regime had explicitly committed itself to place orders with domestic producers, save in those circumstances where no Russian factory could supply the product. Foreign firms could realistically hope to gain access to the Russian market, only by establishing a subsidiary or buying into a Russian company.[67]

The strategies pursued by the various parties clearly betrayed their different intentions. The tsarist government hoped to minimize its purchases from abroad, in order to protect the balance of payments. At the same time, the government hoped to gain access to modern armaments technology. Domestic arms suppliers knew that they were being given a clear run in the expanding Russian market, but their success depended on their ability to demonstrate that their products matched European standards of quality and performance. The surest way of bringing plant and product up to contemporary best practice was to involve foreign companies. The commercial banks acted as brokers in the marriage plans that were drawn up between foreign and Russian firms. Companies such as Vickers, Krupp and Schneider knew that they could never flood the Russian market with weapons and ships manufactured abroad. The only sensible strategy was to participate in the creation or reorganization of Russian firms, using foreign financial resources and technological lead as bargaining counters. For these reasons, foreign investment and technical assistance in the defence industry increased at the very moment when they ceased to play as significant a role as they had hitherto in other sectors of the economy.[68]

Foreign capital and technology played a key part in the modernization of existing enterprises. Technical reports prepared by foreign engineers often revealed how much was to be done, in order to bring dockyards and engineering workshops up to scratch, whether they belonged to the state or were in private hands. The French shipbuilders, Augustin Normand, calculated that it would cost 6 million francs (2.26 million rubles) to modernize the equipment at the Crichton dockyards in St Petersburg. On the other hand, the prize was great: an order for nine torpedo boats, worth a total of 48 million francs, on which profits of 10 million francs could confidently be expected. This represented a return of around 16 per cent on a total investment of 13 million francs over five years. Typically, the French firm committed itself to more than the supply of funds, part of which would be contributed by the Crédit Lyonnais: the deal included the provision of technical support and skilled French workers.[69]

The defence market also opened up opportunities for foreign machine-building firms with a more general profile, whose only means of circumventing the tariff was to set up business on Russian soil. Having once entered the market, there was no telling what opportunities might arise. The Augsburg-based engineering firm, MAN concluded a deal with the Nikolaev dockyards in 1908, in the hope of securing a government contract for diesel engines to be installed in Russian warships. The German firm planned, in addition, to investigate the civilian market for other products. The following year, MAN opened negotiations with the long-established engineering firm of Felzer, based in Riga. The negotiations were protracted, because Felzer attached lengthy conditions to its acceptance of the offer. Eventually, the two parties struck a deal in 1912. But by then the Russian government had already decided to place the order for diesel engines with the conspicuously Russian firm of Kolomna.[70]

The most significant links between foreign capital and the Russian armament industry were those forged between Schneider and the firms under the umbrella of the Russo-Asiatic Bank. Specialist firms such as Baranovskii and Parviainen achieved a position of influence with remarkable speed, thanks to the French technical assistance they could dangle before officials from the War Ministry and Admiralty. Without the backing of Schneider, it is doubtful whether either firm could have made such rapid headway. But these activities were dwarfed by the scale of assistance offered to the Putilov Company. In July 1907, Putilov signed a deal with Schneider, under which the French firm agreed to supply Putilov with technical specifications and working notes for the manufacture of artillery. In return, Putilov undertook to deal solely with Schneider, a clear indication that the underlying aim of the French armaments giant was to challenge Krupp, with whom Putilov had already been in contact. From Putilov's point of view, the agreement had the inestimable advantage that Schneider offered exclusive access to the new technology, giving Putilov a competitive edge over its Russian rivals, including those in the state sector. Putilov undertook to pay Schneider 100,000 francs per annum for its assistance, and an additional eight per cent on any orders it received for artillery from the tsarist government.[71]

Notwithstanding the accountants' criticism of management practices at Putilov (see above), Schneider found it impossible to abandon Putilov. The French firm put pressure on financial institutions in Paris to inject further cash into the business. Too much was at stake: Schneider was keen to retain a position of influence in the potentially lucrative Russian defence market, the more so as Krupp was waiting in the wings. In January 1914, a consortium of German banks offered to assist Putilov in increasing its share capital from 25 to 45 million rubles. This led to a counter-attack from Schneider, which stressed to French bankers and to the government that diplomatic interests required a new French initiative. News of the German offer was leaked to the French press, to the predictable outrage of the public. The eventual outcome, agreed in February 1914, was to give Putilov access to French capital (total equity, with new French investment, now stood at 40 million rubles, excluding bonded debt), in return for French representation on the Putilov board. In addition, the banks extended fresh credit to the Russian company, 55 per cent of which was now in the hands of BUP, the Société Générale de Belgique and Schneider. But Putilov had a huge appetite for capital and its debts piled ever higher: the French connection did not save Putilov from an ignominious financial collapse during the First World War.[72]

In shipbuilding, too, foreign capital was drawn into the web of rearmament, company formation and reorganization. Putilov's penetration of the market hinged upon a deal done with the German firm of Blohm und Voss, which sank 5 million marks in Putilov Wharves; other foreign firms were also tempted to participate. But the most noteworthy expression of foreign activity came in the Black Sea industry. Towards the end of 1910, Kannegiser, the long-suffering chairman and managing director of the Nikolaev dockyards, travelled to Paris to hold talks with representatives of the Société Générale, the company's major creditor. He reached agreement with the bank, on the understanding that the company would do all in its power to obtain an order for at least one battleship for the Black Sea fleet. The Société Générale undertook to lend up to 11 million rubles, in return for payment equivalent to one per cent of the total orders received, in addition to interest payments. The profits would be shared equally between Nikolaev and its creditor. Furthermore, the French bank undertook to help the Russian company find suitable foreign technical assistance. Officials of the company travelled to France and Germany, in order to study contemporary battleship construction and new propulsion technology.

Eventually, with the firm encouragement of the Société Générale, Nikolaev dockyards turned to Vickers and Thorneycroft, both of whom agreed to supply details of battleship and destroyer construction exclusively to the Black Sea yards. Vickers undertook 'to act in an advisory capacity, both as to the layout of the works and to the preparation of tenders, estimates of costs, working plans and guidance of the construction work'. In return, the British firm would receive £45,000 for its drawings and £75,000 for each battleship built at Nikolaev. Several German firms also agreed to supply technical drawings and models for turbines and for a new floating dock. The reorganization of the Russian firm in July 1911 involved a huge consortium of French and Russian banks. Two-thirds of the shares in the new company went to the Société Générale and its French associates. Six Russian banks also took shares and placed their representatives on the board.[73]

The flavour of Vickers' commitment is conveyed best in a letter sent from Nikolaev by the British firm's representative, who sought permission for his staff to become more closely involved: 'they will simply guide the Russian foremen in charge as to how the work is to proceed through the various operations, examine same for correctness and also to arrange with the various chiefs to progress the work in such a way as to avoid delay in the completion'. There is no better expression of the optimism of the technical specialist, faced with a technical challenge – in this instance, the manufacture of turbines. In due course, however, Vickers would be obliged to adopt a more realistic approach to the tasks posed by investment in Russia; subsequent correspondence from Nikolaev made critical comments about the aptitude and work practices of Russian workmen, which we shall consider in the following section.[74]

Such agreements between Russian and foreign corporations indirectly enabled the tsarist government to tap advanced western armaments technology, whilst relieving the government of the need to build additional defence plants. Was it inconceivable that enterprises in the state sector would follow suit?

The attempt by foreign enterprise to reorganize state arsenals signified a shift in government attitudes. Hitherto, the regime discouraged foreign investment in state-owned arsenals and dockyards. The government did not prevent managers from concluding agreements with foreign firms for the provision of technical assistance; indeed, the

Motovilikha works had come to just such an understanding with Krupp in 1904, in order to help with the manufacture of shell. But, in the hot-house atmosphere created by the international arms race, foreign firms queued up to offer not just technical advice, but also investment.

The plant at Motovilikha – large, well-established, but badly in need of an overhaul – represented the greatest prize. In 1913, Russian bankers, with the blessing of Putilov, tied an offer of technical assist-ance from Schneider-Creusot to their unsuccessful application to lease the Perm works from the tsarist government. Soon afterwards, the question arose of producing heavy artillery pieces at Perm. The pro-gramme could only go ahead if the factory were re-equipped with bigger furnaces, more powerful forging presses and workshops. Some of this equipment could be supplied easily enough from domestic sources, but no Russian firm had the experience needed to advise on the creation of a facility for the manufacture of large-calibre ordnance. The technical agreement with Krupp was due to lapse in 1913: in the circumstances, the tsarist government hoped to encourage the maximum possible interest in Perm.

The Department of Mines invited leading foreign armaments firms to submit projects for the projected modernization of the plant, which was due to be completed within two years. Tsarist officials were especially hopeful of bids from Armstrong, Whitworth and Schneider-Creusot, arguing that these are 'first class firms, with great experience and brilliant achievements in the production of large calibre artillery and heavy mines and armour-piercing shells'. Several firms, these included, duly tendered for the project in the autumn of 1913.[75]

By the end of the year, the future of the Perm works had become entangled with international power politics. In December the French government entered the lists, offering to provide the Russian govern-ment with a substantial railway loan, provided, amongst other things, that Russia supported the bid from Schneider-Creusot. This was not the first time that the French had attempted to attach conditions to the loan. French bankers had done this during preliminary negotiations with Kokovtsov in the summer, and the French government had also intervened subsequently to state that it would link a loan to the construction of additional strategic railway lines, details of which were to be stipulated by the French general staff. By the beginning of 1914 the French had agreed to make the funds available to government, but the negotiations could still be jeopardized by the fate of the Schneider bid. Kokovtsov accordingly urged upon Timashev the desirability of pursuing the Schneider option.[76]

Throughout January 1914, a commission headed by Timashev's deputy, Konovalov, considered the various bids. The company offered assistance with the production of shell and artillery over a twelve-year period, not just with the immediate task of supplying heavy artillery pieces. However, the Department of Mines seemed unwilling to make such an open-ended commitment. There were other disadvantages to the Schneider proposal: for instance, it envisaged the creation of a workshop at Perm, capable of producing between seven and eight guns of 14-inch or 16-inch calibre, whereas the tsarist government required a shop with a capacity of twelve guns. The Armstrong proposal attracted support from the government's technical advisers, who noted that the British firm could produce the machine tools required for the production of heavy calibre artillery and could also draw upon its experience in equipping other foreign armaments factories.[77]

The spokesman for the Ministry of Finances took a different view, maintaining that it was unreasonable to ignore the claims of the French firm, particularly when Russia was considering a British bid (by Vickers) to build a new ordnance works at Tsaritsyn. Much was at stake: the value of the projected reconstruction of Perm amounted to around eight million rubles. Upon its completion, Russia would possess a plant similar in scale and technical modernity to other leading European firms. The French authorities were unwilling to see the decision go against Schneider. The new ambassador, Paléologue, held urgent talks with Sazonov, Sukhomlinov, Grigorovich and Bark, finally raising the issue with Nicholas II, when he presented himself at court for accreditation at the beginning of February 1914. The Council of Ministers met to consider the matter at the end of the month. On technical and financial grounds, the Armstrong bid was preferable. But political issues were at stake. In particular, French financiers would be unwilling to lend further funds to the Russian government, if these were to be used to boost the order books of a British arms contractor. The government eventually decided to support the Schneider option, but only after attaching certain conditions: the French had to provide the capacity for twelve guns and to order from Armstrong those machine tools that it could not produce itself.[78]

In the event, therefore, the government bowed to French pressure, but not before they had made it clear that Schneider had to adhere to the technical brief prepared by Armstrong. A Soviet account of the affair suggested that it illustrated Russian subordination to foreign capital, but this is rather a narrow interpretation of the evidence. After all, Russia obtained a loan it badly needed (and on terms acceptable to the Russian General Staff), without making any concessions on the details concerning the technical modernization of a key element of its armaments industry. From the point of view of the defence industry as a whole, the involvement of Schneider improved the potential performance of Motovilikha and encouraged the defeated rival firms to look for another foothold in Russia. Their avid search for Russian partners and for new sites to develop would only add to the overall capacity of the industry.[79]

In Vickers' case, the road from Perm led straight to Tsaritsyn, a town on the Volga. In the years immediately preceding the First World War, the British armaments giant launched an ambitious scheme to establish a large gun foundry factory in the heart of Russia. The projected enterprise constituted a major rival, not only to state-owned works, such as Obukhov and Izhevsk, but also to Motovilikha, the object of Vickers' unsuccessful bid. Plans were drawn up in mid-1912 for a 'Russian Krupp', in which the British firm would supply technical advice on construction and operation, while financial support would be forthcoming from the International Bank and the Loan and Discount Bank. The names of people like Ramseier, Utin, Blokh, Khrulev and Vyshnegradskii again figure prominently. They proposed to form a new company, the 'Russian Artillery Works Company Ltd.' (RAOAZ), with a share capital of 15 million rubles, of which Vickers had an option to purchase one-third. The St Petersburg Metal Company also held an option on shares, giving the proposed venture a foothold in the market for naval armaments for the Baltic fleet. Lesenko and Fedorov, directors of St Petersburg Metal were therefore added to the board. For its part, Vickers would receive 10 per cent of the profits for ten years, rising to 17.5 per cent of any profits in excess of 10 per cent of capital. Vickers undertook to supervise the construction of the plant, to arrange the delivery of any components that needed to be imported, and to send specialist engineers to Tsaritsyn.[80]

The tsarist government responded at once to this initiative, granting the new company an order in May 1913 for large-calibre artillery, even before construction of the plant had commenced (Vickers planned an annual capacity of 20 guns). Such enthusiasm is not difficult to understand. The bid held out the prospect of producing new naval artillery, of a quality unavailable from any other source. In addition, Vickers mooted still more ambitious plans for the new company, which involved the manufacture of armour-plate, shell and even small arms. Neither this scheme nor, indeed, the supply of heavy artillery made any progress before 1915. But the negotiations testified to the close

242   Rearmament and industrial ambition

involvement of foreign armaments firms in the Russian defence industry and the enthusiasm of the government for any Russian venture that entailed greater access to advanced armaments technology. It was hard not to be seduced by Vickers' reputation and the British firm's promise to act as technical consultants to the new enterprise for up to fifteen years. This chapter in Anglo-Russian commercial relations emphasizes yet again the scope that rapid technological change allowed new entrants to the armament industry.[81]

Foreign investment created the opportunity for new firms to enter the sphere of defence production, either as subsidiaries of foreign companies or as entirely new ventures. Foreign companies were keen to exploit the growth in the market for defence and associated products in Russia. Citroen set up a subsidiary in conjunction with the Kolomna Company, which would import gears and other equipment from the parent company in France. Russian Renault followed the same pattern. Schneider set up the Optical Company in 1914, to supply measuring instruments and optical devices to the armed forces. In a slightly different vein, the Russian subsidiary of the Sheffield steelmakers, Thomas Firth, which had traded since the beginning of the century as 'Salamander' of Riga, in 1908 began to supply large calibre shell, building a new plant for that purpose, with machinery imported from Britain. The company history proudly proclaimed that the product – 4.7-inch and 12-inch armour-piercing shell – satisfied the rigorous quality requirements of the tsarist government.[82]

These instances of foreign investment in new ventures paled into insignificance when set alongside the ambitious scheme launched by Vickers, but they demonstrate the key importance of technical assistance obtained from foreign armaments firms. The powerful (for some contemporaries, even hypnotic) combination of foreign capital and technological assistance created a modern shipbuilding industry on the Black Sea and the Baltic littoral, and improved the potential of other sections of the armament industry. Nor did the proposals involve any infringement of Russian sovereignty: no foreign firm could push its luck with a regime that could choose from amongst several avid contenders. The question remains, however, why foreign investment by Vickers, Schneider, Citroen and others assumed a direct form, at a time when indirect investment prevailed in most other sectors of industry. The answer must be, in part, that the complexity of the technological tasks posed by contemporary weapons systems encouraged foreign firms to exercise close supervision over

capital and labour. It is to the issue of employment and work practices
that we now turn our attention.

Employment, work conditions and work practices in the defence industry

Total employment in the Russian defence industry grew from
under 86,000 in 1908 to just over 120,000 in 1913, an increase of 40 per
cent. This was well in excess of the growth of total industrial employment, which grew by 29 per cent during the same period.[83]

The most remarkable feature was the rapid growth of employment in
privately owned shipyards. Largely as a result of this increase, the
private sector accounted for 56 per cent of total employment by 1913,
compared with 44 per cent in 1908. But the influx of government orders
between 1912 and 1914 also led to a sharp increase in employment in
government dockyards and GAU factories. At the state armouries, the
workforce stood at 56,600 in 1914, an increase of two-thirds since 1912.[84]

From what source did these workers originate and how were they
recruited? Evidence on the recruitment practices of state works is
unfortunately quite sparse. Such sources as are available suggest that
labour was recruited, as before, predominantly from the local population. At Izhevsk, the workforce consisted largely of the descendants
of the original workers, who had been ascribed to the factory during
the pre-emancipation period. A study of the St Petersburg Tube Works
reveals that workers came from villages in the neighbouring provinces
of Olonets, Tver, Pskov, Novgorod and Vitebsk, where neither agriculture nor rural industry could support the growing numbers of
people. However, not all recruits to factory production were recent
arrivals from the village: close to a third of those taken on in the early
twentieth century were former army conscripts, whose presumed
obedience to authority commended itself to management. At the
explosives factory at Okhtensk, the workforce was recruited from
neighbouring provinces in the north-west, although some workers
originated from as far afield as the mid-Volga.[85]

The labour force expanded much more rapidly at private shipyards
than it did at state yards. At the Nikolaev yards, the labour force had
fallen from a peak of 2,700 in 1905 to 2,100 in 1908–10. But after 1911, as
the company took on orders for battleships and smaller vessels, the
management hurriedly took on fresh contingents of workers. In April
1913, employment stood at 5,400; twelve months later, it reached 8,300.
Vickers' agents reported that Nikolaev recruited workers from the

Table 5.8. *The labour force in the armaments industry,*
1900, 1908 and 1913

	1900	1908	1913
A *State sector*			
1. GAU factories	27,000	33,000	47,400
2. Department of Mines	25,408	30,730	27,552
3. Shipyards	13,929	11,173	16,970
B. *Private sector*			
1. Shipyards	7,450	8,720	23,100
2. Other armaments[1]	1,600	2,000	5,000
Total	75,387	85,623	120,022

[1] It is impracticable to identify every single private firm within the metalworking and machine-building industry, to calculate the proportion of workers engaged on military production at such factories, and then to sum the figures. Instead, one can derive a rough figure by taking the number of workers employed in these branches of industry and applying a coefficient, representing defence output as a proportion of total output (viz. 26.2 per cent for the defence share of machine-building and 5.3 per cent for chemicals). The authoritative Soviet source, L. E. Mints, *Trudovye resursy SSSR*, Moscow, 1975, p. 87, cites a figure of 352,100 as the workforce in metalworking and machine-building in 1913, private and state enterprise (on USSR territory). The equivalent total for the Russian Empire (applying a coefficient of 0.815) is 432,900. The number of workers employed on defence work was 113,420 (26.2 per cent of 432,900). Applying the same procedure to Mints' figure for chemicals (83,500 workers, including those in state-owned explosives works), we derive a figure of 5,430 workers. This yields a total of 118,850 workers who were employed in the production of manufactured goods for the armed forces. Since the known workforce in defence production in 1913 (less the unknown number for private non-shipbuilding) was 115,000 (cols. A.1, A.2, A.3 and B.1 in table 5.8), the residual figure was around 4,000 (119,000 less 115,000). This figure is probably an underestimate: the labour force at such well-known firms in St Petersburg as Baranovskii (800), Parviainen (1,600), and Lessner (1,260) would alone account for most of this total (figures from E. E. Kruze, *Peterburgskie rabochie v 1912–1914gg.*, Moscow-Leningrad, 1961, p. 41, and Heather Hogan, 'Labor and management in conflict: the St Petersburg metalworking industry, 1900–1914', PhD Michigan, 1981, p. 49). Giant firms such as Kolomna Engineering would also need to be taken into account. On the other hand, some of these big armaments producers also handled shipbuilding contracts (St Petersburg Metal, Putilov), and their labour force may already be accounted for. A figure between 4,000 and 6,000 is probably not too wide of the mark, and thus a figure of 5,000 appears in table 5.8, row B.2, col.2.

surrounding villages. By contrast, the newly-established shipyard Russud was obliged to send recruiting agents to the central industrial region and the north-west in search of skilled workers. Management also increased the length of the working day, wiping out the gains made by workers during the 1905 revolution.[86]

Most of the growth in employment at state works between 1908 and 1913 – and in the private sector, too – is explained by the fact that workers who had been laid off during the postwar slump were once more offered jobs. Throughout the industry, the workforce was predominantly male, although, by 1912, women were being employed as *brakovshchiki*, that is quality controllers, at some GAU arsenals. Women were employed in a supervisory role at the Okhtensk explosives factory; in 1911 they made up a quarter of the total labour force. Most of them, like their counterparts at the Tube Works, were wives of male employees. But the chief beneficiaries of the rearmament boom were younger males. The government set age limits on employment; the GAU regulations did not permit men and women to stay on once they had reached the age of fifty. Juvenile labour was allowed by a law passed in 1906, and around 5 per cent of the workers registered at the Tube Works before 1914 were between fourteen and seventeen years old.[87]

If we assume that the ratio of workers in shipbuilding and non-shipbuilding was the same in 1900 and 1908 as it was in 1913, then the figure for non-shipbuilding in 1900 would be around 1,600 and in 1908 would be around 2,000. These figures appear in table 5.8, row B.2, cols. 1 and 2.
Sources: A.1 from G. K. Miftiev, 'Artilleriiskaia promyshlennost' Rossii v period pervoi mirovoi voiny', kandidatskaia dissertatsiia, Leningrad, 1953, p. 100 (the 1902 figure in the source, 26,117, is adjusted upwards by 4%, in line with the trend in employment at the Tula Cartridge works, as given in A. A. Korolev, 'Finansovo-ekonomicheskaia deiatelnost' Tul'skogo patronnogo zavoda v kontse XIX-nachale XX vv.', Iz istorii Tul'skogo kraia, Tula, 1972, pp. 38–40; Miftiev's figure for 1909, 31,734 is adjusted in line with armaments index in table 5.12 below, to yield an estimate for 1908); A.2 figure for 1900 is taken from Otchet gornogo departamenta za 1900–01, less 27.6%, representing the average proportion of work completed for private customers; the 1908 and 1913 figures are from Smeta gornogo departamenta na 1909 and ibid., na 1913, less 21.6% and 18.3% respectively (proportions from ibid., na 1914, pp. 21–2); A.3 from L. G. Beskrovnyi, Armiia i flot v nachale XX veka, Moscow, 1986, pp. 198–9 and K. F. Shatsillo, Russkii imperializm i razvitie flota nakanune pervoi mirovoi voiny, Moscow, 1968, p. 223. The figures exclude the minor state workshops attached to ports at Kronstadt, Nikolaev and Sevastopol; B. 1 from Beskrovnyi, Armiia i flot, pp. 198–9 and Shatsillo, Russkii imperializm, p. 240, both citing an unpublished dissertation by A. M. Falkov. Figures in B.2 derived by methods explained in the accompanying note. See also note to table 5.10.

The character of work at several GAU factories (although not at the state arsenals) dictated the pattern of recruitment. Most of the work at the Tube Works and the explosives factories was semi-skilled, consisting of straightforward and repetitive operations with simple machine tools. Some craftsmen were employed as brassfounders, pattern-makers and toolmakers, and others operated more complicated kinds of machinery, but these were in the minority. The main skill required at Okhtensk was in the manufacture of percussion compounds, but the bulk of work was semi-skilled or unskilled. Even large ordnance factories and the Urals ironworks required unskilled labour for a range of tasks.[88]

But the state ironworks were not typical of the armament industry. At the arsenals, much higher standards of skill were required. The manufacture of small arms involved a high level of skill. It took 1,424 separate, intricate and precise operations (involving specifications of between 0.127mm and 0.025mm) to produce a rifle. The manufacture of machine-guns involved more operations and an even greater degree of precision. In order to deal with these tasks, management at the Tula armoury and at the Izhevsk arsenal continued to seek to recruit second and third-generation workers from the craft schools attached to the factory. But these did not always provide adequate numbers of new entrants, and it was necessary to think about improving material inducements in the state sector.[89]

The turnover of labour continued to affect the armament industry. After 1908, this was no longer the result of involuntary movement. Instead, workers left of their own volition, causing problems for the hard-pressed managers of arsenals, dockyards and private works. A study of the St Petersburg Tube Works, based upon the analysis of 15,375 workers' passbooks, captures the high rate of labour turnover in the period before the First World War. Between 1908 and 1913, the labour force increased by 2,100, but the net change disguises the fact that more than 6,700 workers were taken on, whilst 4,600 were discharged. The data in table 5.9 demonstrate the tendency for management to lay off workers during slack times (1907, 1909–11). But it also suggests the voluntary severance of workers in 1912–14 from the enterprise, as they sought to improve their prospects by looking for more highly-paid work elsewhere.[90]

At times of intense activity, as at the turn of the century and during the prewar boom in shipbuilding, the management of individual factories risked losing labour to their rivals. What kinds of incentive did management offer, in order to retain the services of skilled

Table 5.9. *Turnover of workers at St Petersburg Tube Works, 1907–1914*

	Taken on	Discharged	Net increase/decrease
1907	52	654	− 602
1908	769	361	+ 408
1909	52	492	− 440
1910	98	448	− 350
1911	126	891	− 765
1912	2,113	522	+ 1,591
1913	3,555	1,888	+ 1,667
1914	4,556	2,518	+ 2,038

Source: S. V. Murzintseva, 'Izuchenie formirovaniia i sostava rabochikh tru-bochnogo zavoda po dannym pasportnykh knig, 1907–1914gg.', *Rabochie Rossii v epokhu kapitalizma: sravnitel'nyi poraionnyi analiz*, Rostov, 1972, pp. 61, 66.

workers? First, managers rewarded workers who stayed at one factory for a minimum length of time. In the state sector, workers who had been employed for more than three years were entitled to up to six weeks' unpaid leave, provided they deposited a surety of two weeks' pay with the administration, a clear sign of management's keenness to retain scarce skilled labour. The management of the Okhtensk works allowed workers a one-month holiday after three years' service, on half-pay, provided that they had behaved 'properly and diligently'. This entitlement was in addition to the statutory holidays (amounting to 25 days in all) at government enterprises. At the Tube Works, management introduced a system of wage scales, differentiated according to length of service. The practice was common elsewhere in the state sector.[91]

Government regulations allowed managers discretion to reward loyal workers in other ways. For example, workers who made a 'necessary and useful' contribution to the work of the factory were entitled to government lodgings, depending on availability, at a subsidized rent. Workers in government dockyards were also offered interest-free loans to cover expenses connected with family events, such as weddings and funerals, and to recoup losses incurred as a result of fire and flood in the home.[92]

How successful were these strategies? Individual arsenals and dockyards engendered powerful loyalties among the workforce. Many workers had been at the Okhtensk explosives factory for ten or twenty years, and 'a person who was working for only five or six years was considered by the others to have arrived recently'. At the St Petersburg Tube Works, half of the workers who were surveyed between 1907 and 1914 had been employed for more than five years. The relative advantages of working in the state sector tended, as before, to instil a sense of loyalty on the part of the workforce.[93]

The shift towards the private sector raises interesting questions, because it implies that work was increasingly being handled by men and women who enjoyed less protection against exploitation than did their counterparts in the state sector. Some of the benefits that state employees received have been mentioned earlier, notably accident insurance and restrictions on the hours of work. Why, then, did workers flock to the new private factories, and what persuaded them to remain?

Government reforms at the beginning of the twentieth century maintained a welfare differential between the state and private sectors. In June 1903, the government promulgated a law for workers in factory industry. The legislation afforded compensation for industrial injury, provided that the worker could demonstrate negligence by the employer. Payments were computed in accordance with average earnings of the employee over the last years of his or her service. State-owned enterprises were explicitly excluded from the act's provisions. Instead, the relevant government departments were asked to prepare fresh regulations for workers in enterprises under their aegis. Supplementary legislation was eventually introduced in June 1904, with effect from 1 January 1906, for workers in state arsenals, and in March 1906 for workers in the dockyards. Many of the provisions of the 1903 law were built into this new legislation, but there were important clauses that gave them an advantage over workers in the private sector. For example, workers in private industry could not claim compensation for industrial injury, if management insisted that the injury was attributable to negligence on the part of the worker. These were not grounds for denying compensation to workers in the state sector.[94]

The procedure for submitting claims was also rather more straightforward for state employees than for workers in private industry. Claims were dealt with by the factory administration, rather than by the factory inspectorate, whose numbers were grossly inadequate to the size of the problem. This arrangement had its disadvantages: managers at state works might, and often did, dispute a claim. With no independent assessment of claims, it was simply the word of the foreman against the worker. Archival evidence testifies to the desper-

ate plight of workers who were left without any source of support
during such disputes. But, if the claim was approved, the terms were
generous by prevailing standards. In the case of the disability allowance, the method of computation was as follows: the worker's earnings over the twelve months preceding the event were divided by the
total number of days worked; this daily average was then multiplied
by 260 (representing the estimated number of days worked in Russian
industry), yielding an annual figure. Two-thirds of this sum was then
paid to the worker if he was completely incapacitated, or paid to his
widow in the event of his death. In practice, workers at Okhtensk
received full pay for up to four months in the event of injury. After that
time, if the worker did not return, he was retired on the pension,
calculated in the above manner. If, upon his death, the employee's
next of kin proved to be incapable of work, because of physical or
mental infirmity, they received a pension for life.[95]

The contrast in provision is also clear in respect of sickness. Government regulations stipulated that workers in state enterprises had the
right to see a doctor free of charge if they were ill and the right to up to
two months' free hospital treatment, if their complaint was the result
of conditions of work. Their relatives were entitled to treatment free of
charge as outpatients, although they had to pay if they were hospita-
lized. The Okhtensk works, already equipped with a small infirmary,
built a seventy-bed hospital in 1910 for workers who needed specialist
treatment, obviating the need for workers to travel to St Petersburg for
treatment. From 1904 onwards, workers at government enterprises
were also compensated in the event of permanent disability as a result
of an illness contracted at work. Should the illness result in their death,
their families were likewise compensated. Artem'ev, the doctor at
Okhtensk, maintained that these regulations were capable of so broad
an interpretation that most workers (especially after the further easing
of the regulations in February 1907), retired on an 'unofficial' pension.
This was worth on average 9.25 rubles per month, equivalent to
one-third of their former earnings.[96]

These provisions found no place in the 1903 statute and thus were of
benefit exclusively to state employees. Factory owners put up prolonged resistance to the extension of sickness insurance to their workforce. The government brought a project to the Duma in 1908, but it
did not reach the statute book until 1912. The law of 23 June 1912
required factory owners to establish sick clubs and insurance associations, extending sickness cover to workers for the first time. But the
legislation did not remove any of the disparities between the state and

private sectors. As in 1903, the laws deliberately excluded workers in government enterprises, leaving them in a more favourable position.[97]

Many of these benefits served to emphasize just how arduous and dangerous work in the armament industry could be. This was obviously the case in the manufacture of explosives. A graphic account of the risks to which workers were exposed was provided in 1911 by the factory doctor attached to Okhtensk. The nature of the job brought the risk of flashes and explosions; 225 such instances recorded between 1897 and 1911 had left six people dead and several more injured. On average, there were between ten and fifteen instances each year, although the pressure of work during the Russo-Japanese War, when work carried on round the clock, led to twenty-four instances in 1904 and fifty-three in 1905. Artem'ev doubted that these accidents were attributable to the carelessness of inexperienced workers: in his opinion, older workers sometimes failed to exercise appropriate care. Other risks included the inhalation of toxic fumes and, still more insidious, the progressive disability that resulted from working with fulminate of mercury in the production of TNT. He noted that the 1,400 workers at Okhtensk, along with their dependents – a total of 5,631 people – made more than 25,000 separate visits to the surgery in 1910.[98]

It would be wrong to minimize the difficult and often dangerous conditions experienced by workers in defence industry. But it seems likely that other workers were more at risk from industrial accidents. High-risk occupations included coal and gold-mining and work on Russia's railways and waterways. Fourteen per cent of railway workers suffered some kind of injury in 1910; 11,255 men were severely injured or killed. In 1908, one-third of all miners in south Russia suffered injury.[99]

Private entrepreneurs recognized the disparity between workers in the state and private sectors. But their deep-seated aversion to legislative interference in worker-employer relations seems to have taken precedence over their concern that they might lose workers to the state sector. Industrialists desperately put off the day when they would be obliged to make concessions to labour. Significantly, their opposition to legislation evaporated in 1912, at the very moment when poaching by the state sector assumed more threatening proportions.[100]

One should neither idealize the situation of workers in state industry, nor think that the businessmen in the arms trade were permanently set against their workforce. The government, for example, did not tolerate trade unions in state-owned premises – a point made by Social Democratic members in the Third Duma – whereas legal collective organizations of workers in the private sector enjoyed a limited existence after March 1906. The government was capable of harsh measures, as in 1913, when it locked out workers at Obukhov who had gone on strike. In September 1913, a special commission on the strike movement in state arsenals threatened 'resolute action' against ringleaders, although it coupled this with a recommendation that wages be increased. By contrast, there were good reasons why private industrialists treated workers relatively more favourably, especially after 1912. Private firms were keen to obtain and retain orders, by demonstrating their competence and reliability. Faced with lucrative defence orders and unwilling to risk fines for delay or non-fulfilment, they dealt gingerly with strikes in the immediate prewar period. Their colleagues in other branches of industry pressed for a much tougher stance, in the face of an upsurge of labour protest after 1912.[101]

Workers in the private sector of defence industry were probably better off in 1913 than they had been five or six years previously, and certainly at an advantage compared to other categories of the labour force. The British engineer, Allan Monkhouse, who spent a year at Kolomna in 1911–12, describes the key role played by the factory inspectors:

> they seem to be state-appointed guardians, to whom the workmen turn every time there is any friction between themselves and the employers. Work-people who claim to have been wrongfully dismissed, under-compensated for accidents or illness, defrauded of pay due to them, or illegally fined for accidents, breakages, etc., immediately take their case to the factory inspector, whose duty it is to take the matter up with the employers and act as arbitrator. In a works as big as this, there is a factory inspector always on the premises.[102]

Yet the factory inspector was but one figure in the landscape of labour relations before the First World War. Management, too, had to adjust to new conditions in the labour market, by adopting a more conciliatory approach to labour.

A different argument has been advanced by Heather Hogan. She demonstrates that employers in St Petersburg sought to recoup the concessions that workers had extracted during the 1905–6 revolution. Managers adopted more subtle tactics, in order to improve the productivity of labour. They could not launch an overt attack upon Russian workers, who now had the legal right to organize. Nor did they place any greater emphasis upon longer hours, or have recourse to punitive measures, in order to enforce discipline. Instead, managers displayed a pronounced tendency to plan for the 'scientific' organization of work.

When these initiatives deskilled the labour process, reduced piece rates and entailed intrusive time and motion studies, workers went on strike. But Hogan's argument does not command universal assent. Her critics acknowledge that some engineering firms did *attempt* to increase the pace of work, and that some of them succeeded, but argue that the industry showed little evidence of the collective *implementation* of scientific management techniques.[103]

Evidence from the shipbuilding industry on the Black Sea shows that entrepreneurs elsewhere faced enormous obstacles in enforcing changes in work routines, even on 'green field' sites. Vickers' English representative complained to his employers that Russian workers were possessed of a 'spirit that is not conducive to rapid progress. They inform you everywhere that when the work at present in hand is completed there will be nothing else to do, so why hurry the work'. In addition, the foremen 'are not interested enough in their work and are very antagonistic to any new methods, and what few suggestions have been adopted is only after great pressure has been brought to bear upon them'. As a result, 'English methods can only be adopted gradually'. The documentation reveals a lack of adequate supervision of labour, reminiscent of some state yards at the beginning of the century. In these circumstances, it is hardly surprising that labour productivity at the Nikolaev dockyards scarcely improved at all between 1908 and 1913. On the other hand, labour productivity at the Nevskii shipyards increased sharply, implying that managerial initiatives enjoyed greater success in St Petersburg than they did in Nikolaev.[104]

The growth of employment in the private sector certainly improved the bargaining power of labour, causing considerable disquiet amongst managers by 1914. The manager of one state yard urged the government to accelerate the delivery of material inputs, lest he be forced to lay off workers and lose them to the private sector. At the privately owned yards of Russud, the management feared that any temporary interruption to supplies would encourage workers to seek work in other yards. They responded by increasing wages and making other concessions. The alternative was to risk incurring tough financial penalties from the government, in respect of delays to the completion of contracts. Worse still, a private firm might find itself starved of work in the future. Some managers did indeed adopt a tough stance towards workers. In the arms trade, however, the potential threat to enterprises of being blacklisted by government loomed larger in the consciousness of industrialists than did the threat to blacklist recalcitrant workers.[105]

Armaments in the industrial economy: an overview

The physical output of individual items of military hardware is not difficult to ascertain, but this disaggregated information is of limited use to the economic historian, who is more likely to be interested in the value of gross output than the manufacture of individual rifles or naval artillery. The historian of rearmament will respond by pointing out the uneven and erratic character of armaments production, which makes it difficult to draw a composite picture of output; this in any case has little meaning from the point of view of tsarist military preparations. Certainly, two obvious features of pre-revolutionary armaments production were the absence of any common trends in the output of different items and the fluctuations in the output of any given item. Such trends in output have to be understood in the context of supply norms. The government placed orders in accordance with prevailing supply norms: if these were satisfactory – if the stocks of shell, for instance, corresponded to the norms laid down – then there was no need to place fresh contracts. To take one example, between 1908 and 1913 the production of cartridges at state factories increased five-fold, whereas the output of fuses and field artillery pieces declined.[106]

Nevertheless, the economic historian cannot evade the responsibility to attempt an exercise in aggregation, in order to establish the position that the armaments industry occupied in the broader economy, as well as to analyze the manner in which available resources were used.

Notwithstanding the difficulties described above, a reasonable approximation can be made of the value of defence production in general and armaments production in particular. The starting-point of any such calculations is the industrial census carried out by Soviet statisticians in the difficult conditions of 1918. The census identified 2,287 enterprises that had operated without interruption between 1913 and 1918. Respondents from this sample of firms were required to categorize their output according to end-product for each successive year. The results established that, in 1913, 5.3 per cent of total industrial production could be classified as 'defence' production, meaning that it was ultimately purchased by or on behalf of military procurement agencies. The same source also yields an estimate of the proportion of machine-building production, destined for military use. In 1913, 26.2 per cent of the output of 120 engineering enterprises represented military production. This included small arms, artillery, ammunition, military vessels and so forth.[107]

Table 5.10. *Aggregate defence production in 1913 (million rubles)*

Total industrial production	Defence production	Military share in production of:		
		Machine-building	Metal-working	Chemicals
7,358	390	138	14	18

Source: col. 1 from *Dinamika rossiiskoi i sovetskoi promyshlennosti*, Moscow-Leningrad, 1929–30, vol. 3, pp. 176–7. Col. 2 represents 5.3% of this total, based upon the proportions reported in *Trudy TsSU*, vol. 26, Moscow, 1926, part 1, p. 41. Col. 3, 26.2% of total reported machine-building, from *Dinamika*, vol. 3, pp. 176–7; col. 4, 5.3% of total reported metal-working; col. 5, 5.3% of total chemicals production, from the same source. The underlying data have been adjusted, in order to incorporate raw materials, which were listed separately.

The application of these percentages to the available data on total industrial production and machine-building production in 1913 yields the results shown in table 5.10. In 1913, armaments production, defined as the output of military hardware (including military vessels) and ammunition probably accounted for 44 per cent of all industrial output destined for the defence sector.

Comparing these estimates with the defence appropriations discussed in chapter 3, the value of total defence production was equivalent to two-fifths of tsarist Russia's defence budget in 1913. It will be recalled that the state armaments budget in 1913 amounted to around 180 million rubles. The estimated value of gross output of all armaments amounted to around 170 million rubles (see table 5.10). Bearing in mind that the government purchased the net output of the arms industry, and that part of armaments spending paid for imports, these estimates are broadly compatible.

How does this compare with the situation in 1908? In principle, it should be possible to reconstruct the value of military output, by drawing upon the scattered information contained in the 1908 industrial census. But the aggregation of this data would involve considerable effort. A less laborious procedure is to backcast from 1913, by applying an index of defence spending. The appropriate index, along with an estimate of military production for the period 1908–13, is shown in table 5.11.

Adopting a similar procedure, we can derive an estimate of armaments production between 1908 and 1913. Table 5.12 implies that

Table 5.11. *Defence production, 1908–1913*

	Index of defence spending	Value of defence production (*million rubles*)
1908	69	269
1909	71	277
1910	73	285
1911	73	285
1912	87	339
1913	100	390

Source: col. 1, total defence expenditure from P. W. Gatrell, 'Industrial expansion in tsarist Russia, 1908–1914', *Economic History Review*, 35, 1982, p. 104, deflated by the index in P. R. Gregory, *Russian National Income, 1885–1913*, Cambridge, 1982, pp. 254–5, table F3; col. 2 from table 5.10, backcast to 1908.

Table 5.12. *Armaments production, 1908–13*

	Index of armaments expenditure	Value of armaments production (million rubles)
1908	43	74
1909	41	70
1910	44	75
1911	57	97
1912	73	125
1913	100	171

Source: col. 1, armaments expenditure from Gatrell, 'Industrial expansion', p. 105, deflated as in table 5.11; col. 2 derived from table 5.10, backcast to 1908.

armaments output accounted for 28 per cent of total military production in 1908, rising to 44 per cent in 1913.

Throughout the period 1908–13, the most significant component in the total output of armaments was shipbuilding. There are no direct figures for the total value of naval construction in 1913. Nevertheless, it is possible to derive the value of output at the four main state shipyards from official figures, and to offer an approximate value for output in the private sector, based upon data on labour productivity at the leading private shipyards. Similar procedures can be adopted for 1908. The results, which should be regarded as approximate, are presented in table 5.13.

Table 5.13. *Military shipbuilding, 1908 and 1913 (million rubles)*

	1908	1913
State yards	30	49
Private yards	18	80
Total	48	129

Source: col. 1, output of state yards taken directly from *Vsepoddaneishii otchet morskogo ministerstva za 1906–09*, St Petersburg, 1911, pp. 186, 202–3, 211; private sector output is calculated by applying a coefficient of output per person in two yards (Nevskii and Nikolaev dockyards), derived from table 5.6, to the labour force in private yards in 1908. The labour force for 1910 is given in L. G. Beskrovnyi, *Armiia i flot Rossii v nachale XX veka*, Moscow, 1986, pp. 198–9, and is estimated for 1908 by applying an index of expenditure on shipbuilding, derived from Gatrell, 'Industrial expansion', p. 105. Col. 2, output of state yards, *Vsepoddaneishii otchet morskogo ministra za 1914*, Petrograd, 1915, pp. 285–96; private sector output is calculated on the same basis as col. 1 above, i.e. 1913 output per person in four shipyards (including Putilov Wharves and Franco-Russian Wharves from table 5.6), multiplied by the private sector workforce in 1913.

Armaments accounted for around 2.2 per cent of gross industrial production in 1913; employment for around 4.2 per cent. These proportions would, of course, be rather higher during the last full year of peace (1913–14). On the face of it, there was scope to reduce the labour force in the armament industry, particularly those workers engaged on military contracts in the Urals ironworks. But crude accounting methods, coupled with a good dose of hindsight, fail to tell the whole story. It is easy to recommend cuts in the labour force; it was difficult to recommend and impossible to implement on a large scale at the time. Employment in the state sector, as we have seen, was bound up with deep-seated concepts of a 'patrimonial' responsibility towards Russian workers, making it inconceivable to envisage a savage programme of redundancies. Even if this strategy had been attempted, the pressing considerations of rearmament would have frustrated it. All enterprises, private and state alike, more than matched increases in their capital stock with additional labour. The armaments industry absorbed workers at a faster rate than any other sector in the industrial economy of prewar Russia. This helps to explain why armaments took over from railways as the motor of growth before 1914.

Russia possessed a large armaments industry, relative to those of other European powers. In France, armaments accounted for less than 1 per cent of total industrial production in 1913, less than half the corresponding figure in Russia. In Britain, the armament industry probably accounted for between 1 and 2 per cent of the total labour force, whereas in Russia the figure was in excess of 4 per cent.[108] In Russian conditions, the frantic pace of rearmament underlined the habitual entrepreneurial tendency to hoard labour in pursuit of satisfactory completion rates. It is hardly surprising that Russian businessmen responded to the challenge of armaments by recruiting large numbers of additional workers, whereas developed industrial societies adopted a more capital-intensive strategy. The greater the demands placed upon Russian defence enterprises, the faster they absorbed labour. This is not to say that the armaments industry lacked new plant, merely that the balance continued to be tilted towards labour, as the relatively cheaper factor of production. Hence, the large contingents of newly-recruited workers found modern and ancient equipment side by side on the factory floor. In this manner, rearmament imperatives disclosed the curious mixture of growth and backwardness that was the hallmark of prewar Russia.

Conclusion

After the hiatus associated with the end of the war in the Far East, and the postwar retrenchment, the armament industry received an avalanche of orders. The technology embodied in modern armaments, as well as the volume of orders, also required – and in some instances inspired – a new kind of productive effort.

The state sector faced criticism from within parliament and from private entrepreneurs. In the event, the state retained and even expanded its direct control over the manufacture of armaments and military vessels. Existing plant was modernized, largely by means of fresh injections of funds from the government budget. The labour force, already large, continued to grow. By 1913, the state sector perhaps had a higher ratio of capital to labour than in 1900 or 1908, but this is not saying much. Whether that investment yielded dramatic improvements in productivity of labour is more difficult to assess. Some managers made rigorous attempts to reduce costs, by cutting their overheads, taking steps to reduce wastage of inputs or by increasing the pace of work on the factory floor. Others appear to have drifted along in complacent fashion, basking in the knowledge that they enjoyed the protection of highly-placed officials in government. Such factories retained large numbers of auxiliary workers and administrative personnel, partly for economic reasons (including the fear that such workers might be permanently lost to the private sector), and partly because they saw the protection or security of labour as one of their chief tasks, enabling them to claim a potential role in wartime.

Proposals to close down some of the least profitable state enterprises and to transfer others, including the Motovilikha factory, to private ownership eventually came to naught. The defence departments had no wish to lose existing armaments capacity. Had Motovilikha been sold or leased, only Obukhov and the St Petersburg Ordnance factory would have been left to supply naval and field artillery respectively. Privatization aroused equally strong feelings in the Mining Department and from conservative groups in the State Council. The involvement of private capital, largely French, in the technical reorganization of the Perm plant represented a significant departure. Schneider's involvement had two desirable consequences, improving the potential performance of a major enterprise and encouraging Vickers, the defeated foreign rival, to look elsewhere for a foothold in the Russian defence industry, thereby adding to overall capacity.[109]

What, then, did the tsarist government obtain for its money? Some of the most prominent names in armaments production consolidated or developed a reputation for good quality. The Izhevsk arsenal, the Baltic shipyards, Izhora and Motovilikha works yielded to no one in the quality of their product and stood the test of international comparison and competition. On the other hand, there is no sign that the state sector was the locus of technical innovation or innovation in management style, as happened in some of the government armouries in the United States.[110]

The government probably took the correct decision in limiting the number of contracts it placed with the state sector. A larger volume of orders to state works would have created additional bottlenecks. But there was no question of the state relinquishing its direct control over armouries and dockyards, nor is there any compelling economic argument why it should have done so. The differential in production costs between the state and the private sectors in 1914 (probably between 10 and 20 per cent) was not so great as to indicate a massive misallocation of resources. In any case, ideological and strategic considerations added to the safety of the state sector from the threat of privatization or emasculation.[111]

The private arms trade faced an uncertain future in the aftermath of the Russo-Japanese War. There was no guarantee that the tsarist procurement authorities would favour the commercial sector with orders for armaments. In 1908, government officials went out of their way to disown the private sector and to display a protective concern for state enterprise. Until 1910, at the earliest, private defence contractors had to satisfy themselves with the crumbs from the table. Thereafter, however, they managed to gorge themselves on the cornucopia of government orders.

The growth of corporate power in the defence industry offered the private sector a way out of the multiple dilemmas that confronted it during the recession. The emergence of a commercial defence industry was marked by a plethora of inter-locking directorships, by collusion between independent ventures in bidding for contracts (see the next chapter), and ultimately by amalgamation and integration. The contacts between foreign firms and established Russian firms or new entrants to the defence industry enabled the private sector to carve a significant slice of the total Russian market for armaments. If the state sector had the advantages that came from its entrenched position, from the support of leading government ministers and from its price competitiveness, the private sector could offer the procurement authorities the opportunity to tap advanced western armaments technology, without the government having to bear the costs of constructing new plant. The confidence exuded by businessmen derived from the realization that the private armaments and shipbuilding industry had become an indispensable element in the tsarist defence effort.

Yet the euphoria that was evident at shareholders' meetings disguised several underlying problems. One was the burden of servicing the huge debt that many new and reconstructed firms had acquired during the boom years. If the government switched orders elsewhere, or the banks pulled the plug on their clients, they would be in desperate straits. Another problem concerned labour practices. The private sector needed to recruit and retain skilled labour; 'deskilling' may have offered one solution to the problem, but there was plenty of working-class resistance to the initiatives contemplated by management. Managers risked a great deal, if they sought outright confrontation with the workforce.

Would the Russian defence effort have been improved, had resources been allocated differently? Why did the regime decide against imports of armaments on a large scale? Should the government have relied more heavily on the private sector, or less? These questions entail a consideration of procurement decision-making, which forms the basis for the following chapter.

6 The economics and politics of defence procurement

Introduction: decision-making in defence procurement

The specific characteristics of defence industry have frequently fostered a close relationship between government and its suppliers. Both parties to the contract are driven together by the high stakes involved. American defence analysts have described the 'non-market, quasi-administrative buyer-seller relationship' that is the hallmark of the process of weapons procurement.[1] The government hopes to acquire the particular product or weapons system within the time-limit and budget stated in the contract. Rigorous quality controls must be implemented, in order to ensure that the product conforms to the required performance standards. For these reasons, firms in the defence industry do not have the same kind of autonomy available to other firms. Their behaviour and performance excite the close interest of government.

For their part, private arms manufacturers press for allowances to be made, in respect of the risks and uncertainty associated with defence production. The creation of new weapons systems entails high development costs, which are borne in the first instance by the arms contractor. Funds are tied up in research laboratories. Uncertainties surround the final costs of any production programme, especially where the technology is new. Furthermore, the purchaser may be required to alter product specifications at short notice, disrupting the production process. The industry is also vulnerable to sudden shifts in government policy, which could force the abandonment of a weapons system. For the contractor, therefore, armaments production can be a risky business. One way of minimizing those risks is to establish a positive working relationship with the customer.

The close relationship between government and industry is evident in the kinds of incentives that are made available to private firms, to

260

offset the obstacles and risks described above. These include guaranteed rates of profit, as well as other forms of financial assistance, such as subsidies and loans. Such terms are often built into defence contracts. Economic historians have used evidence of these and other practices to speak of a partnership between defence firms and government, which extended to the participation of business leaders on government committees that discussed weapons systems and defence procurement. But the 'special relationship' did not yield unmitigated advantages for the private arms trade. The British Admiralty, for instance, in adding new firms to the official list of contractors, could also remove firms. As a result, they would not only lose British government contracts; their damaged reputation would also render them vulnerable to the loss of export orders.

In relying for the most part upon government armouries and shipyards, as well as upon foreign deliveries, the tsarist regime traditionally avoided the peculiarities of a special relationship, prior to the war against Japan. After 1905, that relationship was finally consummated. But to think in terms of 'partnership' would be to underestimate the resistance within some parts of the Russian government to private enterprise. Underlying this opposition was the fear that the arms trade would, by collusion or some such nefarious practice, extract a high price from the regime for its cooperation. Shotgun marriage, rather than partnership, would be a more appropriate term for government–business relations.

Procurement agencies did not yet comprehend how much leverage the arms trade possessed, or in what ways defence producers would seek to exercise that leverage. How much expertise could government officials bring to bear on the complex issues involved in new weapons and shipbuilding technology? How would they respond to the rapid pace of technological change? To these problems were added the vexed question of the acquisition of foreign weapons and military vessels. Here, a delicate balance had to be struck between, on the one hand, the axiomatic insistence that Russia minimize its dependence upon foreign suppliers and, on the other, the need to acknowledge the financial support offered the tsarist state by foreign governments. Procurement officials had to weigh the consequences of their recommendations and decisions, both for domestic industry and for Russia's relations with its main ally.

Weapons procurement in prewar Russia entailed other issues, besides questions of commercial involvement and import strategies. The impetus for reform in defence procurement, unleashed by military defeat and political upheaval, was carried forward as a result of profound changes in the character and scale of rearmament. The adoption of the 'small shipbuilding programme' in 1907, and of additional weapons programmes in 1910 and 1911, imposed new tasks and obligations upon the Ministry of War and the Admiralty. The first and most obvious change was the size of the budget which the procurement authorities now had at their disposal. The provision of extra resources brought additional responsibilities, particularly in view of the parliamentary scrutiny of accounts. In the past, the State Auditor examined departmental budgets with a critical eye, but if he uncovered evidence of the mismanagement of funds, his findings went no further than the offices of state. Now, procurement officials were exposed to the spotlight of publicity; to use a different metaphor, a vigilant parliament might be expected to wash any dirty linen in public.

The difficulties of choosing the right contractor were compounded by the need to keep to a minimum delays in the completion of contracts. Procurement officials bore the ultimate responsibility for the satisfactory completion of work on schedule. This was a heavy burden to bear. Failure to ensure that work was completed on time implied that Russia's armed forces would fall behind their rivals in qualitative terms. The risks attendant upon another Tsushima did not need to be laboured. Officials had little scope to affect the progress of orders, which might be affected by industrial disputes or bottlenecks, whether caused by the Russian climate or other exogenous factors. But, if a major programme were badly delayed, these officials would be charged with negligence or incompetence. The dilemmas that confronted those in charge of military procurement should not be underestimated. They had a duty to ensure that work was delivered promptly; but, at the same time, their masters told them to exercise caution in the award of contracts, in order to obtain maximum value for money. The reconciliation of these objectives would tax the most professional and hardworking official in the defence departments.

Faced with difficult choices – whether to purchase from foreign or domestic suppliers and, if the latter, from state or private works – procurement officials understood that their behaviour and decisions were subject to closer scrutiny than at any time hitherto. They laboured at a considerable disadvantage. The domestic and international context within which they operated had changed dramatically since the beginning of the twentieth century. Yet the conditions in which they worked had not altered. Procurement officials were

poorly paid, had little prospect for career advancement and, in consequence, lacked motivation. A job that called for greater professional-
ism and expertise offered no more tangible rewards by 1914 than it had
a decade previously. We shall begin by examining some of the consequences of government indifference to their career structure.

The arms lobby and the procurement process

Eckhart Kehr argued that arms suppliers manipulated government and public opinion, in order to secure contracts. Leading firms
helped to manufacture war scares, as well as armaments.[2] There is,
however, no evidence that Russian industrialists either manipulated
public opinion or exercised a direct influence over foreign and defence
policy. Industrialists obviously had opinions about the course that
Russian foreign policy should take. For example, many Moscow merchants individually and collectively espoused the cause of Russian
nationalism and favoured an active government policy in the Balkans.
The group around the textile magnate P. P. Riabushinskii was particularly vocal in this respect, and took the opportunity to publicize its
views in the press. But they echoed the widespread view among the
middle class that Russia had a mission to act in Europe on behalf of
fellow slavs. Economic considerations played only a modest part in the
formation of this sentiment. Nor did armament firms engage in the
offensive.[3]

On the other hand, abundant evidence has come to light that arms
suppliers lobbied government officials, in order to secure defence
contracts. This practice is unsurprising: the nature of the product
commits defence contractors to the lobby of government. In Russia,
this behaviour became a hallmark of the newly emergent arms trade.
But did the lobby betoken the strength of monopoly capital, as Soviet
historians used to argue? Or did it reflect, rather, the weakness of the
industry, in the face of budgetary constraints and challenges from
other potential suppliers? Was there, indeed, anything distinctive
about the behaviour of arms suppliers? One of the early historians of
the Russian bourgeoisie believed that lobbying, with its attendant
features of bribery and corruption, was a pronounced element in
business behaviour. According to this account, Russian industrialists
wasted energy and capital on the unproductive pursuit of officialdom,
instead of investing in new technology, as any self-respecting entrepreneur should have done. But in the competitive environment of
many Russian industries, their conduct was perfectly understandable.

In armaments, where conditions of monopsony prevailed, lobbying became an essential business practice.[4]

The representatives of private firms assiduously cultivated contacts with officials in government departments. Former government officials infiltrated company boards. Colonel Soskinovskii, an ex-Admiralty man, represented the Nikolaev yards before the Main Ship-building and Supply Administration (GUKS); Noblessner's interests were looked after by Captain N. Karpov. I. Pushchin, a top official in GUKS, was employed by the Russo-Baltic Company and the Sormovo engineering works; upon retiring, he promptly joined the Russian subsidiary of the German firm Schichau. The shipbuilding conglomerate Nikolaev-Russud scooped the pool, by recruiting Admiral I. F. Bostrem, the former deputy Navy Minister. Other ex-government employees recommended themselves, because they could offer advice on naval technology: Admiral Krylov, for instance, served as a consultant to a number of private shipyards. Other firms made a point of picking up former civil servants from the Ministry of Finances. The Putilov board included several directors – Putilov himself, A. A. Davydov and von Dreier – from this fertile source. Such men were valuable, not only because of their technical expertise, but also because of the links they preserved with government personnel. Yet they were not recruited solely in order to lobby for contracts. Many of them owed their appointment to the big commercial banks, who wished to have their men in positions of influence within the firm.[5]

Arms suppliers regularly made informal approaches to government officials after 1908, to enhance their standing and competitive position. The representatives of the private sector found a receptive audience amongst those responsible for defence procurement. This became clear from the results of a lengthy investigation, conducted during 1910 and 1911 by Senator N. P. Garin into the behaviour of the military procurement agencies, in particular the Main Artillery Administration (GAU) and the Chief Quartermaster's Department (GIU). But Garin's inquiry and subsequent report ranged well beyond the lobby.[6]

Garin investigated defence procurement in the military districts (*voennye okruga*) of St Petersburg, Moscow, Kiev, Odessa and Kazan. Private firms were compelled to make available their commercial correspondence and financial accounts. Garin devoted much of his final report to the financial overspend in the procurement process. He complained that the staff in the GAU and GIU had no incentive to conclude defence contracts on terms that were financially advantageous to the government. Instead, officials connived at the attempts

by potential suppliers to subvert the procurement system. Officials
employed by the GIU were particularly likely to line their pockets
with bribes and other inducements, failing to subject contracts to close
scrutiny. In the GAU, they turned a blind eye to collusion between
arms suppliers.[7]

This aspect of the behaviour of procurement officials attracted a
good deal of attention from Soviet historians. Missing from their
accounts, however, is the explanation that Garin gave for the corruption and inefficiency that prevailed in the main agencies. Garin interpreted the behaviour of procurement officials as a function of the low
quality of personnel that could be recruited, especially given the poor
rates of pay they received. The personnel at the GAU and GIU tended
to be men whom other government departments had turned down;
the unsuccessful candidates were thus deprived of the higher salaries
that they would have otherwise have commanded. Once employed in
defence procurement, they faced a miserable future. The procurement
departments offered nothing in the way of specialist instruction
which might make up for the lack of training available at the cadet
officer schools and other military education establishments. Furthermore, their responsibilities became more complex with each passing
year, but rates of pay did not rise commensurately: salaries remained
at the levels fixed during the reign of Alexander II. Meanwhile, the
army had doubled in size during the intervening half century, and
weaponry had become more sophisticated and expensive. Garin
observed that 'the work falling to each individual official has
increased many times. In addition, whereas formerly many items of
military subsistence were produced in the regimental economy, now
they are procured by the GIU'. Promotion prospects, like the rate of
pay, were poor. A less inspiring and satisfying career would have been
difficult to find.[8]

The men recruited into the administration of procurement thus
tended to be second-rate and poorly paid, and easily prey to bribery
and corruption. Garin exempted most of the GAU officials from this
latter charge, but was no less critical of the artillery administration,
which delayed the confirmation of contracts, made abrupt changes to
specifications and even dispatched the wrong parts to be assembled at
workshops hundreds of miles away. Garin advocated improvements
in training and salaries. He advised that mundane clerical and book-
keeping jobs could be performed equally well, if not better, by civilians, rather than by military men. Officers would then be free to use
their military and technical knowledge in more appropriate ways.

They could at least acquire a degree of professional status, pride and commitment.[9]

The Tsar, however, brought Garin's revealing investigation to an abrupt halt at the end of 1911. Furthermore, he refused to sanction the publication or even internal circulation of Garin's findings. Why the sudden change of policy? Nicholas II appears to have acceded to the wishes of officials in the Ministry of War, backed by the newly installed Sukhomlinov, who objected vigorously to any inquiry that smacked of outside interference. Initially, Sukhomlinov and his staff had gone along with the investigation, because an outright refusal to cooperate would have inflicted further damage on the already heavily criticized Ministry. But they did so reluctantly, and Sukhomlinov managed to withhold information from the team of investigators, such as that relating to the stocks of equipment held in readiness for mobilization. Towards the end of 1910, he warned the Tsar that Garin's inquiries were undermining the confidence and activities of procurement officials in the GIU. Nicholas heeded the implied advice and asked Stolypin and the Ministry of Justice to close the investigation. The government decided not to prosecute the officials who had violated the law.[10]

At first sight, Sukhomlinov's actions provide another damning indictment of his ministerial performance. But this conclusion would not be entirely fair. Sukhomlinov and Garin shared a common vision of a professional bureaucracy. The Minister of War agreed that his personnel should be encouraged to devote their time to military training and education, rather than to the performance of routine administrative and 'policing' duties, which could be entrusted to properly trained civilians. To that extent, there was common ground between the two men. Unfortunately, this admirable vision required a substantial investment of time and money.[11]

Meanwhile, Garin's investigation uncovered evidence that private firms paid retainers to insiders in the GAU and GIU or rewarded them with cash or shares, in exchange for detailed information that would help them in preparing a bid for a government contract. But the level of corruption can hardly be called impressive. Most of the firms named were small fry, such as the Polish firm of Lilpop, Rau and Levenstein and the engineering company, K. Rudzkii, based in Warsaw and Ekaterinoslav: 'between 1899 and 1909 not one order to these firms was approved without bribes'. Two well-documented cases nevertheless revealed that substantial sums of money also changed hands. The newly formed submarine firm, Noblessner channelled bribes to officials in the Admiralty through the Loan and Discount Bank, in order to counter the competition posed by the state-owned Baltic works. The managing director of the long-established Tula Cartridge Company N. E. Ponafidin, systematically paid 1 per cent of the value of contracts for cartridge cases and cupro-nickel to officials in the GAU.[12]

The emergence of an arms lobby and of informal contacts between contractors and procurement officials should be seen in the context of an uncertain market. Arms suppliers desperately needed to bring themselves to the attention of the government and to secure contracts, given their peculiar vulnerability: 'the plant (wrote one leading arms manufacturer) is huge ... any thought that orders for military vessels will stop at some stage is quite frightening'.[13] In addition, Russian entrepreneurs in this unusual industry pleaded for more forward planning (*planomernost'*) in the distribution of orders, a view supported by Garin. Forward planning by the GAU would help to improve productivity: 'if there is some certainty about orders for several years ahead, and about the repetition of similar types of order, then the adoption of best practice techniques will make production more straightforward and advantageous, leading to a significant reduction in costs'.[14] The attempt to forge a relationship with the procurement agencies could be justified, not only as a survival tactic, but also as a device to promote the improved use of available capacity.

Garin advocated a radically new approach to procurement, in which formal negotiations between the government and a network of suppliers would replace the prevailing atmosphere of secrecy and corruption. There was much to be said in favour of the creation of an institutionalized forum in which a working relationship between industry and government could be devised. The establishment of a formal body in which both parties were involved would remove many of the grievances that industrialists currently articulated. It could educate officials about the technical problems associated with the manufacture of different products. It could help to reduce the time lag between the decision to acquire a particular product and the confirmation of a contract. And it could eliminate many of the labyrinthine procedures involved, especially in the procurement of uniforms and boots, dispelling the doubts entertained by some of the best firms and encouraging them to participate.[15]

Some businessmen were certainly guilty of attempts to suborn procurement officials; others probably escaped detection by being too subtle. Large firms had other strategies up their sleeve. They could exercise control over the market, by forming agreements between themselves as did Kolomna and Sormovo in machine-building and the two shipyards of Nikolaev and Russud. They could trade on their indispensability to government. Whether the government could flex its own muscles in response depended upon the performance and potential of the state sector and upon the extent to which the government was prepared to exercise its option to buy from foreign firms.

The introduction of system: the formation of the Shipbuilding Commission

Garin's report made no mention of shipbuilding, but the institutional model he advocated seems to have been based upon the arrangements recently created for the procurement of military vessels. From 1908 until 1917, no major shipbuilding contract was awarded without the approval of a government commission, in which procurement officials, technical experts, accountants and (on occasion) private contractors took part. In deciding the criteria for the award of contracts, this commission busied itself with the internal affairs of state and private enterprises alike. Its deliberations provide valuable insights into prevailing attitudes and procurement practice. The background to its formation also reveals the struggle that surrounded any attempt at institutional reform in late imperial Russia.

The approval of the 'small shipbuilding programme' in 1907 made it imperative to proceed with administrative reform of the Navy Ministry. Its current practices were criticized within the Duma and by liberal and conservative newspapers alike. Stolypin, in particular, believed in the necessity for reform of the Admiralty's existing procurement procedures. He initiated plans for a new authority that could take over naval procurement from the Ministry. However, naval officials did not give up their powers without a fight. When reform was ultimately imposed, Admiralty officials managed to retain considerable authority.

In the autumn of 1908, the Admiralty got wind of a projected 'chief administrative commission for shipbuilding'. Under the draft project, sponsored by the Ministry of Finances and backed by the State Auditor's office, the commission was empowered to consider all aspects of shipbuilding, including technical details of construction. To that end, its chairman could invite 'specialists in various branches of shipbuilding and construction' to take part in its proceedings. The plan made private businessmen, as well as engineers and technical specialists, eligible to participate, in the guise of invited consultants.[16]

From the point of view of the navy, the most offensive aspect of the

Navy vs Army

proposals concerned the dilution of ministerial authority. Two representatives each from civilian ministries (Finance, Trade and Industry,
and State Audit), as well as from the War Ministry, would join
Admiralty officials in administering state shipyards, and planning and
monitoring procurement. The commission would thus – uniquely –
constrain the Admiralty, whose officials also objected to the open-
ended manner in which outsiders might be invited to take part. The
Deputy Navy Minister, S. A. Voevodskii, found these proposals particularly irksome, at a time when (as he put it) the Ministry was making
'every effort' to confront the problems arising from the consequences
of the Russo-Japanese War. The Minister, Dikov, conveyed these views
in writing to Stolypin.[17]

However, the formation of an inter-departmental commission was
not without precedent, as other members of government were quick to
point out. The State Auditor argued that the programme of artillery
rearmament between 1900 and 1908 owed its success to such a body,
which possessed powers in excess of those envisaged by the projected
commission on shipbuilding. In these circumstances, the Ministry had
to accept some kind of control on its activities.[18]

In a parallel draft, prepared by the Admiralty, the navy rejected any
representation from the Ministry of War and from the Council of
Ministers, on the grounds that the commission's brief was to consider
economic aspects of shipbuilding, and not 'questions concerning naval
rearmament in general'. This tactic was designed to counter the arguments put forward by the State Auditor, who urged that the GAU and
General Staff be included on the commission, in order 'to assist the
creation of communication between the fleet and the army'. The
Admiralty also insisted that only 'approved and well-informed' men
could be invited to attend the commission's deliberations, and rejected
the participation of private businessmen, whom it deemed insufficiently informed to participate.[19]

The statutes of the Shipbuilding Commission (Soveshchanie po
sudostroeniiu) eventually received imperial assent on 10 December
1908. In its final form, the Commission had one representative (rather
than two) from the three civilian ministries. The Ministry of War failed
to get any seat at all, putting paid to any hope that the Commission
would serve as a forum for debate between the two defence departments. Nor, to their acute disappointment, were private entrepreneurs
allowed to participate in the deliberations of the new body, except
when summoned to answer questions relating to proposed contracts.
To a considerable extent, therefore, the intense lobbying by the

Admiralty had borne fruit. However, the presence of three representatives from the navy, together with the Chairman (*ex officio*, the Deputy Navy Minister) did not give the Admiralty an automatic majority on the Commission, because along with the three representatives from civilian ministries, the chairman of the Council of Ministers appointed his own nominee. From this point of view, the commission appeared to be finely balanced. The right given the Chairman to nominate temporary members, with equal rights to those of permanent members, could tilt the balance one way or the other.[20]

According to article one of the regulations, the commission had 'to consider the economic and financial questions arising from the proposed measures for construction and equipment of warships and for the supply of new naval bases in accordance with the shipbuilding programme'. The commission could thus consider the prevailing economic circumstances, advise on the choice of particular contractors and examine the conditions under which contracts were to be carried out. In addition, the commission considered requests that might be made by contractors for financial support or (what amounted to the same thing) for relief from financial penalties that attached to delayed completion of work. The only aspect of the naval rearmament programme which was explicitly excluded from its purview were the technical details of ship construction and armament. Once such details had been determined, all remaining matters of procurement were supposed to come before the commission.[21]

The Admiralty had thus gained important concessions during the course of discussions about the formation of the proposed commission, which did not have the power to consider technical questions; still less, didit have the right to raise questions relating to the rearmament programme in general. Its responsibility was confined to the implementation of a given policy. Furthermore, representation from other departments of government had been whittled down. If the chairman found himself unable to agree with a majority decision in the commission, he could take the issue up with the relevant ministry and, if necessary, refer the matter to the Council of Ministers. Finally, a crucial amendment allowed the Chairman the right to pack the new body with supporters of the Ministry.

The commission exemplified many of the best and worst features of tsarist bureaucratic administration. Its members, who included such well-known experts as Admiral A. N. Krylov and K. P. Boklevskii, the dean of the shipbuilding faculty at the St Petersburg Polytechnic, were dedicated and well versed in matters concerning ship construction and naval rearmament. Meeting weekly, often for five hours or more, the commission demonstrated an impressive capacity for the detailed consideration of naval construction programmes and the finances of Russian shipyards. At the same time, the Admiralty tried to subvert the work of the commission, by allocating orders without seeking its prior approval. Some orders were approved directly by the Main Administration for Shipbuilding (GUKS). In such instances, the Ministry incurred the wrath of such men as Boklevskii, and of Stolypin himself, but their displeasure seems to have caused naval officials few sleepless nights.[22]

No less disconcerting were the suspicions that the commission entertained towards private enterprise, suspicions that Boklevskii, in particular, did his best to counter. Boklevskii was at one time portrayed in Soviet historiography as the 'delegate of monopoly capital'. In fact, he maintained an objective stance towards the private and public sectors, arguing that the commission should be guided in the main by considerations of available capacity, production costs and completion schedules, rather than by preconceived ideas about the desired destiny of contracts. Quite simply, the shipbuilding commission never became the poodle of private enterprise. Leading private businessmen, such as S. I. Mikhin, A. K. Voigt and Tokarskii (representing, respectively, Sormovo, Putilov and the Confederation of Northern and Baltic Engineering Industry) had been invited to attend a special meeting to consider the 1907 shipbuilding programme. But they were conspicuous by their absence from the new commission. Private enterprise, therefore, had to fight its own corner, without any institutionalized access to government. If a 'special relationship' did exist, it was not to be found in the corridors of the shipbuilding commission.[23]

Foreign or domestic supply?

The principle that the Russian government should give priority to domestic suppliers in awarding defence contracts had often been enunciated, but repetition simply served to underline its ineffectiveness in practice. As long ago as 1860, an imperial edict had instructed government departments to order finished goods from Russian factories wherever possible. However, the ministries chiefly responsible for purchasing manufactured goods (the Admiralty and the ministries of War and Transport) made no such undertaking and ignored the ruling. In 1902, following the recommendations of a special commission, government regulations for the first time required each department to provide the Ministry of Finances with a schedule of orders that had been placed abroad. But the Ministry had no power to veto contracts awarded to foreign suppliers, and the information it gathered was allowed to gather dust in government files. The events of 1904–5 in any case rapidly undermined the position of the Ministry of Finances. During the war against Japan, the government placed substantial defence orders with foreign firms.[24]

When the war ended, however, the government took more purposeful steps to control ministerial purchasing overseas. In February 1907, the government introduced fresh regulations, requiring each department to inform the newly established Ministry of Trade and Industry of any proposed foreign order in excess of 10,000 rubles, and to justify the award of such contracts to foreign firms. The Ministry had the right to challenge such contracts and to raise specific cases with the Council of Ministers. Russian industrialists, deep in the throes of the recession, hailed this move as a much-needed concession; others hid their private delight behind fulsome praise for the decision to put 'national interests' first, by protecting the balance of payments. One leading banker and industrialist noted that 'our balance of payments suffers from foreign orders for defence, and especially for naval purposes'. But words were not enough. A battle began to ensure that this new principle was upheld and, in particular, that orders would only be placed abroad if the items in question could not be supplied by domestic producers.[25]

Abundant opportunities existed to circumvent the new regulations. Municipal authorities and railway companies, as well as central government departments, placed orders with Russian merchant houses, which imported goods from Britain or Germany, in order to lessen the risk of detection. Another tactic was to ensure that the value of each order did not exceed 10,000 rubles, the limit at which the regulations came into effect. Procurement agencies could also insist on a certain product specification, in the knowledge that only foreign suppliers could meet those terms.[26]

These regulations did not apply to private enterprise, which could only be prevented from ordering goods abroad by an outright ban on imports. This was out of the question. The government did encourage private customers to seek out domestic sources of supply. New regulations had been introduced in 1903, enabling the State Bank to extend loans to domestic shipping companies that bought Russian-built vessels. The Bank could advance up to two-thirds of the cost, at a privileged rate of interest. Between 1903 and 1906 these loans averaged just under 2 million rubles per annum. However, the practice fell victim to government retrenchment, and the loans ceased in 1906. In any case, domestic producers laboured under other disadvantages. Foreign suppliers received (or insisted upon) more generous advances, and their products were subject to less stringent inspection procedures than those applied to domestic goods.[27]

The Admiralty paid lip-service to the principle of import substitution, but subverted the principle as occasion demanded. There were, of course, several advantages in ordering naval vessels from foreign suppliers, notably speed of delivery and (often, but not always) price. But these tactics brought the Admiralty into frequent conflict with the Ministry of Trade and Industry, and sometimes, as over implementation of the 1907 shipbuilding programme, with the government as a whole. The cornerstone of the small shipbuilding programme was the planned construction of four new battleships. Admiralty officials urged that the order for turbines and boilers be given to a firm in the forefront of naval technology. Vickers appeared to be the most obvious choice. In June 1907, the Deputy Navy Minister informed the Council of Ministers that the Ministry had prepared a draft contract with Vickers for two battleships. Under the terms of this contract, Vickers would receive £386,000 for turbines, £219,000 for boilers and £400,000 for other work associated with the construction of the first battleship. The construction of the hulls and fitting out the ships would take place in Russia, using Russian labour and materials.[28]

These proposals immediately encountered opposition from the Ministry of Trade and Industry. Shipov argued that there was no need to involve Vickers or any other foreign firm in the implementation of the shipbuilding programme. Turbines and boilers alike could be manufactured, under licence from Parsons, by the Franco-Russian Company in St Petersburg. The matter came up for consideration at the Council of Ministers in November. The Navy Minister amplified his arguments in favour of Vickers. Apart from the fact that it was a leading supplier of turbines and boilers, and could be relied upon to deliver these items promptly, Vickers offered further advantages, in helping to define the specification of armaments on the vessels. The British firm outlined a project for the construction of a battleship of 21,000 tons, fitted with a total of twelve 12-inch guns, distributed between four turrets. By contrast, the state shipyards offered to fit only ten guns, mounted in five turrets. Other members of the Council of Ministers were not impressed by these arguments. Instead, they took the view, outlined already in a memorandum submitted by the

Confederation of Trade and Industry, that 'domestic and not foreign factories should be involved in such crucial national matters as the rebuilding of the Russian fleet'. The cabinet took the view that the Russian shipbuilding industry currently experienced the 'utmost difficulty'. Economic, rather than technical aspects of the question were of paramount importance.[29]

This did not signal the end of the Admiralty's attempt to involve foreign enterprise in the production of battleships. After the cabinet meeting on 13 November, the government set up an inter-departmental commission to arrange for tenders to be submitted. By March 1908, eighteen tenders had been received, including eight from foreign companies and five from Russian factories (the remainder were projects submitted by Russian engineers). Among the foreign projects was one submitted by Vickers, a somewhat futile gesture in view of the fate of the previous contract. The commission tried to circumvent the wishes of the government and came out in support of a tender from the Hamburg firm of Blohm und Voss. When he heard of this proposal, Kokovtsov fired off a sharp note to Dikov. However, Kokovtsov's objections to the proposed deal did not draw upon the traditional argument about domestic industry; instead, he observed that 'such an assessment by the commission of the various projects may have an extremely unfavourable impact on French public opinion and seriously affect the progress of our negotiations for indispensable foreign credit'.[30]

No doubt with this warning in mind, the Main Administration of Shipbuilding and Supply recommended to the Council of Ministers that the contract be given to the state-owned Baltic yards. The contract stipulated that the state shipyard would supply the hulls for two battleships and that the order for turbines would be subcontracted to the Franco-Russian Company. However, the key element in the contract was the technical assistance to be provided by the British shipbuilders John Brown. This proved to be the pattern for the future. Yet, notwithstanding the decision that had been reached, the Admiralty succeeded in ordering at least one turbine from the German firm AEG, on the pretext that disagreements over the terms of the contract with the relevant Russian supplier held up progress.[31]

The Ministry of Trade and Industry continued to urge the defence departments to purchase industrial equipment from Russian suppliers. In 1908, Shipov cited the depression of trade in support of this policy. The Deputy Navy Minister made a lame attempt to demonstrate that orders for machine tools normally went to Russian firms. What he did not mention was that these were essentially agencies that imported foreign manufactured goods. The government held firm to the principle that priority be given to Russian firms. In 1913, for example, the State Auditor secretly acknowledged that the cost of the 1912 shipbuilding programme (421 million rubles) could have been reduced by almost 30 per cent, if the government had approved the award of contracts to foreign producers. But fiscal arguments were now outweighed by the need to use domestic industrial productive capacity to the full.[32]

This policy should not be seen as a straightforward concession to private enterprise. Balance of payments considerations played the major part in government thinking on this subject. But, once the government had agreed a set of principles for foreign orders, Russian businessmen could legitimately urge the government to enforce the 1907 regulations. In the depth of the 1908 slump, the Confederation of Trade and Industry sent evidence to Stolypin that the navy had ordered torpedo boats and barges from British firms. Stolypin extracted an assurance from the Admiralty that no such orders had been placed. This did not satisfy the industrialists, but they could make the government aware of the strength of feeling and attach their rhetoric to the government regulations in force.[33]

What weakened their position, however, was the availability of state-owned capacity. A decision to award contracts to Russian factories did not necessarily entail an order to the private sector. Generally speaking, orders for hulls and naval armaments went to Russian producers, not because of lobbying by the private sector, but rather because of pressure from sections of government, in particular, the Ministry of Trade and Industry, and from the Shipbuilding Commission, on which the shipbuilders were unrepresented. Increasingly, as firms such as the Franco-Russian Company and the St Petersburg Metal Company moved into the production of turbines and boilers, domestic factories received orders for more complex items, as well as for hulls and naval armaments. The major factor now was the realization that foreign enterprise would supply technical assistance and advice. As Vezhbitskii put it in 1908, 'there are already signs of specific technical agreements between Russian factories and foreign firms, which recognize that they can only use their productive capacity by a certain kind of businesslike agreement with the Russian enterprise'.[34]

The bulk of orders before 1907 comprised defence products (see tables 6.1 and 6.2). The beginnings of a decline in foreign orders can be detected in 1909, but it is difficult to tell whether this trend was

Table 6.1. *Orders placed abroad by government departments, 1901–1910 (million rubles)*

	War	Navy	Transport	Total	% Defence
1901	3.05	19.02	2.23	25.93	85
1902	2.18	17.41	1.43	22.26	88
1903	2.55	10.09	1.50	15.70	80
1904	16.91	21.33	1.57	41.83	91
1905	73.13	68.42	4.93	148.05	95
1906	4.44	18.08	2.38	27.78	81
1907	5.61	12.37	3.46	25.34	71
1908	3.15	7.07	2.24	16.22	63
1909	2.56	5.72	1.78	14.53	57
1910	4.93	n.a.	1.48	n.a.	–

Note: figures include import duties
Source: Otchet otdela promyshlennosti za 1911, St Petersburg, 1912, pp. 146–7.

Table 6.2. *Foreign share of military orders, 1907–1910*

	War			Navy		
	Weapon outlays	Foreign orders		Shipbuilding	Foreign orders	
	(million rubles)		%	(million rubles)		%
1907	35.1	5.6	16	34.8	12.4	36
1908	35.3	3.2	9	31.3	7.1	23
1909	36.9	2.6	7	24.6	5.7	23
1910	39.4	4.9	12	26.2	n.a.	n.a.

Source: as for table 6.1; expenditures derived from *Proekt gosudarstvennoi rospisi dokhodov i raskhodov*, St Petersburg, 1907–10.

sustained or reversed as rearmament gathered pace in 1910. The War Ministry ordered around ten per cent of its weaponry from overseas suppliers between 1907 and 1910. By contrast, nearly one-quarter of orders for naval vessels went to foreign firms.[35]

The significance of the foreign contribution to the rearmament drive is made difficult to assess by the absence of figures for orders placed after 1910. The government preferred to place orders with domestic suppliers, counting on their contacts with foreign firms. However, this strategy seems to have come under pressure on the eve of the First World War. In 1913, for example, the GAU was authorized to spend ten million rubles, in order to bring its reserves of shell up to strength, but three million rubles went to the Rhine Iron and Steel Company in Düsseldorf. The GAU spent over 19 million rubles on foreign orders in 1914, although the sum was earmarked mostly for purchases of machine tools and other equipment for the armaments enterprises, rather than on military goods.[36]

The government's preoccupation with the balance of payments coincided neatly with business interests. Both parties sought to create the conditions for import substitution in defence procurement. However, this strategy – it can hardly be called a policy – was constantly being subverted, particularly by the Admiralty. One answer lay in seeking foreign technical assistance to domestic firms. But the lengthy negotiations that preceded such agreements put Russian participants at a disadvantage and their aspirations could easily come unstuck when the pace of defence procurement intensified.

State and private enterprise: the internal arms race

The dichotomy between state and private enterprise in Russia was charged with more significance than in any other contemporary industrial power. To weaken the traditional grip of the state over armament production entailed a corresponding growth in the opportunities afforded private enterprise. The prospect that the production of armaments might one day come to depend on the whim of Russian capitalists and the vagaries of the marketplace alarmed tsarist officials to distraction. They intended to preserve the tsarist state from the loss of sovereignty implied in the supremacy of capitalism. At the very least, the extension of armaments production to the private sector would call for a partnership between capitalists and government, unmediated – in the worst case – by the possibility of calling upon the services of state-owned enterprise.[37]

It was not simply self-interest that prompted a spokesman for the Obukhov shipyards to defend state ownership of assets: 'foreign and private firms are keen to offer their services, but the state ought not to make its defence completely dependent upon the political mood of foreign suppliers or on the pecuniary appetites of native industrialists'.[38] This was a widespread view. Even S. I. Timashev, the Minister of Trade and Industry, in no way a committed opponent of private enterprise, expressed the view that 'in the matter of production of armaments, the government must not depend upon private factories'. The Minister of Finances and the State Auditor shared this opinion.[39]

Government representatives stuck to this conviction, even during the depths of industrial recession, when the government faced a fierce onslaught by Russian businessmen. The prolonged depression not only exposed the frailty of private firms, but also highlighted the privileges enjoyed by the state sector. The jealous assault by industrialists on state enterprise reached a crescendo during the conference on the iron and steel and machine-building industries in 1908. Few industrialists could resist the opportunity to attack the government's support for state enterprises, at a time when the private sector was depressed. The most outspoken critic of government policy, the maverick Moscow industrialist Jules Goujon, demanded that the state withdraw entirely from industrial production. He urged the sale or closure of government-owned steel and engineering works, 'which yielded the government nothing but losses, because of poor management practices'. Noting that state enterprises did not have to pay fines for delays in delivery, Goujon called for such discrimination to be scrapped. Other business leaders rehearsed the arguments against state enterprise, pointing out that the inefficient performance of particular state factories was concealed by government subsidies, which allowed them to compete unfairly with the private sector. The competitive advantage of the state sector was artificially maintained by the fact that overheads, as well as tax and insurance payments, did not figure in their cost schedules. State factories also received advances, varying from 50 to 75 per cent of the value of the contract, which freed them of the need to borrow from financial institutions at prevailing rates of interest. Stories also circulated of corruption in the procurement agencies. Officials reportedly advised state armouries of the price at which the government intended to purchase a product, enabling them to undercut their rivals in the private sector.[40]

This concerted attack on the state sector provoked a vigorous response from the Ministry of Trade and Industry, whose spokesman (N. A. Iossa) denied that state-owned ironworks competed with private factories. He rejected the specific charge, levelled by Goujon, that the large armoury at Motovilikha was a fundamentally unsound enterprise. Although he acknowledged that some state works were demonstrably inefficient, Iossa pointed to the deleterious consequences that would follow their closure: 'this question is connected with the question of the conditions of numerous workers'. Similar arguments had been advanced by other government officials, who raised the spectre of unemployment and social instability. In 1911, the State Auditor maintained that 'the government should come to the aid of the private sector, only after state factories have been fully supplied with work'. These arguments cut no ice with private entrepreneurs. Vezhbitskii, one of the spokesmen of heavy industry, was unimpressed by the official justification of procurement policy. He insisted that state enterprises themselves should come to the rescue of struggling private firms: 'in the event of a general decline in demand, state works should give some of their orders up to private enterprise'.[41]

The consensus amongst Russian industrialists was that the state sector occupied an anomalous position in Russia. Only the equalization of conditions for state and private enterprise – by the extension of commercial principles to the former – would begin to give satisfaction to the industrialists. After 1908, as the depression lifted, so too did many of the dismissive comments of private entrepreneurs. But they retained a belief in the fundamental unfairness of a system that regarded state shipyards and armouries as having a prior claim on government contracts.

Whatever their shortcomings, the tsarist government never contemplated the privatisation of its arsenals and shipyards in their entirety. As we have seen, even the state ironworks, the weakest link in the chain, escaped this fate, albeit not without a struggle. The most persuasive argument used against privatization proposals was a familiar one: state ownership of works such as Motovilikha guaranteed that the government would not be bound by prices set by the private sector. This was a sensitive issue, for economic as well as ideological reasons: the government believed that the iron and steel syndicate, Prodamet, had forced up prices, and had no wish to see the armament industry fall victim to a private monopoly. It was wholly inappropriate to transfer ownership in the foreseeable future: 'the removal of the Perm ordnance works from state administration, and the transfer of responsibility to a private joint-stock company, must be regarded as unwelcome and even harmful from the point of view of the proper supply of armaments to the army and navy, at the cheapest possible price'.[42]

The attacks mounted by businessmen challenged the foundations upon which state enterprise rested, and demanded a response. The government continued to attach crucial importance to the functions fulfilled by state shipyards and armouries. A semi-official statement insisted that 'the armouries and arsenals weaken the dependence of the state in wartime upon private industry for the supply of defence goods, and in peacetime regulate the prices for armaments on the domestic market'.[43]

At the heart of the procurement decision-making process, therefore, lay the belief that the prices charged by state factories established a benchmark against which private bids could be judged. This information could be used to drive a hard bargain with private enterprise. How successful was this strategy? When the occasion demanded – that is, when they wished to enter the market – private firms deliberately undercut the state armouries and shipyards. In 1908, for example, Putilov offered to deliver 3-inch quick-firing artillery pieces at 1,030 rubles, equivalent to the (cost) price charged by Obukhov. The circumstances were unusual: Putilov put together what looked like an attractive bid, in order to get business during a slump, by submitting a very low bid on gun carriages (22 per cent below the Obukhov price), as a device to obtain the contract for the guns. Having made provision for a loss on the carriages, Putilov still made a profit of 35 per cent on the artillery contract. Subsequently, as the depression lifted, Putilov developed a reputation for charging high prices, and the government's attempt to stimulate competition and control prices succeeded only in the short term.[44]

Nor did it always follow that new entrants undercut their rivals in the state sector. The shipbuilding commission tried to play off two suppliers of submarines, the state-owned Baltic shipyards and the newly formed company, Noblessner, in order to force the private firm to lower its bid. But Noblessner insisted that it could not reduce its price, because of the high start-up costs involved. Sometimes, too, new entrants found it impossible to reduce their prices, because of the need to pay a licence fee to a foreign firm. In these circumstances, the rivalry of state yards did not enter into the calculations of the arms trade.[45]

The government's basic strategy also came unstuck when firms colluded, as they frequently did. In 1910, for instance, Putilov, St Petersburg Metal and Nikolaev agreed on the bids they would submit for the contract to supply naval gun turrets, in order to defeat the Admiralty's attempt to force down prices. Garin observed that 'the existence of actual competition in respect of artillery procurement is a rare enough occurrence; the industry is not organized into a permanent syndicate, but collaborates over virtually every contract'. When the pace of rearmament quickened, the government found it difficult to respond to this kind of tactic. The prior existence of the state sector made little difference, at a time when the government needed to call upon all available capacity.[46]

Underlying the entrepreneurial rhetoric against state works lay the assumption that they could not compete *on equal terms* with private firms. How much truth was there in this belief; did state enterprises operate with higher unit costs than equivalent firms in the private sector? In powder production, the cost differential amounted to around 28 per cent. This gap reflected, in part, the fact that the state works had to buy inputs of saltpetre and pyrites from Russian suppliers, whereas the privately-owned Schlüsselburg powder works obtained cheaper supplies from abroad. But this did not entirely account for the higher costs at Okhtensk. The state works maintained a larger workforce per unit of output, including a white-collar staff that was nearly three times the size of the contingent at Schlüsselburg. Housing and other facilities also had to be found for the larger workforce at Okhtensk. Taken together, the overhead costs associated with a large plant condemned Okhtensk to a high-cost regime.[47]

It is more difficult to establish the extent of the differential in military shipbuilding. When government shipyards were required to operate as commercial enterprises, the prices they charged for armoured cruisers and battleships typically exceeded the trade price by between 10 and 18 per cent. This probably gives a fair indication of the cost differential between the state and private shipyards around 1911. By 1913, as they acquired more experience in manufacturing modern vessels, private yards opened up a slightly larger productivity gap with the state sector. But it was unlikely to have exceeded 22 per cent. Costs were also affected by the price of raw material and other inputs. Private yards probably obtained relatively cheaper inputs, by importing steel or acquiring it at a discount from steel mills within their orbit. There was, therefore, some truth in the industrialists' charge that the state sector was less efficient than the private sector.[48]

Notwithstanding the decision to place government shipyards on a commercial footing after 1908, they still retained many of the features that distinguished them from private enterprise in an earlier period. Government armouries and ironworks belonged to a different world. Managers were recruited from the civil service, not from the commercial sector. Workers retained an attachment to a particular factory, much as their forefathers had been obliged to do since the Petrine era. A distinct culture pervaded the state shipyards and armouries, one of fervent commitment to the government's armament programme and belief in the inviolability of state-owned enterprise. This culture turned the manufacture of weaponry into a duty, not just a shopfloor routine. The introduction of self-financing did not undermine a belief that the quality of output, and an adherence to the broader goals of government, mattered more than the balance sheet. The First World War would do nothing to weaken the resolve of government officials to support the state sector. Nor, however, did it dent the conviction of private entrepreneurs that they alone were capable of displaying the 'energy and knowledge' demanded in the modern machine age.[49]

The professionalization of procurement and the decline of the regimental economy

The ordinary soldier doubtless regarded the supply of decent clothing, footwear and food as a rather more important matter than the production and supply of armaments. Recognizing the element of self-interest involved in the provision of such basic items of consumption, the tsarist state had entrusted generations of ordinary soldiers with the task of producing finished goods for their own use. The responsibility of the Quartermaster's Department (GIU) was confined to the supply of raw materials and semi-finished products to Russian regiments. However, the dismal experience of the Russo-Japanese War led the government to reassess its procedures. One of the main lessons drawn from the war was the need to dismantle the regimental economy, which had become discredited in the eyes of army officials and soldiers alike. Critics pointed out that 150,000 soldiers, or 12 per cent of men in uniform, spent their entire time supposedly on duty but actually engaged upon the manufacture of uniforms and boots. The leading Russian expert on military procurement asserted that 'the emancipation of troops from the burden of economic responsibilities, and the transfer of those tasks to a procurement agency has conferred an advantage on foreign armies', which needed to be redressed, if the Russian army were to realize its full potential.[50]

The government responded by taking upon itself the responsibility to supply troops with finished goods. In 1906, new legislation gave the Quartermaster's Department authority, not only to procure materials, but also to supply the army with manufactured goods. It was a popular and overdue decision, but it burdened officials in the GIU with additional responsibilities, at a time when their behaviour and performance were coming under intense scrutiny. After 1908, as Garin emphasized, the GIU budget increased rapidly, but the training and salaries of its personnel made a much more modest advance.[51]

Henceforth, the Quartermaster's Department subcontracted work to state and private workshops, and maintained a network of repair shops, close to army units. Attempts were also made to enlist more small-scale producers (*kustari*) and cooperative producers in the manufacture of boots and uniforms. The War Ministry offered preferential terms to cooperatives and individual craftsmen, for example by no longer requiring them to deposit a security against the raw materials they received. The GIU also undertook not to enforce penalties in the event of delays in the completion of contracts. By 1909, more than 50 per cent of clothing, as well as all bed-linen was being supplied by various cooperative enterprises. Footwear was mostly produced in small workshops or by gangs of workers (*arteli*). These decisions demonstrated a deliberate government policy to sustain small-scale enterprise, as happened in other instances as well.[52]

However, the new arrangements did not escape criticism. As Garin discovered during his investigations, an unscrupulous contractor could obtain a contract to supply cloth or finished goods, pocket the advance and escape to a different town. Perhaps with this problem in mind, the State Auditor recommended that the GIU deal with large-scale suppliers, who also offered a cheaper and more reliable product. In his view, small businesses had sufficient working capital and were thus liable to be late in handing over the finished product. It is difficult to ascertain whether this was a widely-held view, and nor is it straightforward to establish the extent to which the balance shifted towards large enterprise. Recent research has tended to draw attention to the vitality of small-scale enterprise, and it would be unwise to assume that large firms automatically reigned supreme. According to the standard source on the subject, small-scale industry contributed around 90 per cent of all output in the footwear and saddlery trades. The small producer received the prepared leather from the factory, and cut, stitched and nailed the boots himself. In this industry, unlike armaments, where the costs of entry were quite modest, it is likely that rising levels of defence procurement opened the door to numerous small businesses across the country.[53]

Meanwhile, the GIU relied less and less on semi-public auctions as a means of acquiring semi-finished goods, such as cloth and leather. Here, the War Ministry did follow the advice of the State Auditor, dealing with larger and well-established (although not necessarily more scrupulous) merchants. The GIU drew up lists of recognized *fabrikanty*, with whom contracts were concluded in advance. Nevertheless, these new arrangements did not eliminate the longstanding problem of poor quality materials. The quality of cloth and leather continued to give cause for concern, not so much because of the creeping impact on military morale, but because of the waste of resources involved.[54]

This sphere of defence procurement did not escape the reform initiatives that affected other branches of procurement. The GIU created new economic committees (*khoziaistvennye komitety*) at the uniform and equipment workshops under its administration. The aim was to introduce the same kind of financial discipline that had been imposed in other spheres of state enterprise. The committees monitored costs of production and checked on the uses to which equipment and materials were put. Workshops were required to operate within a definite budget and to seek GIU approval for any overspend. The intention was admirable, but inflation in the price of raw materials played havoc with the regime of self-financing. The problems were compounded by the difficulties of finding qualified personnel for these management tasks.[55]

With what success, therefore, did the GIU meet its new tasks in the aftermath of the Russo-Japanese War? Some difficulties persisted, although these did not always reflect shortcomings in the procurement system itself. For example, Russian producers failed to keep pace with military demand for leather, and the GIU had to order from foreign suppliers. This happened on two occasions: after the Russo-Japanese War, when vigorous attempts were being made to improve the quality of footwear, and on the eve of the First World War, when demand reached a new peak. Whether this reflects success or failure, of course, depended upon one's point of view. Russian manufacturers bemoaned the reliance on imports, but the Russian army would have adopted a much more positive attitude, applauding the flexibility demonstrated by the Quartermaster's staff.[56]

A contemporary report commented that the GIU was making 'every effort' to improve the quality of footwear assigned to the rank and file troops. However, these efforts were hampered by financial constraints, and the GIU was sometimes forced to sacrifice quality for quantity. In 1913, the War Ministry drew up estimates of expenditure, based upon past consumption norms, as well as upon the average price that prevailed in 1912 and 1913. But prices rose rapidly during the first half of 1914 and the estimates rapidly became outdated: the Quartermaster's Department reckoned to pay 6.35 rubles for a pair of boots, but suppliers demanded 7.40 rubles.[57]

In dismantling the regimental economy, therefore, the tsarist regime required an overstretched and underpaid staff to shoulder additional responsibilities. In the circumstances – rapid growth in the size of the armed forces, inflation in raw material prices – the GIU personnel acquitted themselves reasonably well. If Russian soldiers went to war insufficiently clothed and sheltered, the blame attached to military planners, rather than to procurement officials, who responded to the norms handed down by the General Staff. The other conclusion to be drawn is that the mutual distrust that characterized the relationship between business and government was very much evident in the procurement of 'soft' items. The Confederation of Trade and Industry called for the establishment of a committee, which would allow government and business jointly to consider military procurement. The proposal sank without trace, as if the decision to dismantle the regimental economy and to deal directly with private enterprise para-doxically convinced government officials of the need to keep business-men at arm's length.[58]

The procurement and production of armaments: performance indicators

The performance of the Russian armament industry can be assessed in conjunction with the performance of the procurement system. At stake are three key issues. First, arms suppliers must manu-facture a high-quality product, and it is the task of the procurement agency to ensure that standards are observed. The second element in the contract relates to prices; the procurement system should operate in such a way as to keep prices as close as possible to those specified in the contract, subject to any unforeseen factors that may alter the original terms agreed. Finally, the success of the procurement agency will be judged on its ability to obtain the finished product within the specified time. How successful was the Russian procurements system according to these criteria? Finally, to what extent did it contribute to raising the technological level of the Russian armament industry?

In the early years of the century, the government faced several complaints from the military about the quality of finished goods. Initially, the government simply responded by urging its suppliers in the state sector to improve performance. The Ministry of Trade and Industry instructed the Urals ironworks that an unacceptably high proportion of output of shell and guns was defective. That these criticisms gradually became less vocal suggests that the reform of factory administration had left its mark. By 1913, for instance, officials compared the quality of ordnance produced at Motovilikha very favourably with similar products made abroad.[59]

Senator Garin had harsh things to say about the quality of output at some of the leading private firms, such as Putilov and Sormovo. But not everyone shared his poor opinion. In any case, the quality of output improved as these firms gained greater experience in manufacture of weapons. In shipbuilding, for instance, Vickers' advisers in Russia made sarcastic comments about the management and layout of local plant, but they were impressed by the quality of finished products.[60]

No less important was the question of delivery dates. The experience of small arms suggests that the industry improved its delivery schedules during the late nineteenth century. It took sixteen years to re-equip the Russian soldier with the Berdan rifle during the 1860s, but only ten to complete the re-equipment of the army with the Mosin rifle during the 1890s. Russian dockyards also handled the 1895 shipbuilding programme reasonably well, although its completion owed a good deal to frenzied activity during the Russo-Japanese War. What of the period after 1905? Delays were common in state and private enterprise alike, as Garin discovered. The annual reports of the State Auditor testified to delays at Motovilikha, especially between 1907 and 1909. Arrears (*nedoimki*) in production at the Perm plant were equivalent to 173 per cent of its total output in 1913. Sometimes, delays could be explained quite simply, for instance by pointing to problems with the supply of foreign parts for military vessels. But there were other, more systemic problems at work. One of these was the excessive observation of formalities at the level of individual enterprises in the state sector. Another problem had to do with the constant changes in product specification which were imposed on contractors, a problem that also had implications for costs. The files of the Shipbuilding Commission are filled with complaints about the fickleness of the procurement agencies. Vickers' strongest criticism of tsarist procurement practice was reserved for the constant changes made to product specifications after contract terms had been agreed.[61]

The government tried to alleviate these problems in various ways, including the imposition of fines on private enterprise for delays in completion of work. This tactic had broader repercussions. For example, engineering firms in the capital preferred to make concessions to workers' demands, rather than risk the interruption of production schedules by stoppages of one kind or another, and thus the threat of financial penalties. More important than the financial penalty was the realization that they might forfeit their chance of orders in the future. However, it is difficult to establish the extent of this strategy.[62]

Government officials sought to keep down procurement prices, directly, through inviting firms to submit tenders and, indirectly, through the procurement of raw materials at auction. But private firms often undermined this objective, by colluding between themselves to submit an agreed price, and compensating the losers. The State Auditor reported in 1913 that an informal syndicate of private ship-builders had forced up the prices: 'taking advantage of the favourable opportunity to grab government orders, and receiving lavish subsidies from the commercial banks, Russian firms have formed alliances in order to apportion orders according to their discretion. This has complicated and certainly held up the shipbuilding programme'.[63]

The government expressed the hope that the competition between state and private sectors would act as a restraint on price inflation. The evidence on this last point is, as we saw earlier, inconclusive. The State Auditor believed that competition succeeded in restricting the rate of price increases in defence procurement. On the other hand, Senator Garin argued that state works sometimes charged *higher* prices than the private sector, thereby undermining the principle that they should 'regulate' procurement prices.[64]

Whatever moderating influence may have been exerted on prices by such rivalry, the fact remains that the general tendency was for costs and prices to rise, as a result of the inflation in raw materials prices before 1914. The tariff on iron and steel raised the cost of inputs (crude steel and sheet steel sold for between 0.95 and 1.20 rubles per pud in south Russia, but cost 1.45 rubles in St Petersburg. The equivalent cost in Britain was between 0.75 and 0.90 rubles). These factors, rather than the activities of Prodamet, helped to inflate the price of finished armaments. In shipbuilding, too, specific forces operated to inflate procurement prices, such as the transition to more advanced and costlier technologies in propulsion and armament.[65]

Other factors operated to maintain high costs and to delay the completion of contracts. In particular, neither the GAU nor GUKS allocated orders in a systematic manner to individual factories. A special report, prepared for the State Council by three councillors, including Rödiger, the former Minister of War and Dmitriev, a specialist on naval shipbuilding articulated this view. Explaining the relative time taken to construct vessels in Russia, Germany and the UK, as well as the high costs of construction in Russia compared to these other countries, the authors rejected some of the conventional explanations, such as the lack of a well-developed indigenous commercial shipbuilding industry and the high cost of raw materials, which were offset by the relative cheapness of labour. Instead, they argued that the Admiralty had a haphazard attitude towards procurement. Without a clear indication of the size of orders, without any guarantee that the orders would not be changed in a capricious fashion and, above all, without a real commitment from the Ministry to the domestic industry, the state yards were in a difficult position. Their capacity was under-utilized and, as a result, they had high overhead costs to bear.[66]

How did the Russian armament industry perform relative to the industry elsewhere? Construction costs were usually lower elsewhere, even though wages were higher: in the British shipbuilding industry, wages were up to twice as high as the corresponding rates in Russia, and three or four times higher in the USA. In 1908–9, a British-built battleship (*bronenosets*) cost 674 rubles (£71) per ton, compared to 764 rubles (£80) in Germany, 791 rubles (£83) in the USA and 809 rubles (£85) in Russia. Only the French industry came out higher, at 833 rubles (£87), for reasons that remain obscure. The well-informed authors of a contemporary study of the world shipbuilding industry drew attention to the low level of labour productivity in Russian shipbuilding, a function of insufficient on-the-job training and of pre-industrial work routines. Russian workers took up to twenty-eight days' holiday each year, compared to between six and nine days elsewhere.[67]

How do these inter-country differentials compare with other branches of industry? The cost differential between the Russian and the European construction industry was considerably greater than the figures for shipbuilding. In manufacturing industry, armaments appears no worse (and no better) than cotton textiles, where low rates of labour productivity likewise cancelled out the cost advantage conferred on Russian industry by the prevailing low wages. Russian manufacturing industry laboured under inherent disadvantages (compounded by tariff protection); these appear to have affected some branches of industry more seriously than armaments.[68]

To what extent did the Russian armament industry begin to attain the European or world level of technology? Direct evidence on this point is lacking. The large number of technical agreements Russian firms concluded with their counterparts in France and the UK certainly held out the possibility of raising the technological level of the Russian armament industry to comparable levels. The Russian government took a deliberate decision to promote technological transfer; for instance, the Ministry of Trade and Industry insisted that Russud employ foreign advisers: 'the use initially of foreign expertise in the manufacture of gun turrets and steam turbines is absolutely essential in order to develop military shipbuilding in Russia and to reduce production costs'. However, as late as 1913, the State Auditor complained that Russian factories had to order turbines and boilers from abroad, 'a further reminder of the technological backwardness of our shipbuilding industry'. The gap between Russia and its industrial rivals narrowed between 1905 and 1914, but it had definitely not been bridged.[69]

Conclusion

The prewar history of Russian military procurement demonstrated that the system began to acquire more modern features. Some sections of the bureaucracy developed a more professional stance, notably in shipbuilding, where haphazard devices for awarding contracts gave way to a more systematic arrangement under the Shipbuilding Commission. The creation of this body permitted more considered and informed decisions to be taken. A still more dramatic change took place with the dismantling of the traditional regimental economy and the substitution of government supplies of finished goods.

Taken as a whole, however, the procurement system suffered from significant defects. Officials were poorly paid and, at least in the Chief Quartermaster's Department, poorly motivated as well. Until they received adequate remuneration, and thorough training in the complex technical, administrative and economic tasks of procurement, they would remain ill-equipped for the job. Procurement officials laboured under other constraints, especially financial pressures, and had to respond to often aggressive and well-organized bids from private entrepreneurs. These conditions would have taxed even the best-paid and most highly-qualified personnel to the utmost.

The claims of private enterprise challenged the prerogatives of the state sector and forced the government to concede that the arms trade had a role to play. Yet the private sector hardly enjoyed a complete triumph. The armament industry was especially vulnerable to shifts in government spending priorities. In addition, the state sector served as a counterweight to the burgeoning commercial arms trade. The government owned fixed capital in armaments and shipbuilding, and might conceivably add to that capacity in future. Such a strategy did not lack advocates in prewar Russia. The government also sought to harness non-corporate and small-scale industry to the task of industrial production. Hence the support given to organized cottage industry, in the manufacture of basic military goods, such as boots and uniforms. If the arms race handed the laurels to private enterprise in Russia, the victory was bought on highly conditional terms.

Imports of armaments represented another challenge to the nascent arms trade. In practice, however, Russian arms suppliers could discount this threat. In an emergency, as happened during the Russo-Japanese War, the government hurriedly held out the begging bowl to foreign suppliers. But peace brought attempts to manage the balance of payments deficit, and thus a deliberate policy to substitute for imports. Some sections of the tsarist government, notably the Ministry of Trade and Industry, also attached significance to the need to establish an indigenous industry. In armaments production, few military planners countenanced a strategy that relied heavily upon imports. Fortunately for Russian armament producers, these policies dovetailed neatly after 1905.

The complex tasks of rearmament during the early twentieth century emphasized that no realistic alternative could be found to the involvement of large-scale private enterprise in the programme. State shipyards and armouries, despite massive investment and the sizeable labour force at their disposal, were in no position to cope single-handedly with the demands of the arms race. Cottage industry might manufacture boots and belts, but could not build battleships and heavy artillery. Rearmament yielded orders for a small handful of enterprises, which possessed the capital and labour force to cope with the demands of production. Yet the countervailing force of state enterprise, as well as the incipient threat of involving foreign suppliers in the business of rearmament was sufficient reminder that corporate power did not bring about the subordination of the tsarist government to big business. In the twilight years of the old regime, government ministers and civil servants kept their distance from private enterprise and barely disguised their suspicion of the arms trade. Only rarely does the historical record show any awareness of the possibility that the tsarist government could harness private enterprise, in order to create a dynamic partnership with the established state sector.[70] Thus, the 'internal arms race' between state and private enterprise differed fundamentally from the rivalries evident in other continental economies before 1914. The difference reflected the fierce and deep-seated aversion in sections of the tsarist regime to private enterprise. Prewar rearmament brought these tensions to the surface. Nothing in western Europe paralleled the resulting antagonisms.

7   Military preparedness and defence capability on the eve of the First World War

Introduction: Constructing the last argument of tsarism

A mere ten years separated Russia's disastrous engagement with Japan from the cataclysm of European war. But this decade was associated with some profound changes in Russia's body politic and economic conditions. To embark on war in 1914 was to mobilize social and political forces very different from those that operated in 1904; to engage in armed conflict was not only to unleash larger and more sophisticated armaments and personnel upon the enemy, but also to call upon the resources of a more developed industrial economy. After 1905, and for the first time, Russia possessed an embryonic parliamentary regime. To the extent that the Duma exerted limited control over defence appropriations, the tsarist government had to take parliamentary opinion into account when formulating defence policy. Whether, in wartime, the Duma would behave as a pliant instrument of the regime, or as the focal point of broader social tensions, remained to be seen. Another major change involved the system of land tenure. The government of P. A. Stolypin embarked on a thorough reorganization of land tenure, in an attempt to recast the relationship between peasantry and the state, by making it possible for peasants to jettison communal strips of land for individual, enclosed plots, thereby strengthening a sense of property in land and other agricultural assets. On the international stage, Russian diplomacy committed the country more firmly than before to the alliance with France, holding out the prospect that Russia could share the burden of defence with at least one partner. Whether Russia would assert its own multifarious diplomatic interests, in the face of France's overwhelming preoccupation with Germany, was a different matter. Finally, the prewar years witnessed an upsurge in the rate of growth of the Russian economy. After a painful period of financial uncertainty and retrenchment, the economy began to grow rapidly once more, allowing the regime to improve its credit-worthiness, to build up its gold reserves and to devote substantial resources to rearmament. The defence industry had been restructured and expanded, creating opportunities that had not hitherto existed for private enterprise. What did administrative reform, rearmament and economic growth imply for Russia's defence capability?

Defence capability includes military manpower, the organization and disposition of the armed forces, as well as their provision with weapons, equipment and other goods. It subsumes, in other words, the more limited issue of military preparedness: did Russia possess adequate stocks of robust and easily accessible military hardware? It extends to the functions entrusted to men in uniform and to the arrangements for the realization of those functions. It includes the plans made to transport soldiers, food, munitions and equipment – and, in the pre-1914 armies, horses and fodder as well – to the theatre of operations. However, to confine oneself to these questions is to adopt a narrow definition of defence capability. A broader conception is required, taking account of the extent to which society as a whole was prepared for war, and of the capacity of the economy to sustain a war effort. Military planning before 1914 did not take these issues into account, on the assumption that the outcome on the battlefield would be decided in the first few weeks and months of confrontation and engagement. In the crucial opening phase, what mattered was the success or failure of the military to adhere to and realize their carefully-drafted mobilization plans. Within twelve months, economic exhaustion would force the warring parties to conclude peace, giving the spoils of war to the countries whose troops had gained the decisive advantage on the battlefield.[1]

The First World War confounded these expectations, and the experience of war revealed in due course that no belligerent power could count on the supplies of munitions, let alone manpower, that were available at the outbreak of war – considerations that dominated most discussions of military preparedness before 1914. Instead, the European powers had to recruit fresh soldiers from the ranks of the civilian population. What did this mean for Russia, whose regime had forfeited any residual popular sympathy during the 1905 revolution and its bitter aftermath? On the face of it, Russia (unlike other European powers) had a seemingly inexhaustible reserve of manpower, but this advantage could easily be outweighed by the relative backwardness of the education system, by deficiencies in training and by a lack of

But not necessarily ~~from~~ forever

popular commitment to the war effort and the diplomatic goals of the regime.

The questions posed by the prospect of a prolonged engagement became no less acute in respect of the country's economic potential. To what extent could Russia count on its extractive and processing industries to supply the raw materials and manufactured goods that would be required during a protracted war – and by civilians as well as by men in uniform? What impact would the collapse of trade have on the delicate Russian balance of payments? How secure were food supplies in Russia, particularly when rural labour and freight wagons were absorbed in new military tasks? Could Russia, the 'poorest of all civilized nations', manage to share the costs of war with its allies, as it did the costs of preparing for war?[2]

There was something of a paradox in Russian attitudes towards the impending conflict. Planners and politicians took comfort from Russia's relative advantages of size, abundant manpower and food-producing potential. Backwardness might be a virtue, in helping Russia to avoid the penalties of economic disruption, to which more advanced belligerent economies were liable. This had been a standard refrain for at least a generation. But, having witnessed the effects of the Russo-Japanese War, Russian observers were less impressed by the potential for social cohesion in wartime. A lengthy continental engagement might provide a focus for popular discontent, sufficient to unravel Russian society and topple the old regime. From this point of view, an early resolution of the confrontation made greater sense than pinning one's hopes on Russia's apparent superiority in resources.[3]

How could Russian military planners increase the likelihood that they could achieve victory on the battlefield within weeks or months? The complex tasks confronting Germany offered Russia a window of opportunity. Germany planned a lightning attack into France, before turning its forces on Russia; if Germany were bogged down in France, Russian forces might be able to deal a decisive blow on the enemy's eastern front, or at least to wear down the German army in a positional war. The fly in the ointment, however, was Austria-Hungary, whose forces were capable of inflicting heavy damage in Galicia. To deal with the combined forces of the central European powers required a massive expansion of Russian land forces. But, in terms of the financial commitment, the army took second place to naval rearmament, until the very eve of the war. Better, perhaps, to pursue a defensive strategy, in the hope that Germany would be prevented from embarking upon war, at least until Russia's land and sea preparations had been completed. Russia would be much better prepared to fight by 1917. Unfortunately, neither France – which needed its ally to commit forces against Germany at a moment's notice – nor Germany – which finally launched a preemptive strike against its opponents – were willing to wait.[4]

Whatever immediate military preparations were set in motion on the eve of the First World War, they counted for nothing once war breached the initial timetable and stalemate set in. Having reached that point, the belligerent powers were compelled to discard the mobilization plan and the railway timetable; instead, they needed reserves of social stability, an adaptable economy and institutional flexibility, capable of providing their citizens with the means to cope with the demands of modern warfare.[5]

Russia had much to gain from victory, if such were vouchsafed to the armies of the Tsar. Victory would unquestionably yield enhanced prestige on the international stage. A successful joint prosecution of the war with its allies would strengthen international confidence in the ruble and unlock the French and British money markets to an even greater extent than hitherto. Russia could also count on more immediate tangible gains, by tasting the fruits of commercial supremacy over a defeated Germany. Under the terms that could confidently be expected in a revised trade treaty, Russia would gain access to the German market for foodstuffs on more advantageous terms, whilst restricting German competition in manufactured goods in the domestic market. This is not to say that Russian officials made any definite proposals for the economic emasculation of Germany. Although they believed it right and proper to sequestrate the landed estates of German nationals, and although they expected to suspend payments to enemy nationals, they did not intend to seize commercial and industrial assets held by the enemy. Not until 1915 did the Russian government assume the power to liquidate enemy businesses; and only in 1916 did it adopt the principle that wartime economic policy should be directed towards 'the release of the economic system of the country from German influence'.[6]

First, however, Russia had to achieve victory over the powers of the Triple Alliance. What resources did it have at its disposal, and how were they to be mobilized and combined in pursuit of the overall strategy?

The armed forces, military doctrine and Russian society

The Russian army numbered 1.423 million men on the eve of
the First World War, far in excess of its allies and adversaries (France
entered the war with 582,000 men in uniform, and Germany 597,000).
The 'great army programme', adopted in 1914 – to the relief and
delight of the French – envisaged the conscription of a further 480,000
men. But the outbreak of war prevented the unhurried realization of
this programme.[7]

In March 1906, the Tsar had reduced the length of service in the
infantry and field artillery to three years. Other ranks served four
years. Seven out of ten soldiers served in the infantry. Most soldiers,
therefore, served for three years, before entering the reserves. The
composition of the infantry and artillery was overwhelmingly peasant
and, with a relatively short term of service, it is difficult to believe that
many ordinary soldiers lost their close sense of affiliation with the
world of the village (the peasant element was less preponderant in the
cavalry and in engineering units). Many soldiers experienced a huge
gulf between themselves and their commanding officers, even though
some of the latter were themselves of humble origin. There was a
widespread mistrust of authority, particularly when it was exercised
by officers who treated their men no less contemptuously than landlords had their serfs in former times. The Russian army had already
shown its mistrust of authority, by mutiny on a widespread scale
during 1905 and 1906. Discipline had only been restored when it
became clear to the disaffected rank and file that there existed no other
alternative source of authority than that of the Tsar. The prevalent use
of harsh punishment for petty infringements of military discipline
continued after the 1905 revolution, undermining any basic trust
between the ordinary soldier and his superior officers.

Much less certain is the extent to which common soldiers possessed
a firm sense of loyalty to the Tsar. Any residual belief by peasants and
workers in the benevolence of despotism had been rudely shaken
during the revolution, and would be difficult to recapture. True, the
Stolypin land reforms were designed to create a property-owning
peasantry, whose interests would be identical with those of the state,
which alone guaranteed property rights and internal security. Government officials made strenuous efforts to reorganize land tenure and to
provide rural credit, with some degree of success by 1914. But the
reforms had not proceeded sufficiently far to transform peasant

attitudes, which remained distrustful of outsiders, particularly those who represented authority. This was an uncertain social bedrock from which to conscript an additional half million men in peacetime, let alone the millions who were called to the colours during the war.[8]

In addition to this deep-seated mistrust of authority, another factor complicated the picture of military motivation. The army believed that its role ought to be confined to the security of the Empire from external aggression. The propensity of the regime to turn the army into an internal security force to suppress peasant unrest and protest by ethnic minorities could only alienate soldiers still further from the regime. That this attitude had also taken root among junior and senior officers called into question the fundamental reliability of the entire army as a fighting force.

This alienation of the Russian army mattered, because the army was regarded as one of the chief props of the old regime. It mattered in yet another sense. The prevailing military doctrine after the Russo-Japanese War emphasized, as it had throughout the previous generation, the importance of the individual soldier's commitment to advance in the heat of battle. This ethos had been identified as a significant factor in Japanese success on the battlefield. Japanese infantry had mounted well prepared assaults on Russian fortifications. But more remarkable than the support offered to the Japanese troops by artillery or the care they took to advance under cover of darkness was their fighting spirit. The attacks on Russian positions caused great loss of life among Japanese infantry. The lesson of the campaign was that troops had to accept heavy casualties, as the price to be paid for tactical assaults. If the same kind of commitment or morale were absent or weakly developed, the Russian army had little to fall back upon but the traditional weapon of military discipline, namely the knout, whose limited usefulness had already been exposed by the mutinies of 1905 and 1906.

But it was one thing to pinpoint the significance of morale; to realize the concept proved much more difficult. In practice, something could be done to educate the soldier, provided that time, care and personnel could be found for this purpose. The reform of the regimental economy freed more time for strictly military pursuits. So, too, did the final admission – 'far too late', in the opinion of one recent study – that the army should be freed of its commitment to maintain internal security. Apart from extending the time available to familiarize the common soldier with the care and use of weapons and other military equipment, additional hours were released for education. More resources were found for military training. However, the relatively short period of service in the Russian army hardly offered much opportunity to engage in these laudable pursuits. The army, short of NCO's and short of time, could do little more than train its soldiers in the elementary use of weapons.[9]

This provides a clue as to the army's enthusiastic espousal of the doctrine of morale, despite the evident lack of this quality during the Russo-Japanese War and its immediate aftermath. The numerical size of the armed forces and the growth of munitions provision were insufficient to compensate for the technological superiority of other powers in Europe. If all else failed, the Russian soldier should be called upon to stand fast and to use his bayonet. A similar explanation was doubtless at work in the navy, where the notion of the 'spiritual life [*dukhovnaia zhizn'*] of the ship' prevailed. Despite the rearmament drive, the investment in fortresses and in military vessels, the Russian army and navy remained technologically backward. As we shall see, Russia lacked well-developed communications, so vital given the extended territory in which troops were obliged to operate. Insufficient investment in railways, despite French cajoling, as well as a dearth of radio communication, deprived the army of crucial ability to communicate decisions from the central command to field commanders and from field commanders to troops on the ground.

Finally, notwithstanding the investment that had been made in education during the late nineteenth and early twentieth centuries, many conscripts possessed little more than the rudiments of literacy. Against this background, military doctrine substituted a vision of personal bravery and reliance on the bayonet for the use of concentrated firepower, personal initiative and modern methods of military communication. Comprehension of one's function and responsibility in a troop unit played only a small part in the preparation of the imperial Russian army for war.[10]

Rearmament and military supply

What was the outcome of the Russian commitment to rearmament? To what extent did the resources devoted to defence yield an adequately equipped army and navy? According to that eloquent, energetic and deeply conservative advocate of a rapprochement with Germany, Peter Durnovo, Russia remained a relatively weak military power, a state of affairs he ascribed largely to the existence of the Duma. It was bad enough that the parliament deprived the Tsar of his autocratic power; that (as Durnovo alleged) the Duma compounded its misdemeanours by failing to support the programmes brought before it by the defence ministries, a sure sign that 'dilettante' opinions had prevailed over those of the expert. Turning to specific areas of concern, Durnovo pointed out that the Russian army was especially deficient in heavy artillery and in machine guns. Russia would therefore remain, as at present (in February 1914), ill-equipped to fight against Germany and Austria-Hungary.[11]

The record of military reverses during the First World War appeared to vindicate Durnovo's gloomy assessment of Russian prospects. But it is not necessary to resort to hindsight in order to corroborate his most telling criticisms of the state of Russian armaments supply. The provision of heavier field artillery and machine guns did indeed fall significantly short of the supply norms that the army had approved. Russia entered the war with inadequate stocks, particularly of powerful field howitzers (mortars), which the German army possessed in greater numbers and which proved particularly important in trench warfare. Stocks of machine guns barely exceeded four-fifths of estimated requirements (see table 7.1). Here is evidence of years of neglect and of problems addressed only belatedly. A mere 10 per cent of total resources were devoted to artillery under the 1910 programme. True, this deficiency was to be made good under the 'great programme for strengthening the army', but the completion of the programme was destined to take place only in 1917. The Russian army went to war with three times fewer field howitzers per division than its German counterpart.[12]

In other respects, the situation appeared much less alarming, as even Durnovo had to admit. Stocks of rifles, 3-inch artillery, 3-inch shell and light artillery on the eve of the war corresponded closely to the norms that had been laid down by the Russian General Staff during 1910 and 1912. Whether such norms were sufficient was a different matter. The Deputy Minister of War, A. A. Polivanov, who took charge of these preparations, calculated on a war lasting between two and twelve months. The norms for cartridges and shell fell short of those adopted by France and Germany. But higher norms would have required additional allocations, which the army sought in 1907 and in 1912, without being completely successful. On the first occasion, the army was the victim of Kokovtsov's knife, receiving only 70 per cent of the sum requested for cartridges. On the second, the demands of the fortress programme took priority; the proposal to increase shell norms by 50 per cent (to 1,500 shell per piece) was sacrificed on the altar of

Table 7.1. *Munitions stocks at the outbreak of war, July 1914*

	Mobilization Plan (1912)	Stocks held[1] (July 1914)	Percentage surplus/shortfall
Rifles (mill.)	4.559[2]	4.652[2]	103
Revolvers	436,000	424,000	97
Machine guns	4,990	4,152	83
Cartridges (mill.)	2,745	2,655	97
3-inch field guns	6,261	6,265	100
3-inch shell (mill.)	6.261	6.433	103
3-inch horse artillery	493	407	86
3-inch mountain artillery	481	440	91
4.2-inch howitzers	84	88	105
4.2-inch shell	91,200	22,344	25
4.8-inch howitzers	586	534	91[3]
4.8-inch shell	512,000	449,477	88
6-inch guns	180	173	96
6-inch shell	164,000	99,910	61

Note: [1] including reserves
[2] 3-line Mosin rifle and 4.2 line Berdan
[3] front-line stocks (512 pieces) corresponded to 1912 plan
Source: A. A. Manikovskii, *Boevoe snabzhenie russkoi armii v mirovuiu voinu*, 2nd edn, Moscow 1930, vol. 2, pp. 120, 147, 152–3, 172, 286–7, 307, 377–9, 398.

fortress modernization. None the less, by the standards of the Russo-Japanese War, and in view of the short campaign that everyone anticipated, the supply norms were adequate and did not cause any alarm in military circles. In addition, military experts believed that Russian stocks of rifles, artillery and shell made up in quality what they may have lacked in quantity.[13]

Faced with quantitative shortcomings, and notwithstanding the praise showered on the rifle and the artillery piece, the Russian army counted on the substitution of manpower for material, or labour for capital. The French did the same: both armies went to war with around 200 soldiers per gun, a far more generous ratio than Germany and Austria, whose armies had one gun for every 135 soldiers (see table 7.2).

Military preparedness was not confined to the supply of hardware. The provisioning of large contingents of troops had caused enormous problems in the past. To what extent had they been overcome by 1914? Substantial improvements were made in the provision of basic goods to the army. Reserve supplies of linen, footwear and greatcoats fell

Table 7.2. *Comparative military strength of the European powers, 1914*

	Total army (millions)	Army corps	Infantry divisions	Cavalry divisions	Artillery batteries	Artillery pieces
Russia	1.42	37	122.5	28	c.792	c.6,720
France	0.85	21	86	10	1,054	4,248
Britain	0.38	–	6	1	84	492
Germany	0.81	25	102	11	1,045	6,004
Austria-Hungary	0.42	16	55.5	11	569	3,090
Romania	n.a.	5	20	2	192	768

Source: A. M. Zaionchkovskii, *Podgotovka Rossii k imperialisticheskoi voine: ocherki voennoi podgotovki i pervonachal'nykh planov*, Moscow, 1926, p. 101; Russian army strength from L. G. Beskrovnyi, *Armiia i flot v nachale XX veka*, Moscow, 1986, p. 15; other data from Q. Wright, *A Study of War*, Chicago, 1941, pp. 670–1.

only marginally short of estimated requirements. However, the short-fall of more than 10 per cent in stocks of uniforms ought to have given cause for concern (see table 7.3).

Whether Russian manufacturing industry could cope with a sudden increase in military demand for uniforms, footwear and similar goods remained to be seen. The recruitment of wave upon wave of reservists and new conscripts after 1914 meant that factories and workshops were expected to provide such items by the million. But in this respect, as in other branches of army supply, military planners gave no thought to the question of industrial mobilization.

Naval rearmament and naval strategy

The military objectives behind Russian naval rearmament were difficult to fathom, as Durnovo acknowledged in 1914. He regarded Russia as a continental, rather than a maritime power. Silent on the question of the Baltic and Black Sea fleets, Durnovo explicitly attacked the maintenance of a fleet in the Far East. But his antipathy placed him at odds with the Tsar, who yielded nothing to the German Emperor in his enthusiasm for a strong fleet, and who found plenty of adherents for this doctrine, who wielded greater influence than Durnovo. The Navy Minister, Admiral Grigorovich spoke grandly, if vaguely, of a 'partnership' between the three navies of the Triple Entente. But the lack of substance in his vision could hardly be

Table 7.3. *Stocks of military matériel, 1914*

	Required reserve (millions)	Stocks (millions)	Percentage shortfall
Uniforms	2.403	2.132	88.7
Greatcoats	2.402	2.259	94.1
Linen sheet (pairs)	2.402	2.311	96.3
Footwear (pairs)	2.582	2.467	95.5

Source: derived from Beskrovnyi, *Armiia i flot*, 1986, p. 158.

concealed. Might an expanded Russian fleet be justified as a 'deterrent', along the lines of the Tirpitz plan for a greatly enlarged German battleship fleet? It is scarcely conceivable that such considerations seriously entered the minds of Russian naval strategists. German preparations were a response to British naval supremacy, an attempt to ensure that Britain could ultimately never threaten Germany's global interests. Russian plans bore no direct relationship to those of Germany or Britain.[14]

On the other hand, the expansion of the Russian navy did not entirely lack an economic rationale. This view gained greater currency during the blockade of the Straits in 1912. Newspaper articles drew attention to the potential damage to Russia's grain trade, threatening the balance of payments. Certainly, Russia depended very heavily on a maritime export trade: in 1909–13, 73 per cent of all exports were despatched by sea, including 43 per cent (by value) through the Dardanelles. In crude terms, the Russian navy could protect the export trade. But only 46 per cent of imports arrived by sea (mostly at the Baltic ports); and the fleet was irrelevant to the growing overland trade across central Europe. From a different economic viewpoint, Russia would have done better to invest heavily in a merchant fleet, reducing its liabilities to foreign shipping and insurance companies.[15]

Even if one conceded the dubious point that the Russian fleet possessed an economic rationale, the tasks that it confronted were enormous. Germany, much more dependent on maritime trade than Russia, had to contend with one potential adversary, in the shape of the British navy. Russia would encounter both German and Ottoman naval forces. To secure the grain trade, Russia would have to match any increase in the naval strength of its chief rival for supremacy of the Black Sea.

But if earlier budgetary data (handwritten margin note)

In struggling to finance the modernization of three fleets – no one in authority was prepared to abandon the Far Eastern fleet completely – Russia surely attempted too much. Resources were thinly spread, in an attempt to compete with Germany, Turkey and Japan. Funds had been released for the strengthening of the Baltic fleet, but this was not enough for Grigorovich and Sazonov, responsible respectively for the navy and foreign affairs, who wanted a strong naval presence in the Black Sea. Norman Stone has written that Russia ended up with two 'half-navies'. Although his verdict underestimates the capability of the Baltic fleet, exaggerates the significance of the Black Sea fleet and overlooks the (admittedly paltry) Pacific fleet, nevertheless there is a substantial element of truth in the charge that the Russian navy was confronted with too many strategic responsibilities and could not shoulder them all simultaneously.[16]

A German threat to Russian foreign trade could not realistically be prevented by a large Russian fleet, whose mobility and capacity for action could be (and was) curtailed at a stroke. The outbreak of war made nonsense of these confused and ambitious plans, because the navy was immobilized by the German blockade of the Baltic and the closure of the Dardanelles. The closure of the Baltic deprived Russia of an outlet that accounted for around one-third of its foreign trade. Meanwhile, the remaining Russian fleet, trapped in the Black Sea, had to confine itself to the intermittent and militarily dubious harassment of Turkish maritime trade.[17]

What of the condition in which the Russian navy found itself in the summer of 1914? Had Durnovo turned his attention to the navy, he would have been obliged to acknowledge that rapid advances had been made since Tsushima. Partly, these were a function of the immense resources devoted to the acquisition of modern military vessels. In 1908, around one-third of the naval budget was earmarked for new vessels; five years later the proportion had risen to well over half. The Russian fleet had been strengthened by the measures taken in 1907 and 1912. Plans were afoot to create a navy with dreadnoughts, which would be accompanied by older battleships and an appropriate complement of cruisers and torpedo boat destroyers. The 'small ship-building programme' was due to be completed in 1914, although delays meant that the navy did not reach full strength until after the outbreak of war.[18]

Construction of new vessels does not tell the whole story. The Russian navy also made more effective use of the ships it had, because of the efforts that had been made to recruit and train personnel. In

Table 7.4. *The Russian fleet, 1909–1917*

	Battleships		Armoured cruisers		Light cruisers		Destroyers		Submarines	
	a	b	a	b	a	b	a	b	a	b
1909	12	139	6	66	7	46	82	35	30	–
1914	8	110	6	66	8	50	120	43	32	–
1917	15	275	10	195	16	100	150	90	26	–

a: number of vessels
b: 000 displacement tons
Source: Rossiia v mirovoi voine, Moscow, 1925, p. 95.

1908, only half of all Russian military vessels were prepared for naval action. The rest were under repair or, more commonly, in use as training vessels. A substantial number of ships were required to train ratings, since their low level of literacy and skill required them to undergo lengthy periods of instruction. The situation improved by 1914, because additional resources were invested in education and on-shore training, for instance in cadet schools. This meant that the new vessels could be put to sea without delay.[19]

Problems remained, of course: Russia obtained relatively less per ruble of expenditure than did its allies and adversaries, for the reasons offered earlier. In addition, delays in the completion of ship construction, the result of a poorly thought-out procurement policy, as well as a shortage of skilled craftsmen and engineers, allowed competitors to steal a march on Russia. This was an inevitable consequence of the decision to rely upon domestic sources of supply.

Whatever the tangible improvements made to the size and capabilities of the Russian navy since the debacle at Tsushima, the tsarist fleet failed to capture the imagination of 'census society'. As if to confirm the gulf between themselves and the Tsar's entourage, many educated Russians did not hold the navy dear. There was nothing of the widespread academic and mass trumpeting of the virtues of naval strength, such as characterized late imperial Germany. The Russian naval union, important though it was in keeping alive the cause of naval rearmament, paled into insignificance beside the German Flottenverein, with its membership of half a million and more. Russia also lacked the popular maritime tradition upon which British naval strategists could count in support of the dreadnought programme. Russian businessmen supported the claims of the navy, and the Tsar's personal preference for an imperial battleship fleet won the day. But popular blessing for the navy was conspicuous by its absence. Russian peasants had other things on their mind than battleships and submarines. The Russian nobility, many of them fiercely anti-industrial, could hardly be counted upon to press the claims of a navy whose construction filled the pockets of the business class. The professional intelligentsia who in Germany gave Admiral Tirpitz their vocal support opposed tsarism at almost every turn. Russia's 'half-navies', therefore, occupied a disembodied position in society. This massive public indifference was a poor return for the millions of rubles that poured into Russian shipyards, boosting total industrial output and employment.[20]

Railways and military communications

The conscription of hundreds of thousands of men in wartime, together with munitions, equipment and horses depended critically upon the performance of the railway network. All sides believed that the outcome of the war hinged upon the speed at which men and material could be mobilized: hence the importance attached to the military timetables. Discussions between Russian and French military planners were dominated by these issues. But, despite the efforts made to build new lines and to add extra track to existing lines, some contemporary observers remained unimpressed. The influential German historian Theodor Schiemann discounted additions to the railway network, pointing out that Russia lacked the capacity to deal with the task of mobilization: 'the network of strategic railways is inadequate. The railways possess a rolling stock sufficient, perhaps, for normal traffic, but not commensurate with the colossal demands which will be made upon them in the event of a European war'.[21] How much truth was there in these charges, which would surface again during the First World War?

Between 1908 and 1914, a feverish programme of military construction got under way. The construction of a link between Bologoe (on the St Petersburg to Moscow line) and Siedlice (east of Warsaw) signalled Russian intentions to improve the speed and carrying capacity of strategically important lines. The German General Staff conceded that this one line, completed in 1908, would reduce by three days the time taken to mobilize Russian troops on the German frontier. Further additions in Russian Poland took place during 1910. This investment in strategic lines represented a dramatic improvement over the situation that existed ten years earlier. Now it was the turn of the Austrian military planners to express alarm, over the extension of lines that linked the north-west with the south-west, such as the links between Lgov (west of Kursk) and Mitau (close to Riga), between Orel and Narva, and the line connecting the Kuban with the north Caucasus. By the spring of 1914, the Austrian General Staff pointed out that Russia could now mobilize the same number of troops on the Austrian frontier as its adversary, but take only twenty days, eleven fewer than the Dual Monarchy. Finally, the German General Staff noted in the summer of 1914 that the completion of railway construction in progress would reduce the time for full mobilization to eighteen days, whereas at present only two-thirds of the troops would be mobilized within that time.[22]

Despite these efforts, the railway network in European Russia was thinly spread. On the eve of the war, Russia had just over one kilometre of track per square kilometre, whereas France and Germany had ten and twelve times as much respectively, and even Austria-Hungary had seven times more track. One contemporary estimate suggested that Russia needed to build at least 8,000km of track each year, in order to improve the density and carrying capacity of the network; the rate of construction actually achieved between 1908 and 1913 barely amounted to one-tenth of the desired rate. Three-quarters of the entire network consisted of single-track lines, the most notorious example being the trans-Siberian railway: elsewhere in Europe between two-fifths and three-fifths of the network comprised single-track. In addition, insufficient investment in locomotives and wagons during the prewar decade inevitably subjected the existing rolling-stock to greater wear and tear. The shortfall of locomotives and wagons was put at 2,000 and 80,000 respectively, corroboration enough of Schiemann's dismissive comments.[23]

The technological level of Russian railway transport also left much to be desired. Most operations, such as switching track and changing signals, were performed manually and unsystematically. Locomotives and wagons did not conform to any common standard. The majority of wagons lacked a roof. Locomotives were fuelled in a haphazard, laborious and dangerous fashion. Expert opinion commented on the lack of attention given to the maintenance of rolling-stock. Couplings frequently broke under the strain imposed on them by more powerful locomotives.[24]

Having pinpointed these deficiencies, it needs to be asked whether additional railway construction and investment in rolling-stock would have enhanced Russia's security. There are limits to the effectiveness of any railway system. The enemy can sever communications, by blowing up track and bridges. Even if railways remain intact, they can easily become clogged with traffic, no matter how many lines are available. Extra rolling stock requires additional fuel. Would the new locomotives have been cared for any better than the existing stock? Russia might have benefited from more track and more stock, but equally these increased supplies might have overloaded a poorly managed system. What counted at the moment of mobilization and during the heat of a campaign, particularly when it was accompanied by an incessant flow of refugees and prisoners, was that the system should be well administered. Unfortunately, the complex demands imposed by war exposed the deficient administration of the Russian railway network. Military authorities vied with each other and with civilian agencies for control over lines at the front. Finally, no amount of investment in railway construction could disguise the difficulties that all belligerents encountered in wartime, namely how to move large numbers of men and equipment from the railhead to the field of battle.[25]

In this respect, Russia was woefully unprepared. The General Staff decided in 1910 to improve the stocks of motorized vehicles, but its proposals were held up by the War Ministry. In July 1914, the Russian army had at its disposal no more than 710 motorized vehicles, including only 418 lorries. The extent of underinvestment in motorized transport is implied in wartime levels of consumption: between July 1914 and June 1916, the army took delivery of 30,000 vehicles, not including motor bikes. Here, more than in most spheres of military supply, Russia lagged behind the other European belligerents. Of Russian aviation, there is not much to be said. In 1909, the War Ministry purchased four airplanes, but on the eve of the war the aviation budget did not exceed 3 million rubles. In 1912, the General Staff created a department of military aviation, but procurement policy was haphazard and caused disagreements between the General Staff and the purchasing agencies. Russia boasted a mere handful of trained pilots. The motley stock of planes at their disposal displayed a frustrating plethora of Russian frames and imported engines.[26]

Other forms of military communication, no less important in modern warfare, also attracted little attention at the time. The war against Japan had taught the Russian army the value of telegraph and telephone communication in the field. But, on the eve of the First World War, radio communication in the Russian army was in its infancy (the German army suffered from a similar defect). The total length of telegraph lines increased from 320,000km in 1894 to 800,000km in 1913, but this represented a relatively thin coverage of the imperial land mass. According to plans drawn up in 1912, each army corps was to be supplied with 20 telegraph apparatus, 193 field telephones and 350km of cable. These norms were reportedly met, although doubts remained about the ability of Russian officers to make proper use of the facilities at their disposal. The position in the rear gave even more cause for concern, because stocks of equipment fell far short of what was needed. Army depots disposed of 5,854 telephones, when there should have been twice as many, and 500 field telegraphs, when there should have been 700. The war quickly revealed the inadequacy of these preparations and called forth a desperate bid to supply far greater quantities. Within eighteen months of the outbreak of hostilities, the army had ordered nearly 4,000 telegraphs and 120,000 telephones, ten times as many as it had at its disposal in 1914. By the end of 1916 the army called for 300,000 telephones. Here, as in other branches of military supply, the war wreaked havoc with peacetime estimates of demand and posed yet another difficult challenge to domestic industry.[27]

Defence industry and industrial capacity

Durnovo buttressed his argument about the dangers inherent in armed conflict between Russia and Germany, by pinpointing inadequacies in Russia's defence industry. He maintained that the armaments industry had failed to supply the armed forces with adequate stocks of military matériel. There is little point in discussing this accusation further: it was in the interests of suppliers to process with all possible speed the orders they received from the procurement authorities. If supplies were inadequate, this reflected not so much the backwardness of Russian industry, but rather the government's purchasing policy, which was directly related to the norms fixed by the military. More telling was Durnovo's complaint that, given the 'low productivity of our factories', armaments factories could not supply military matériel in sufficient quantity to compensate for the likely closure of Russia's borders by her enemies. This charge would be echoed after 1917, by historians who sought an explanation for military shortcomings during the war.[28]

However, such blanket condemnation of the Russian defence industry is undermined by the evidence presented earlier, indicating that rearmament had begun to create a more modern defence industry. The reactionary Durnovo could hardly be expected to applaud the growing involvement of the private sector in the defence industry, still less to welcome the participation of French and British capital in Russian industry. But, in so far as his analysis overlooked evidence of new investment in manufacturing industry and the restructuring of defence enterprise, Durnovo failed to see how much had changed since the turn of the century.

Military planners acknowledged that defence industry had made rapid strides, but some of them were convinced that the government needed to exercise closer control over enterprises in this sector. Lukomskii, the author of an article in the Admiralty's staff journal, took this argument a great deal further, proposing that the government should intervene in all branches of industry that related to national defence. The government, he argued, had a duty to secure supplies of basic materials, such as metals, coal and grain, by taking control over production and distribution. Private owners would be compensated by the state for the loss of their assets. The inevitable addition to the national debt was a small price to pay for enhanced security: 'the loan would be granted for a definite purpose, not merely for cosmetic reasons'. The expropriation of up to three-quarters (sic) of a given sector would allow the government to determine prices, ensuring both price stability and a welcome increase in government revenue. Other consumers would surely applaud this initiative. More extensive state control of the armaments industry would facilitate the 'rational' organization of work at all levels, from the central administration down to the factory shop. At each stage of the planning process, technical questions and financial management would be kept separate. Work routines on the shopfloor could be closely monitored, in order to improve labour productivity. The government could begin by tackling the management of the arsenals currently in state hands, whose competitive position left much to be desired.[29]

Lukomskii thus offered a technocratic solution to the problem of industrial unpreparedness, although he did not venture to discuss how the new arrangements, if implemented, would be greeted by businessmen and workers. He offered a taste of things to come during the war, which provided officials in the War Ministry with the opportunity to extend state control over defence industry. His vision of public control over the production and distribution of raw materials enjoyed a still wider appeal in wartime, especially by the beginning of

1917, when the commercial press was filled with articles concerning 'compulsory syndicalization.'[30]

It was all very well to argue in favour of increased state control of industry, but this did not provide a solution to the immediate problems that would likely confront Russian manufacturing industry in the event of war. To the extent that some branches of industry depended heavily upon imports, Durnovo was correct to identify Russian vulnerability to any disruption to normal trade flows. Many sectors relied on imports of raw materials, machine parts and finished goods. Notwithstanding the production of wool and cotton in central Asia, Russia imported around two-fifths of cotton fibre and one-third of wool fibre. Dependence upon imports figured to a still greater extent where leather, tanning materials and dyestuffs were concerned, all of them products crucial to the war effort. Some basic industrial chemicals were supplied by domestic industry, but soda came from Germany and pyrites from Portugal and Norway. All but 2 per cent of Russian demand for lead was met by imports; zinc output, largely confined to Poland, accounted for only one-third of domestic consumption. Russia completely lacked domestic sources of supply of aluminium, nickel and tin. In the electrical engineering industry, Russia imported around 35 per cent of its needs, a proportion that was much higher in the case of high voltage plant, transformers, valves and incandescent lamps. Russia imported most of its textile machinery and steam engines. Finally, and most significant of all, all but 30 per cent of machine tools were imported by 1913.[31]

This catalogue of import dependence hardly betokened a capacity to survive a long war without profound disruption to industrial production. However, military planners neither analyzed the issue of potential resource shortages nor offered a strategy for promoting import substitution in wartime. Their assumptions about the nature and duration of continental warfare rendered them blissfully unaware of the problems that would befall industry.

Tsarist Russia's narrow industrial base was likely to cause a different kind of problem in the event of a prolonged war.[32] The relatively small number of domestic engineering firms could cope with a sudden increase in demand for high-explosive shell, but a simultaneous increase in demand for other munitions, or for the machine tools with which to manufacture munitions would tax those firms to the limit. When the 'shell shortage' burst forth during the winter of 1914, orders for munitions were hurriedly placed with leading engineering firms. This hardly made rational use of available capacity; lesser-ranking

Industrial evacuation

firms should have been encouraged to manufacture straightforward items, such as shell, leaving more experienced factories to handle contracts for rifles, machine-guns and machine tools. Instead, the government tolerated the diversion of highly-skilled workers and sophisticated equipment to shell production. The failure to implement a more rational strategy in wartime bedevilled armament supply. It typified more widespread failures of decision-making in tsarist Russia; but it also reflected the limited options available within the industrial economy.[33]

Nevertheless, one should judge industrial capacity according to other criteria as well, not just against the yardstick of a war whose dreadful dimensions and demands could scarcely be glimpsed in 1914. Measured against its size and technological level in 1900 or 1908, Russian industry had made enormous strides. The estimated value of the industrial capital stock increased from 2,200 million rubles in 1900 to just under 2,900 million rubles in 1908. By 1913, it stood at over 4,100 million rubles. The bare figures do no more than hint at the quantity and quality of new equipment placed at the disposal of Russian workers.[34]

Many of these workers, however, were vulnerable to the demands of the recruiting office in 1914. Some firms lost up to one-fifth of their labour force at the outbreak of war, and had to take energetic and time-consuming steps in order to replace them or persuade the army that their skills were better put to use in the factory than at the front. No less serious a problem arose from the location of Russian industry. A rough calculation suggests that Russia forfeited around one-fifth of available industrial capital when German and Austrian troops occupied its territory. Textile factories and ironworks in Russian Poland were abandoned to the enemy with alarming suddenness. An unknown proportion of industrial capital did eventually find its way into the Russian heartland: for example, important engineering works along the Baltic littoral were evacuated. The beleaguered industrial economy could ill afford the time-lag involved in this complex effort of administration and transportation. But these difficulties were caused by the accidents of Russian geography and resource endowment, rather than by industrial backwardness. The more developed Soviet industrial economy faced similar problems in 1941.[35]

Financial preparedness and the Russian balance of payments

'The development of our armed forces will not create genuinely strong military potential if the state is financially and economically weak'. With this assertion, Kokovtsov expressed the prevailing orthodoxy within the Russian Ministry of Finances. Writing, as he did, in the immediate aftermath of the war against Japan, the argument in favour of restraint carried conviction. Nor did the rapid recovery of the Russian economy after 1908 predispose Kokovtsov to approve ambitious rearmament programmes: it made little sense to rearm, if the outcome was simply to bankrupt the state, or to accumulate debts that placed an intolerable burden on future generations. But the tsarist state did take on new commitments, including participation in the European arms race. What did these commitments imply for Russian finances on the eve of war in 1914?[36]

The first point to register is that the government budget grew rapidly between 1905 and 1914: recurrent revenue and expenditure increased by around 60 per cent in those years (table 3.1 and 3.5). By means of judicious adjustments to the published figures, Kokovtsov regularly presented the public at home and abroad with a balanced budget, thereby confirming the health of tsarist finances. He succeeded in maintaining public confidence, without making any fundamental changes to the structure of government taxation. Additional revenue derived from the increased level of economic activity. No controversy over death duties or income tax disturbed the surface of Russian budgetary politics, as it did elsewhere in Europe. Only a brief ripple of dissent emerged from time to time, as when Kokovtsov told his colleagues in cabinet that higher levels of defence spending required a sharp increase in the price of vodka.[37]

What of Russia's ability to meet its international financial obligations? Russia accumulated multiple commitments to foreign creditors. They included payments on state debt held abroad, as well as interest payments to holders of municipal debt and dividends payable to foreign investors. Russia maintained a large foreign debt, which in January 1914 stood at 3,971 million rubles. In addition, securities issued on behalf of the railway companies and held abroad totalled 975 million rubles. Municipal authorities had issued stock abroad to the tune of 380 million rubles. Finally, the foreign obligations of private corporations amounted to 2,602 million rubles. Russia traditionally secured a healthy surplus on the merchandise account, but it covered only part of these commitments and it depended heavily upon the size of the grain harvest, whose vulnerability was all too apparent to contemporary observers. To cover the remaining deficit on the balance of payments current account, Russia resorted to additional borrowing, whether from foreign governments or private investors. The government floated guaranteed railway loans on the foreign stock markets, with the encouragement of the French government and military advisers.[38]

Russia thus depended upon a continuous inflow of fresh infusions of foreign capital, and thus new additions to the state debt. Any expressions of disquiet about the financial prospects of imperial Russia were habitually silenced by pointing to the substantial reserves of foreign currency held by the Russian Treasury, amounting to 464 million rubles in January 1914. The Treasury used this reserve, in order to support the ruble exchange rate. Most of the reserve was held on deposit in France and Germany, with smaller amounts in Britain, Holland, Austria-Hungary and the USA. On the eve of the war, the government moved its holdings out of Germany, one instance in which defence considerations directly governed financial policy.[39]

The size and location of the gold and foreign currency reserves did not dispose all members of the ruling elite to adopt a sanguine attitude towards government finances. The most notorious dissident, unsurprisingly, was Count Witte. Attending a meeting of the Finance Committee in March 1914, he expressed the opinion that 'from a financial point of view, we are considerably less well prepared for war than we were ten years earlier'.[40] Underlying Witte's gloomy assessment was a belief that his successor had failed to adhere sufficiently closely to the conventions of the gold standard; financial preparedness, in Witte's view, meant sufficient gold reserves to support the convertibility of the ruble to the last note. Prewar developments did not inspire him with confidence. Noting that total Russian gold reserves had increased from 903 to 1,688 million rubles between 1906 and 1913, he pointed to a threefold increase in the volume of paper rubles in circulation, from 578 to 1,665 million rubles. Since part of Russia's gold reserve was held abroad, the ruble was not entirely covered by gold. Nor, in Witte's opinion, did this exhaust Russian vulnerability. In the likely event of a financial panic, the State Bank would have great difficulty in meeting the claims of depositors, because a large proportion of its assets took the form of long-term commitments. The state, he believed, would only be able to finance a war by resorting to the printing press, undoing the achievements of the past decade and a half.[41]

Expectations of a short conflict conditioned views of the likely impact of war on Russia's ability to meet outstanding commitments to its creditors, as well as its capacity to bear the direct costs associated with war. No one expected that any country could afford more than a brief rupture to international commerce. In these circumstances, Russia would continue, as before, to export grain and other primary products to help settle its obligations. Russia's reserves of gold and foreign currency would act as collateral for fresh loans.[42]

The government can be accused of possessing a narrow vision of financial preparedness. Evidently, official discussions were dominated by the size of the gold reserve. Other issues failed to get an airing in the corridors of power. No one asked how Russia would pay for large quantities of military supplies and raw materials, in the event of a protracted conflict, and whether existing creditors would be prepared to extend fresh credit on a significant scale. The stability of the ruble continued to be of paramount concern, being a hallmark of Russia's international economic status and attractiveness to potential investors. The traditional preoccupation with 'sound money' dictated the government's adherence to balanced budgets, which advertised Russian solvency to its numerous creditors. Few observers believed that war would inflict significant damage on the currency, let alone that it would bankrupt Russia. It was confidently expected that Russia would be able to pay for imports of raw materials or finished goods by exporting primary products. Bewitched by the concept of a short war, few contemporaries expected significant changes to the state budget: a few marginal changes to taxation represented the boundaries of official thinking. No one contemplated the necessity of calling upon the civilian population to subscribe to state debt on an unprecedented scale, as a means of mobilizing savings for the war effort.

The war confounded expectations that Russia would be relatively immune from financial disturbances. Russia abandoned the gold standard as soon as the war broke out, much faster than anyone expected. Taxes were forced higher; the government, in desperation, even contemplated an income tax. For the most part, Russia paid for the war by printing money at an unprecedented rate and by obtaining loans at home and abroad. Russia borrowed from Britain and especially France to finance its purchases overseas, as well as to try and maintain the purchasing power of the ruble. By borrowing in this manner, the tsarist government spent much less on the war, relative to its normal peacetime expenditure, than most other belligerents, with the exception of Austria-Hungary.[43]   *Hardach 1977, p. 153*

Burden sharing and the Franco-Russian alliance

The Franco-Russian alliance brought together two of Europe's largest economies: Russia, whose national income in 1913 amounted to 20 billion rubles, and France, with a national income of just under 12

314   **Rearmament and industrial ambition**

billion rubles. Confronting these countries were Germany and Austria-Hungary, with a combined national income equivalent to 34 billion rubles, making the two continental blocs evenly matched. The partners to the Franco-Russian alliance differed, not only in the size of their respective economies, but also in their level of economic development. Here, the roles were reversed. In terms of national income per head of population, France was more than twice as rich as Russia (and Germany more than three times as rich). France produced 1.95 tons of coal per head of population, Russia a mere 0.21 tons (compare Germany, with 4.3 tons). France produced 120 kg of crude steel per head, whereas Russia could manage only 29 kg (Germany manufactured 270 kg per head). The alliance not only joined together two unevenly matched economies; it also represented a mix of two quite different political and social systems, autocratic Russia and republican France, united by the common concern for the ambitions of imperial Germany.[44]

The Franco-Russian alliance was first and foremost a military alliance. Did the relative poverty of tsarist Russia and its reliance on French finance turn Russia into the junior, or dependent partner? Certainly, the alliance appeared to offer more to France than to Russia. It afforded France the opportunity to share with Russia the costs of challenging German supremacy in Europe and of one day making Germany pay for the humiliation inflicted on France in 1871. In the decade prior to the outbreak of war in 1914, the military agreement was refined. Before 1912, the military agreement between France and Russia provided for regular meetings of general staff officers. These occasions seem to have been largely confined to mutual attendance at military manoeuvres. During 1912, ceremonial encounters gave way to more substantive meetings. French politicians and military leaders – in the persons of Prime Minister Raymond Poincaré and the Chief of General Staff Joseph Joffre – mounted a concerted effort to convert their Russian counterparts to a French view of defence preparations. In particular, the manifest deficiencies (as it seemed) of the Russian railway network obsessed French military planners, and eventually impelled the French government to approve the release of funds dedicated to the construction of new lines on the Polish border.[45]

The crux of the matter concerned the Russian timetable for mobilization. The original Russian mobilization plan provided for troops to be deployed well inside Russian territory: this plan appalled the French general staff, who were concerned that this disposition would hamper a speedy and direct assault on Germany. At the annual conference of the joint general staffs in 1913, Joffre and his colleagues successfully insisted that Russia deploy its troops in a large concentration around Warsaw, much further west than the 1912 plan had called for, in order to permit a more concerted Russian attack on Berlin. In the event, Russia sent 29-and-a-half divisions against Germany and 46-and-a-half against Austria-Hungary.[46]

One reading of the discussions between Joffre and Zhilinskii, his Russian counterpart, is that they revealed the wholesale subordination of Russia to France: in his memoirs, Sukhomlinov describes the military agreement as 'a gamble with Russian cannon fodder'. This conclusion is unjustified, in as much as prewar preparations corresponded to important strands in Russian military thinking, no less than to French preferences. In 1908, General Alekseev had identified shortcomings in the railway network, which hampered attempts to concentrate Russian troops quickly and effectively along the border with Germany, Austria and Romania, whose forces threatened to overwhelm their opponents. Its potential enemies had nearly three times as many lines as Russia and could handle 530 trains daily, compared to a mere 211 trains on the Russian side. The prewar negotiations between Russia and France simply reflected a traditional preoccupation amongst many Russian military planners with the defence of the western borders. The Russian military, for example, not the French, planned a new line connecting Riazan and Warsaw. In improving the potential access of Russian troops through Polish territory, as well as regenerating the old fortresses along the imperial frontiers, French financial assistance satisfied Russian strategists no less than Joffre.[47]

The final version of the military convention, which took effect in September 1913, provided for both countries to mobilize immediately and without consultation, should Germany itself mobilize; in the event that either Italy or Austria mobilized, France and Russia agreed that prior consultations would have to take place before any response was made. The agreement satisfied the French preoccupation with the need to threaten Germany with a war on two fronts. Russia agreed to maintain fortifications and a large army close to the Polish border.[48]

From a French viewpoint, the alternative strategy would have been to strengthen the French army, but the slow rate of growth of population rendered this virtually impossible, at least until the eve of the First World War. Far better to draw instead on the apparently 'inexhaustible' reserves of Russian manpower to threaten Germany on its eastern frontier. Nor did the advantages to France of the alliance stop there. French rentiers not only received a regular, fixed return on their investments in Russian government bonds; they also avoided the increases in taxation that would otherwise have been necessary to support a larger French army. No doubt this helped to reconcile French investors to the tsarist regime, whose record on human rights would otherwise hardly have predisposed them to lend it their support.[49]

In August 1913, the French approved loans for the construction of more than 5,000km of new track and 3,050km of complementary lines, as well as for improving the capacity of existing lines. Particular attention was given to doubling the lines connecting Kiev with Poland and with the south-east, a programme that was scheduled to begin in 1914 and to be completed by 1918. The loan for strategic lines alone amounted to between 750 and 900 million rubles, and was granted on the understanding, not only that Russia would build these strategic lines, but also that the size of the Russian army would be increased.[50]

Some members of the Duma castigated as 'shameful' the ill-disguised pressure exerted by the French, but this view is difficult to sustain, particularly in the light of French failure to extract an undertaking that Russia would purchase military equipment exclusively from France. Plans were already afoot to increase the size of the Russian army by around 365,000 men. Where criticism can be directed is at the military planners of both countries for dwelling so heavily on the movement of troops to the frontier, whilst overlooking the need for investment to improve the carrying capacity of lines to Archangel and Vladivostok, the two ports which would replace the Black Sea and Baltic ports in the event of war. There is no better illustration of the military fixation with 'war by timetable'.[51]

The extent and significance of what would nowadays be termed burden-sharing was not always appreciated by contemporaries. Durnovo overlooked the extent to which Russia collaborated with France, in order to maximize the combined effectiveness of their troops. As someone whose sympathies lay with Berlin, rather than Paris, this was hardly surprising. Collaboration between the partners in the Triple Entente, particularly between France and Russia, undoubtedly featured in the pre-1914 defence effort. Nor should it be assumed that 'economic backwardness' condemned Russia to play the role of the subordinate. As the negotiations in 1913–14 over the railway loan demonstrated, both parties depended on one another in order to enhance their respective visions of national security.[52]

That these visions were restricted does not alter the point that the burden was shared. The Franco-Russian alliance distributed the

[handwritten marginalia: "Not clear from plates" and other annotations]

burden of defence equally between the two partners, provided one looks at more than one measure of the burden. In terms of the share of national income committed to defence, Russia contributed more heavily than France (see table 3.5); with its higher level of development, France might have made a bigger contribution. On the other hand, France maintained a larger proportion of its population in uniform. In 1914, the French army represented 0.95 per cent of total population, whereas no more than 0.76 per cent of the Russian population served in the army. Whatever the tensions that surfaced from time to time, neither France nor Russia can be accused of having a free ride in the alliance.[53]

Food production and food supply

In his analysis of the dangers that faced Russia on the eve of war Durnovo said nothing about food supply, presumably because he shared the common perception that, whatever other difficulties it faced, Russia would not be thwarted by a shortage of food. The risk of wartime starvation was much higher in island Britain (few contemporaries publicly voiced any concern about the German food balance). Russia, with its vast steppe, seemed immune from the threat to maritime trade. Indeed, it was thought that Russia alone stood to benefit from the disruption to trade, in so far as the collapse of grain exports in wartime would yield between 10 to 15 per cent of the gross cereal harvest for domestic consumption. The prewar behaviour of Russian food production did not cause strategists any anxiety, and recent recalculations of the volume and value of grain production suggest that they were right not to be alarmed at trends in this component of total agricultural output. Net grain output, for example, more than kept pace with the rate of growth of population; the per capita value of grain production increased by 23 per cent between 1904/8 and 1909/13.[54]

This benign picture, however, concealed some serious weaknesses. Livestock remained a weak element of the aggregate agricultural sector. The growth in grain output fails to reveal significant shifts in regional production patterns that took place during the early twentieth century. In the central industrial region and the north-west, food producers had converted their fields from cereal to technical crops, such as flax. This was not in itself a negative development: on the contrary, it suggested the kind of regional specialization associated with economic progress. Yet these changes in regional production patterns entailed the uninterrupted transport of grain from the central black-earth region and the southern steppe to the main consuming regions of the country. So long as this supply could be guaranteed, the balance of agricultural production was fairly stable. But a major shock, such as war, particularly when accompanied by pronounced shifts in population and disruption to transport, could easily upset this delicate balance. Here was the chief danger in the prewar food economy.[55]

Those who concerned themselves with military preparedness before 1914 paid no attention to such overarching considerations, being more preoccupied with the details of food procurement. Under Witte, the Ministry of Finances had taken the lead in procuring grain on behalf of the armed forces, largely as a means of intervening in the domestic grain market, in order to stabilize prices. After 1905, with the blessing of Kokovtsov, the army increasingly assumed responsibility for its own grain procurements, acquiring grain directly from producers or from district and provincial zemstvo boards, thereby cutting out the Ministry of Finances. Unfortunately, the new arrangements proved extremely costly for the Ministry of War. During the Witte era, the government had paid an additional 1.5 million rubles each year for grain, representing the difference between the prevailing market price and the fixed price on which the estimates were based. Between 1903 and 1906, when it assumed responsibility for grain procurement, the Ministry of War spent an extra 8.5 million rubles, the difference between the (falling) market price and the procurement price. Subsequently, as grain prices rose, this differential narrowed. By 1912, the army's own personnel had become less closely involved in procurements, ceding this task to the staff of the zemstvos and the stock exchange committees. The evidence points once more to the growing professionalization of the Russian army, in this instance allowing civilian agencies to assume responsibility for grain procurement, leaving military personnel to concentrate on matters pertaining more strictly to military provision.[56]

When war came, it demonstrated Russia's ability to feed its soldiers well, many of them enjoying a better diet than they had done during peacetime. This reflected the priority given to the maintenance of military consumption. Meanwhile, the supply of foodstuffs to the civilian population broke down completely by the winter of 1916. This was not primarily a consequence of declining grain output. Aggregate grain production held up well during the first two years of war, notwithstanding the loss of able-bodied men to the army and the decline in the supply of capital equipment to the agricultural sector.

Peasants maintained production by utilizing the remaining family labour more intensively. Only in 1916 and 1917 did grain production fall significantly, and even then the overall grain balance was favourable. But the regional patterns of production and consumption were thrown into chaos, not least by the wartime mobilization and evacuation of people and equipment, which disrupted traffic flows. In addition, peasants demonstrated a marked reluctance to market additional quantities of grain, because they could maintain and even increase the prewar level of their purchasing power, by marketing normal quantities of grain at higher prices, by forfeiting their purchase of vodka (now the subject of prohibition) and by drawing upon transfer payments. With abundant cash in hand, peasants tended to increase household consumption of grain (this included feed for livestock), rather than to market the surplus quantities. Finally, by 1916–17 the lack of consumer goods and the decline in the value of the ruble constituted powerful disincentives to sell grain. This outcome revealed the extent of military hubris. The war effort demanded not just the acquisition of modern military hardware, but investment in food production, and appropriate policies to extract grain from the agricultural sector.[57]

Conclusion

What kind of security did Russian military expenditure purchase in 1914, compared to 1906? For several years after the Russo-Japanese War, Russian security remained at a desperately low ebb. A joint meeting of the army and navy chiefs of staff, held in April 1908, concluded that the defence of St Petersburg could not be guaranteed, given the lack of officers, military specialists and, above all, mines and mine-layers. The war against Japan had all but eliminated the reserves of military goods. Retrenchment severely curtailed the scope for replenishment and rearmament. In these circumstances, according to Deputy Minister of War Polivanov, 'in 1908 our army was incapable of fighting [*byla neboesposobna*]'. This depressing view was echoed by Rödiger, the outgoing Minister of War, by Alekseev, attached to the General Staff, and by Palitsyn, the Chief of Staff, who reported that 'the most important branch of state affairs – the defence of the realm – is far from corresponding to the international situation of Russia and its inherent power'.[58]

Nor did its allies and potential adversaries think any more highly of Russia's military strength in the years immediately following the war

against Japan. In part, this jaundiced view reflected the losses incurred
by the army and navy during 1904 and 1905. But it also reflected a poor
assessment of military morale, transport and supply. In addition,
informed military observers drew attention to the problems posed by
rural and urban unrest, which continued throughout 1906 and into
1907. The German General Staff reckoned in 1906 that Russia could
deploy no more than four-fifths of its available troops in any
engagement on the frontiers of the country, the others being required
for internal security duties.[59]

All observers agreed that Russian military potential improved out of
all recognition between 1905 and 1914. This did not stop Durnovo from
trying to impress upon the Tsar that a war in Europe would be a
foolish gamble. Some of Durnovo's observations, as we have seen,
rang true. Yet, it is difficult to avoid the conclusion that Durnovo
exaggerated Russian military weakness, in order to strengthen the case
for a rapprochement between Russia and Germany. A far more positive assessment was made by German military planners and foreign
office officials, who entertained no doubts about the military capacity
of their potential enemy. Moltke, the chief of the German General
Staff, noted in February 1914 that Russian military preparedness 'is
now much greater than ever before'; 'even level-headed politicians
(wrote the German Chancellor, Bethmann Hollweg, on the eve of the
war) are worried at the increases in Russian strength and the
imminence of Russian attack'. Russia possessed powerful armaments,
in addition to the large army.[60]

The perception of Russian military strength held by foreign
observers was all the more remarkable in view of the way in which the
resources were managed by the military establishment. Despite the
resource constraints they faced, Russia's military planners failed to
create a proper balance between the claims of different elements in the
armed forces. Instead, they tried indiscriminately to meet a welter of
competing strategic imperatives. In practice, this meant a desperate
attempt to maintain adequate troops in readiness for an offensive
against both Germany and Austria-Hungary, without ignoring the
defence of Russia's borders in the Far East and in central Asia. As if this
were not enough, the Tsar insisted that Russia be provided with a fleet
that had an offensive as well as a defensive capability. To manage
these competing and divergent claims for resources would have taxed
the most ingenious and astute political brain. Political guidance,
however, was a commodity in short supply in imperial Russia. A
balance between defence claimants had been sought by the Council for

State Defence, but this voice was silenced in 1909, and there emerged no effective personal or institutional counterweight to the Tsar, capable of pressing the claims of the army against those of the navy. The initiatives taken during 1913 and 1914, under the 'great army programme', did not compensate for a decade of relative neglect of heavy field artillery, communications equipment and training, particularly of reserve troops.[61]

Military planning during the last years of peace was conducted in close association with the French General Staff. Unfortunately, this collaboration yielded a joint adherence to an entirely inflexible plan for troop mobilization, epitomized by the adoption of the 1912 mobilization document. Military plans imposed a kind of tunnel vision on the Russian military, in which everything was subordinated to the task of concentrating troops in large numbers, not just on the border with Germany (as Joffre and Sukhomlinov intended), but also on the frontier with Austria-Hungary. This compromise plan was bad enough in itself. At the same time, all the broader questions – of contingency arrangements for evacuation, of railway capacity in the rear of the country, of supplies to the civilian population, of industrial mobilization – never entered the military field of vision. To be fair, Moltke and Bethmann Hollweg were no less blinkered than Zhilinskii and Goremykin. Generals and civilian officials alike concentrated on the size and equipment of the Russian army, to the exclusion of other aspects of the tsarist defence capability. They failed to spot that Russia was prepared to fight on paper, but was unable to conduct a prolonged and complex conflict.

Russia entered the war with its uniformed and civilian population unprepared for a long war. No one realistically expected the campaign to last beyond a few months, and those who did contemplate the unthinkable expressed sanguine views about Russia's capacity to survive. But, in the absence of a speedy military solution, Russian military and civilian society eventually unravelled. The constant emphasis in prewar military doctrine on the soldier's morale did not compensate for the thin veneer of patriotism, which concealed a much stronger seam of discontent. The army did not mask, but instead manifested all too clearly the tensions in Russian society, between the privileged and the dispossessed, between the 'patrician' and the 'plebeian', between Russian and non-Russian. The bulk of educated opinion supported a war in defence of slav liberties, but this support was not granted unconditionally. Russian liberals, for the most part professional people, soon demanded greater participation in the

But it did not
do more a fact

affairs of state, as the price for supporting a protracted campaign
against the Triple Alliance. This was one source of potential domestic
instability. Ordinary people had little interest in a war that undermined their living standards and deprived them of able-bodied
youths, in the cause of a war whose purpose may have been disclosed
but whose broader meaning could not easily be fathomed. Herein lay
another source of discontent. Unlike France, whose peasantry 'became
Frenchmen' between 1870 and 1914, and in the process acquired an
acute sense of the need for a military solution to their national grievances, militarism in that form never struck deep roots in Russian
society. Of all the belligerent powers in Europe, Russia was least
prepared psychologically for war.[62]

Conclusion

Historians of late imperial Russia must confront the degree to which the tsarist regime adapted to the consequences of rapid change at home and in the wider world. Economic historians of Russia need to focus on the extent of innovation in the economic system, as well as on the economic consequences of decisions about the allocation of resources. These issues have generated a substantial literature, and this book belongs firmly within a well-established historiographical tradition. The present study demonstrates that the tsarist government embarked on a major programme of reform and rearmament in the aftermath of war and revolution, in order to improve its defence capability, but that the regime proved less adept at addressing the consequences of these policy shifts. Rearmament saddled the old regime with economic and political problems which it was ill-equipped to handle. Imperial Russia had to deal simultaneously with the tasks of economic recovery, structural change and rearmament; the attempt to reconcile these tasks, in the midst of an international scramble for influence, exposed the fragile foundations upon which the entire edifice rested.

I

None the less, this book has shown that military and industrial objectives, far from being incompatible, could be reconciled. Rearmament brought recovery for Russia's beleaguered industrialists. Broadly speaking, it encouraged capital investment, generated increased levels of industrial employment and stimulated more modern forms of industrial organization. Profitability provided one criterion of recovery: profits improved dramatically between 1907 and 1914. But this is to adopt too narrow a focus. More important, bigger profits provided funds for reinvestment in new plant. Rearmament provided the back-

323

drop to a significant increase in the size and quality of the industrial capital stock. The associated investment in shipyards, industrial equipment and new manufacturing facilities gave a pronounced impetus to industrial recovery and to potential expansion in new markets.[1]

This implies that there were no alternatives to rearmament as the mainspring of industrial growth. In principle, Russian industry might have secured recovery without the need for a heavy commitment of government funds to rearmament. In 1907–8, Russian industry stood at the bottom of the trade cycle. Recovery would have come sooner or later, as industry moved out of the trough of the cycle. Rearmament offered industry a breathing-space. But what kind of recovery might otherwise have taken place? Likely as not, the government would have been involved, either through the supply of credit by the State Bank to the commercial banking system or, more directly, through state ownership of transport infrastructure.

Leading industrialists certainly hoped and expected as much. In May 1915, representatives of the Russian engineering industry urged the government to guarantee orders with firms for several years ahead. Heavy industry required a continued commitment by government to purchase capital goods. In these uncertain times, industrialists remained wedded to non-market transactions, as the best hope of continued prosperity. However, their pleas to government officials in the traditional manner showed also how little had changed in industrial politics.[2]

The question of alternative market opportunities was closely bound up with the creation of new products. What were the signs that Russian industry developed new products, other than armaments? Factories continued to turn out a broad range of manufactured goods; production runs in all product lines were short. The Russian market had not yet developed to the extent that entrepreneurs could risk specialization. Armaments joined the long list of products which Russian industry manufactured. Nor does investment in new capital equipment appear to have provided a base from which to launch an offensive to capture markets from foreign competitors; on the eve of the First World War, Russia continued to import large quantities of industrial equipment. The success of import substitution in armaments production was not matched in electrical engineering or in machine tools.

Russian entrepreneurs did not have a monopoly in armaments. Granted, the tsarist government all but renounced the purchase of armaments from foreign suppliers, both for balance of payments and

Hostility to private enterprise

for security considerations. But the government could turn to its own shipyards and armouries. To minimize this risk, Russian arms producers mounted an attack on the integrity of the state sector, complaining that it enjoyed an unfair competitive advantage, and that its administration and work practices were outmoded. Whatever the truth of these charges – which conveniently ignored the reforms in progress at state enterprises – the case for their closure could never succeed on purely economic grounds. The old regime had political, ideological and security reasons for promoting the survival of the state sector. Politically, government dockyards and armouries formed a counterweight to the emergent industrial elite. Ideologically, they demonstrated that the tsarist state could not be compromised by the power of capital. Strategically, their purpose was to provide the government with its first line of defence in any future production campaign in wartime.[3]

Russian industrialists, therefore, were forced to accept limitations on their economic strength, as well as strict subordination within the existing political system. The 1905 revolution was not a triumph for the industrial bourgeoisie, and the new parliament reflected a widespread public antipathy to private enterprise. The industrial pressure-groups that substituted for genuine political power did their best to mobilize Russian entrepreneurs in defence of their market share. Eventually, the private sector obtained a handsome slice of the rearmament cake, as a kind of compensation for political leverage. Mounting corporate strength provided comfort in straitened times, although it served to confirm, rather than to modify public hostility to industrial endeavour.

It may be objected that too much emphasis has been placed on the hostility of the tsarist government to private enterprise. After all, the imperial regime did not obstruct private investment in the iron and steel industry during the late nineteenth century. Even in armaments production, the state sanctioned orders to firms producing cartridges and military vessels. In addition, the Russian government put together a rescue package for private firms at the turn of the century. These measures hardly indicate outright opposition to private enterprise, and the perennial lack of government unity suggests that some departments of state did champion the cause of capitalism. Nevertheless, much of its practice was devoted to the regulation, if not the close supervision of management and workforce alike. Many government officials, even in the Ministry of Trade and Industry, hoped to control industrialists' behaviour, or to keep it within acceptable bounds. The Ministry of Finances regarded the development of private enterprise as a convenient source of revenue, not a policy to pursue as an end in itself. If Russia's industrialists continued to generate profits and to build new businesses, they did so in an atmosphere of official antagonism and public distaste.

The highly conditional toleration of the principle of private enterprise certainly betokened no weakening of the bonds of state enterprise. The government could not abandon its own arsenals and shipyards, because the stakes were too high. Wherever entrepreneurs turned, they confronted evidence of 'patrimonial' authority and patriarchal attitudes: in the favours showered on state enterprises, in the protection afforded workers in government employment, and in the fiscal system, which treated industry as a productive milch-cow. Nor did these attitudes and institutions change fundamentally after 1905. Having nearly succumbed to the forces of revolution and having been obliged to accept parliamentary constraints on its authority in such sensitive spheres as defence and budgetary matters, the imperial regime was unwilling to sacrifice still more of its traditional prerogatives. The support extended to state enterprise must be seen in this light.

Hostility to private enterprise went hand in hand with ignorance. The old regime never came to terms with the needs of a modern industrial economy. Its tariff policy offered little effective protection to the infant machine tool industry. The government had no coherent policy for improving industrialists' access to credit. Its tax policy did not encourage industrial investment. The government was unwilling to consult or consort with industrialists, showing no inclination to establish a regular forum in which business leaders could articulate their views. This communication gap was not peculiar to Russia: it is hard to find evidence across Europe of adequate institutional arrangements before 1914 for the exchange of views between government and business. But few European governments demonstrated the peculiar tsarist combination of ideological antipathy and administrative obstacles towards private enterprise.[4] (Owen)

One is justified, therefore, in attaching significance to the notion of an 'internal arms race'. The state sector was the guardian of an older tradition of paternalism, in which the state protected 'the people' who toiled on its behalf. To the extent that government employees laboured for the security of the tsar's state, this can even be thought of as a 'patrimonial' tradition, although the argument should not be pressed too far. None the less, it is not too fanciful to suggest that, by upholding the state sector, the government sought to defend the fiscal interests of the population; hence the rhetoric of 'the people's kopek' (*narodnaia kopeika*).[5]

II

Enormous efforts were expended in the defence of the Russian empire, but to what end? Asked to justify elaborate defence preparations, tsarist officials would have argued that their measures provided security against external aggression. However, this argument celebrated a vision of imperial grandeur that went down better in St Petersburg than in the borderlands of empire. Far from being regarded as a threatening intrusion, external aggression may have been welcomed by some of the restless ethnic groups which found themselves subject to tsarist domination. As the events of 1918 were to show, national 'independence movements' could forge fruitful links with Germany.[6]

Russian defence preparations assumed a no more benign character in the eyes of the majority of Russians. Educated society – in the words of Huckleberry Finn, 'the quality' – accepted rearmament as part of a package of responsibilities, whereby the greatest slav nation offered protection to other slav populations. By contrast, Russian workers and peasants (Huck's 'ornery' folk) saw things in a different light. Russian troops stood guard on the borders of the empire, but they were also accommodated in garrisons the length and breadth of the country, where they could be deployed to deal with internal unrest. That many soldiers and officers disliked the policing role they were asked to assume hardly made their function and behaviour any more palatable to the oppressed peasant and the striking worker.

Nicholas II set great store by naval rearmament. This was undoubtedly a gamble, because of the huge resources required. Russia was not alone in investing heavily in naval rearmament: the German naval programme staggered contemporaries, and justifiably so. But the decision to acquire a modern battleship fleet had different implications in Russia and in Germany. In Germany, naval expansion generated fears of additional taxation, including death duties. In Russia, the main implication was not fiscal – the government could borrow, and economic growth generated additional revenue – but administrative. Who would control the programme: would it be entrusted to the established men of influence, or to a new generation of professionally trained men, technocratic in outlook, men who wanted to 'get things done', rather than to observe the niceties of courtly ritual? Could it be left to the large state shipyards in St Petersburg; could the state afford to construct entirely new shipyards to handle the Black Sea pro- gramme? Naval rearmament became the sphere in which all the interlocking problems of imperial Russia came to the fore: finance, parliamentary politics, personnel recruitment and training, inter- national relations, technological change and entrepreneurial endeavour.

These were the overriding dilemmas of reform in late imperial Russia: whether the political system could cope with the consequences of rapid change in the economy, in society and in international rela- tions. This, it seems to me, is the relevance of the argument advanced a generation ago by less orthodox Soviet historians, namely that instabi- lity was a function of the struggle between different structures of production relations (non-capitalist and capitalist), rather than of the contradictions generated by capitalism. The rivalry between the state and private sectors brought into the open antagonisms within govern- ment, which lacked the mechanisms to handle them.[7]

Could tsarist Russia have done any better? From the perspective of 1905, the answer must surely be no, for so much had been achieved. With hindsight, however, one is bound to advocate not policies to generate faster economic growth, but a different allocation of resources. Less, certainly, on a fancy naval programme (shades of the 'Potemkin village'?) and on fortresses that would be abandoned at an early opportunity. More on transportation, including motorized trans- port; more on heavier artillery, to put the entrenched positions of the enemy under greater pressure. More on training, on the creation of more professional procurement officials, capable of responding to demands for munitions, food and other items. Unhappily for Russia, international events dictated that the armies of the Tsar would embark on war at least three years before the rearmament programmes were to reach fruition.

Ultimately, however, one must step sufficiently far back from the detailed pattern of rearmament to ask what purpose it served. Russia and Germany were economic partners, as well as economic rivals, a point that the arch-conservative Durnovo was perceptive enough to recognize. Should not Russian diplomacy have sought to reconcile the objectives of these two European giants? This is easy enough to advocate with hindsight. But, if Fritz Fischer is right, then Russia had everything to fear from German expansionism, and Russia's war plans were justified, as a means of protecting its interests in the Black Sea. Besides, Russia and Austria were rivals for the mastery of slav popu-

lations in south-eastern Europe: popular concern for fellow slavs in the
Balkans had a powerful resonance in St Petersburg. Germany would
not – and did not – abandon its Austrian partner. Seen in this light, the
Franco-Russian alliance made sense.[8]

Needless to say, pan-slavism had little resonance in the factories and
villages of the Russian empire. But the tsarist government showed
little understanding of the aims and aspirations of workers and
peasants. In other spheres, the regime acted as if it knew what workers
and peasants wanted ('police trade unions' in 1903; 'freedom' from the
land commune in 1906). Should one be surprised that the government
chose with equal presumption to act on their behalf in the sphere of
foreign and defence policy?

When war broke out, all social groups fell victim to the aspirations of
the regime. Workers and peasants were conscripted to serve at the
'frontier of hell and death'. The ensuing revolution spared neither
government ministers, the court nor Russian industrialists. The war,
with its sickening consequences for human beings, its appalling consumption of resources, its reliance on mass mobilization and new
industrial technology, its extension of government intervention and
the breakdown of international cooperation truly marked the beginning of the 'real, not the calendar century', and eventually exposed the
recklessness of the gamble undertaken by the imperial regime.[9]

Notes

Introduction

1 A. Gerschenkron, 'Problems and patterns of Russian economic development', in C. E. Black, ed., *The Transformation of Russian Society*, Cambridge, Mass., 1960, p. 71.

2 *Ibid.*, pp. 52–8; A. Gerschenkron, 'The early phases of industrialization in Russia: afterthoughts and counterthoughts', in W. W. Rostow, ed., *The Economics of Take-Off into Self-Sustained Growth*, London, 1963, pp. 151–69.

3 Gerschenkron, 'Problems and patterns', pp. 51–2. For the latest assessment of Gerschenkron's hypotheses, see R. Sylla and G. Toniolo, eds., *Patterns of European Industrialization: The Nineteenth Century*, London, 1991.

4 T. Shanin, *Russia as a 'Developing Society': Volume One, The Roots of Otherness*, London, 1985, pp. 126–9, 184, 202.

5 D. C. B. Lieven, *Russia's Rulers Under the Old Regime*, London, 1989, for the upper reaches of the tsarist bureaucracy. The 'peasant impoverishment' thesis was challenged by J. Y. Simms, 'The crisis in Russian agriculture at the end of the nineteenth century: a different view', *Slavic Review*, 36, 1977, pp. 377–98; the subject receives sophisticated treatment in S. G. Wheatcroft, 'Crises and the condition of the peasantry in late imperial Russia', in E. Kingston-Mann and T. Mixter, eds., *Peasant Economy, Culture and Politics of European Russia, 1800–1921*, Princeton, 1991, pp. 128–72. On the subject of foreign investment and its political significance, see V. I. Bovykin, 'O nekotorykh voprosakh izucheniia inostrannogo kapitala v Rossii', in A. L. Sidorov, ed., *Ob osobennostiakh imperializma v Rossii*, Moscow, 1963, pp. 250–313; for a non-Soviet perspective, consult Olga Crisp, *Studies in the Russian Economy before 1914*, London, 1976, and J. P. McKay, *Pioneers for Profit: Foreign Entrepreneurship and Russian Industrialization, 1885–1913*, Chicago, 1970.

6 D. Geyer, *Russian Imperialism: The Interaction of Foreign and Domestic Policy, 1860–1914*, Leamington Spa, 1987, p. 309.

7 G. Kennedy, *The Economics of Defence*, London, 1975, pp. 111–12.

8 By defence market is meant the sum total of goods and services to which military customers lay claim by means of outlays on capital items (such as weapons and buildings) and current requirements (such as food and uniforms).

9 These words belong to Kenneth Boulding, cited in G. Hardach, *The First World War, 1914–1918*, London, 1977, pp. 53–4.
10 E. Kehr, 'Munitions industry', *Encyclopedia of the Social Sciences*, 15 vols., New York, 1930–5, vol. 11, pp. 128–34; 'Class struggle and the armament industry', in E. Kehr, *Economic Interests, Militarism and Foreign Policy*, ed. G. A. Craig, Berkeley, 1977, pp. 50–75. See also W. H. McNeill, *The Pursuit of Power: Technology, Armed Force and Society since A.D. 1000*, Chicago, 1982, p. 277. Some support for Kehr's position may be found in V. Berghahn, *Germany and the Approach of War*, London, 1973, pp. 92, 109–15.
11 K. E. Boulding and A. Gleason, 'War as an investment: the case of Japan', *Peace Research Society Papers*, 3, 1965, pp. 11–12. A. S. Milward, *War, Economy and Society, 1939–1945*, London, 1987, p. 12. However, Milward goes on to draw attention to other sources of support for German expansionism. On Britain, see R. C. Trebilcock, 'Legends of the armaments industry', *Journal of Contemporary History*, 5, 1970, pp. 3–19; but compare S. Pollard and P. L. Robertson, *The British Shipbuilding Industry, 1870–1914*, Cambridge, Mass., 1979, p. 220.
12 S. C. Sarkesian, ed., *The Military Industrial Complex: A Reassessment*, Beverly Hills, 1972; A. Giddens, *The Nation-State and Violence*, Cambridge, 1985, pp. 244–54.
13 Kennedy, *Economics of Defence*, pp. 122–5 provides a fuller discussion.
14 M. J. Peck and F. M. Scherer, *The Weapons Acquisition Process: An Economic Analysis*, Boston, 1962, pp. 48, 61, 208–10; F. M. Scherer, *The Weapons Acquisition Process: Economic Incentives*, Cambridge, Mass., 1962, p. x.
15 Joseph Bradley, *Guns for the Tsar: The State, Labor and Technology Transfer in the Russian Small Arms Industry*, DeKalb, 1990. See also E. R. Goldstein, 'Military aspects of Russian industrialization: the defense industries, 1890–1917', PhD thesis, Case Western Reserve University, 1971; and V. V. Polikarpov, 'Gosudarstvennoe proizvodstvo vooruzheniia v Rossii nachalo XXv. (istoriografiia voprosa)', *Istoriia i istoriki*, 1987, pp. 16–37.
16 A. S. Milward, *The German Economy at War*, London, 1967, and R. Overy, 'Hitler's war and the German economy: a reinterpretation', *Economic History Review*, 35, 1982, pp. 272–91, for contrasting views of the significance of Blitzkrieg. British peacetime preparations are discussed by A. Offer, *The First World War: An Agrarian Interpretation*, Oxford, 1989.
17 An exception is the latest book by W. C. Fuller, Jr., *Strategy and Power in Russia, 1600–1914*, New York, 1992.
18 K. F. Shatsillo 'O disproportsii v razvitii vooruzhennykh sil Rossii nakanune pervoi mirovoi voiny, 1906–1914gg.', *Istoricheskie zapiski*, 83, 1969, pp. 123–36; and *Rossiia pered pervoi mirovoi voinoi: vooruzhennye sily tsarizma v 1905–1914gg.*, Moscow, 1974. The quotation is from A. L. Sidorov, *Istoricheskie predposylki Velikoi Oktiabr'skoi sotsialisticheskoi revoliutsii*, Moscow, 1970, p. 56 (my italics).
19 W. M. Pintner, 'The burden of defense in imperial Russia, 1725–1914', *Russian Review*, 43, 1984, pp. 231–59.
20 W. C. Fuller, Jr., *Civil–Military Conflict in Imperial Russia, 1881–1914*, Princeton, 1985.

1 The eve of the Russo-Japanese War

1 B. Eklof, J. Bushnell and L. Zakharova, eds., *The Great Reforms in Russia, 1860–1874: A New Perspective*, Bloomington, Indiana, 1993.
2 The most helpful guide is Geyer, *Russian Imperialism*.
3 P. R. Gregory, *Russian National Income, 1885–1913*, Cambridge, 1982, pp. 153–63; P. W. Gatrell, *The Tsarist Economy, 1850–1917*, London, 1986, pp. 29–47.
4 Gregory, *Russian National Income*, appendices I, J, L; A. Kahan, 'Capital formation during the period of early industrialization in Russia, 1890–1913', in P. Mathias and M. M. Postan, eds., *Cambridge Economic History of Europe*, vol. 7, part 2, Cambridge, 1978, pp. 265–307.
5 For an excellent study of the relationship between government and one leading propertied social group, see A. J. Rieber, *Merchants and Entrepreneurs in Imperial Russia*, Chapel Hill, 1982.
6 *Documents diplomatiques français, 1871–1914*, Paris, 1929–1936, série 1, vol. 9, pp. 615–16; A. Z. Manfred, *Obrazovanie russko-frantsuzskogo soiuza*, Moscow, 1975.
7 L. E. Shepelev, *Tsarizm i burzhuaziia vo vtoroi polovine XIX veka*, Leningrad, 1981, is the best guide to policy shifts in the Ministry of Finances.
8 John Bushnell draws some of the threads together in 'Miliutin and the Balkan war: military reform versus military performance', in Eklof et al., eds., *The Great Reforms*.
9 Geyer, *Russian Imperialism*, p. 125; D. C. B. Lieven, *Russia and the Origins of the First World War*, London, 1983, p. 21; R. Girault, *Emprunts russes et investissements français en Russie, 1887–1914*, Paris, 1973, p. 242.
10 A. Malozemoff, *Russian Far Eastern Policy, 1881–1904*, Berkeley, 1958; I. Nish, *The Origins of the Russo-Japanese War*, London, 1985. By contrast, Franco-Russian relations were closely bound up with developments in central Asia. In 1899, the French government loaned fresh funds to Russia, but attached tight strings to the loan. See Geyer, *Russian Imperialism*, pp. 154–5, 182–3; Girault, *Emprunts russes*, pp. 335–8; B. V. Anan"ich, *Rossiia i mezhdunarodnyi kapital, 1897–1914*, Leningrad, 1970, pp. 39–49.
11 L. G. Beskrovnyi, *Armiia i flot v XIX veke*, Moscow, 1973, pp. 312–13; Geyer, *Russian Imperialism*, pp. 346–8, 362.
12 Quoted in Fuller, *Civil–Military Conflict*, p. 57. For other details, see Beskrovnyi, *Armiia i flot*, p. 521; Geyer, *Russian Imperialism*, pp. 202–19.
13 Beskrovnyi, *Armiia i flot*, p. 519. The disparity between the Russian and German fleets in 1898 is revealed in K. A. Kuznetsov et al., *Baltiiskii sudostroitel'nyi 1856–1917*, Leningrad, 1970, p. 153. For government contracts, see P. P. Migulin, *Russkii gosudarstvennyi kredit*, 3 vols., St Petersburg, 1907, vol. 3, p. 1,072.
14 Tsentral'nyi Gosudarstvennyi Arkhiv Voenno-Morskogo Flota (hereafter TsGAVMF) f.420, op.1, d.23, ll.2–5; Beskrovnyi, *Armiia i flot*, p. 522.
15 F. T. Jane, *The Imperial Russian Navy*, 2nd edn, London, 1904, reprinted 1983, pp. 307, 356–64, 421–2; P. I. Belavenets, *Nuzhen-li nam flot i znachenie ego v istorii Rossii*, St Petersburg, 1910, pp. 255, 261.
16 A full discussion of the battle between the defence departments and the

Ministry of Finances is provided in Fuller, *Civil–Military Conflict*, pp. 59–62, 65–7. Budget figures derive from P. A. Khromov, *Ekonomicheskoe razvitie Rossii v XIX i XX vekakh*, Moscow, 1950, pp. 518–23. For the 1899 decision, see *Vsepoddaneishii otchet gosudarstvennogo kontrolera za 1900* (hereafter *VOGK*), St Petersburg, 1901, p. 15, and Fuller, *Civil–Military Conflict*, pp. 68–9.

17 Beskrovnyi, *Armiia i flot*, p. 62; Pintner, 'The burden of defense', p. 245.

18 The extent of military training continued to cause problems until 1914. See chapter 7.

19 *VOGK za 1902*, St Petersburg, 1903, p. 21; *VOGK za 1903*, p. 22; *VOGK za 1904*, p. 19.

20 *VOGK za 1900*, p. 26; *VOGK za 1903*, p. 11; Beskrovnyi, *Armiia i flot*, pp. 451–2.

21 Quoted in S. N. Prokopovich, *Voina i narodnoe khoziaistvo*, Moscow, 1918, p. 4, and by Fuller, *Civil–Military Conflict*, p. 64. Fuller interprets this, not entirely convincingly, as an indication that Vyshnegradskii subscribed to the conventional view of the soldier's battlefield morale. Kuropatkin believed that the fiscal policies pursued by the government had weakened the morale of the peasant conscript.

22 These workers were for the most part soldier-conscripts (*nizhnie chiny*), whereas their counterparts in the GAU factories and the government dockyards were normally civilians. See N. M. Lisovskii, *Rabochie v voennom vedomstve*, St Petersburg, 1906, pp. 6–7, noting the wry comment by the War Minister that 'we are simply plantation owners and our workers are our negro slaves'.

23 See A. Kahan, *The Plow, the Hammer and the Knout*, Chicago, 1985, pp. 95–101.

24 *Voennaia entsiklopediia*, 18 vols. (no more published), St Petersburg, 1911–15, vol. 10, entry under 'zavody artilleriiskie'.

25 The standard factory history of Putilov is by M. Mitel'man et al., *Istoriia Putilovskogo zavoda, 1801–1917gg.*, 4th edn, Moscow, 1961, but it does not meet the needs of the modern historian. The history of the Nikolaev yards after 1900 figures heavily in the work of the Soviet historian Shatsillo (see below). There is no up-to-date history of Nevskii.

26 See the entries on individual government arsenals and dockyards in *Voennaia entsiklopediia*; also E. K. Germonius, 'Izhevskii oruzheinyi zavod i rol' kazennykh zavodov v dele oborony', *Russian Economist*, 2, 1922, p. 2,901; V. N. Ashurkov, 'Predpriiatiia voennogo vedomstva kak element mnogoukladnoi ekonomiki Rossii', in *Voprosy istorii kapitalisticheskoi Rossii*, Sverdlovsk, 1972, pp. 109–17.

27 Ashurkov, 'Predpriiatiia', pp. 110–11, 113–15, and Iu. F. Subbotin, 'Voennaia promyshlennost' Rossii vo vtoroi polovine XIX-nachale XXv., 1868–1914gg.', kandidatskaia dissertatsiia, Moscow State University, 1975.

28 Germonius, 'Izhevskii zavod', pp. 2,909–10.

29 M. P. Viatkin, *Gornozavodskii Ural v 1900–1917gg.*, Moscow-Leningrad, 1965, pp. 11–16.

30 Tsentral'nyi Gosudarstvennyi Istoricheskii Arkhiv (hereafter TsGIA) f.37, op.77, d.136, 11.1–2; *VOGK za 1908*, St Petersburg, 1909, pp. 139–40, 145. The State Auditor commented that the state ironworks also supplied high quality steel to British customers, though at a loss.

31 *VOGK za 1900*, St Petersburg, 1901, p.28; *VOGK za 1903*, p. 25; Beskrovnyi, *Armiia i flot*, p. 359.

32 A. A. Korolev, 'Iz istorii russkoi voennoi promyshlennosti: vozniknovenie chastnogo patronnogo zavoda', *Uchenye zapiski Tul'skogo gosudarstvennogo pedagogicheskogo instituta*, kafedra istorii, vyp. 2, Tula, 1969, pp. 78–98. In 1890, Tula charged 20 per cent more than the state sector for its cartridges.

33 *Otchet gornogo departamenta za 1900–1901*, St Petersburg, 1902.

34 J. Kipp, 'The Russian navy and the problem of technological transfer: technological backwardness and military-industrial development, 1853–1876', in Eklof et al., eds., *The Great Reforms*, forthcoming.

35 N. I. Dmitriev and V. V. Kolpychev, *Sudostroitel'nye zavody i sudostroenie v Rossii i za granitsei*, St Petersburg, 1909, pp. 889–902.

36 Tsentral'nyi Gosudarstvennyi Voenno-istoricheskii Arkhiv (hereafter TsGVIA) f.369, op.1, d.133, ll.1–13ob.; TsGAVMF f.420, op.1, d.23, ll.2–15, citing State Auditor's reports; Dmitriev and Kolpychev, *Sudostroitel'nye zavody*, pp. 902–4; Kuznetsov et al., *Baltiiskii sudostroitel'nyi*, p. 71.

37 Dmitriev and Kolpychev, *Sudostroitel'nye zavody*, p. 916; I. A. Baklanova, *Rabochie sudostroiteli Rossii v XIX veke*, Moscow-Leningrad, 1959, pp. 7–8.

38 Dmitriev and Kolpychev, *Sudostroitel'nye zavody*, pp. 817, 832–3.

39 *Ibid.*, pp. 801–5.

40 *VOGK za 1900*, St Petersburg, 1901, p. 25; Germonius, 'Izhevskii zavod', pp. 2,903–5; N. N. Golovin, *Voennye usiliia Rossii v mirovoi voine*, 2 vols., Paris, 1939, vol. 2, p. 427.

41 *Svod voennykh postanovlenii*, vol. 13, 3rd edn, St Petersburg, 1910, paras. 8, 16, 65–6, 75.

42 A commission of enquiry took evidence during 1903 and made several suggestions for improvements in accounting procedures, but nothing was done in the short term. See I. Kh. Ozerov, *Gornye zaovdy Urala*, Moscow, 1910, p. 120.

43 Dmitriev and Kolpychev, *Sudostroitel'nye zavody*, p. 916.

44 The 1901 edition of the regulations for state shipyards stipulated that the principle of commercial administration be maintained at the Obukhov and Baltic yards. But Izhora and the Admiralty yards continued to receive an annual appropriation from the Treasury, to which they were required strictly to adhere. TsGAVMF f.420, op.1, d.23, ll.2–15, 37ob.; *Svod morskikh postanovlenii*, 1901 edn.

45 For background, see Baklanova, *Rabochie*, pp. 47, 97; 'Iz istorii Shostenskogo zavoda', *Krasnyi arkhiv*, 75, 1936, no. 2, pp. 192–6.

46 The cotton industry was the largest, employing nearly 400,000 workers. The coal industry employed 109,000 workers. Industries of comparable size include chemicals (60,000), paper and printing (78,000) and woodworking (80,000). Figures from A. G. Rashin, *Formirovanie rabochego klassa Rossii*, Moscow, 1958, pp. 48, 61.

47 See table 5.8. In 1902, the workforce permanently employed at GAU factories and workshops stood at just over 29,000. A further 45,700 workers were engaged in military engineering projects, and 15,200 in the construction and upkeep of barracks. See Lisovskii, *Rabochie*, pp. 8–9. Other data are

taken from *Dinamika rossiiskoi i sovetskoi promyshlennosti v sviazi s razvitiem narodnogo khoziaistva za sorok let (1887–1925gg.)*, 3 vols., Moscow-Leningrad, 1929–30, vol. 1, pp. 96–7. The proportion of the male labour force employed in the British armaments industry was no more than two per cent in 1900, according to W. Ashworth, 'Economic aspects of late Victorian naval administration', *Economic History Review*, 22, 1969, p. 492. The Swedish industry accounted for half of one per cent of the total industrial labour force. In Russia, armaments accounted for close on four per cent of the total labour force.

48 V. I. Grinevetskii, *Poslevoennye perspektivy russkoi promyshlennosti*, Kharkov, 1919, p. 159. For further discussion, see Crisp, *Studies*, pp. 36–44; Gatrell, *Tsarist Economy*, pp. 157–67.

49 TsGIA f.37, op.77, d.136, 11.15–27; Baklanova, *Rabochie*, pp. 125–6. On Tula, see V. N. Ashurkov, 'Rabochie zavodov artilleriiskogo vedomstva v epokhu kapitalizma: osobennosti ikh polozheniia i klassovoi bor'by', in *Rabochie Rossii v epokhu kapitalizma*, Tula, 1972, p. 168. The author quotes the despairing remarks of the Bolshevik activist V. D. Bonch-Breuvich: 'the worker in the factory is at the same time master of the house. He sends back home work on samovars and guns, and rigorously exploits other workers, who cannot find work in the factory'. The whole question is explored for the earlier period by Bradley, *Guns for the Tsar*.

50 *Svod morskikh postanovlenii*, vol. 5, 1910, para. 119. These regulations were abolished in 1910.

51 On hours of work in military shipbuilding, see Baklanova, *Rabochie*, p. 72. For non-defence industry, see Iu. I. Kir'ianov, *Zhiznennyi uroven' rabochikh Rossii, konets XIX-nachalo XXv.*, Moscow, 1979, p. 84. The 1897 law applied only to enterprises that employed more than twenty workers.

52 S. N. Semanov, *Peterburgskie rabochie nakanune pervoi russkoi revoliutsii*, Moscow, 1966, p. 39; A.R., 'Rabochie Sormovskikh zavodov', *Narodnoe khoziaistvo*, 4, 1902, pp. 84–94.

53 Lisovskii, *Rabochie*, pp. 187–90; Baklanova, *Rabochie*, pp. 112–14. Tula had 90 places, Sestroretsk 60 and Izhevsk 120. For workers' complaints in 1905 about the kind of provision that was made, see *Revoliutsiia 1905–1907gg. v Rossii: nachalo pervoi russkoi revoliutsii, ianvar'-mart 1905g.*, Moscow, 1955, pp. 135–7.

54 A. A. Manikovskii, *Boevoe snabzhenie russkoi armii v mirovuiu voinu, 1914–1918gg.*, 2 vols., Moscow, 1930, vol. 1, p. 78; *Svod voennykh postanovlenii*, vol. 13, 1910, appendix; *Svod morskikh postanovlenii*, vol. 5, 1910, para. 120; Germonius, 'Izhevskii zavod', pp. 2,902–3. Fewer than half of one per cent of Russian factories in 1895 made direct provision for schooling, according to V. Luknitskii, 'O vol'nonaemnykh rabochikh artilleriiskikh tekhnicheskikh zavedenii', *Artilleriiskii zhurnal*, 1, 1899, p. 99.

55 Germonius, 'Izhevskii zavod', p. 2,902; S. I. Zav'ialov, *Izhorskii zavod*, 2 vols., Leningrad, 1976, vol. 1, p. 175.

56 Rashin, *Formirovanie*, pp. 503–4; O. Crisp, 'Labour and industrialization', in *Cambridge Economic History*, vol. 7, part 2, pp. 381–2, citing a work by Otto Goebel.

57 A.R., 'Rabochie Sormovskikh zavodov'.
58 *Svod morskikh postanovlenii*, vol. 5, 1910, para. 126; *Workmen's Insurance and Compensations Systems in Europe*, 2 vols., Washington, 1911, vol. 2, pp. 2,259–67. In 1891, workers at government dockyards were offered sick pay and the right to claim a disability pension: Baklanova, *Rabochie*, pp. 101, 176. See also I. I. Shelymagin, *Zakonodatel'stvo o fabrichno-zavodskom trude v Rossii v 1900–1917gg.*, Moscow-Leningrad, 1952, p. 72.
59 On provisions for pensions at the state shipyards, see *Workmen's Insurance*, pp. 2,255, 2,297–8, and S. V. Murzintseva, 'Iz istorii ekonomicheskogo polozheniia rabochikh na predpriiatiakh voennogo i morskogo vedomstv v 1907–1914gg. v Peterburge', *Uchenye zapiski LGU*, 270, 1959, p. 234. On the vexed question of workers' links with the land, see Gatrell, *Tsarist Economy*, pp. 88–94.
60 The background history of the Popov commission is described in Lisovskii, *Rabochie*, introduction and p. 236. See also Baklanova, *Rabochie*, pp. 110–19.
61 There were some signs that things were beginning to change. In 1900, the GAU insisted that workers pay a commercial rent for the plots of land they occupied after emancipation: 'Iz istorii Shostenskogo zavoda', pp. 192–6.
62 The Mosin rifle was a more reliable, accurate and lighter version of the 3-line breech-loading rifle. *VOGK za 1901*; Beskrovnyi, *Armiia i flot*, pp. 315–20.
63 Subbotin, 'Voennaia promyshlennost'', p. 106; Beskrovnyi, *Armiia i flot*, p. 323.
64 *Ibid.*, p. 359; R. Ropponen, *Die Kraft Russlands*, Helsinki, 1968, pp. 184–5, citing a report prepared for the Austro-Hungarian General Staff. Plans already in place provided for a stock of 6,831 artillery pieces within four years.
65 TsGAVMF f.420, op.1, d.23, ll.2–15; Baklanova, *Rabochie*, pp. 125–6.
66 Dmitriev and Kolpychev, *Sudostroitel'nye zavody*, p. 777.
67 Modern treatments of the subject are J. Bushnell, 'Peasants in uniform: the tsarist army as a peasant society', *Journal of Social History*, 13, 1980, pp. 565–76 and D. Beyrau, *Militär und Gesellschaft im vorrevolutionären Russland*, Cologne-Vienna, 1984, pp. 313, 360.
68 A. P. Voznesenskii, 'O voennom khoziaistve', *Obshchestvo revnitelei voennykh znanii*, 1906, kniga 1, p. 101; F. Maksheev, *Voenno-administrativnoe ustroistvo tyla armii*, 3 vols., St Petersburg, 1893–95, vol. 3, 1895, p. 161; *VOGK za 1900*, St Petersburg, 1902, pp. 20–1.
69 *Voennaia entsiklopediia*, vol. 10, 1912, entry under 'zavedeniia intendantskie'.
70 Khromov, *Ekonomicheskoe razvitie*, pp. 452, 454, 457. The average annual growth rate of industrial production derives from Kondratiev, as reported in A. Gerschenkron, 'The rate of industrial growth in Russia since 1885', *Journal of Economic History*, supplement 7, 1947, pp. 144–74.
71 Percentage shares calculated from Khromov, *Ekonomicheskoe razvitie*, p. 457.
72 McKay, *Pioneers for Profit*, pp. 113–36.
73 M. Ia. Gefter, 'Tsarizm i monopolisticheskii kapital v metallurgii iuga Rossii do pervoi mirovoi voiny', *Istoricheskie zapiski*, 43, 1953, p. 77. See also A. L.

Tsukernik, *Sindikat 'Prodamet' 1902–1914gg.: istoriko-ekonomicheskii ocherk*, Moscow, 1959, p. 13; McKay, *Pioneers*, pp. 117, 339, 391–4.

74 L. A. Mendel'son, *Teoriia i istoriia ekonomicheskikh krizisov i tsiklov*, 3 vols., Moscow, 1959–64, vol. 2, pp. 456, 458, 460; P. I. Liashchenko, *Istoriia narodnogo khoziaistva SSSR*, 2 vols., Moscow, 1952, vol. 2, p. 324. The output of iron and steel in physical terms declined much less sharply between 1900 and 1902.

75 *Stenogramma soveshchaniia o polozhenii metallurgicheskoi i mashinostroitel'noi promyshlennosti*, St Petersburg, 1908, p. 46; McKay, *Pioneers*, p. 140.

76 *Ibid.*, p. 134.

77 *Otchet gornogo departamenta za 1900–01*, St Petersburg, 1902, pp. 268–71; Viatkin, *Gornozavodskii Ural*, pp. 11–16, and the older but still valuable work by Ozerov, *Gornye zavody Urala*.

78 *Smeta dokhodov i raskhodov gornogo departamenta na 1914*, St Petersburg, 1913, pp. 39, 49; Ozerov, *Gornye zavody*, pp. 120, 128; Viatkin, pp. 46–7, 116.

79 The first soviet census distinguished 160 classes of product (*nomenklatura izdelii*) in the machine-building industry. See B. N. Sarab'ianov, *Metallopromyshlennost' Rossii*, Moscow, 1921, p. 25.

80 The main source on the Russian engineering industry is Ia. S. Rozenfel'd and K. I. Klimenko, *Istoriia mashinostroeniia SSSR*, Moscow, 1961; see also *Ocherki istorii tekhniki v Rossii, 1861–1917gg.*, Moscow, 1973, p. 328.

81 Rozenfel'd and Klimenko, *Istoriia*, pp. 50, 53, 136; P. G. Ivanov, *Ocherk istorii i statistiki russkogo zavodskogo parovozostroeniia*, Petrograd, 1920; D. P. Il'inskii and V. P. Ivanitskii, *Ocherk istorii russkoi parovozostroitel'noi i vagonostroitel'noi promyshlennosti*, Moscow, 1929, pp. 75–8.

82 *Ibid.*, p. 67; *Ocherki istorii tekhniki*, pp. 328–32, 345.

83 Dmitriev and Kolpychev, *Sudostroitel'nye zavody*, pp. 812–14; *Ocherki istorii tekhniki*, pp. 245–6.

84 Dmitriev and Kolpychev, *Sudostroitel'nye zavody*, pp. 793–5.

85 Details in Rozenfel'd and Klimenko, *Istoriia*, p. 87.

86 Horsepower per worker increased by between 29 and 43 per cent; output per worker increased by between 8 per cent (rolling-stock) and 38 per cent (agricultural machinery). *Ibid.*, p. 86.

87 Tsukernik, *Sindikat 'Prodamet'*, pp. 13, 37. The South Russian Iron and Steel Association petitioned the government to buy up steel-making factories and close them down. Other details from Mendel'son, *Istoriia*, vol. 2, pp. 459–60; Liashchenko, *Istoriia*, vol. 2, p. 324; McKay, *Pioneers*, pp. 281–2; Crisp, *Studies*, pp. 177–8.

88 Tsukernik, *Sindikat 'Prodamet'*, pp. 12–18. For French misgivings, see Crisp, *Studies*, pp. 177–8, and Girault, *Emprunts russes*, pp. 354–8. On the various forms of government assistance, see I. F. Gindin, 'Politika tsarskogo pravitel'stva v otnoshenii promyshlennykh monopolii', in *Ob osobennostiakh imperializma*, pp. 86–123. Shares in Prodamet were not traded on the stock exchange, and any firm that left the syndicate had to turn its shares over to the other members. Firms' export orders were not subject to Prodamet control until 1912. See *Monopolii v metallurgicheskoi promyshlennosti, 1900–1917gg.*, Moscow, 1963, pp. 301, 579–80.

89 Liashchenko, *Istoriia*, vol. 2, pp. 308–10; McKay, *Pioneers*, p. 283.
90 Liashchenko, *Istoriia*, pp. 310–12.
91 McKay, *Pioneers*, pp. 229–32.
92 During the 1890s, Druzhkovka produced only rails; 88 per cent of Hughes' output was also rails. By 1903, these proportions had fallen to around 72 per cent. See Crisp, *Studies*, pp. 34, 227; Tsukernik, *Sindikat 'Prodamet'*, pp. 78–88.
93 *Monopolii*, pp. 25–7; N. Shteinfel'd, 'Politika kazennykh zakazov', *Narodnoe khoziaistvo*, 1902, 8, pp. 149–54; Liashchenko, *Istoriia*, vol. 2, p. 320; A. L. Tsukernik, 'Iz istorii monopolizatsii zheleznogo rynka v Rossii', *Istoricheskie zapiski*, 42, 1953, pp. 173–4.
94 Il'inskii and Ivanitskii, *Ocherk*, pp. 91–2, 95. The original members of Prod parovoz were Kolomna Engineering, the Russian Locomotive and Engineering Company, Hartmann, Briansk, Putilov and Sormovo. The Nevskii engineering works joined in 1907. Details in V. I. Bovykin, *Formirovanie finansovogo kapitala v Rossii*, Moscow, 1984, p. 218; T. D. Krupina, 'K voprosu o vzaimootnosheniiakh tsarskogo pravitel'stva s monopoliiami', *Istoricheskie zapiski*, 57, 1956, p. 147. According to Il'inskii and Ivanitskii, p. 95, government subsidies were worth 300 rubles per goods wagon, 800 rubles per passenger wagon and 3,000 rubles per locomotive. Applying these figures to the output data, subsidies were equivalent to 21 per cent of wagon production and three per cent of locomotive production in 1907.
96 Cited in V. Ia. Laverychev, *Gosudarstvo i monopolii v dorevoliutsionnoi Rossii*, Moscow, 1982, pp. 124–5.
97 For the British case, see Clive Trebilcock, 'War and the failure of industrial mobilization: 1899 and 1914', in J. Winter, ed., *War and Economic Development*, Cambridge, 1975, pp. 139–64.

2 War and revolution, retrenchment and recession

1 Quoted in A. L. Sidorov, *Finansovoe polozhenie Rossii v gody pervoi mirovoi voiny*, Moscow, 1960, p. 20. See also S. Harcave, ed., *The Memoirs of Count Witte*, New York, 1990, pp. 424–5.
2 G. Surh, *1905 in St Petersburg: Labor and Government*, Stanford, 1989; L. Engelstein, *Moscow, 1905: Working-Class Organization and Political Conflict*, Princeton, 1982; T. Emmons, *The Formation of Political Parties in Russia and the First National Elections in Russia*, Stanford, 1983.
3 W. J. Kelly, 'Crisis management in the Russian oil industry: the 1905 revolution', *Journal of European Economic History*, 10, 1981, pp. 291–342.
4 Details of the negotiations are provided by Anan"ich, *Rossiia*, pp. 114–15, 123–8. A leading German Foreign Office spokesman, Rudolf Martin, argued that Russia remained creditworthy, so long as grain exports were maintained. See B. Lohr, *Die 'Zukunft Russlands': Perspektiven russischer Wirtschaftsentwicklung und deutsch-russische Wirtschaftsbeziehungen vor dem ersten Weltkrieg*, Wiesbaden, 1985, pp. 21–7.
5 The chief published source of information on government economic policy remains the memoirs of V. N. Kokovtsov, *Iz moego proshlogo: vospominaniia*, 2

vols., Paris, 1933; an abbreviated English edition, annotated by H. H. Fisher, appeared under the title *Out of My Past: The Memoirs of Count Kokovtsov*, Stanford, 1935.

6 The outstanding monograph on business-government relations in this period is L. E. Shepelev, *Tsarizm i burzhuaziia v 1904–1914gg.*, Leningrad, 1987.

7 Kokovtsov noted that improvements were also made to the capacity of the Chinese Eastern Railway. *Iz moego proshlogo*, vol. 1, p. 39. See also Newton A. McCully, *The McCully Report: The Russo-Japanese War, 1904–1905*, Annapolis, 1977, pp. 17–18, 23. The carrying capacity of the trans-Siberian railway in 1900 had been limited to three trains daily. Troop strengths are taken from Ropponen, *Die Kraft Russlands*, p. 39.

8 TsGIA, f.1393, op.2, d.456, ll.365–6. For further discussion of the Garin report, see chapter 6.

9 B. A. Romanov, *Ocherki diplomatichesoi istorii russko-iaponskoi voiny*, Moscow-Leningrad, 1955, p. 303, notes that there were 1,037 12-inch shells at Vladivostok, but no 12-inch guns, and only 153 such shells at Port Arthur, where they were badly needed. The army received heavier howitzers only in the summer of 1905, far too late to affect the outcome of the war. On the crucial shortage of communication equipment, see McCully, *Report*, pp. 32, 47.

10 The quality of footwear supplied to Russian troops is described in I. Kh. Ozerov, *Kak raskhoduiutsia v Rossii narodnye dengi*, Moscow, 1907, p. 151. On peacetime arrangements, see chapter 1.

11 Quoted in Shatsillo, *Rossiia*, p. 14. See also *Ocherki istorii SSSR, 1905–1907*, Moscow-Leningrad, 1955, p. 52.

12 Romanov, *Ocherki*, p. 303; P. A. Zaionchkovskii, *Samoderzhavie i russkaia armiia na rubezhe XIX–XX stoletii, 1881–1903*, Moscow, 1973, pp. 339–40.

13 Raymond Spear, *Report on the Russian Medical and Sanitary Features of the Russo-Japanese War to the Surgeon General U.S. Navy*, Washington, 1906, pp. 9, 12–13; T.I. Pol'ner, *Obshchezemskaia organizatsiia na Dal'nem Vostoke*, Moscow, 1908. Food shortages are discussed in Fuller, *Strategy and Power*, 1992, p. 401.

14 McCully, *Report*, pp. 243–56; *Ocherki istorii SSSR*, pp. 64–66.

15 V. A. Marinov, *Rossiia i Iaponiia pered pervoi mirovoi voinoi, 1905–1914gg: ocherki istorii otnoshenii*, Moscow, 1974, pp. 11–13; Shatsillo, *Rossiia*, p. 13; figures on naval casualties derive from Ia.I. Kefeli, *Poteri v lichnom sostave russkogo flota v voinu s Iaponiei: statisticheskoe issledovanie*, St. Petersburg, 1914, p. 118.

16 B. A. Romanov, ed., 'Konets russko-iaponskoi voiny', *Krasnyi arkhiv*, 28, 1928, pp. 182–204.

17 Figures from *Stenogramma soveshchaniia*, pp. 104–5. French and German manufacturers competed for Russian custom during the war. The renewal of the Russo-German trade agreement at the end of 1904 alarmed French industrialists, who urged the government to ensure that any loan to Russia be made conditional on orders to French iron and steel producers. Kokovtsov tartly remarked in private that 'Russia is not Turkey'. However, he did inform Bompard, the French ambassador, that Russia regarded France as a

major source of military supplies. See Anan"ich, *Rossiia*, pp. 119–22; Girault, *Emprunts russes*, pp. 405–11; M. Epkenhans, *Die wilhelminische Flottenrüstung, 1908–1914*, Munich, 1991, p. 470.

18 *Stenogramma soveshchaniia*, pp. 105, 116–17; *Istoriia Tul'skogo oruzheinogo zavoda, 1712–1972*, Moscow, 1973, pp. 91, 101–4.

19 TsGAVMF, f.420, op.1, d.13, ll.1–5.

20 L. G. Beskrovnyi, 'Proizvodstvo vooruzheniia i boepripasov dlia armii v Rossii v period imperializma, 1898–1917', *Istoricheskie zapiski*, 99, 1977, pp. 105–7; A. A. Korolev, 'Finansovo-ekonomicheskaia deiatelnost' Tul'skogo patronnogo zavoda, 1899–1907', *Iz istorii Tul'skogo kraia*, Tula, 1972, pp. 26–41.

21 Beskrovnyi, 'Proizvodstvo', pp. 105–7; *Otchet gornogo departamenta za 1900–01gg.*; ibid., *za 1905*; G. A. Miftiev, 'Artilleriiskaia promyshlennost' Rossii v period pervoi mirovoi voiny', kandidatskaia dissertatsiia, Leningrad State University, 1953, appendix 2.

22 Dmitriev and Kolpychev, *Sudostroitel'nye zavody*, p. 777. According to McCully, *Report*, p. 3, 'the Emperor visited all the ships under construction and by personal addresses and offers of rewards urged the workmen to increased efforts'.

23 TsGAVMF f.427, op.1, d.1998, ll.151–62; Dmitriev and Kolpychev, *Sudostroitel'nye zavody*, pp. 905, 912; Zav'ialov, *Izhorskii zavod*, p. 171.

24 TsGIA, f.1393, op.2, d.456, ll.365–365ob.; TsGAVMF f.512, op.1, d.1781, ll.9ob., 21ob.; d.1782, l.39. Ozerov, *Kak raskhoduiutsia*, p. 116 notes that Putilov also received orders for coastal vessels. See also S. B. Okun', ed., *Putilovets v trekh revoliutsiiakh: sbornik materialov po istorii Putilovskogo zavoda*, Leningrad, 1933, p. xvi; Liashchenko, *Istoriia*, p. 585; R. Girault, 'Finances internationales et relations internationales: à propos des usines Poutiloff', *Revue d'histoire moderne et contemporaine*, 13, 1966, p. 220.

25 Subbotin, 'Voennaia promyshlennost'', pp. 117, 121.

26 TsGIA f.37, op.77, d.136, l.10; *Gosudarstvannaia Duma: Stenograficheskie otchety* (hereafter *SOGD*), III, 4th session, sitting 77, col. 1,251; Viatkin, *Gornozavodskii Ural*, p. 113.

27 *VOGK za 1905*, St Petersburg, 1906, p. 32.

28 Kokovtsov, speaking to the State Council in 1908, is quoted in Mendel'son, *Teoriia*, vol. 3, p. 130.

29 Ibid., p. 137; Bovykin, *Formirovanie*, pp. 52–3.

30 *Stenogramma soveshchaniia*, pp. 6–7; Il'inskii and Ivanitskii, *Ocherk*, p. 91; Mendel'son, *Teoriia*, pp. 131, 135.

31 Mendel'son, *Teoriia*, pp. 133–6. The 1904 harvest was 24 per cent higher than the average for the previous quinquennium. The quotation is from G. Meerson, 'Promyshlennaia depressiia v Rossii, 1906–1909gg.', *Vestnik Kommunisticheskoi Akademii*, 9, 1924, p. 148.

32 A. L. Blek, 'Usloviia truda rabochikh na peterburgskikh zavodakh po dannym 1901g.', *Arkhiv istorii truda v Rossii*, 2, 1921, pp. 65–85.

33 Ozerov pointed out acerbically that it would be cheaper to reform labour law and prevent massive labour disputes than to pay the police bill incurred by the Ministry of the Interior: Ozerov, *Kak raskhoduiutsia*, p. 121. See

also Rieber, *Merchants and Entrepreneurs*, pp. 261–6; T. McDaniel, *Autocracy, Capitalism and Revolution in Russia*, Berkeley, 1988, pp. 107–8.

34 U. A. Shuster, *Peterburgskie rabochie v 1905–1907gg.*, Leningrad, 1976, p. 93; Emmons, *Formation of Political Parties*, p. 128. Kokovtsov's memoirs are silent on his meeting with the employers.

35 For a general survey of industrialists' attitudes and behaviour in 1905, see A. Ermanskii, 'Krupnaia burzhuaziia v 1905–1907gg.', in Iu. Martov et al., eds., *Obshchestvennoe dvizhenie v Rossii v nachale XXv.*, 4 vols., St Petersburg, 1909–14, vol. 2, part 2, 1910, pp. 30–100.

36 Shepelev, *Tsarizm i burzhuaziia*, pp. 74–77. For documentation, see B. A. Romanov, ed., *Rabochii vopros v komissii V. N. Kokovtsova v 1905g.*, Moscow, 1926. See also Ermanskii, 'Krupnaia burzhuaziia', pp. 50–1, for the industrialists' claim to participate in the deliberations of the Bulygin commission. The quotation in the text is from McDaniel, *Autocracy*, p. 115.

37 See the remarks of Goujon, cited in McDaniel, *Autocracy*, p. 108; V.Ia. Laverychev, *Po tu storonu barrikad: iz istorii bor'by Moskovskoi burzhuazii s revoliutsii*, Moscow, 1967, pp. 34–5.

38 Ermanskii, 'Krupnaia burzhuaziia', pp. 33, 44–5; Laverychev, *Po tu storonu*, pp. 34–5; Emmons, *Formation*, p. 129; Rieber, *Merchants*, pp. 346–7.

39 Laverychev, *Po tu storonu*, pp. 44, 58.

40 Shepelev, *Tsarizm*, 1987, pp. 77–8; Ermanskii, 'Krupnaia burzhuaziia', p. 52. Lieven, *Russia's Rulers*, p. 320 discusses the law relating to membership of the State Council.

41 Ermanskii, 'Krupnaia burzhuaziia', p. 58; Emmons, *Formation*, pp. 127–42; Rieber, *Merchants*, pp. 273–81.

42 V. V. Reikhardt, 'Partiinye gruppirovki i predstavitel'stvo interesov krupnogo kapitala v 1905–1906gg.', *Krasnaia letopis'*, 1930, 6, pp. 5–39; S. E. Sef, ed., *Burzhuaziia v 1905g. po neizdannym arkhivnym materialam*, Moscow-Leningrad, 1926, pp. 88–100.

43 Shepelev, *Tsarizm i burzhuaziia*, p. 80; Laverychev, *Po tu storonu*, p. 40; Rieber, *Merchants*, pp. 270–1, 298–99.

44 For a full account, see J. H. Hartl, *Die Interessenvertretungen der Industriellen in Russland, 1905–1914*, Vienna, 1978.

45 Shepelev, *Tsarizm i burzhuaziia*, pp. 83–5; Rieber, *Merchants*, p. 337.

46 In February 1906, the Confederation of Trade and Industry stated publicly that 'the landed elements in our society are ill-informed about the real significance of trade and industry ... and regard industrialists and merchants as a parasitic money-making class which can bear the burden of heavy taxation without much difficulty'. Quoted by Ermanskii, 'Krupnaia burzhuaziia', pp. 59–60; Sef, ed., *Burzhuaziia*, pp. 18–21; Rieber, *Merchants*, p. 321.

47 H. Reichman, *Railwaymen and Revolution*, Berkeley, 1989, pp. 149–57.

48 According to the German General staff, twelve of the sixty infantry divisions were tied up in the task of maintaining order in Russia. See Ropponen, *Die Kraft Russlands*, p. 219; J. Bushnell, *Mutiny amid Repression: Russian Soldiers in the Revolution of 1905–1906*, Bloomington, 1985.

49 An exception to the general strike movement in St Petersburg was the

gun-cotton works administered by the Admiralty, whose workforce failed to respond to the call from workers at the Baltic and Tube factories in January 1905. See *Nachalo pervoi russkoi revoliutsii*, pp. 21–3, 135–7, 190–1.

50 *Ibid.*, pp. 135–7, 190–1. See also V. A. Tsybul'skii, 'Sestroretskie rabochie v revoliutsii 1905–1907gg.', in Iu. D. Margolis, ed., *Novoe o revoliutsii 1905–1907gg. v Rossii*, Moscow, 1989, pp. 132–9.

51 *Nachalo*, pp. 124–5, 149–50, 198–200. For further evidence of anti-war sentiment, see Surh, pp. 270–1.

52 *Nachalo*, pp. 141–2, 166–9.

53 *Ibid.*, pp. 198–200; Shuster, *Peterburgskie rabochie*, p. 101.

54 *Nachalo*, pp. 202–3; *Revoliutsionnoe dvizhenie v Rossii vesnoi i letom 1905g., aprel'-sentiabr'*, part, 1, Moscow, 1957, p. 270.

55 *Ibid.*, part 2, 1961, pp. 28–9.

56 *Ibid.*, pp. 41–4, 47–8; *Vserossiiskaia politicheskaia stachka v oktiabre 1905g.*, part 1, Moscow, 1955, pp. 131–9; *Vysshii pod"em revoliutsii 1905–1907gg: vooruzhennye vosstaniia noiabr'-dekabr' 1905g.*, part 2, Moscow, 1955, pp. 841–2, 846–9.

57 Details in Zav'ialov, *Izhorskii zavod*, pp. 208–9, 235–6, 249, and Surh, *1905 in St Petersburg*, pp. 194–6. For Obukhov, see P. A. Berlin, *Russkaia burzhuaziia v staroe i novoe vremia*, Moscow, 1922, pp. 235–6.

58 *Revoliutsionnoe dvizhenie v Tul'skoi gubernii 1905–1907gg.*, Tula, 1956, pp. 77–8, 99–104. For Sestroretsk, see Tsybul'skii, 'Sestroretskie rabochie'; SR influence in Perm is discussed in C. Rice, *Russian Workers and the Socialist-Revolutionary Party through the Revolution of 1905–1907*, London, 1988, pp. 51–2, 165–76.

59 See E. Maevskii, 'Massovoe dvizhenie s 1904 po 1907gg.', in Martov, ed., *Obshchestvennoe dvizhenie*, vol. 2, part 1, p. 157.

60 *Nachalo*, pp. 469–70. On Lange, see *Revoliutsiia 1905–1907gg. v Latvii: dokumenty i materialy*, Riga, 1956, pp. 29, 92–3.

61 *Revoliutsionnoe dvizhenie v Tul'skoi gubernii*, pp. 59–62.

62 During the December massacre, twenty-three people were killed: details in *Krasnyi Arkhiv*, vol. 65–6, no. 4–5, 1934, pp. 193–247. On the exaction of financial penalties, see TsGIA f.1393, op.2, d.456, l.147. For Nevskii and Putilov, see *Revoliutsionnoe dvizhenie v Rossii vesnoi i letom 1905g.*, part 1, Moscow, 1957, pp. 281–2; *Revoliutsionnoe dvizhenie v Tul'skoi gubernii*, pp. 112–3.

63 TsGIA f.1393, op.2, d.456, ll.151-ob.; D. Kol'tsov, 'Rabochie v 1905–1907gg.', *Obshchestvennoe dvizhenie*, vol. 2, part 1 p. 189. Putilov paid the wages of delegates to the St Petersburg Soviet: Berlin, *Russkaia burzhuaziia*, p. 236.

64 Completion rates are derived from Manikovskii, *Boevoe snabzhenie*, vol. 1, p. 129; Beskrovnyi, 'Proizvodstvo', pp. 90–2.

65 TsGIA f.37, op.77, d.136, l.7. The average daily wage at Zlatoust was 1.10 rubles in 1904; by 1906 it had risen to 1.46 rubles. See also Shuster, *Peterburgskie rabochie*, p. 100.

66 On the gains made by other workers, see Kir'ianov, *Zhiznennyi uroven'*, pp. 101–32; on spatial concentration, see Shuster, *Peterburgskie rabochie*, p. 117; Surh, *1905 in St Petersburg*, p. 358.

67 In March 1903, Kuropatkin indicated that a war lasting eighteen months

would cost around 600 million rubles; a year later, Kokovtsov put the likely cost at around 750 million rubles. See B. A. Romanov, ed., *Russkie finansy i evropeiskaia birzha v 1904–1906gg.*, Moscow-Leningrad, 1926, pp. 31–62, 82–4, 307–8. On the financial outcome, see Sidorov, *Finansovoe polozhenie*, pp. 15–21; Anan"ich, *Rossiia*, pp. 153–77; and Girault, *Emprunts russes*, pp. 430–49.

68 *Russkie finansy*, pp. 239–41; Girault, *Emprunts russes*, pp. 398, 416, 445–6.

69 *Russkie finansy*, 336–40.

70 See A. L. Sidorov, ed., 'Finansovoe polozhenie tsarskogo samoderzhaviia v period russko-iaponskoi voiny i pervoi russkoi revoliutsii', *Istoricheskii arkhiv*, 1955, 2, pp. 141–2; *Russkie finansy*, p. 358.

71 From 1906 until his death in 1915, Witte chaired the Finance Committee, a non-executive body. Kokovtsov held the post of Minister of Finances between February 1904 and October 1905; after an interval of six months, during which I. P. Shipov served as Minister of Finances, he took back the portfolio. On the Finance Committee, see N. P. Eroshkin, *Istoriia gosudarstvennykh uchrezhdenii dorevoliutsionnoi Rossii*, 3rd edn, Moscow, 1983, pp. 162–3. Biographical details are culled from Shepelev, *Tsarizm i burzhuaziia*, and Anan"ich, *Rossiia*, p. 259.

72 Sidorov, *Finansovoe polozhenie*, pp. 26–7.

73 Anan"ich, *Rossiia*, pp. 257–261; Harcave, ed., *Memoirs*, pp. 561–72; Kokovtsov, *Out of My Past*, pp. 98, 459–60.

74 Sidorov, *Finansovoe polozhenie*, pp. 27–8.

75 See *Russkie finansy*, pp. 349–66, and Anan"ich, *Rossiia*, pp. 254–60.

76 K. F. Shatsillo, 'O disproportsii v razvitii vooruzhennykh sil Rossii nakanune pervoi mirovoi voiny, 1906–1914', *Istoricheskie zapiski*, 83, 1969, p. 124, fn.5. The total naval budget in 1900–4 averaged 102 million rubles. According to A. L. Vainshtein, *Narodnoe bogatstvo i narodnokhoziaistvennoe nakoplenie predprevoliutsionnoi Rossii*, Moscow, 1960, p. 292, the value of all vessels, merchant and naval, including those under construction, amounted to 783 million rubles on 1 January 1914. Bearing in mind the huge shipbuilding programme that was under way after 1907, and discounting the merchant fleet, the value of the stock of military shipping in 1904 must have been well under 400 million rubles.

77 Shatsillo, 'O disproportsii', p. 128, fn.28; Ozerov, *Kak raskhoduiutsia*, p. 139.

78 TsGIA f.,1276, op.2, d.444, ll.2–3. See also K. F. Shatsillo, *Russkii imperializm i razvitie flota nakanune pervoi mirovoi voiny, 1906–1914gg.*, Moscow, 1968, pp. 53–6.

79 TsGIA, f.1276, op.4, d.530, l.24ob.; *ibid.*, op.2, d.444, l.50ob; Shatsillo, *Russkii imperializm*, pp. 53–7. Birilev is described in Witte's memoirs as an 'honourable, knowledgeable naval man ... he is not stupid, has a sharp tongue and a sharp pen, and can be amusing'. He despised the Grand Duke, whom Witte himself called 'hare-brained': Harcave, ed., *Memoirs*, pp. 719, 721.

80 Shatsillo, *Russkii imperializm*, pp. 24, 61; Shatsillo, *Rossiia*, p. 36.

81 TsGIA f.1276, op.4, d.530, ll.25–7. The strategy in the Black Sea was designed to forestall any hostile attempt to penetrate the Straits (Russia's own navy was forbidden to leave the Black Sea). For reference to new naval

technology, see *ibid.*, op.2, d.444, ll.1–8, and Shatsillo, *Russkii imperializm*, pp. 57–9, 105.

82 TsGIA f.1276, op.2, d.444, ll.41–2; *ibid.*, op.4, d.530, ll.32–9; Shatsillo, 'O disproportsii', p. 128. For Dikov – 'very decent', chosen 'not for his abilities, but for lack of a suitable and willing candidate' – see Harcave, ed., *Memoirs*, p. 721.

83 Shatsillo, *Russkii imperializm*, pp. 49–50.

84 Iu. V. Rummel', *Otechestvennyi flot kak sredstvo oborony i mezhdunarodnoi politiki*, St Petersburg, 1907, pp. 58–9, 81–6; A. P. Semenov-Tian-Shanskii, *O napravlenii v razvitii russkogo flota*, St Petersburg, 1907; Belavenets, *Nuzhenli nam flot*; Shatsillo, *Russkii imperializm*, p. 49. Rummel''s work was also couched in terms of a plea for the creation of a merchant fleet. His son was a leading figure in the south Russian iron and steel industry and played a major role in Prodamet.

85 A. G. Kavtaradze, 'Iz istorii russkogo general'nogo shtaba', *Voenno-istoricheskii zhurnal*, 1972, 7, pp. 87–92; 1974, 12, pp. 80–6; Shatsillo, 'O disproportsii', p. 126.

86 Sidorov, *Finansovoe polozhenie*, p. 55; A. Zhilin, 'Bol'shaia programma po usileniiu russkoi armii', *Voenno-istoricheskii zhurnal*, 1974, 7, pp. 90–7; N. Stone, *The Eastern Front, 1914–1917*, London, 1975, pp. 23, 30–1.

87 Shatsillo, *Rossiia*, pp. 39, 106.

88 TsGIA f.1276, op.4, d.530, l.17; Stone, *Eastern Front*, pp. 19–20.

89 Shatsillo, *Rossiia*, pp. 39–40.

90 TsGIA f.1276, op.4, d.530, ll.24–29ob. Eroshkin, *Istoriia*, p. 227, and M. Perrins, 'The Council for State Defence, 1905–1909: a study in Russian bureaucratic politics', *Slavonic and East European Review*, 58, 1980, pp. 370–98.

91 *Artilleriiskii zhurnal*, 1908, p. 975 (Rodzevich).

92 TsGIA f.37, op.77, d.136, l.10; Viatkin, *Gornozavodskii Ural*, p. 113.

93 TsGIA f.37, op.77, d.136, l.7; *VOGK za 1908*, p. 143.

94 TsGIA f.37, op.77, d.136, ll.15–27, report by Professor V. N. Lipin on his visit to the Perm Cannon Works, 27 December 1906 to 19 January 1907. At Zlatoust, one-quarter of output in the gun shop was rejected. See *VOGK za 1908*, p. 143.

95 Ozerov, *Kak raskhoduiutsia*, pp. 111–37, 158–9.

96 *Stenogramma*, pp. 12–13. Tokarskii's comments were endorsed by Ozerov.

97 *SOGD*, III, 4th session, 72 sitting, cols. 1,404–5; Shatsillo, *Russkii imperializm*, pp. 169–73.

98 A. F. Iakovlev, *Ekonomicheskie krizisy v Rossii*, Moscow, 1955, pp. 314, 339–43. Mendel'son, *Teoriia*, vol. 3, pp. 137–51, takes a different view, but is not convincing.

99 Meerson, 'Promyshlennaia depressiia', pp. 147–74, who emphasizes the 'crisis of overproduction'; Bovykin, *Formirovanie*, p. 56. See also TsGIA f.268, op.3, d.1049, l.124.

100 Mendel'son, *Teoriia*, vol. 3, pp. 148–9.

101 L. E. Shepelev, *Akstionernye kompanii v Rossii*, Leningrad, 1973, pp. 135, 225;

I. F. Gindin, *Russkie kommercheskie banki*, Moscow, 1948, pp. 118, 124; Mendel'son, *Teoriia*, vol. 3, pp. 142–4.
102 Liashchenko, *Istoriia*, p. 310.
103 Laverychev, *Gosudarstvo*, pp. 120–1.
104 *Ibid.*, for the conventional Soviet view, as well as A. P. Pogrebinskii, 'Komitet po zheleznodorozhnym zakazam i ego likvidatsiia v 1914g.', *Istoricheskie zapiski*, 83, 1969, pp. 233–43.
105 Quotations in Liashchenko, *Istoriia*, p. 325. See M.Ia. Gefter, 'Bor'ba vokrug sozdaniia metallurgicheskogo tresta v Rossii v nachale XXv.', *Istoricheskie zapiski*, 47, 1954, pp. 124–48.
106 Gefter, 'Bor'ba', p. 131. Gefter emphasized inter-firm division; Rieber, *Merchants and Entrepreneurs*, pp. 340–4, places much greater stress upon ministerial opposition, which whipped up consumer frenzy.
107 G. M. Gorfein, 'Iz istorii obrazovaniia Ministerstva torgovli i promyshlennosti', S. N. Valk, ed., *Ocherki po istorii ekonomiki i klassovykh otnoshenii v Rossii kontsa XIX-nachala XX veka*, Moscow-Leningrad, 1964, pp. 161–79. Shepelev, *Tsarizm i burzhuaziia*, pp. 37, 42–6. Timashev went on to pursue a career in finance, thereby confirming his colleagues' worst fears.
108 *Ibid.*, pp. 54–8, drawing a contrast with A. V. Krivoshein, in the Chief Administration of Land Reorganization and Agriculture.
109 The classic statement about the dilemmas of political reform and social change in the first Russian revolution remains M. Weber, 'Zur Lage der bürgerlichen Demokratie in Russland', reprinted in W. J. Mommsen and D. Dahlmann, eds., *Max Weber: Zur Russischen Revolution von 1905*, Tübingen, 1989, pp. 71–280.
110 Rieber, *Merchants and Entrepreneurs*, p. 333.

3 The defence burden, 1907–1914

1 General Brinken, chief of staff of the Petersburg military district, reported in 1907 that the Tsar was 'hypnotized' by the idea of a large modern navy: Shatsillo, *Russkii imperializm*, p. 61. See also V. A. Sukhomlinov, *Vospominaniia*, Berlin, 1924, pp. 225–6. Nicholas complained when ministerial reports 'failed to provide detailed insights into the real conditions of the fleet or the qualifications of new recruits', according to A. Verner, *The Crisis of Russian Autocracy: Nicholas II and the 1905 Revolution*, Princeton, 1990, pp. 23–5, 60, 65.
2 C. Schmidt, ed., *The Economics of Military Expenditure*, London, 1987, pp. 141–2, 193–4; David M. MacDonald, *United Government and Foreign Policy in Russia, 1900–1914*, Cambridge, Mass., 1992.
3 Offer, *First World War*, for a full treatment.
4 Marinov, *Rossiia i Iaponiia*, is the main source for Russo-Japanese relations before 1914.
5 A. M. Zaionchkovskii, *Podgotovka Rossii k mirovoi voine v mezhdunarodnom otnoshenii*, Moscow-Leningrad, 1926, pp. 118–20; *Documents diplomatiques français*, série 2, vol. 9, pp. 273–4; vol. 10, pp. 185, 491–3; vol. 11, p. 789; Ropponen, *Die Kraft Russlands*, p. 228.

6 V. I. Bovykin, *Ocherki istorii vneshnei politiki Rossii*, Moscow, 1960, p. 88; Ropponen, *Die Kraft Russlands*, pp. 215–7; Zaionchkovskii, *Podgotovka*, p. 202.
7 Cited in Shatsillo, *Rossiia*, p. 31. See also Lieven, *Russia*, pp. 31–2, 74–5.
8 Undated memorandum, cited in Marinov, *Rossiia i Iaponiia*, p. 104. See also Kokovtsov, *Out of My Past*, pp. 231–5.
9 Marinov, *Rossiia i Iaponiia*, pp. 105–7.
10 *Ibid.*, pp. 46–9, 85, 101–4.
11 Lieven, *Russia*, pp. 38, 69; Fuller, *Strategy and Power*, pp. 433–8.
12 F. A. Golder, *Documents of Russian History, 1914–1917*, New York, 1927, pp. 3–23; Lieven, *Russia*, pp. 80–3.
13 Geyer, *Russian Imperialism*, p. 300.
14 A. M. Zaionchkovskii, *Podgotovka Rossii k imperialisticheskoi voine: ocherki voennoi podgotovki i pervonachal'nykh planov*, Moscow, 1926; G. Frantz, *Russlands Eintritt in den Weltkrieg: der Ausbau der russischen Wehrmacht und ihr Einsatz bei Kriegsausbruch*, Berlin, 1924; Fuller, *Strategy and Power*. David Stevenson is completing a major study of the European arms race.
15 TsGIA f.1276, op.4, d.530, ll.424–65, 'Kratkii svod otzyvov grazhdanskikh vedomstv po voprosu o plane gosudarstvennoi oborony'.
16 Zaionchkovskii, *Podgotovka*, pp. 74–80, 348–54 (Memorandum from General Alekseev, 17 December 1908).
17 *SOGD*, III, 4 session, 71 sitting, cols. 1,302–3. See also Harcave, ed., *Memoirs*, p. 729. In his *Political Memoirs, 1905–1917*, Ann Arbor, 1967, p. 168, Paul Miliukov described Koliubakin as an ex-officer 'with a hot temper'.
18 TsGIA f. 1276, op. 4, d. 530, l. 150ob.
19 Details in Sukhomlinov, *Vospominaniia*, pp. 154–5. Witte used a different metaphor: 'what we had from 1905 to 1909 was something like a trunk with two heads'. Harcave, ed., *Memoirs*, p. 730. The General Staff also failed to keep the GAU properly informed of its plans, according to E. Z. Barsukov, *Podgotovka Rossii k mirovoi voine v artilleriiskom otnoshenii*, Moscow-Leningrad, 1926, p. 60.
20 The Tsar initially declared his intention to chair the SGO but, typically, changed his mind. See Kavtaradze, 'Iz istorii', pp. 87–92; L. G. Beskrovnyi, *Armiia i flot Rossii v nachale XXv.*, Moscow, 1986, pp. 49–51.
21 A. F. Rödiger, 'Istoriia moei zhizni', *Voenno-istoricheskii zhurnal*, 6, 1990, pp. 82–7. Rödiger had already incurred the Tsar's displeasure by opposing the decision to hive off the General Staff from the War Ministry, according to Kokovtsov, *Memoirs*, p. 229. For Rödiger's resignation, see W. T. Wilfong, 'Rebuilding the Russian army, 1905–1914', PhD thesis, University of Indiana, 1977, pp. 86–95, 115.
22 A. A. Polivanov, *Iz dnevnikov i vospominanii po dolzhnosti voennogo ministra i ego pomoshchnika, 1907–1916gg.*, Moscow, 1924, pp. 27–8. Sukhomlinov worked his way through four staff chiefs between 1909 and 1914. Stone, *Eastern Front*, p. 26 interprets this turnover as a deliberate attempt by the new War Minister to impose his authority over the General Staff. Sukhomlinov was the subject of numerous uncomplimentary portraits, as in S. I. Shidlovskii, *Vospominaniia*, 2 vols., Berlin, 1923, vol. 1, pp. 214–17, and N. N.

Golovine, *The Russian Army in the World War*, New Haven, 1931, pp. 11–14. His rehabilitation began with Sidorov, *Finansovoe polozhenie*, pp. 52–4, 74, and was continued by Norman Stone and W. T. Wilfong.

23 'Iz zapisok A. F. Rödigera', *Krasnyi arkhiv*, 60, 1930, 5, pp. 104, 123; Sukhomlinov, *Vospominaniia*, p. 270; Beskrovnyi, *Armiia i flot*, p. 12; Wilfong, 'Rebuilding', pp. 69–75.

24 TsGIA f. 1276, op. 4, d. 530, l. 15ob.; Barsukov, *Podgotovka*, p. 58.

25 Polivanov, *Iz dnevnikov*, p. 28; Wilfong, 'Rebuilding', pp. 97–137; Fuller, *Strategy and Power*, p. 427. For a critique of Sukhomlinov's policy towards fortresses, see Zaionchkovskii, *Podgotovka*, pp. 141–54. Each fortress cost between 50 and 100 million rubles to build and equip, according to Rödiger, in *SOGD* III, 1st session, 74 sitting, 27 May 1908, col. 1,616.

26 TsGIA f. 1726, op. 4, d. 530, ll. 192–4, 219–20, 231–40ob., Council for State Defence, 9 May 1908; Shatsillo, *Rossiia*, pp. 41–2, 106.

27 TsGIA f. 1276, op. 4, d. 530, ll. 343–76, Kokovtsov to Stolypin, 1 April 1908; Polivanov, *Iz dnevnikov*, p. 39; Kokovtsov, *Memoirs*, pp. 218–19, 229–30. Sukhomlinov captured the frostiness of his relationship with Kokovtsov in his own memoirs: when Kokovtsov became Prime Minister (in 1911), Sukhomlinov relates that he 'was obliged to tell him that it won't be possible to fire money at the enemy and that all his gold reserves and other funds would simply find their way into the pockets of our conquerors, in the event of a national disgrace'. Sukhomlinov, *Vospominaniia*, pp. 218–19.

28 Barsukov, *Podgotovka*, pp. 58–69, 269–70; Zaionchkovskii, *Podgotovka*, pp. 85–90; Ropponen, *Die Kraft Russlands*, pp. 198–200.

29 *Ibid.*, pp. 202–3; Barsukov, *Podgotovka*, pp. 63–8; Stone, *Eastern Front*, pp. 31–2.

30 A. Zhilin, 'Bol'shaia programma po usileniiu russkoi armii', *Voenno-istoricheskii zhurnal*, 7, 1974, p. 91; Beskrovnyi, 'Proizvodstvo vooruzheniia', pp. 106–7.

31 Sukhomlinov, *Vospominaniia*, pp. 194, 269; B. Bukin, 'Zheleznye dorogi v mirovuiu voinu ikh blizhaishie zadachi v podgotovke strany k oborone', *Voina i revoliutsiia*, 1926, 3, pp. 100–18; 4, pp. 87–100.

32 Shatsillo, *Rossiia*, pp. 43–9; A. L. Sidorov, ed., 'Iz istorii podgotovki Rossii k pervoi mirovoi voine', *Istoricheskii arkhiv*, 1962, 2, p. 143.

33 K. F. Shatsillo, 'Poslednie voennye programmy Rossiiskoi imperii', *Voprosy istorii*, 7–8, 1991, p. 230; Zhilin, 'Bol'shaia programma', p. 91; G. Krumeich, *Armaments and Politics in France on the Eve of the First World War: The Introduction of Three-Year Conscription, 1913–1914*, Leamington Spa, 1984.

34 The 'large programme' absorbed and replaced the 'small' military programme.

35 Barsukov, *Podgotovka*, pp. 81–94; Zhilin, 'Bol'shaia programma', pp. 91–5; Shatsillo, 'Poslednie voennye programmy', pp. 230–1.

36 Zhilin, 'Bol'shaia programma', p. 96; Beskrovnyi, *Armiia i flot*, p. 15; D. W. Spring, 'Russia and the Franco-Russian alliance, 1905–1914: dependence or interdependence', *Slavonic and East European Review*, 66, 1988, pp. 564–92 remarks that 'it was not the dependence of Russian strategy on France which called for the speeding up of Russia's mobilization and an early

attack on east Prussia. It was the deterioration of relations with the central powers and the correctly foreseen strategy of Germany in a two-front war'.

37 Cited in Shatsillo, *Russkii imperializm*, pp. 346, 323.

38 *Ibid.*, pp. 163–201; A. Zvegintsev, 'The Duma and imperial defence', *Russian Review*, 1912, 3, pp. 49–63.

39 I. V. Bestuzhev, 'Bor'ba v Rossii po voprosam vneshnei politiki nakanune pervoi mirovoi voiny, 1910–1914', *Istoricheskie zapiski*, 75, 1965, pp. 45–85; Shatsillo, *Russkii imperializm*, pp. 90–162; idem, 'Poslednie voennye programmy', p. 229. Grigorovich replaced Voevodskii, who served from 1909 until 1911 and was, in Witte's view, 'not to be taken seriously'.

40 TsGIA f. 1276, op. 5, d. 494, ll. 25–7, 'Zhurnal Osobogo soveshchaniia po rassmotreniiu programmy razvitiia morskikh vooruzhennykh sil Rossii', 3 August 1909; Shatsillo, *Russkii imperializm*, pp. 65–7.

41 TsGIA f. 1276, op. 5, d. 494, ll. 28–34.

42 *Ibid.*, ll. 84–9, 'Zhurnal Osobogo soveshchaniia', 21 August 1909; *ibid.*, op. 4, d. 530, ll. 405–11, Navy Minister to Council of Ministers, 15 January 1910; *ibid.*, d. 444, ll. 405–11, Council of Ministers, 15 January 1910; 'Iz istorii podgotovki', pp. 120–5.

43 Shatsillo, *Russkii imperializm*, pp. 193–5.

44 TsGIA f. 1276, op. 2, d. 444, ll. 232–240ob., Council of Ministers, 4 August 1911; TsGAVMF f. 401, op. 6, d. 1, ll. 196–205ob., Commission on Shipbuilding, 2 December 1911.

45 TsGAVMF f. 401, op. 6, d. 272, l. 177, Secret report on progress of 1912–16 shipbuilding programme (1913); Shatsillo, *Russkii imperializm*, pp. 72–77, 158–61. For an unconvincing attempt to argue that the Duma was responsible for Russia's failure to achieve naval parity with Germany by 1914, see N. S. Chirikov, 'Plan voiny, podgotovka i mobilizatsiia imperatorskogo flota v 1914 godu', *Voennaia byl'*, 75, 1965, pp. 12–18.

46 N. V. Savich, 'Morskie raskhody i sudostroitel'naia programma', *Novyi ekonomist*, 5, 1914, pp. 4–7.

47 *Vestnik finansov*, 1914, 13, p. 623; *Proposed Budget for the Russian Empire*, St Petersburg, 1908, p. 103; *Proekt gosudarstvennoi rospisi dokhodov i raskhodov na 1908*, St Petersburg, 1908, pp. 120–1. The 1907 total includes 186 million rubles 'extraordinary' expenditure, connected with the Russo-Japanese War; the 1913 figure includes 135 million rubles for 'economic-operational' expenditures. These figures exclude sums assigned for railway construction, some of which were earmarked for military lines.

48 For Kokovtsov's assessment, see TsGIA f. 1276, op. 4, d. 530, l. 353, and Sidorov, *Finansovoe polozhenie*, pp. 48, 55–8.

49 *SOGD*, III, 1st session, 74 sitting, 27 May 1908, col. 1,658; 4th session, 62 sitting, 21 February 1911, col. 2,341 (Alekseenko). See also Fuller, *Civil–Military Conflict*, p. 48 and Pintner, 'Burden' p. 248, who puts defence spending at 25.2 per cent of the budget in 1910–14.

50 *Proekt .. na 1915*, Petrograd, 1915, pp. 138–9, noting that 73 million rubles were assigned to the construction budget; *Proekt gosudarstvennoi rospisi ... na 1917*, Petrograd, 1916, p. 119; Fuller, *Civil–Military Conflict*, p. 220; Pintner, 'Burden', p. 243.

51 Nikanor Savich (1869–?) subsequently appeared on the Progressive Bloc's slate as the preferred candidate for the post of Navy Minister in 1915. He held office briefly under the Provisional Government. For the budget figures, see *Proekt ... na 1913*, pp. 126–7; Pintner, 'Burden', p. 244. The figures relate to ordinary spending.

52 Gregory, *Russian National Income*, appendix F, pp. 252–3.

53 Fuller, *Civil–Military Conflict*, p. 68.

54 Savich remained concerned by the power vested in the Admiralty by virtue of the 'colossal' sums assigned it: see Savich, 'Morskie raskhody'. Zvegintsev (1869–1915) entered politics via the Voronezh zemstvo; during the First World War, his airplane was shot down by 'friendly fire'. Alekseenko (1847–1917) outlived him by just two years. Guchkov (1862–1936) served briefly as chairman of the Third Duma (1910), but reached the pinnacle of his fame as chairman of the central war industries committee. He died in Paris. Shingarev (1869–1918) served in the Provisional Government, but was murdered in his hospital bed by Bolshevik sailors.

55 Grigorovich (1853–1930), unusually, remained in his post until February 1917. He receives a good press in Zvegintsev, 'The Duma and state defence', in Kokovtsov, *Memoirs*, pp. 218–19, and (grudgingly), in Witte's memoirs, where he is compared favourably with his predecessors. For Stolypin's view on the role of the Duma, see *SOGD*, III, 1st session, 72 sitting, 24 May 1908, cols. 1,400–4; Sukhomlinov, *Vospominaniia*, pp. 221, 223; J. D. Walz, 'State defense and Russian politics under the last Tsar', PhD thesis, Syracuse University, 1967; and Fuller, *Civil–Military Conflict*, pp. 225–30.

56 V. N. Mukoseev, 'Gosudarstvennoe khoziaistvo', in Martov et al. *Obshchestvennoe dvizhenie*, vol. 1, pp. 182–95. The Duma could not challenge payments earmarked for the state debt. See P. E. Shchegolev, ed., *Padenie tsarskogo rezhima*, 7 vols., Leningrad, 1924–7, vol. 7, p. 11 (Shingarev); Shatsillo, *Russkii imperializm*, p. 166.

57 *SOGD*, III, 4th session, 62 sitting, col. 2,342; *ibid.*, 126 sitting, col. 737–8; Kokovtsov, *Memoirs*, p. 371. See also Ozerov, *Kak raskhoduiutsia*, p. 159, and Sidorov, *Finansovoe polozhenie*, pp. 71–2.

58 In 1911, 16 per cent of the appropriations to the War Ministry remained unspent; by 1913, this figure had fallen to one per cent. See Sidorov, *Finansovoe polozhenie*, p. 75; also *SOGD* III, 5th session, 126 sitting, cols. 737–8 (Rozanov), for the GAU budget.

59 *SOGD*, III, 4th session, 62 sittings, cols. 2,342–444. Kokovtsov's memoirs reveal his undisguised contempt for Shingarev.

60 TsGIA f. 1393, op. 2, d. 455, l. 98; Fuller, *Civil–Military Conflict*, p. 285.

61 The extent of corruption is discussed in chapter 6.

62 Savich, 'Morskie raskhody'.

63 TsGIA f.1276, op.4, d.530, ll.343–74, Kokovtsov to Stolypin, 2 January 1910; Kokovtsov, *Memoirs*, p. 345.

64 Shepelev, *Tsarizm i burzhuaziia*, p. 49. Rukhlov (1853–1918) held office until October 1915. Born into a peasant family in Vologda province, he made a rapid rise through the government, helped by his association with the extreme rightwing Union of Russian People.

65 V. S. Diakin, 'Iz istorii ekonomicheskoi politiki tsarizma v 1907–1914gg.', *Istoricheskie zapiski*, 109, 1983, pp. 25–63. Krivoshein (1858–1921) held the post of Minister of Agriculture from 1908 until 1915.

66 TsGIA f. 1276, op. 4, d. 530, ll. 32–9, 367–70, Kokovtsov to Stolypin, 2 January 1910.

67 R. H. Gorlin, 'Problems of tax reform in imperial Russia', *Journal of Modern History*, 49, 1977, pp. 246–65; Sidorov, *Finansovoe polozhenie*, pp. 33–48; Iu. N. Shebaldin, 'Gosudarstvennyi biudzhet tsarskoi Rossii v nachale XXv. do pervoi mirovoi voiny', *Istoricheskie zapiski*, 65, 1959, pp. 163–90.

68 Shepelev, *Tsarizm i burzhuaziia*, pp. 162–4.

69 *Promyshlennost'* i torgovlia, 1911, 8, pp. 343–5. The net profits of state railways increased from 161 million rubles in 1908 to 473 million in 1913; other details from Shepelev, *Tsarizm i burzhuaziia*, pp. 222–8.

70 Mukoseev, 'Gosudarstvennoe khoziaistvo', p. 181; *Explanatory Memorandum to the Russian Budget*, St Petersburg, 1913, vol. 1, p. 97.

71 M. Miller, *The Economic Development of Russia, 1905–1914*, London, 1926, pp. 132–6.

72 G. D. Dement'ev, 'Svobodnaia nalichnost' gosudarstvennogo kaznacheistva', *Vestnik finansov*, 1912, 9, appendix, pp. 34–5; A. I. Bukovetskii, 'Svobodnaia nalichnost' i zolotoi zapas tsarskogo pravitel'stva v kontse XIX-nachale XXv.', in *Monopolii i inostrannyi kapital v Rossii*, Moscow-Leningrad, 1962, p. 363. See also Kokovtsov, *Memoirs*, p. 460; *Explanatory Memorandum*, p. 97; Anan"ich, *Rossiia*, pp. 233–54, 266–7. The 1908–9 negotiations are also described in Sidorov, *Finansovoe polozhenie*, p. 31; Shebaldin, 'Gosudarstvennyi biudzhet', pp. 178–9 and Girault, *Emprunts russes*, pp. 487–91.

73 Bukovetskii, 'Svobodnaia nalichnost"', pp. 364–5; Sidorov, *Finansovoe polozhenie*, p. 104.

74 TsGIA f. 1276, op. 4, d. 5340, ll. 363–4; Sidorov, *Finansovoe polozhenie*, pp. 27–34; Anan"ich, *Rossiia*, pp. 254–60.

75 *SOGD*, III, 1st session, 74 sitting, col. 1,602, 27 May 1908 (Bab'ianskii); *Vestnik finansov*, 1914, 13, p. 623; Alvin Johnson, 'The expansion of military expenditures', *Documents of the American Association for International Conciliation*, New York, 1911, pp. 3–9. Different figures, from a German source, are given in Hardach, *First World War*, p. 150: Germany $7.4, France $8.0, Britain $7.8, Austria $3.3 and Russia $2.8.

76 *SOGD*, III, 1st session, 74 sitting, col. 1,602, for other estimates of defence spending as a proportion of national income: in Russia, between 8.3 and 10 per cent, in Austria, 5 per cent, in Germany 4 per cent and in France between 5 and 6.2 per cent.

77 P. K. O'Brien, 'The costs and benefits of British imperialism, 1846–1914', *Past and Present*, 120, 1988, pp. 163–200.

78 Quoted in Quincy Wright, *The Study of War*, Chicago, 1940, p. 260. See also M. Pearton, *The Knowledgeable State: Diplomacy, War and Technology since 1870*, London, 1982, pp. 132–9 and Harcave, ed., *Memoirs*, pp. 55–7.

79 Witte's 1903 statement appears in G. Drage, *Russian Affairs*, London, 1904, p. 279. For the very different view he held in 1913 – 'the vast sums spent on

armaments come from the sweat of the poor; they sap our productive strength, while poverty, sickness and mortality increase' – see Harcave, ed., *Memoirs*, pp. 57–8; and *Explanatory Memorandum to the Russian Budget*, 1913, vol. 1, p. 94.

80 G. Kennedy, *Defense Economics*, London, 1983, provides a clear guide to the issues.

81 *SOGD*, III, 1st session, 74 sitting, col. 1,627 (Belousov). Kokovtsov's views appear in Kokovtsov, *Memoirs*, pp. 260–1. Durnovo is quoted in Lieven, *Russia's Rulers*, p. 224.

82 A. Kahan, 'Government policies and the industrialization of Russia', *Journal of Economic History*, 27, 1967, pp. 460–77.

83 J. Brooks, 'The zemstvo and the education of the people', in T. Emmons and W. Vucinich, eds., *The Zemstvo in Russia: An Experiment in Local Self-Government*, Stanford, 1982, pp. 270–1.

84 The quote is from B. Eklof, 'Peasants and schools', in B. Eklof and S. P. Frank, eds., *The World of the Russian Peasant*, London, 1990, p. 118. It might be argued that the government should have done more to advance the educational opportunities of the urban population. On the other hand, factories – including state-owned enterprises – did provide some schooling for young workers. The argument about 'social capabilities' derives from Moses Abramovitz, 'Catching up, forging ahead and falling behind', *Journal of Economic History*, 46, 1986, pp. 385–406.

85 Figures from S. C. Ramer, 'The zemstvo and public health', in Emmons and Vucinich, eds., *Zemstvo*, pp. 302, 307.

86 M. Bulgakov, *A Country Doctor's Notebook*, London, 1990.

87 Kennedy, *Defense Economics*, pp. 193–203.

88 Geyer, *Russian Imperialism*, p. 287, perhaps exaggerates the relative weakness of the Black Sea fleet, *vis-à-vis* that of the enhanced Turkish navy. On the need for both defensive and offensive capabilities, see the comments of Stolypin and Sukhomlinov, in Shatsillo, *Russkii imperializm*, p. 323.

4 The economics and politics of industrial recovery

1 Gerschenkron, 'The rate of industrial growth', p. 152.

2 I. Kh. Ozerov, *Na temy dnia: k ekonomicheskomu polozheniiu Rossii*, St Petersburg, 1912, p. 296; A. Finn-Enotaevskii, *Sovremennoe khoziaistvo v Rossii*, St Petersburg, 1911, pp. 248–50; M. I. Tugan-Baranovskii, *K luchshemu budushchemu*, St Petersburg, 1912, pp. 177–83; Lyashchenko, *History*, p. 685; I. F. Gindin, *Russkie kommercheskie banki*, Moscow, 1948, pp. 160–1, 165; Mendel'son, *Teoriia*, vol. 3, p. 205.

3 Gerschenkron, *Economic Backwardness*, p. 22; M. E. Falkus, *The Industrialization of Russia, 1700–1914*, London, 1972, pp. 79–80; Crisp, *Studies*, pp. 34, 52, 149.

4 *Promyshlennost' i Torgovlia*, 1911, 7. Avdakov (1851–1915) came from an Armenian professional background. After training at the Institute of Mines in St Petersburg, he established himself as a leading figure in the south Russian iron and steel industry. He held directorships in Nikolaev Ship-

building, Lena Goldfields, Makeevka Coal and Briansk Iron and Steel; he was briefly head of the coal syndicate Produgol'. He also served on the State Council. Details in *Materialy po istorii SSSR*, vol. 6, Moscow, 1959, p. 745; Shepelev, *Tsarizm i burzhuaziia*, pp. 98–9; and Rieber, *Merchants and Entrepreneurs*, pp. 229–30.

5 The government did, however, offer indirect support to industry; in particular, the State Bank underwrote the operations of the commercial banking system.

6 TsGIA f.1276, op. 4, d.217, ll.1–1ob. The delay was caused by the sudden death of Filosofov and his replacement by I. P. Shipov. For their careers and ideas, see Shepelev, *Tsarizm i burzhuaziia*, pp. 39–43. The conference proceedings are contained in *Stenogramma soveshchaniia* and in TsGIA f.268, op.3, d.1049; f.1276, op.4, d.296.

7 TsGIA f.268, op.3, d.1049, ll.135–40.

8 *Ibid.*, ll.136–136ob.; *Zapiska soveta s"ezdov o merakh k pod"emu otechestvennoi zheleznoi promyshlennosti i mashinostroeniia*, St Petersburg, 1908.

9 *Stenogramma*, pp. 47–8 (V. A. Karaulov). Vol'skii estimated that only six million puds were required for the new Donets railway, only one-fifth of the iron and steel supplied to the railways in 1907: *Zapiska soveta s"ezdov*, pp. 7, 28; *Stenogramma*, pp. 75 (Farmakovskii), 83–5 (Tokarskii).

10 See the report on the Conference (by Shipov) to the Council of Ministers, TsGIA f.268, op.3, d.1049, ll.124ob.–125.

11 Rieber, *Merchants and Entrepreneurs*, pp. 195–8; Crisp, *Studies*, pp. 28–31.

12 Shepelev, *Tsarizm i burzhuaziia*, pp. 231–2; Gindin, 'Politika', p. 103. Miller died prematurely in 1911. He was succeeded by P. L. Bark (1858–1937), later Minister of Finances between 1914 and February 1917.

13 *Promyshlennost' i torgovlia*, 1914, 2, p. 69, cited in Shepelev, *Tsarizm i burzhuaziia*, p. 240; Gindin, 'Politika', pp. 104–5.

14 Shepelev, *Tsarizm i burzhuaziia*, pp. 232–3.

15 Laverychev, *Gosudarstvo i monopolii*, pp. 70–5. Further details in Gindin, 'Politika'. A brief summary in English is provided in Rieber, *Merchants and Entrepreneurs*, pp. 369–70.

16 TsGIA f.268, op. 3, d.1049, l.124; *Svod zakonov Rossiiskoi imperii*, izd. 1887, vol. 10, part 1, 'Polozhenie o kazennykh podriadakh i postavkakh', new edn, 1900, revised 1915; *Stenogramma*, pp. 125, 128. See also Subbotin, 'Voennaia promyshlennost'', p. 127.

17 Shepelev, *Tsarizm i burzhuaziia*, pp. 251–3.

18 TsGIA f.1276, op.4, d.166, ll.4–4ob.

19 Rieber, *Merchants and Entrepreneurs*, p. 370.

20 See Bovykin, *Formirovanie*, and H. Haumann, *Kapitalismus im zaristischen Staat, 1905–1917*, Königstein, 1980.

21 Urban population increased from 16.55 million in 1908 to 18.60 million in 1913. Urban consumption patterns are discussed in G. A. Dikhtiar, *Vnutrenniaia torgovlia v dorevoliutsionnoi Rossii*, Moscow, 1960, pp. 47–58.

22 Strumilin derived an estimate of the capital stock of industry from two sources: published balance sheets, which yielded information about the 'acquisition cost' of assets, and (for investment in non-corporate industry)

tax statistics. Tax statistics recorded gross turnover for various categories of enterprise; by applying a coefficient for the rate of turnover of basic capital, Strumilin estimated the value of capital employed. S. G. Strumilin, *Statistiko-ekonomicheskie ocherki*, Moscow, 1958, pp. 519, 530–1.

23 Gindin, *Russkie kommercheskie banki*, pp. 177–86, 192, 331–40; Crisp, *Studies*, pp. 144–53.

24 Details from Khromov, *Ekonomicheskoe razvitie*, p. 457; *Zapiska*, pp. 7–9; Gefter, 'Tsarizm', p. 104; Tsukernik, *Sindikat 'Prodamet'*, p. 189; V. S. Ziv, *Inostrannye kapitaly v russkoi gornozavodskoi promyshlennosti*, Petrograd, 1917, p. 9.

25 *Svod statisticheskikh dannykh po zheleznodelatel'noi promyshlennosti*, St Petersburg, 1911–13; *Gornozavodskoe delo*, 51, 1915, p. 12,512; *Statistischeskii sbornik za 1913–1917gg.*, Petrograd, 1915, p. 25; I. Kh. Ozerov, *Ekonomicheskaia Rossiia i ee finansovaia politika*, St Petersburg, 1905, p. 118; N. N. Savvin, *K voprosu o potreblenii metalla i metallicheskikh izdelii v Rossii*, St Petersburg, 1913, p. 6; Gefter, 'Tsarizm', pp. 82–5; Liashchenko, *Istoriia*, vol. 2, p. 127.

26 *Torgovo-promyshlennaia gazeta*, 7 January 1914; *Finansovoe obozrenie*, 1914, 10, p. 29.

27 Savvin, *K voprosu*, p. 4.

28 *Otchet otdela promyshlennosti za 1910*, St Petersburg, 1911, p. 171. Pig iron sold at 45 kopeks per pud in 1908 and 46 kopeks in 1910; structural shapes (*sortovoe zhelezo*) sold for 90 kopeks per pud in 1908 and 120 kopeks in 1910.

29 TsGIA f.23, op.27, d.120.

30 Litvinov-Falinskii (1868–1928) began his career as a factory inspector in St Petersburg. He wrote several books on factory inspection, labour law and economic policy. At this time he headed the department of industry in the new Ministry of Trade and Industry. He left Russia after the revolution.

31 TsGIA f.23, op.27, d.120, ll.3–12.

32 Liashchenko, *Istoriia*, vol. 2, pp. 314–15. Compare G. D. Feldman, *Iron and Steel in the German Inflation, 1918–1923*, Princeton, 1977, p. 32.

33 Details of output and marketing of rolled iron and steel may be found in *Obshchii obzor glavneishikh ostraslei gornoi i gornozavodskoi promyshlennosti*, 2 vols., St Petersburg/Petrograd, 1913–15, vol. 1, p. 37; vol. 2, p. 219, and *Svod statisticheskikh dannykh*, p. 73.

34 Liashchenko, *Istoriia*, vol. 1, pp. 314–15; *Monopolii*, pp. 68, 102.

35 TsGIA, f.23, op.27, d.120, 1.16.

36 *Otchet otdela promyshlennosti za 1913*, Petrograd, 1914, pp. 111–12.

37 TsGAVMF f.401, op.4, d.36, ll.101–6, 110–14, d.37, ll.72–83, 131–7ob., 176–80, sessions of the Commission on Shipbuilding, 13 and 27 April, 28 September, 16 November and 21 December 1912. Liashchenko, *Istoriia*, vol. 2, pp. 316–17 argues, without offering any evidence, that Prodamet hindered pre-war defence preparations.

38 TsGAVMF f.420, op.1, d.76, ll.66–66ob., Minister of Trade and Industry to Admiralty, 6 October 1908.

39 TsGIA f.23, op.27, d.120, 1.20ob.

40 *Otchet otdela promyshlennosti za 1914*, Petrograd, 1915, pp. 59–60. No decision was taken about the rate of duty that would apply.

41 Viatkin, *Gornozavodskii Ural*, pp. 126, 226; *Ocherki istorii tekhniki*, p. 142.
42 Tsukernik, *Sindikat 'Prodamet'*, pp. 239–41.
43 TsGIA f.23, op.27, d.120, l.4ob.; Tsukernik, *Sindikat 'Prodamet'*, pp. 239–41; McKay, *Pioneers*, pp. 112–40, 197–200. For a German comparison, see S. L. Webb, 'Tariffs, cartels, technology and growth in the German steel industry', *Journal of Economic History*, 40, 1980, pp. 309–29.
44 Tsukernik, *Sindikat 'Prodamet'*, pp. 244–51; McKay, *Pioneers*, pp.197–200.
45 The best guide to this subject remains D. I. Shpolianskii, *Monopolii ugol'no-metallurgicheskoi promyshlennosti iuga Rossii v nachale XX veka*, Moscow, 1953, pp. 120–1. Other details from *Obshchii obzor*, vol. 2, p. 173; V. L. Tukholka, 'Zheleznye rudy', *Bogatstva SSSR*, 1925, 3, p. 39; Ziv, *Inostrannye kapitaly*, pp. 60, 68; P. I. Fomin, *Gornaia i gornozavodskaia promyshlennost' iuga Rossii*, 2 vols., Kharkov, 1915–22, vol. 2, pp. 113–14; Tsukernik, *Sindikat 'Prodamet'*, pp. 41–51; McKay, *Pioneers*, pp. 391–4.
46 Rieber, *Merchants and Entrepreneurs*, p. 227, notes that the distinctive voice of the 'southern entrepreneurial group', founded on a mix of engineering skill and managerial acumen, began to weaken after 1908, as the investment banks took charge.
47 *Dinamika*, vol. 3, pp. 52–79, 116. Figures in Gregory, *Russian National Income*, appendix I, imply a 32 per cent increase between 1912 and 1913.
48 Private company purchases are detailed in Il'inskii and Ivanitskii, *Ocherk*, p. 97. Two per cent of wagons and five per cent of locomotives were imported: see V. I. Zhdanov, *Dovoennaia moshchnost' metallopromyshlennosti i ee znachenie v ekonomike strany*, Moscow-Leningrad, 1925, p. 41. For locomotives, see Ivanov, *Ocherk*; *Istoriia Khar'kovskogo parovozostroitel'nogo zavoda, 1895–1932gg.*, Kharkov, 1956, pp. 233, 235, 240–1, 251, 295; Rozenfel'd and Klimenko, *Istoriia*, p. 102.
49 Il'inskii and Ivanitskii, *Ocherki*, pp. 99–101; I. F. Gindin, 'Antikrizisnoe finansirovanie predpriiatii tiazheloi promyshlennosti, konets XIX-nachalo XXv.', *Istoricheskie zapiski*, 105, 1980, pp. 105–49, for Nevskii; N. Savin, 'The machine industry', in A. Raffalovich, ed., *Russia: Its Trade and Commerce*, London, 1818, p. 206, for the car industry in Riga. Motor car production is mentioned briefly in *Doklad Soveta s"ezdov o merakh k razvitiiu proizvoditel'nykh sil Rossii*, Petrograd, 1915, p. 239.
50 E. M. Izmailovskaia, *Russkoe sel'skokhoziaistvennoe mashinostroenie*, Moscow, 1920, pp. 16–17, 26–7, 34, 95–9; *Otchet otdela promyshlennosti za 1914*, Petrograd, 1915, pp. 37–48.
51 G. Holzer, 'The German electrical industry in Russia, 1890–1910', PhD thesis, Lincoln, Nebraska, 1970, p. 68; L. Ia. Eventov, *Inostrannye kapitaly v russkoi promyshlennosti*, Moscow, 1931, pp. 72–3; Sarab'ianov, *Metallopromyshlennost'*, p. 25; L. G. Davydova, *Ipsol'zovanie elektricheskoi energii v promyshlennosti Rossi*, Moscow, 1966, p. 158; Rozenfel'd and Klimenko, *Istoriia*, pp. 109–11; J. Coopersmith, *The Electrification of Russia*, Ithaca, 1992.
52 Zhdanov, *Dovoennaia moshchnost'*, p. 41; Rozenfel'd and Klimenko, *Istoriia*, pp. 107–8; G. B. Borisov and S. Vasil'ev, *Stankostroitel'nyi im. Sverdlova: ocherk istorii Leningradskogo stankostroitel'nyi im. Sverdlova: ocherk istorii Leningradskogo stankostroitel'nogo zavoda, 1867–1961gg.*, Leningrad, 1962, pp. 34, 56, 57.

53 TsGVIA f.369, op.1, d.31, l.247; Rozenfel'd and Klimenko, *Istoriia*, p. 105; M. Ol'shevskii, 'Russkoe mashinostroenie i deistvuiushchii tamozhennyi tarif', *Promyshlennost' i torgovlia*, 1914, 11, pp. 567–71; *Trudy pervogo s"ezda predstavitelei metalloobrabatyvaiushchei promyshlennosti*, Petrograd, 1916, p. 22.
54 *Doklad Soveta s"ezdov*, 1915, p. 172; S. N. Vankov, 'O normalizatsii metalloo-brabatyvaiushchei promyshlennosti', *Nauchno-tekhnicheskii vestnik*, 1921, 4–5, pp. 1–18; Rozenfel'd and Klimenko, *Istoriia*, pp. 105–8.
55 TsGIA f.1393, op.2, d.456, ll.161ob.–162.
56 Ol'shevskii, 'Russkoe mashinostroenie'; N. N. Savvin, 'O poshlinakh na stanki po obrabotke metallov', *Vestnik inzhenerov*, 1915, 7, pp. 269–72; Kannegiser, *Zadachi*, pp. 9–10.
57 Il'inskii and Ivanitskii, *Ocherk*, pp. 74, 87; Rozenfel'd and Klimenko, *Istoriia*, p. 137.
58 Grinevetskii, *Poslevoennye perspektivy*, p. 139; N. Charnovskii, 'Mashinostroitel'naia promyshlennost' v Rossii', *Narodnoe khoziaistvo v 1916 godu*, Petrograd, 1921, 4, p. 52; *Trudy pervogo s"ezda*, 1916; S. N. Vankov, 'O sostoianii nashei metalloobrabatyvaiushchei promyshlennosti k nachalu 1914 g. i vo vremia voiny', *Nauchno-tekhnicheskii vestnik*, 1921, 6, pp. 1–18.
59 *Finansovoe obozrenie*, 1914, 7, p. 9. Total share capital increased from 121.5 million rubles (December 1911) to 223.4 million rubles (December 1913).
60 Ia. I. Livshin, '"Predstavitel'nye" organizatsii krupnoi burzhuazii v Rossii v kontse XIX–nachale XXvv.', *Istoriia SSSR*, 1959, 2, pp. 95–117; R. A. Roosa, 'Russian industrialists and "state socialism", 1906–1917', *Soviet Studies*, 23, 1972, pp. 395–417.

5 The armaments industry

1 Derived from table 5.8 below.
2 TsGAVMF f.420, op.1, d.23, ll.16–41ob.; *VOGK za 1911*, St Petersburg, 1912, p. 75; Shatsillo, *Russkii imperializm*, p. 211.
3 *Svod morskikh postanovlenii*, vol. 5, 1910, paras. 5, 18. The new regulations said nothing about the possibility of borrowing from commercial banks, nor is there any evidence that the state yards ever tried to do so.
4 The Baltic yards made a profit of 500,000 rubles in 1908, but only 292,000 rubles in 1910; the Admiralty yards' profits dropped from 434,000 to 126,000 rubles. The Baltic yards maintained an amortization fund of around two million rubles, but half of this would vanish, if the yards bought new machine tools and installed modern foundry facilities. See TsGAVMF f.401, op. 6, d.178, ll.2–17.
5 TsGAVMF f.427, op. 1, d.2114, ll.27–52ob., f.427, op.1, d.1998, ll.1–3, 151–62, 286; *Vsepoddaneishii otchet morskogo ministra za 1911*, St Petersburg, 1912, p. 278.
6 TsGAVMF f.427, op. 1, d.1998, ll.38–49ob.; f.420, op. 1, d.188, l.115; f.401, op. 6, d.178, ll.15–17, 33; f.410, op. 3, d.1246,. ll.2–6, 14–20.
7 TsGAVMF f.410, op. 3, d.822, ll.75ob.–76; d.1246, ll.8–9.
8 The comments of General Gross, director of Izhora, are reported in Zav'ialov, *Izhorskii zavod*, p. 265; see also TsGAVMF f.410, op. 3, d.1066, l.10; *ibid.*,

d.37, l.188; *Vsepoddaneishii otchet morskogo ministra za 1913*, St Petersburg, 1914, p.302; Shatsillo, *Russkii imperializm, pp.221–23.*

9 TsGAVMF f.410, op. 3, d.1246, ll.8–9.

10 TsGAVMF f.410, op. 3, d.822, l.193; f.441, op. 1, d.1998, ll.1–3, 286, 293. For the State Auditor's remarks, see *ibid.*, 314–20ob.; for the Ministry of Finances' opposition (Weber to Stolypin, 31 October 1909), *ibid.*, f.410, op.1, d.1998, ll.322–4. The cabinet resolution appears in *ibid.*, 11.349–57ob.

11 The sums involved in writing off debts were substantial, amounting to 15 million rubles. For details see TsGAVMF f.401, op. 6, d.178, ll.2–17; *Vsepoddanneishii otchet morskogo ministerstva za 1912*, St Petersburg, 1913, p. 122.

12 TsGAVMF f.427, op. 1, d.1998, ll.2, 274, 286; *Vsepoddaneishii doklad morskogo ministru* (hereafter *VDMM*) *za 1912*, St Petersburg, 1913, p. 122; *VDMM za 1913*, p. 323.

13 TsGAVMF f.427, op. 1, d.1998, ll.151–62, 286; f. 427, op.1, d.1999, ll.2–80; f.401, op.6, d.178, ll.183, 186; *Vsepoddaneishii otchet morskogo ministra za 1913*, St Petersburg, 1912, p. 283.

14 TsGAVMF f.401, op. 6, d.37, l.186; *Vsepoddaneishii otchet morskogo ministra za 1913*, St Petersburg, 1914, pp. 308–11.

15 TsGAVMF f.401, op. 6, d.36, ll.146ob.–147, Shipbuilding Commission, 20 July 1912; *ibid.*, ll.149–54, 5 July 1912.

16 TsGAVMF f.401, op. 6, d.37, ll.5ob., 176, 188–90; *ibid.*, d.274, ll.106–112ob., Council of Ministers, 4 January 1913.

17 TsGAVMF f.401, op. 3, d.822, ll.120–122ob., Council of Ministers, 9 February 1912, on the breakdown of the 1908 regulations. In September 1914, in response to continued pressure from the Duma, the government appointed a 'Chief Inspector of State Shipyards', with responsibility for promoting collaboration between state yards.

18 Assets estimated from Vainshtein, *Narodnoe bogatstvo*, p. 403.

19 The figures in the final column of table 5.3 have been divided by my estimate of the GAU labour force in 1908 and 1913, given in table 5.8.

20 *VOGK za 1913*, St Petersburg, 1914, pp. 37–8.

21 *VOGK za 1909*, pp. 58–9; *VOGK za 1910*, p. 64; *VOGK za 1911*, 1911, pp. 56–7; *SOGD*, III, 4th session, 71 sitting, cols. 1,251–60, 20 March 1910. Guchkov welcomed the decision to build 'in the secure heartland of Russia' (*ibid.*, 5th session, 126 sitting, col. 724).

22 Germonius, 'Izhevskii oruzheinyi zavod', pp. 2,909–10.

23 *VOGK za 1913*, St Petersburg, 1914, pp. 38–9; *VOGK za 1914*, p. 38; Manikovskii, *Boevoe snabzhenie*, vol. 1, pp. 127–9.

24 *Smeta dokhodov i raskhodov gornogo departamenta na 1913*, St Petersburg, 1912, p. 37; Ozerov, *Gornye zavody*, p. 120; Viatkin, *Gornozavodskii Ural*, p. 116.

25 Viatkin, *Gornozavodskii Ural*, pp. 109, 113–15, 118.

26 *Ibid.*, p. 116.

27 *Smeta dokhodov ... na 1914*, pp. 39, 49.

28 Ozerov, *Gornye zavody*, p. 128; *Smeta dokhodov ... na 1911, pp. 73–8.*

29 *Otchet gornogo departamenta na 1911*, St Petersburg, 1912, p. 225; *Smeta gornogo departamenta na 1914*, Petrograd, 1915, p. 37; *VOGK za 1911*, St Petersburg, 1912, p. 130.

30 TsGIA f.37, op.77, d.136, ll.103–6ob., dated September 1912; *VOGK za 1914*, Petrograd, 1915, p. 44; Ozerov, *Gornye zavody*, p. 137.
31 TsGIA f.37, op.77, d.136, ll.101–2ob.
32 Viatkin, *Gornozavodskii Ural*, pp. 260–4.
33 TsGIA f.37, op.77, d.131, ll.107–12ob.; Viatkin, *Gornozavodskii Ural*, p. 263.
34 R. C. Trebilcock, *The Vickers Brothers: Armaments and Enterprise, 1854–1914*, London, 1977; Epkenhans, *Die Wilhelminische Flottenrüstung*; R. P. T. Davenport-Hines, 'The British marketing of armaments, 1885–1935', in Davenport-Hines, ed., *Markets and Bagmen: Studies in the History of Marketing and British Industrial Performance, 1830–1939*, London, 1986, pp. 146–91; and work in progress by C. Beaud on Schneider-Creusot. Note, however, that even at the peak of rearmament, military output rarely exceeded 40 per cent of Krupp's total output.
35 TsGIA f.268, op.3, d.1049, 1.125.
36 Biographical details are culled from various sources, chiefly *Materialy po istorii SSSR*, Moscow, 1956, vol. 6, pp. 745–75; Kokovtsov, *Out of My Past*, pp. 539–94; and V. I. Bovykin and K. F. Shatsillo, 'Lichnye unii v tiazheloi promyshlennosti Rossii nakanune pervoi mirovoi voiny', *Vestnik MGU, istoriia*, 1962, 1, pp. 55–74. Additional details in Harcave, ed., *Memoirs*, p. 553 and Rieber, *Merchants and Entrepreneurs*, 1982, p. 374.
37 The quotation appears in Shatsillo, *Russkii imperializm*, p. 300. Plotnikov, like Meshcherskii, gave evidence to the Bolshevik commission of investigation into the Russian admiralty during 1918, but his fate is not known.
38 For Meshcherskii, see P. V. Volobuev and V. Z. Drobizhev, 'iz istorii goskapitalizma v nachal'nyi period sotsialisticheskogo stroitel'stva v SSSR', *Voprosy istorii*, 9, 1957, pp. 107–22. Khrulev's works include *Finansy Rossii v sviazi s ekonomicheskom polozheniem ee naseleniia*, 2nd edn, St Petersburg, 1908; and *Finansy Rossii i ee promyshlennost'*, 2nd edn, Petrograd, 1916; they sing the praises of private enterprise.
39 The three groups were identified in 1914 by Racouza-Soutschevsky, in a report prepared for the BUP, cited in Girault, *Emprunts russes*, pp. 356–7.
40 Details in *Finansovoe obozrenie*, 1914, 4, p. 21; 1914, 8, p. 23; and *Fabrichno-zavodskie predpriiatiia Rossiiskoi imperii*, St Petersburg, 1908; 2nd edn, Petrograd, 1914. The chief secondary sources are V. I. Bovykin, 'Banki i voennaia promyshlennost' Rossii nakanune pervoi mirovoi voiny', *Istoricheskie zapiski*, 64, 1959, pp. 82–135; V. I. Bovykin and K. N. Tarnovskii, 'Kontsentratsiia proizvodstva i razvitie monopolii v metalloobrabatyvaiushchei promyshlennosti Rossii', *Voprosy istorii*, 1957, 2, pp. 19–31; Iu. N. Subbotin, 'Iz istorii voennoi promyshlennosti Rossii kontsa XIX-nachala XXv.', *Vesnik LGU*, 20, 1973, 3, pp. 45–52; and N. I. Torpan, 'Finansovo-monopolisticheskie gruppirovki v voennoi promyshlennosti na territorii Estonii v 1911–1917gg.', *Izvestiia AN Estonskoi SSR, obshchestvennye nauki*, 1984, 2, pp. 112–23; 3, pp. 228–39.
41 *Finansovoe obozrenie*, 1914, 2, p. 19; I. F. Gindin, *Banki i promyshlennost' v Rossii*, Moscow–Leningrad, 1927, p. 67.
42 *Finansovoe obozrenie*, 1914, 3, p. 19; 1914, 7, p. 8; Gindin, *Banki*, p. 67.
43 TsGIA f.1393, op. 2, d.456, l.147; *Finansovoe obozrenie*, 1914, 2, p. 29; G. P.

358 Notes to pages 221–231

Efremtsev, *Istorii Kolomenskogo zavoda*, 2nd edn, Moscow, 1984; A. G. Golikov, 'Obrazovanie monopolisticheskogo ob"edineniia "Kolomna-Sormova"', *Vestnik MGU, istoriia*, 1971, 5, pp. 74–87.

44 Details from *Fabrichno-zavodskie predpriiatiia*, and Bovykin and Shatsillo, 'Lichnye unii'.

45 In addition to the sources cited in note 44, see *Materialy*, pp. 328–41 for the firm's participation in the shell syndicate.

46 TsGIA f.1276, op.11, d.248, 1.6 (inquiry into the affairs of Putilov, March–April 1915); *Finansovoe obozrenie*, 1914, 5, p. 21; 1914, 8, p. 23; Bovykin, 'Banki', pp. 85, 96–8; Okun', ed., *Putilovets*, p. xxvi.

47 *Finansovoe obozrenie*, 1914, 4, p. 4.

48 TsGIA f.23, op.15, d.354, l.13ob.; A. V. Pankin, 'Memoirs', manuscript, Lenin Library no. 304, 1.6; *Fabrichno-zavodskie predpriiatiia*; Goldstein, 'Military Aspects' p. 29. I have no information about the financial support offered to Schlüsselburg.

49 Gindin, *Banki*, p. 67; Beskrovnyi, *Armiia i flot*, pp. 83–5.

50 *Finansovoe obozrenie*, 1914, 10, p. 27; *ibid.*, 12, p. 9. Parviainen received orders worth three million rubles in 1913 and seven million in 1914. On Putilov, see Girault, 'Finances internationales', pp. 217–36; Bovykin, 'Banki', p. 83; Miftiev, 'Artilleriiskaia promyshlennost'', p. 115.

51 Girault, 'Finances internationales', p. 225; Bovykin' 'Banki', pp. 85–90.

52 TsGIA f.1393, op. 2, d.456, 1.147; Golikov, 'Obrazovanie', pp. 80–1.

53 *Ibid.*, pp. 83–7.

54 Based upon information provided in *Materialy*, pp. 745–75.

55 TsGAVMF f.420, op.1, d.41, ll.149–50ob., Kokovtsov to Dikov, 19 September 1908.

56 Details from Gindin, 'Antikrizisnoe finansirovanie', pp. 105–49.

57 TsGIA f.1276, op.11, d.248, 1.6; *Materialy*, pp. 535, 545–50, 554–5; K. Dembovskii, 'Mekhanicheskaia i mashinostroitel'naia promyshlennost' v Rossii pri nastoiashchei kon"iunkture', *Promyshlennost' i torgovlia*, 1914, 14, pp. 67–71; Bovykin, 'Banki', pp. 90–1.

58 TsGIA f.23, op.12, d.1371, 1.50.

59 TsGIA f.23, op.12, d.1371, ll.66–70ob., 72–3; *ibid.*, op.11, d.248, ll.1–19; *Materialy*, pp. 543–5.

60 Details from *VDMM za 1914*, Petrograd, 1915, summary tables; Bovykin and Shatsillo, 'Lichnye unii', p. 72; E. E. Kruze, *Peterburgskie rabochie v 1912–1914gg.*, Moscow–Leningrad, 1961, pp. 26, 43; and K. F. Shatsillo, 'Monopolii i stroitel'stvo podvodnogo flota v Rossii nakanune i v period pervoi mirovoi voiny', *Vestnik MGU, istoriia*, 1960, 3, pp. 27–42.

61 J. H. Grout, U.S. Consul, Odessa, to State Department, 18 July 1911, US State Department Papers, US National Archives, RG 92, series M316, frame 367–9. See also Dmitriev and Kolpychev, *Sudostroitel'nye zavody*, p. 812.

62 TsGAVMF f.512, op. 1, d.1782, ll.19, 28–9; K. F. Shatsillo, 'Formirovanie finansovogo kapitala v sudostroitel'noi promyshlennosti iuga Rossii', in *Iz istorii imperializma v Rossii*, Moscow–Leningrad, 1959, p. 28.

63 TsGIA f.1333, op.2, d.21, ll.1–7ob.; Shatsillo, 'Formirovanie', pp. 28–9.

64 TsGIA f.1333, op.2, d.21, ll.46–51 (Vickers agreement); TsGAVMF f.512, op.1,

d.285, ll.1–5, 39–46ob. (AGM, Paris, 29 July 1912); Shatsillo, 'Formirovanie', pp. 30–5. The rapid influx of Russian workers into the port of Nikolaev entailed less pleasant consequences. The US Consul in Odessa reported that the company had forced Jewish inhabitants out of the town, in order to make room for immigrant workers.

65 Shatsillo, 'Formirovanie', pp. 35–9.

66 *Ibid.*, pp. 40–50; TsGAVMF f.512, op.1, d.522, ll.2–7; d.1782, ll.9–9ob.; f.401, op.6, d.777, ll.13, Filippovich to Bloch, 12 December 1914.

67 See McKay, *Pioneers*, p. 378, who comments that 'a Russian entrepreneur could increasingly shrug off the admonishments of the stern old French uncle, while still paying him an occasional visit – with palm outstretched'. Some foreign firms did develop an interest in the defence market during the 1860s, but their activity proved short-lived.

68 R. C. Trebilcock, 'British armaments and European industrialization', *Economic History Review*, 26, 1973, pp. 254–72; McKay, *Pioneers*, pp. 233, 236–41; Gindin, *Russkie kommercheskie banki*, pp. 395–403.

69 McKay, *Pioneers*, pp. 105–6, citing Crédit Lyonnais archives.

70 W. Kirchner, *Die deutsche Industrie und die Industrialisierung Russlands, 1815–1914*, St. Katharinen, 1986, p. 163.

71 TsGIA f.1393, op.2, d.316, ll.1–5ob.

72 Girault, 'Finances internationales', pp. 228, 234; Bovykin, 'Banki', pp. 91–2; Claude Beaud, 'De l'expansion internationale à la multinationale: Schneider en Russie, 1896–1914', *Histoire, Economie et Société SEDES*, 1985, 4, pp. 575–602.

73 Vickers Archives (hereafter VA), microfilm no. 735, technical agreement between Société Générale and Naval shipyards, January 1911.

74 VA microfilm no. R.214, Charles Evans to Vickers' London office, 25 November 1912.

75 Viatkin, *Gornozavodskii Ural*, p. 265.

76 V. I. Bovykin, 'Iz istorii proniknoveniia inostrannogo kapitala v Rossii (Permskoe delo)', *Nauchnye doklady vysshei shkoly*, 1958, 1, pp. 66–73; *Documents diplomatiques français*, série 3, vol. 9, pp. 56–7; Anan"ich, *Rossiia*, pp. 271–9; Girault, *Emprunts russes*, pp. 563–8. The French finally agreed a loan of 249 million rubles.

77 Bovykin, 'Iz istorii', pp. 68–9.

78 TsGIA f.37, op.77, d.136, ll.163–82ob.

79 Bovykin, 'Iz istorii', pp. 70–2; *Documents diplomatiques français*, vol. 9, pp.570–1, Dolcet to Doumergue, 12 March 1914 (n.s.).

80 VA, files 51 and 1219; Bovykin, 'Banki', pp. 122–4.

81 VA, files 51 and R215; TsGIA f.1333, op.2, d.21, ll.46–51 (Vickers agreement); TsGAVMF f.512, op. 1, d.285, ll.1–5, 39–46ob. (AGM, Paris, 29 July 1912); TsGAVMF f.401, op.6, d.272, l.276ob., for the Admiralty's contract, for 12 16-inch and 50 smaller naval guns per annum, worth 10 million rubles over a ten-year period, 1916–25. See also E.R. Goldstein, 'Vickers Ltd. and the tsarist regime', *Slavonic and East European Review*, 58, 1980, pp. 561–71; G. Jones and C. Trebilcock, 'Russian industry and British business, 1910–1930: oil and armaments', *Journal of European Economic History*, 11, 1982,

pp. 61–103; and V. V. Polikarpov, 'Iz istorii voennoi promyshlennosti v Rossii, 1906–1917gg.', *Istoricheskie zapiski*, 104, 1979, pp. 126–36.

82 A. C. Marshall and N. Newbould, *The History of Firth's*, Sheffield, 1924, pp. 89–90, 95. I owe this reference to Dr A. J. Marrison. Other details from *Fabrichno-zavodskie predpriiatiia*, Petrograd, 1914.

83 L. E. Mints, *Trudovye resursy SSSR*, Moscow, 1975, p. 40.

84 The number of auxiliary workers at Motovilikha appears to have fallen by 12 per cent between 1908 and 1912. But this may have been a result of changes in the classification of workers. For details, see *Otchet gornogo departamenta za 1908*, pp. 534–5; *Smeta dokhodov . . . na 1914*, pp. 23–36; and Miftiev, 'Artilleriiskaia promyshlennost'', p. 100.

85 See Germonius, 'Izhevskii oruzhcinyi zavod', p. 2,902, and S. V. Murzint-seva, 'Izuchenie formirovaniia i sostava rabochikh trubochnogo zavoda po dannym pasportnykh knig, 1907–1944gg.', in *Rabochie Rossii v epokhu kapitalizma: sravnitel'nyi poraionnyi analiz*, Rostov, 1972, pp. 59–68.

86 TsGAVMF f.512, op.1, d.285, ll.13, 15.

87 Evidence on the background of workers is hard to come by. Kruze, *Peterburgskie rabochie*, pp. 75–7 provides one of the few attempts to explore the question. For other details, see A. A. Artem'ev, 'Usloviia rabot v tekhnicheskikh zavedeniiakh Artilleriiskogo vedomstva i postanovka zdes' meditsinskoi pomoshchi rabochim', *Trudy vtorogo Vserossiiskogo s"ezda fabrichnykh vrachei i predstavitelei fabrichno-zavodskoi promyshlennosti*, Moscow, 1911, vol. 1, pp. 15–17.

88 Murzintseva, 'Izuchenie', pp. 59–68.

89 Manikovskii, *Boevoe snabzhenie*, vol. 1, p. 78; *Svod voennykh postanovlenii*, vol. 13, 1910, appendix; *Svod morskikh postanovlenii*, vol. 5, 1910, para. 120; Germonius, 'Izhevskii oruzheinyi zavod', pp. 2,902–3.

90 Murzintseva, 'Izuchenie', pp. 61, 66.

91 *Polozhenie o vol'nonaemnykh i pravila o naime masterovykh i rabochikh v tekhnicheskikh artilleriiskikh zavedeniiakh*, Petrograd, 1915, para. 15; *Svod morskikh postanovlenii*, vol. 5, 1910, appendix, pp. 73–4; Artem'ev, 'Usloviia rabot', p. 16; Kir'ianov, *Zhiznennyi uroven'*, p. 77; S. V. Murzintseva, 'Iz istorii ekonomicheskoi polozhenii rabochikh na predpriiatiiakh voennogo i morskogo vedomstv v 1907–1914gg. v Peterburge', *Uchenye zapiski LGU*, 270, 1959, p. 231.

92 *Svod voennykh postanovlenii*, vol. 13, 1910, appendix, para. 26.

93 Artem'ev, 'Usloviia rabot', p. 10; Ashurkov, 'Predpriiatiia'.

94 *Workmen's Insurance*, vol. 2, pp. 2,259–67.

95 Murzintseva, 'Iz istorii', pp. 235–8; Artem'ev, 'Usloviia', p. 30; *Svod morskikh postanovlenii*, vol. 5, 1910, paras, 128–9, 136.

96 Artem'ev, 'Usloviia', pp. 27–8, 30–2, noting that the daily wage in 1910 ranged from 0.90 rubles to 1.40 rubles. See also *Polozhenie*, 1915, para 30.

97 Shepelev, *Tsarizm i burzhuaziia*, pp. 174–87; Shelymagin, *Zakonodatel'stvo*, pp. 232, 246; V. Ia. Laverychev, *Tsarizm i rabochii vopros v Rossii*, Moscow, 1972, p. 241.

98 Artem'ev, 'Usloviia', pp. 13–14. Artem'ev took up his post in 1906, but what became of him after 1911 is unclear. He was certainly no longer attached to

Okhtensk by 1915. See *Obshchii sostav uchebnykh i tekhnicheskikh artiller-iiskikh zavedenii, podvedomstvennykh GAU na 1915*, Petrograd, 1915.
99 E. E. Kruze, *Usloviia truda i byta rabochego klassa Rossii v 1900–1914gg.*, Leningrad, 1981, pp. 44–51.
100 Shelymagin, *Zakonodatel'stvo*, pp. 237–8. See also P. E. Liubarov, 'Tret'ia gosudarstvennaia Duma i vopros o strakhovanii rabochikh kazennykh predpriiatii', *Vestnik MGU, istoriia*, 1967, 2, pp. 36–48.
101 R. B. McKean, *St Petersburg between the Revolutions: Workers and Revolutionaries, June 1907–February 1917*, London, 1990, p. 282.
102 Allan Monkhouse, *Moscow, 1911–1933*, London, 1933, pp. 37, 47, However, Monkhouse went on to comment that state employees 'found themselves considerably better off than the majority of those employed in private enterprises'.
103 H. Hogan, 'The reorganization of work processes in the St Petersburg metalworking industry, 1901–1914", *Russian Review*, 42, 1983, pp. 163–90. See also V. E. Bonnell, *Roots of Rebellion: Workers' Politics and Organization in St. Petersburg and Moscow, 1900–1914*, Berkeley, 1983, pp. 195–202; S. V. Murzintseva, 'Iz istorii razrabotki antirabochego zakonodatel'stva na zavodakh voennogo i morskogo vedomstv v 1907–1914gg.', in V. V. Mavrodin, ed., *Rabochie oruzheinoi promyshlennosti v Rossii i russkie oruzheiniki v XIX-nachale XXv.*, Leningrad, 1976, pp. 101–12. The debate has been joined more recently by McKean, *St Petersburg*, pp. 12, 261.
104 VA, microfilm MF214, T. Jones to T. Owens, 29 August 1913.
105 TsGAVMF f.401, op.6, d.546, l.226, Shipbuilding Commission 16 May 1914; *ibid.*, l.239ob., 23 May 1914.
106 Beskrovnyi, 'Proizvodstvo vooruzheniia'.
107 'Promyshlennaia i professional'naia perepis' 1918g: fabrichno-zavodskaia promyshlennost' v period 1913–1918gg.', *Trudy TsSU*, vol. 26, parts 1 and 2, Moscow, 1926. See also N. Ia. Vorob'ev, *Ocherki po istorii promyshlennoi statistiki v dorevoliutsionnoi Rossii i SSSR*, Moscow, 1961, and M. N. Chernomorskii, 'Pervaia promyshlennaia perepis' 1918g. kak istoricheskii istochnik', *Trudy Moskovskogo gosudarstvennogo istorichesko-arkhivnogo instituta*, 12, 1959, pp. 245–66.
108 Ashworth, 'Economic aspects', p. 492; F. Crouzet, 'Recherches sur la production d'armements en France, 1815–1913', *Revue historique*, 251, 1974, p. 72.
109 In 1915, however, Motovilikha was still being described as 'poorly equipped'. TsGIA f.1276, op.11, d.248, l.5.
110 Merritt Roe Smith, *Harpers Ferry Armory and the New Technology*, Ithaca, 1977.
111 See below, p. 281.

6 The economics and politics of defence procurement

1 Scherer, *The Weapons Acquisition Process*, p. x.
2 Kehr, 'Munitions Industry', pp. 128–34.
3 Rieber, *Merchants and Entrepreneurs*, pp. 297, 320; Bestuzhev, 'Bor'ba', pp. 44–85.
4 Berlin, *Russkaia burzuaziia*, pp. 177–8.

5 See chapter 5, note 36, and A. N. Krylov, *Moi vospominaniia*, 8th edn, Leningrad, 1984. Bostrem figures briefly in Harcave, ed., *Memoirs*, pp. 721–2. Other details from Shatsillo, *Russkii imperializm*, pp. 296–9.
6 On the origins of the inquiry, see TsGIA f. 1393, op. 2, d. 456, ll. 1–393. The corresponding file on the GIU is in *ibid.*, d. 455, ll.1–101ob. Garin (1860–?) was employed in the Ministry of the Interior, where he served for a short time as Trepov's deputy, in 1904. In 1916, he became deputy Minister of War, where he assumed particular responsibility for foreign supply on the Special Council for State Defence. Witte dismissed Garin as someone who wrote reports in florid prose and who was 'servile to those in high places'. Harcave, ed., *Memoirs*, p. 689.
7 TsGIA f. 1393, op. 2, d. 456, l. 367.
8 *Ibid.*, d. 455, l. 98; Ia. I. Livshin, 'K voprosu o voenno-promyshlennykh monopoliiakh v Rossii v nachale XX veka', *Voprosy istorii*, 1957, 7, pp. 55–70; V. I. Bovykin, 'Monopolisticheskie soglasheniia v russkoi voennoi promyshlennosti, po materialam senatorskikh revizii', *Istoriia SSSR*, 1958, 1, pp. 125–9; T. D. Krupina, 'K voprosu o vzaimootnosheniiakh tsarskogo pravitel'stva s monopoliiami', *Istoricheskie zapiski*, 57, 1956, pp. 158–9; Laverychev, *Gosudarstvo*, pp. 66–83.
9 TsGIA f.1393, op.2, d.455, ll.99–100; d. 456, ll. 369ob.–70ob., 391.
10 Fuller, *Civil–Military Conflict*, pp. 239–40, 255; A. A. Korolev, 'Reviziia senatorom N. P. Garinym Tul'skogo patronnogo zavoda', in *Iz istorii Tul'skogo kraia*, Tula, 1972, pp. 54–62. Garin, like D. B. Neidhardt, another senator responsible for investigations into business-government links, was closely associated with Stolypin (Neidhardt had married Stolypin's sister). A recent account of Stolypin's career suggests that Neidhardt, a former governor of Odessa, helped secure the appointment of his brother-in-law to the Ministry of the Interior. See P. N. Zyr'ianov, 'Petr' Arkad'evich Stolypin', *Voprosy istorii*, 1990, 6, p. 59.
11 His views are set out in Sukhomlinov, *Vospominaniia*, pp. 253–4. Amongst several attacks in parliament on the competence of the GAU, see the speech of Guchkov in *SOGD*, III, 5th session, 126 sitting, 7 May 1912, cols. 720–36: 'In five years of close study of the budget of the War Ministry, I have not come across a department as fundamentally disorganized as the GAU', and the remarks of Academician A. V. Vasil'ev, reported in *Gosudarstvennyi Sovet, Stenograficheskii otchet* (hereafter SOGS), 4th session, 35th sitting, 11 May 1909, cols. 1,966–7. See also Ozerov, *Kak raskhoduiutsia*, pp. 158–60.
12 TsGIA f.1333, op.1, d.2, l.6; f.1393, op.2, d.455, and Korolev, 'Reviziia'.
13 Shatsillo, *Rossiia*, p. 71, citing an unnamed director of Russud.
14 TsGAVMF f.410, op.3, d.761, l.1–10ob. In two instances, the government did begin to make a longer-term commitment to private enterprises; contracts were promised to the Vickers' plant at Tsaritsyn and a new powder works in Vladimir, for a ten-year period. *Ibid.*, f.401, op.2, d.272, l.276ob.
15 TsGIA f.1393, op.2, d.455, ll.95–7, 100.
16 For background, see TsGAVMF, f.410, op.3, d.761, ll.1–5 (undated report by Rerberg, 1907); f.420, op.1, d.92, ll.3–4, Voevodskii to Dikov, 15 September 1908.

17 *Ibid.*, ll.12–12ob., Dikov to Stolypin, 14 November 1908.

18 The reference was to the artillery commission, formed on 29 February 1900, which considered economic and technical aspects of the artillery programme. This commission had powers to dictate to the GAU which suppliers, procurement method and prices it should adopt. TsGIA f.1276, op.14, d.623, ll.34–5, 40–1.

19 *Ibid.*, ll.18ob., 20–25 ob.

20 The managers of the four state yards were entitled to attend, but without voting rights. TsGAVMF f.410, op.3, d.1357, ll.5–7; TsGIA f.1276, op.14, d.623, ll.1–1ob.

21 TsGAVMF f.420, op.1, d.92, ll.84ob.–86; f.401, op.6, d.1, l.35; d.178, l.175.

22 *Ibid.*, f.420, op.1, d.149, ll.1–3. K. P. Boklevskii, appointed to the Commission by Stolypin, complained bitterly that the Admiralty concluded contracts behind its back. *Ibid.*, f.401, op.6, d.41, ll.34, 64 (sessions of 29 April and 17 June 1911).

23 The Shipbuilding Commission makes a brief appearance in Krylov, *Vospominaniia*, pp. 185–7, where he launches a scathing attack on the competence of its civilian members. Krylov also recounts how copies of its secret proceedings were sold by an enterprising printer employed by the Navy Ministry, but there is no other corroboration of this anecdote. The standard Soviet view of Boklevskii features in Shatsillo, *Russkii imperializm*, pp. 289–92.

24 *Otchet otdela promyshlennosti za 1910*, St Petersburg, 1911, pp. 134–9; *Otchet otdela promyshlennosti za 1911*, 1912, pp. 146–7; debates in *Stenogramma*, p. 14. It is worth recalling that the petition presented to the Tsar in January 1905 by the Assembly of Russian Workers included the condition that 'contracts for orders of the war and naval departments are to be placed in Russia and not abroad'. See the text of the petition, in H. D. Mehlinger and J. M. Thompson, *Count Witte and the Tsarist Government in the 1905 Revolution*, Bloomington, Indiana, 1972, p. 347.

25 Khrulev, *Finansy Rossii*, p. 215. Khrulev was chairman of the International Bank and the Nikopol-Mariupol Ironworks, and a member of the board of the Tula Cartridge Company.

26 *Stenogramma*, pp. 14, 118.

27 TsGIA f.268, op.3, d.1049, ll.123–4; *Stenogramma*, pp. 107–11, 277–89.

28 TsGAVMF f.420, op.1, d.42, ll.3ob.–4, Memorandum dated 30 June 1907.

29 *Ibid.*, ll.52–57ob., 60–65ob.; Shatsillo, 'Inostrannyi kapital', p. 76.

30 TsGAVMF f.420, op.1, d.42, ll.139–ob., 3 September 1908.

31 *Ibid.*, ll.156–158ob., 19 October 1908; d.76, ll.159–159ob., ll.165–66ob.

32 *Ibid.*, ll.66–66ob., Shipov to Dikov, 6 October 1908; see also TsGAVMF f.401, op.6, d.272, l.178ob.

33 TsGIA f.1276, op.4, d.166, ll.4–6, Confederation of Trade and Industry to Stolypin, 16 June 1908; Stolypin to Dikov, 18 June 1908; Dikov to Stolypin, 21 June 1908.

34 See, for example, the session on 4 January 1912, TsGAVMF, f.401, op.6, d.36, ll.6–12; *Stenogramma*, 1908, p. 286; Shipov made the same point in 1909. TsGAVMF f.420, op.1, d.76, ll.128–9, Council of Ministers, 18 February 1909.

35 I have assumed that the figures given in table 6.1 were exclusively for weaponry and for vessels.

36 A. Bart, 'Na fronte artilleriiskogo snabzheniia', *Byloe*, 34, 1925, pp. 147–91; A. L. Sidorov, 'Otnosheniia Rossii s soiuznikami i inostrannye postavki vo vremia pervoi mirovoi voiny, 1914–1917gg.', *Istoricheskie zapiski*, 15, 1945, p. 130.

37 See Lisovskii, *Rabochie*, pp. 24–6, where he emphasizes the guarantees that can be extracted from the state sector.

38 Quoted in TsGAVMF f.427, op.1, d.2114, l.37ob., Report of fire and safety commission, 1910.

39 Timashev is quoted in Viatkin, *Gornozavodskii Ural*, p. 126. See also TsGAVMF f.420, op.1, d.42, ll.149 50, Kokovtsov to Dikov, 19 September 1908; *ibid.*, f.401, op.6, d.35, l.23ob.

40 *Stenogramma*, pp. 53–55. The Ministry of Trade and Industry also admitted to the Shipbuilding Commission, in July 1911, that 'penalties and damages are nothing but a fiction, so far as state factories are concerned'. TsGAVMF f.401, op.6, d.1, l.104. As long ago as 1870, industrialists complained that 'in peacetime, the state works are a drain on the public purse, whilst in wartime their capacity is insufficient'. Cited in Ashurkov, 'Predpriiatiia', pp. 113–14.

41 TsGAVMF f.401, op.6, d.35, l.23ob., State Auditor's report for 1911, marked 'secret'; *Stenogramma*, pp. 122–9.

42 TsGIA f.37, op.77, d.136, l.103; Viatkin, *Gornozavodskii Ural*, pp. 262–4.

43 *Voennaia entsiklopediia*, vol. 10, 1912, entry under 'zavody artilleriiskie'.

44 TsGIA f.1393, op.2, d.456, l.93.

45 TsGAVMF f.401, op.6, d.36, ll.185–7; *ibid.*, d.37, ll.25–35.

46 TsGIA f.1333, op.2, d.21, ll.7–7ob. *ibid.*, f.1393, op.2, d.456, l.367.

47 *Ibid.*, ll.182ob., 190, 203ob.

48 TsGAVMF f.420, op.1, d.42, l.64ob., op.6, d.35, l.24; *VOGK za 1911*, St Petersburg, 1912, p. 75. See TsGIA f.1393, op.2, d.456, l.193, for an illustration of relative input prices. This advantage may have been illusory, however: state rolling mills also transferred steel from one factory to another.

49 For the views of Manikovskii, later head of the GAU, see *Boevoe snabzhenie*, *passim*. He was opposed by technical specialists, such as the engineer P. I. Balinskii, quoted in TsGVIA f.369, op.1, d.133, ll.1–13ob. Balinksii called for a 'Russian Krupp, free from bureaucratic interference' and capable of displaying 'energy and knowledge'.

50 Some regiments 'employed' as many as 200 tailors and shoemakers, working slowly and without supervision. See Voznesenskii, 'O voennom khoziaistve', p. 118; Bushnell, 'Peasants in uniform', p. 567, notes that up to 40 per cent of troops were engaged in activities other than military training. The quotation from Maksheev appears in *SOGS*, 4th session, 35th sitting, 11 May 1909, col. 1,966 (Vasil'ev).

51 TsGIA f.1393, op.2, d.455, l.98. The GIU budget in 1913 amounted to 356 million rubles, including 125 million rubles representing food and fodder purchases, and 48 million rubles for equipment. Military demand for leather and fur products was put at 15–20 million rubles: *Doklad soveta*

s"ezdov, pp. 53–9. The supply of food to the army is dealt with briefly in T. M. Kitanina, *Khlebnaia torgovlia Rossii v 1875–1914gg.*, Leningrad, 1978, pp. 201–21.

52 Described in *VOGK za 1909*, St Petersburg, 1910, pp. 31–8; *VOGK za 1910*, St Petersburg, 1911, p. 48. On other initiatives to encourage small-scale industry, see K. N. Tarnovskii, 'Kustarnaia promyshlennost' i tsarizm, 1907–1914gg.', *Voprosy istorii*, 1986, 7, pp. 33–46.

53 *VOGK za 1911*, St Petersburg, 1912, pp. 33–4; *VOGK za 1913*, Petrograd, 1914, p. 28. Also Ozerov, *Kak raskhoduiutsia*, pp. 158–9. Other details from A. A. Rybnikov, *Mel'kaia promyshlennost' Rossii*, Moscow, 1922, pp. 7–8; V. Varzar, 'Factories and workshops', in Raffalovich, ed., *Russia*, p. 142.

54 TsGIA f.1393, op.1, d.455, ll.81–2. *VOGK za 1913*, p. 29; *VOGK za 1914*, Petrograd, 1915, p. 32.

55 *Voennaia entsiklopediia*, vol. 10, 1912, entry under 'zavedeniia intendantskie'. Beskrovnyi, *Armiia i flot*, p. 151, mistakenly gives the date as 1910.

56 *VOGK za 1907*, St Petersburg, 1908, p. 23; Beskrovnyi, *Armiia i flot*, p. 157.

57 *VOGK za 1914*, p. 30; *Obshchaia ob"iasnitel'naia zapiska ... na 1914*, appendix 4.

58 TsGIA f.1393, op.2, d.455, l.97.

59 TsGIA f.23, op.12, d.1371, ll.66–70ob.; f.1393, op.2, d.316, ll.1–5ob.; *VOGK za 1908*, St Petersburg, 1909, pp. 142–3.

60 VA, microfilm R214.

61 TsGAVMF f.410, op.3, d.822, ll.75ob.–76; *VOGK za 1912*, St Petersburg, 1913, p. vi; *Svod voennykh postanovlenii*, vol. 18, 1907, para. 11; Jones and Trebilcock, 'Russian industry', pp. 61–103. Ozerov, *Kak raskhoduiutsia*, pp. 159–60 is one of many critics of the procurement agencies' tendency to make abrupt changes to specifications.

62 McKean, *St Petersburg*, pp. 273–5. In 1912, only one in ten of the leading engineering firms in the capital voted to fine workers who went on strike.

63 TsGAVMF f.401, op.6, d.272, l.184.

64 TsGIA f.1393, op.2, d.456, ll.367–8.

65 Dmitriev and Kolpychev, *Sudostroitel'nye zavody*, p. 1,017.

66 TsGAVMF f.410, op.3, d.761, ll.1–100ob. The report corroborates many of Garin's findings.

67 Dmitriev and Kolpychev, *Sudostroitel'nye zavody*, pp. 1,014–9.

68 Grinevetskii, *Poslevoennye perspektivy*, p. 159; Gatrell, *Tsarist Economy*, pp. 158–9, 163.

69 TsGIA f.23, op.12, d.1167, l.28, 8th July 1911; TsGAVMF f.401, op.6, d.272, l.181, State Auditor's comments on the Admiralty's annual statement, 1913.

70 For an unusual statement of the potential for cooperation between the two sectors (in the context of armour-plate production), see the remarks of an Admiralty official, quoted in Ozerov, *Kak raskhoduiutsia*, p. 154.

7 Military preparedness on the eve of the First World War

1 Sidorov, *Ekonomicheskoe polozhenie*, pp. 5–8; L. Burchardt, *Friedenswirtschaft und Kriegsvorsorge: Deutschlands wirtschaftliche Rüstungsbestrebungen vor 1914*, Boppard-am-Rhein, 1968.

2 The phrase belongs to the Russian economist S. N. Prokopovich.

3 See A. Gulevich, *Voina i narodnoe khoziaistvo*, St Petersburg, 1898, and the discussion in Prokopovich, *Voina*, chapter 1. Gulevich concluded that Britain would be the first to suffer a food shortage, within six months of the outbreak of war; the same fate would befall Germany within ten months. For a sanguine view of Russia's advantages of natural resources and manpower, see A. L. Rafalovich, 'Voina i ee vliianie na nashe narodnoe khoziaistvo', *Promyshlennost' i torgovlia*, 1914, 21, pp. 406–8. For German General Staff and British Admiralty fears about the intolerable economic burden implicit in a long conflict, see Offer, *First World War*, pp. 348, 350.

4 Moltke's views on Russia's gathering military strength are recorded in Ropponen, *Die Kraft Russlands*, p. 249.

5 The article by S. Lukomskii, 'Razvitie i organizatsiia zavodskoi deiatel'nosti v riadu ostal'nykh uslovii mogushchestva gosudarstva', *Morskoi sbornik*, 1914, 2, pp. 113–31, provides an exception to the narrow approach adopted by most military planners. Lukomskii identified five components of military preparedness: the size of the armed forces (including their weaponry); prevailing technical conditions (this included the quality of weaponry and vessels, and the potential speed with which mobilization could be effected); education and training of troops; the morale of the troops; and, finally, the ability of the country to supply its military and civilian population with necessary materials and products. He assumed that Russia faced difficulties in supplying the military, but (in common with his contemporaries) he was confident in the capacity of the economy to satisfy civilian needs.

6 B. E. Nolde, *Russia in the Economic War*, New Haven, 1928, pp. 17, 55. Nor is it the case that the Russian government immediately closed the Russian market to German goods; on the contrary, the government pinned its hopes on continued access to German oils and fats, non-ferrous metal and machinery. The tsarist regime did not prohibit trade with the enemy until the end of 1916.

7 Wright, *A Study of War*, pp. 670–1, gives the size of the Russian army in 1914 as 1.3 million. For the figure cited in the text, as well as for the intended impact of the 'great army programme', see Beskrovnyi, *Armiia i flot*, pp. 14–15.

8 A full account of peasant society during the Stolypin years remains to be written. E. Vinogradoff, 'The Russian peasantry and the elections to the fourth state Duma', in L. H. Haimson, ed., *The Politics of Rural Russia, 1907–1914*, New York, 1978, pp. 219–60, is persuasive in identifying the peasants' fundamental preoccupation with their claim to private estates, to the exclusion of other issues. But see D. A. J. Macey, 'The peasant commune and the Stolypin reforms: peasant attitudes, 1906–1914', in R. Bartlett, ed., *Land Commune and Peasant Community in Russia*, London, 1990, pp. 219–36, for a discussion of the complex issues involved in arriving at an understanding of peasant attitudes. On the Russian army before 1914, the first chapter of Allan Wildman, *The End of the Russian Imperial Army: The Old Army and the Soldiers' Revolt*, Princeton, 1980 offers a good discussion.

9 Fuller, *Civil–Military Conflict*, pp. 220, 255, 257.
10 Walter Pintner, 'Russian military thought: the western model and the shadow of Suvorov', in P. Paret, ed., *Makers of Modern Strategy*, New York, 1986, pp. 354–75. The treatment of military education and training in Beskrovnyi, *Armiia i flot*, pp. 26–8, does not go very far. Makarov, the chief advocate of morale in the navy, is discussed briefly in a study by P. A. Zhilin, *Russkaia voennaia mysl'*, Moscow, 1986, pp. 137–8. Stone, *Eastern Front*, chapter 2, offers an interesting analysis. For a thoughtful discussion of the complex question of military motivation, see the final chapter of John Keegan, *The Face of Battle*, London, 1976.
11 Golder, ed., *Documents*, p. 11.
12 N. N. Golovine, *The Russian Army in the World War*, New Haven, 1931, pp. 32–4, and Stone, *Eastern Front*, p. 32.
13 TsGVIA f.369, op.1, d.124, ll.10–11, undated memo (January 1916?): 'our ordnance, shell and rifles are of a high quality and the war has not revealed any defects'. See also Manikovskii, *Boevoe snabzhenie*, vol. 1, pp. 285–7, 305–6. Stone, *Eastern Front*, pp. 38–9 notes that the German concentration on trench mortars reflected the peculiarities of the military budget; deprived by the Reichstag of the power of conscript additional men, the German army substituted heavy artillery for troops. The planned bombardment of Russian and French fortresses also influenced this use of resources.
14 Golder, ed., *Documents*, pp. 7, 13. Durnovo points out that Russian control of the Straits would still leave it vulnerable to British naval supremacy in the Mediterranean. For the Tsar's attitude, see Sukhomlinov, *Vospominaniia*, pp. 225–6.
15 M. Soboleff, 'Foreign trade of Russia', in Raffalovich, ed., *Russia*, pp. 303–5. In 1913, fewer than one vessel in five that arrived at Russian ports was registered in Russia. See also Lohr, *Die 'Zukunft Russlands'*, p. 29.
17 Nolde, *Russia*, pp. 44–6.
18 See *Explanatory Memorandum*, 1913; *VDMM za 1912*, St Petersburg, 1913, pp. 72–7; *VDMM za 1914*, Petrograd, 1915, pp. 66–74.
19 *SOGD*, III, 4th session, 71 sitting, col.1,265 (L'vov); *SOGS*, VI, session 33 (27 March 1911), cols.1,576–7 (P. F. Rerberg); Savich, 'Morskie raskhody', pp. 4–7.
20 Kennedy, *Rise of the Anglo-German Antagonism*, pp. 361–85.
21 Golder, ed., *Documents*, p. 11; Ropponen, *Die Kraft Russlands*, p. 265.
22 *Ibid.*, pp. 220, 242, 256, 269. For the situation in 1900, consult Fuller, *Strategy and Power*, p. 381.
23 Bukin, 'Zheleznye dorogi', p. 103; Sidorov, *Ekonomicheskoe polozhenie*, pp. 567–9.
24 But see John Westwood, 'The railways', in R. W. Davies, ed., *From Tsarism to the New Economic Policy*, London, 1990, pp. 173–5, who notes that older locomotives were withdrawn.
25 *Ibid.*, p. 177. Westwood notes that the military tended to hoard goods wagons. Stone, *Eastern Front*, p. 41, makes the point that the rapid addition to railway track between 1910 and 1914, improving the system's carrying capacity, was sufficient to cause the German General Staff to believe that

the Schlieffen Plan was rapidly becoming obsolete. Hence, the imperative need to launch an offensive in 1914.

26 TsGVIA f.369, op.2, d.10, l.190; op.8, d.1, ll.1–5; d.74, ll.3–4; Beskrovnyi, *Armiia i flot*, p. 131.

27 Figures from *ibid.*, p. 147.

28 Golder, *Documents*, p. 11.

29 Lukomskii, 'Razvitie zavodskoi deiatel'nosti', pp. 119–29.

30 The most famous statement of government attempts to take control of the armaments industry is found in Manikovskii's programme for new construction in 1916. See Sidorov, *Ekonomicheskoe polozhenie*, pp. 424–49. There is a large contemporary literature on 'compulsory syndicalization', of which a representative sample is the series of articles by V. Ziv in *Birzhevye vedomosti*, 3–6 May 1917.

31 Varzar, 'Machine industry', pp. 200–26; *Narodnoe khoziaistvo v 1915g.*, Petrograd, 1918; *Ocherki istorii tekhniki*, p. 332.

32 Textiles and food-processing together accounted for one-half of gross industrial production in 1914. Extractive industries, including oil, metallurgy and engineering combined to produce less than one-third of total industrial output. See Crisp, *Studies*, pp. 34–6.

33 TsGVIA f.369, op.3, d.78, ll.170–2 (memorandum dated 18 January 1916); Krylov, *Moi vospominaniia*, p. 251; V. P. Litvinov-Falinskii, cited in Manikovskii, *Boevoe snabzhenie*, vol. 2, pp. 293–7. For similar complaints, which were widespread in wartime, see *ibid.*, pp. 342–7; N. Savin, 'God voiny i tekhnicheskaia mobilizatsiia promyshlennosti', *Promyshlennost' i torgovlia*, 1915, 13–14, pp. 5–8; *Trudy soveshchanii po izgotovleniiu korpusov 3-dium. granat*, Moscow, 1916, p. 130 ('those factories that have begun to manufacture shell should refuse to accept further orders and should produce machine tools instead'), and Charnovskii, 'Mashinostroitel'naia promyshlennost'', p. 52.

34 Strumilin, *Statistiko-ekonomicheskie ocherki*, p. 519. These figures, which include non-incorporated industry, should be treated with caution. But all authors who have examined this subject (such as V. A. Gukhman and M. A. Barun in the 1920s) agree on the rapid growth in industrial capital between 1908 and 1913.

35 *Khoziaistvennaia zhizn' i ekonomicheskoe polozhenie naseleniia Rossii za pervye deviat' mesiatsev voiny*, Petrograd, 1916, p. 32; L. S. Gaponenko, *Rabochii klass Rossii v 1917 godu,*, Moscow, 1970, pp. 75–6; Efremtsev, *Istoriia*, p. 105. Estimates of industrial capital stock on territory subsequently occupied by the enemy are derived from Vainshtein, *Narodnoe bogatstvo*, pp. 368–9. Evacuation procedures are discussed in Sidorov, *Ekonomisheskoe polozhenie*, pp. 216–23.

36 Quoted in Romanov, ed., *Russkie finansy*, p. 358, Kokovtsov to Stoplypin, 14 November 1906.

37 Anan''ich, *Rossiia*, p. 267. In January 1914, the Tsar dismissed Kokovtsov. His successor as Minister of Finances, Peter Bark, was expressly encouraged to shift the emphasis in the budget from taxes on consumption (particularly the consumption of vodka) towards taxes on productive economic activity.

In the short term, however, a balanced budget required that Russia adhere to the traditional fiscal regime. See Shepelev, *Tsarizm i burzhuaziia*, pp. 162–3.

38 Vainshtein, *Narodnoe bogatstvo*, pp. 444–5; Anan"ich, *Rossiia*, pp. 261, 267–8, 271; Gregory, *Russian National Income*, pp. 313–37.

39 Bukovetskii, 'Svobodnaia nalichnost'', pp. 359–76; Sidorov, *Finansovoe polozhenie*, pp. 98, 104–5. A more pessimistic mood amongst German financiers in 1914 is captured in Lohr, *Die 'Zukunft Russlands'*, pp. 171–80.

40 Sidorov, *Finansovoe polozhenie*, 102.

41 In response to Witte's criticisms, the Finance Committee decided to reduce the amount of gold held abroad, in order to ensure that a larger proportion of the currency in circulation was covered by domestic resources.

42 Unlike Britain or France, Russia did not own extensive property overseas. There were a few enterprises and other assets in China, Manchuria, Mongolia and Persia, chief amongst them the Chinese Eastern Railway. The chief remaining assets included gold reserves held overseas. These combined assets amounted to 917 million rubles in January 1914, which, in theory, could be sold to help finance the war effort. Vainshtein, *Narodnoe bogatstvo*, pp. 444–5.

43 See Hardach, *First World War*, p. 153.

44 Britain contributed a further 21 billion rubles to the Triple Entente. Data from Gregory, *Russian National Income*, pp. 155–7.

45 For background discussion, see Zaionchkovskii, *Podgotovka Rossii*.

46 Stone, *Eastern Front*, pp. 51–3.

47 Sukhomlinov, *Vospominaniia*, pp. 191–2; Sidorov, *Ekonomicheskoe polozhenie*, pp. 576–7; Anan"ich, *Rossiia*, pp. 275, 279; Spring, 'Russia and the Franco-Russian alliance'. There is another consideration to take into account: the alliance allowed Russia to draw upon French support for tsarist ambitions in the Far East. See Fuller, *Strategy and Power*, pp. 392–3.

48 *Documents diplomatiques français*, série 3, vol. 8, pp. 85–93.

49 This point is made by Pearton, *The Knowledgeable State*, pp. 103–4. The three-year law, passed in 1913, is discussed in G. Krumeich, *Armaments and Politics in France on the Eve of the First World War: The Introduction of Three-Year Conscription, 1913–1914*, Leamington Spa, 1984.

50 Anan"ich, *Rossiia*, p. 283.

51 See the reports in *ibid.*, pp. 287–8, quoting the Cadet Shingarev and the rightist Markov, who complained that Russia had been offered very poor terms. Consult the map in Girault, *Emprunts russes*, p. 518.

52 See Girault, *Emprunts russes*, pp. 563–8.

53 For the data, see table 3.6. and Wright, *Study of War*, pp. 670–1. On the subject of military alliances, see Kennedy, *Defense Economics*, pp. 32–44.

54 Gulevich, *Voina*, discussed the German food situation. The only references to food in Durnovo's memorandum are to the imminent disruption to British food imports likely to be caused by a German blockade and to the desirability of promoting Russian exports to Germany, provided the trade treaty could be renegotiated in Russia's favour. On British preparations for a naval blockade of Germany, see Offer, *First World War*, part three. My

estimates of grain output per capita derive from Gregory, *Russian National Income*, appendix D, p. 235. The mean value of net grain output was 15.1 rubles per person in 1904/08 and 18.6 rubles in 1909/13 (both figures expressed in 1913 prices).

55 This section draws upon S. G. Wheatcroft, 'The balance of grain production and utilization in Russia in war and revolution', Birmingham, n.d.

56 Kitanina, *Khlebnaia torgovlia*, pp. 255–65, provides a full discussion.

57 R. Claus, *Die Kriegswirtschaft Russlands bis zur bolschewistischen Revolution*, Berlin, 1922, pp. 138–40; N. D. Kondrat'ev, *Rynok khlebov i ego regulirovanie v voine i revoliutsii*, Moscow, 1922, pp. 48, 330; Wheatcroft, 'Balance of grain production'.

58 Polivanov is quoted in Sidorov, *Finansovoe polozhenie*, p. 54, Palitsyn by Kavtaradze, 'Iz istorii', p. 87. See also Rödiger's memoirs, excerpted in *Voenno-istoricheskii zhurnal*, 1990, 6, pp. 82–7; 1991, 1, pp. 57–63; for Alekseev, see Zaionchkovskii, *Podgotovka*, pp. 348–54.

59 Ropponen, *Die Kraft Russlands*, pp. 213–35.

60 Quoted by Stone, *Eastern Front*, pp. 37, 42. See also Lohr, *Die 'Zukunft Russlands'*; and Niall Ferguson, 'Germany and the origins of the First World War: new perspectives', *Historical Journal*, 35, 1992, pp. 725–52.

61 For a modern view, see Fuller, *Strategy and Power*. An interesting observation on the drift in prewar priorities was provided by Fisher, the First Sea Lord, in 1908. Finding himself seated between Stolypin and Izvol'skii at an official dinner, Stolypin asked Fisher '"What do you think we want most?" He fancied I should answer "so many battleships, so many cruisers etc. etc.", but instead I said "Your western frontier is denuded of troops and your magazines are depleted. *Fill them up* and then talk of fleets!...". Stolypin looked hard at me and said not another word'. Quoted in J. A. Fisher, *Fear God and Dread Nought: The Correspondence of Admiral of the Fleet Lord Fisher of Kilverstone*, ed. A. J. Marder, 3 vols., London, 1952–59, vol. 2, p. 194 (Fisher's italics).

62 The terms 'patrician' and 'plebeian' are used by Norman Stone. For France, see E. Weber, *Peasants into Frenchmen*, London, 1977; on Britain, see Offer, *The First World War*, pp. 313–61.

Conclusion

1 The magnitude of the improvement is difficult to gauge, and the entire subject requires more investigation. A start might be made with the article by I. F. Gindin, 'Balansy aktsionernykh predpriiatii kak istoricheskii istochnik', in *Maloissledovannye istochniki po istorii SSSR, XIX–XXvv.*, Moscow, 1964, pp. 74–147. See also Gerschenkron, *Economic Backwardness*, p. 22; and 'Rate of industrial growth'.

2 *Doklad soveta s"ezdov*, p. 155.

3 Manikovskii, *Boevoe snabzhenie*, vol. 2, pp. 61–78; V. S. M[ikhailov], 'Ob organizatsii voennoi promyshlennosti', *Voennaia nauka i revoliutsiia*, 1922, 1, pp. 138–54. Both authors advocated that the most technologically complex armaments be produced exclusively at state works. Other goods, par-

ticularly those with a dual civilian-military purpose (optical instruments, medical supplies, electrical equipment), could be supplied by the private sector.

4 For further thoughts on this topic, consult T. C. Owen, *The Corporation under Russian Law, 1800–1917: A Study in Tsarist Economic Policy*, Cambridge, 1991.

5 *SOGD*, III, 1st session, 74 sitting, 27 May 1908, col. 1,662 (Kurakin, deputy from Yaroslavl).

6 J. Reshetar, *The Ukrainian Revolution*, Princeton, 1952.

7 See the contributions to *Voprosy istorii kapitalisticheskoi Rossii*, Sverdlovsk, 1972, as well as Polikarpov, 'Gosudarstvennoe proizvodstvo vooruzheniia', pp. 16–37 and the bad-tempered debate between Bovykin and Polikarpov in the pages of *Voprosy istorii* during 1989.

8 F. Fischer, *War of Illusions: German Policies from 1911 to 1914*, London, 1975.

9 Anna Akhmatova, 'Poema bez geroia', *Sochineniia*, 2 vols., Munich, 1968, vol. 2, p. 118. The other phrase belongs to Joyce Cary.

Bibliography

1. Archives

St Petersburg

Central State Historical Archive (TsGIA)
fond 23   Ministry of Trade and Industry
fond 32   Confederation of Trade and Industry
fond 37   Department of Mines
fond 268   Department of Railway Affairs, Ministry of Finances
fond 1276 Council of Ministers
fond 1333 Inspections undertaken by Senator D. B. Neidhart
fond 1393 Inspections undertaken by Senator N. P. Garin

Central State Archive of the Navy (TsGAVMF)
fond 401   Commission on Shipbuilding
fond 410   Admiralty Office
fond 420   Office of the Navy Minister
fond 427   Main Administration of Shipbuilding and Supply (GUKS)
fond 441   Council for the Administration of the Affairs of State Shipyards
fond 512   Board of Nilolaev Shipbuilding Company

St Petersburg State Historical Archive (formerly LGIA)
fond 1307 Baranovskii Company
fond 1314 Parviainen Company
fond 2108 Nikolaev Shipbuilding Company
fond 2145 Russo-Baltic Shipbuilding Company

Moscow

Central State Military – Historical Archive (TsGVIA)
fond 369   Special Council for State Defence

Lenin Library, Manuscript Division
A. V. Pankin, Reminiscences, March 1952

Other Archives

Cambridge University Library
Vickers Papers:
Files R214, R215, R307, 57, 735, 1219 relating to Vickers' business in Russia
  before 1917
United States National Archives, Washington, D.C.
Record Group 92, series 316, Department of State Records relating to internal
  affairs of Russia and the Soviet Union
Record Group 165, War College Division, Office of Chief of Staff

2. Official publications (place of publication St Petersburg unless otherwise
   stated)

Gosudarstvennaia Duma: Stenograficheskie otchety, 1906–17.
Gosudarstvennyi Sovet: Stenograficheskie otchety, 1906–17.
Explanatory Memorandum to the Russian Budget, 1913.
Ezhegodnik Rossii (after 1910 *Statisticheskii ezhegodnik Rossii*), 11 vols.,
   1905–18.
Fabrichno-zavodskie predpriiatiia Rossiiskoi imperii, 1908; 2nd edn, 1914.
Narodnoe khoziaistvo v 1915 godu, Petrograd, 1918.
*Ob"iasnitel'naia zapiska Ministerstva finansov k proektu gosudarstvennoi rospisi
   dokhodov i raskhodov na 1913*, 1912.
Obshchaia ob"iasnitel'naia zapiska k smete Voennogo ministerstva na (1910–1913) god,
   4 vols., 1910–13.
Obshchii obzor glavneishikh otraslei gornoi i gornozavodskoi promyshlennosti, 2 vols.,
   1913–15.
*Obshchii sostav uchebnykh i tekhnicheskikh artilleriiskikh zavedenii, podvedomstven-
   nykh GAU na (1911–1915) god*, 1911–15.
Otchet Gornogo departamenta za (1891–1911) god, 1892–1913.
*Otchet Gosudarstvennogo kontrolera po ispol'neniiu gosudarstvennoi rospisi i
   finansovykh smet za (1866–1914) god*, 1868–1915.
Otchet otdela promyshlennosti za (1910–1914), 1910–14.
*Polozhenie o vol'nonaemnykh i pravila o naime masterovykh i rabochikh v tekhni-
   cheskikh artilleriiskikh zavedeniiakh*, 1915.
Pravila o naime masterovykh i rabochikh v tekhnicheskikh artilleriiskikh zavedeniiakh,
   2nd edn, 1906.
Proekt gosudarstvennoi rospisi dokhodov i raskhodov na 1908, 1908.
'Promyshlennaia i professional'naia perepis' 1918g: fabrichno-zavodskaia
   promyshlennost' v period 1913–1918gg.', *Trudy TsSU*, vol. 26, parts 1 and 2,
   Moscow, 1926.
Proposed Budget for the Russian Empire, St Petersburg, 1908.
Smeta dokhodov i raskhodov gornogo departamenta na (1864–1917), 1863–1916.
Smeta voennogo ministerstva na (1864–1915) po GAU, 52 vols., 1863–1915.
Smeta voennogo ministerstva po chrezvychainym raskhodam na (1910–1917) god, 7
   vols., 1909–16.
Statisticheskii ezhegodnik na (1912–1914), 1913–15.

Svod morskikh postanovlenii: vol. 5, tekhnicheskie zavedeniia morskogo vedomstva, 2nd edn (1901), 1902; 3rd edn (1910), 1910.
Svod statisticheskikh dannykh po zhelezodelatel'noi promyshlennosti za 1912, 1913.
Svod voennykh postanovlenii: vol. 12, zavedeniia intendantskie, 2nd edn, 1891; 3rd edn, 1914.
Svod voennykh postanovlenii: vol. 13, zavedeniia artilleriiskie, 3rd edn, 1910.
Svod zakonov Rossiiskoi imperii, izd. 1887, vol. 10, part 1, 'Polozhenie o kazennykh podriadakh i postavkakh', new edition, 1900, revised 1915.
Vsepoddaneishii doklad po morskomu ministerstvu za (1910–1916), 1911–17.
Vsepoddaneishii otchet gosudarstvennogo kontrolera za (1864–1915) god, 1865–1916.
Vsepoddaneishii otchet po morskomu ministerstvu za (1856–1914) god (after 1910, *Vsepoddaneishii otchet morskogo ministra*), 1859–1915.

3. Unpublished works

E. R. Goldstein, 'Military aspects of Russian industrialization: the defense industries, 1890–1917', PhD thesis, Case Western Reserve University, 1971.
H. Hogan, 'Labor and management in conflict: the St Petersburg metalworking industry, 1900–1914', PhD thesis, University of Michigan, 1981.
G. Holzer, 'The German electrical industry in Russia, 1890–1910', PhD thesis, Lincoln, University of Nebraska, 1970.
G. A. Miftiev, 'Artilleriiskaia promyshlennost' Rossii v period pervoi mirovoi voiny', kandidatskaia dissertatsiia, Leningrad State University, 1953.
Iu. F. Subbotin, 'Voennaia promyshlennost' Rossii vo vtoroi polovine XIX-nachale XXv., 1868–1914gg.', kandidatskaia dissertatsiia, Moscow State University, 1975.
J. D. Walz, 'State defense and Russian politics under the last Tsar', PhD thesis, Syracuse University, 1967.
S. G. Wheatcroft, 'The balance of grain production and utilization in Russia in war and revolution', Centre for Russian and East European Studies, University of Birmingham, n.d.
W. T. Wilfong, 'Rebuilding the Russian army, 1905–1914: the question of a comprehensive plan for national defense', PhD thesis, University of Indiana, 1977.

4. Periodicals and Newspapers

Artilleriiskii zhurnal
Birzhevye vedomosti
Finansovoe obozrenie
Morskoi sbornik
Novyi ekonomist
Promyshlennost' i torgovlia
Torgovo-promyshlennaia gazeta
Vestnik finansov
Vestnik inzhenerov

5. Published books and articles

A. K. L., 'O polozhenii rabochikh v tekhnicheskikh artilleriiskikh zavede-niakh', *Artilleriiskii zhurnal*, 1904, 9, pp. 1,005–21.

A. R., 'Rabochie Sormovskikh zavodov', *Narodnoe khoziaistvo*, 1902, 4, pp. 84–94.

Abramovitz, Moses, 'Catching up, forging ahead and falling behind', *Journal of Economic History*, 46, 1986, pp. 385–406.

Anan"ich, B. V., *Rossiia i mezhdunarodnyi kapital, 1897–1914*, Leningrad, 1970.

Artem'ev, A. A., 'Usloviia rabot v tekhnicheskikh zavedeniiakh Artilleriiskogo vedomstva i postanovka zdes' meditsinskoi pomoshchi rabochim', *Trudy vtorogo Vserossiiskogo s"ezda fabrichnykh vrachei i predstavitelei fabrichno-zavodskoi promyshlennosti*, vypusk 1, Moscow, 1911, pp. 13–34.

Ashurkov, V. N., 'Rabochie zavodov artilleriiskogo vedomstva v epokhu kapi-talizma: osobennosti ikh polozheniia i klassovoi bor'by', *Rabochie Rossii v epokhu kapitalizma*, Tula, 1972, pp. 93–101.

'Predpriiatiia voennogo vedomstva kak element mnogoukladnoi ekonomiki Rossii', in *Voprosy istorii kapitalisticheskoi Rossii*, Sverdlovsk, 1972, pp. 109–17.

Ashworth, W., 'Economic aspects of late Victorian naval administration', *Economic History Review*, 22, 1969, pp. 491–505.

Baklanova, I. A., *Rabochie sudostroiteli Rossii v XIX veke*, Moscow-Leningrad, 1959.

Barsukov, E. Z., *Podgotovka Rossii k mirovoi voine v artilleriiskom otnoshenii*, Moscow, 1926.

Bart, A., 'Na fronte artilleriiskogo snabzheniia', *Byloe*, 34, 1925, pp. 147–91.

Beaud, Claude, 'De l'expansion internationale à la multinationale: Schneider en Russie, 1896–1914', *Histoire, Economie et Société*, *SEDES*, 1985, 4, pp. 575–602.

Belavenets, P. I., *Nuzhen-li nam flot i znachenie ego v istorii Rossii*, St Petersburg, 1910.

Berghahn, V., *Germany and the Approach of War in 1914*, London, 1973.

Berlin, P. A., *Russkaia burzhuaziia v staroe i novoe vremia*, Moscow, 1922.

Beskrovnyi, L. G., *Armiia i flot v XIX veke: voenno-ekonomicheskii potentsial Rossii*, Moscow, 1973.

'Proizvodstvo vooruzheniia i boepripasov dlia armii v Rossii v period imperializma, 1898–1917', *Istoricheskie zapiski*, 99, 1977, pp. 88–139.

Armiia i flot Rossii v nachale XX v.: ocherki voenno-ekonomicheskogo potentsiala, Moscow, 1986.

Bestuzhev, I. V., 'Bor'ba v Rossii po voprosam vneshnei politiki nakanune pervoi mirovoi voiny, 1910–1914', *Istoricheskie zapiski*, 75, 1965, pp. 45–85.

Beyrau, D. *Militär und Gesellschaft im vorrevolutionären Russland*, Cologne-Vienna, 1984.

Blek, A. L., 'Usloviia truda rabochikh na peterburgskikh zavodakh po dannym 1901g.', *Arkhiv istorii truda v Rossii*, 2, 1921, pp. 65–85.

Bobrov, S., *Indeksy Gosplana*, Moscow, 1925.

Bogolepov, M., 'Gosudarstvennoe khoziaistvo', in Iu. N. Martov et al., eds.,

Obshchestvennoe dvizhenie v Rossii v nachale XX veka, 4 vols., St Petersburg, 1909–1914, vol. 1, pp. 151–82.

Bonnell, V. E., *Roots of Rebellion: Workers' Politics and Organization in St Petersburg and Moscow, 1900–1914*, Berkeley, 1983.

Borisov, G. B., and S. Vasil'ev, *Stankostroitel'nyi im. Sverdlova: ocherk istorii Leningradskogo stankostroitel'nogo zavoda, 1867–1961gg.*, Leningrad, 1962.

Boulding, K. E., and A. Gleason, 'War as an investment: the case of Japan', *Peace Research Society Papers*, 3, 1965.

Bovykin, V. I., 'Iz istorii proniknoveniia inostrannogo kapitala v Rossii (Permskoe delo)', *Nauchnye doklady vysshei shkoly*, 1958, 1, pp. 66–73.

'Monopolisticheskie soglasheniia v russkoi voennoi promyshlennosti, po materialam senatorskikh revizii', *Istoriia SSSR*, 1958, 1, pp. 125 9.

'Banki i voennaia promyshlennost' Rossii nakanune pervoi mirovoi voiny', *Istoricheskie zapiski*, 64, 1959, pp. 82–135.

Ocherki istorii vneshnei politiki Rossii, Moscow, 1960.

'O nekotorykh voprosakh izucheniia inostrannogo kapitala v Rossii', in A. L. Sidorov, ed., *Ob osobennostiakh imperializma v Rossii*, Moscow, 1962, pp. 250–313.

Formirovanie finansovogo kapitala v Rossii, konets XIX veka-1908g., Moscow, 1984.

Bovykin, V. I., and K. N. Tarnovskii, 'Kontsentratsiia proizvodstva i razvitie monopolii v metalloobrabatyvaiushchei promyshlennosti Rossii', *Voprosy istorii*, 1957, 2, pp. 19–31.

Bovykin, V. I., and K. F. Shatsillo, 'Lichnye unii v tiazheloi promyshlennosti Rossii nakanune pervoi mirovoi voiny', *Vestnik MGU, istoriia*, 1962, 1, pp. 55–74.

Bradley, Joseph, *Guns for the Tsar: The State, Labor and Technology Transfer in the Russian Small Arms Industry*, DeKalb, 1990.

Brooks, J., 'The zemstvo and the education of the people', in T. Emmons and W. Vucinich, eds., *The Zemstvo in Russia: An Experiment in Local Self-Government*, Stanford, 1982, pp. 243–78.

Bukin, B., 'Zheleznye dorogi v mirovuiu voinu i ikh blizhaishie zadachi v pogdotovke strany k oborone', *Voina i revoliutsiia*, 1926, 3, pp. 100–18; 4, pp. 87–100.

Bukovetskii, A. I., 'Svobodnaia nalichnost' i zolotoi zapas tsarskogo pravitel'stva v kontse XIX-nachale XXv.', in *Monopolii i inostrannyi kapital v Rossii*, 1962, Moscow-Leningrad, pp. 359–76.

Bulgakov, M., *A Country Doctor's Notebook*, London, 1990.

Burchardt, L., *Friedenswirtschaft und Kriegsvorsorge: Deutschlands wirtschaftliche Rüstungsbestrebungen vor 1914*, Boppard-am-Rhein, 1968.

Bushnell, J., 'Peasants in uniform: the tsarist army as a peasant society', *Journal of Social History*, 13, 1980, pp. 565–76.

Mutiny amid Repression: Russian Soldiers in the Revolution of 1905–1906, Bloomington, Indiana, 1985.

Charnovskii, N., 'Mashinostroitel'naia promyshlennost'', *Narodnoe khoziaistvo v 1916 godu*, Petrograd, 1921, 4, pp. 43–77.

Chernomorskii, M. N., 'Pervaia promyshlennaia perepis' 1918g. kak istoricheskii istochnik', *Trudy Moskovskogo gosudarstvennogo istorichesko-arkhivnogo instituta*, 12, 1959, pp. 245–66.

Chirikov, N. S., 'Plan voiny, podgotovka i mobilizatsiia imperatorskogo flota v 1914 godu', *Voennaia byl'*, 75, 1965, pp. 12–18.

Claus, R., *Die Kriegswirtschaft Russlands bis zur bolschewistischen Revolution*, Berlin, 1922.

Coopersmith, J., *The Electrification of Russia*, Ithaca, 1992.

Crisp, Olga, *Studies in the Russian Economy before 1914*, London, 1976.

'Labour and industrialization', in P. Mathias and M. M. Postan, eds., *Cambridge Economic History of Europe*, vol. 7, part 2, Cambridge, 1978, pp. 308–415.

Crouzet, F., 'Recherches sur la production d'armements en France (1815–1913)', *Revue historique*, 251, 1974, pp. 45–84.

Davenport-Hines, R. P. T., 'The British marketing of armaments, 1885–1935' in Davenport-Hines, ed., *Markets and Bagmen: Studies in the History of Marketing and British Industrial Performance, 1830–1939*, London, 1986, pp. 146–91.

Davydova, L. G., *Ispol'zovanie elektricheskoi energii v promyshlennosti Rossii*, Moscow, 1966.

Diakin, V. S., 'Iz istorii ekonomicheskoi politiki tsarizma v 1907–1914gg.', *Istoricheskie zapiski*, 109, 1983, pp. 25–63.

Dikhtiar, G. A., *Vnutrenniaia torgovlia v dorevoliutsionnoi Rossii*, Moscow, 1960.

Dinamika rossiiskoi i sovetskoi promyshlennosti v sviazi s razvitiem narodnogo khoziaistva za sorok let (1887–1926gg.), 3 vols, Moscow-Leningrad, 1929–30.

Dmitriev, N. I., and V. V. Kolpychev, *Sudostroitel'nye zavody i sudostroenie v Rossii i za granitsei*, St Petersburg, 1909.

Documents diplomatiques français, 1871–1914, série 1, 16 vols., série 2, 14 vols., série 3, 11 vols., Paris, 1929–36.

Doklad soveta s"ezdov o merakh k razvitiiu proizvoditel'nykh sil Rossii, Petrograd, 1915.

Efremtsev, G. P., *Istoriia Kolomenskogo zavoda*, 2nd edn, Moscow, 1984.

Eklof, B., 'Peasants and schools', in B. Eklof and S. P. Frank, eds., *The World of the Russian Peasant*, London, 1990, pp. 115–32.

Eklof, B., J. Bushnell and L. Zakharova, eds., *The Great Reforms in Russia: A New Perspective*, Bloomington, Indiana, 1993.

Emmons, T., *The Formation of Political Parties in Russia and the First National Elections in Russia*, Stanford, 1983.

Epkenhans, M., *Die wilhelminische Flottenrüstung, 1908–1914*, Munich, 1991.

Ermanskii, A., 'Krupnaia burzhuaziia v 1905–1907gg.', in Iu. N. Martov et al., eds., *Obshchestvennoe dvizhenie v Rossii v nachale XXv.*, 4 vols., St Petersburg, 1909–14, vol. 2, part 2, 1910, pp. 30–100.

Eroshkin, N. P., *Istoriia gosudarstvennykh uchrezhdenii dorevoliutsionnoi Rossii*, 3rd edn, Moscow, 1983.

Eventov, L. Ia., *Inostrannye kapitaly v russkoi promyshlennosti*, Moscow-Leningrad, 1931.

Falkus, M. E., *The Industrialization of Russia, 1700–1914*, London, 1972.

Feldman, G. D., *Iron and Steel in the German Inflation, 1918–1923*, Princeton, 1977.

Ferguson, N., 'Germany and the origins of the First World War: new perspectives', *Historical Journal*, 35, 1992, pp. 725–52.

Finn-Enotaevskii, A., *Sovremennoe khoziaistvo v Rossii*, St Petersburg, 1911.

Fischer, F., *War of Illusions: German Policies from 1911 to 1914*, London, 1975.

Fisher, J. A., *Fear God and Dread Nought: The Correspondence of Admiral of the Fleet Lord Fisher of Kilverstone*, ed. A. J. Marder, 3 vols., London, 1952–9.

Fomin, P. I., *Gornaia i gornozavodskaia promyshlennost' iuga Rossii*, 2 vols., Kharkov, 1915, 1922.

Frantz, G., *Russlands Eintritt in den Weltkrieg: der Ausbau der russischen Wehrmacht und ihr Einsatz bei Kriegsausbruch*, Berlin, 1924.

Fuller, W. C., Jr., *Civil–Military Conflict in Imperial Russia, 1881–1914*, Princeton, 1985.

Strategy and Power in Russia, 1600–1914, New York, 1992.

Gaponenko, L. S., *Rabochii klass Rossii v 1917 godu*, Moscow, 1970.

Gatrell, P. W., 'Industrial expansion in tsarist Russia, 1908–1913', *Economic History Review*, 35, 1982, pp. 99–100.

The Tsarist Economy, 1850–1917, London, 1986.

Gefter, M. Ia., 'Tsarizm i monopolisticheskii kapital v metallurgii iuga Rossii do pervoi mirovoi voiny', *Istoricheskie zapiski*, 43, 1953, pp. 70–130.

'Bor'ba vokrug sozdaniia metallurgicheskogo tresta v Rossii v nachale XXv.', *Istoricheskie zapiski*, 47, 1954, pp. 124–48.

Germonius, E. K., 'Izhevskii oruzheinyi zavod i rol' kazennykh zavodov v dele oborony', *Russian Economist*, 2, 1922, pp. 2,901–25.

Gerschenkron, A., 'The rate of industrial growth in Russia since 1885', *Journal of Economic History*, supplement 7, 1947, pp. 144–74.

'Problems and patterns of Russian economic development', in C. E. Black, ed., *The Transformation of Russian Society*, Cambridge, Mass., 1960, pp. 42–72.

Economic Backwardness in Historical Perspective, Cambridge, Mass., 1962.

'The early phases of industrialization in Russia: afterthoughts and counterthoughts', in W. W. Rostow, ed., *The Economics of Take-Off into Self-Sustained Growth*, London, 1963, pp. 151–69.

Geyer, D., *Russian Imperialism: The Interaction of Foreign and Domestic Policy, 1860–1914*, Leamington Spa, 1987.

Giddens, A., *The Nation-State and Violence*, Cambridge and Oxford, 1985.

Gindin, I. F., *Banki i promyshlennost' v Rossii*, Moscow-Leningrad, 1927.

Russkie kommercheskie banki, Moscow-Leningrad, 1948.

'Balansy aktsionernykh predpriiatii kak istoricheskii istochnik', in *Maloissledovannye istochniki po istorii SSSR, XIX–XXvv.*, Leningrad, 1964, pp. 74–147.

'Politika tsarskogo pravitel'stva v otnoshenii promyshlennykh monopolii', in *Ob osobennostiiakh imperializma*, Moscow, 1963, pp. 86–123.

'Antikrizisnoe finansirovanie predpriiatii tiazheloi promyshlennosti, konets XIX-nachalo XXv.', *Istoricheskie zapiski*, 105, 1980, pp. 105–49.

Girault, R., 'Finances internationales et relations internationales: à propos des usines Poutiloff', *Revue d'histoire moderne et contemporaine*, 13, 1966, pp. 217–36.

Emprunts russes et investissements français en Russie, 1887–1914, Paris, 1973.

Golder, F. A., *Documents of Russian History, 1914–1917*, New York, 1927.

Goldstein, E. R., 'Vickers Ltd. and the tsarist regime', *Slavonic and East European Review*, 58, 1980, pp. 561–71.

Golikov, A. G., 'Obrazovanie monopolisticheskogo ob"edineniia "Kolomna-Sormovo"', *Vestnik MGU, istoriia*, 1971, 5, pp. 74–87.

Golovin, N. N., *Voennye usiliia Rossii v morovoi voine*, 2 vols., Paris, 1939.

Golovine, N. N., *The Russian Army in the World War*, New Haven, 1931.

Gorfein, G. M., 'Iz istorii obrazovaniia Ministerstva torgovli i promyshlennosti', in S. N. Valk, ed., *Ocherki po istorii ekonomiki i klassovykh otnoshenii v Rossii kontsa XIX-nachala XXv.*, Moscow-Leningrad, 1964, pp. 161–79.

Gorlin, R. H., 'Problems of tax reform in imperial Russia', *Journal of Modern History*, 49, 1977, pp. 246–65.

Gregory, Paul, *Russian National Income, 1885–1913*, Cambridge, 1982.

Grinevetskii, V. I., *Poslevoennye perspektivy russkoi promyshlennosti*, Kharkov, 1919.

Gulevich, A., *Voina i narodnoe khoziaistvo*, St Petersburg, 1898.

Harcave, S., ed., *The Memoirs of Count Witte*, New York, 1990.

Hardach, G., *The First World War, 1914–1918*, London, 1977.

Hartl, J. H., *Die Interessenvertretungen der Industriellen in Russland, 1905–1914*, Vienna, 1978.

Haumann, H., *Kapitalismus im zaristischen Staat, 1905–1917*, Königstein, 1980.

Hogan, H., 'The reorganization of work processes in the St Petersburg metalworking industry, 1901–1914', *Russian Review*, 42, 1983, pp. 163–90.

Iakovlev, A. F., *Ekonomicheskie krizisy v Rossii*, Moscow-Leningrad, 1955.

Il'inskii, D. P., and V. P. Ivanitskii, *Ocherk istorii russkoi parovozostroitel'noi i vagonostroitel'noi promyshlennosti*, Moscow, 1929.

Industrielle Mobilmachungen: Statistische Untersuchungen, Hamburg, 1936.

Istoriia Khar'kovskogo parovozostroitel'nogo zavoda, 1895–1923gg., Kharkov, 1956.

Istoriia Tul'skogo oruzheinogo zavoda, 1712–1972, Moscow, 1973.

Ivanov, P. G., *Ocherk istorii i statistiki russkogo zavodskogo parovozostroeniia*, Petrograd, 1920.

'Iz istorii Shostenskogo zavoda', *Krasnyi arkhiv*, 75, 1936, no. 2, pp. 192–6.

'Iz zapisok A. F. Rödigera', *Krasnyi arkhiv*, 60, 1930, 5, pp. 92–133.

Izmailovskaia, E. M., *Russkoe sel'skokhoziaistvennoe mashinostroenie*, Petrograd, 1920.

Jane, F. T., *The Imperial Russian Navy*, 2nd edn, London, 1904, reprinted 1983.

Johnson, Alvin, 'The expansion of military expenditures', *Documents of the American Association for International Conciliation*, New York, 1911.

Jones, G., and C. Trebilcock, 'Russian industry and British business, 1910–1930: oil and armaments', *Journal of European Economic History*, 11, 1982, pp. 61–103.

Kahan, A., 'Government policies and the industrialization of Russia', *Journal of Economic History*, 27, 1967, pp. 460–77.

'Capital formation during the period of early industrialization in Russia, 1890–1913', in Mathias, P., and M. M. Postan, eds., *Cambridge Economic History of Europe*, vol. 7, part 2, Cambridge, 1978, pp. 265–307.

The Plow, the Hammer and the Knout: An Economic History of Eighteenth-Century Russia, Chicago, 1985.

Kannegiser, I., *Zadachi protektsionizma v metalloobrabatyvaiushchei promyshlennosti*, Petrograd, 1915.

Kavtaradze, A. G., 'Iz istorii russkogo general'nogo shtaba', *Voenno-istoricheskii zhurnal*, 7, 1972, pp. 87–92; 12, 1974, pp. 80–6.

Keegan, John, *The Face of Battle*, London, 1976.

Kefeli, Ia. I., *Poteri v lichnom sostave russkogo flota v voinu s Iaponiei: statisticheskoe issledovanie*, Petrograd, 1914.

Kehr, E., 'Munitions industry', *Encyclopedia of the Social Sciences*, 15 vols., New York 1930–35, vol. 11, pp. 128–34.

Economic Interests, Militarism and Foreign Policy, ed. G. A. Craig, Berkeley, 1977, pp. 50–75.

Kelly, W. J., 'Crisis management in the Russian oil industry: the 1905 revolution', *Journal of European Economic History*, 10, 1981, pp. 291–342.

Kennedy, G., *The Economics of Defence*, London 1975; rev. edn published as *Defense Economics*, 1983.

Kennedy, P. M., *The Rise of the Anglo-German Antagonism, 1860–1914*, London, 1980.

Khoziaistvennaia zhizn' i ekonomicheskoe polozhenie naseleniia Rossii za pervye deviat' mesiatsev voiny, Petrograd, 1916.

Khromov, P. A., *Ekonomicheskoe razvitie Rossii v XIX i XX vekakh*, Moscow, 1950.

Khrulev, S. S., *Finansy Rossii v sviazi s ekonomicheskom polozheniem ee naseleniia*, 2nd edn, St Petersburg, 1908.

Finansy Rossii i ee promyshlennost', 2nd edn, Petrograd, 1916.

Kirchner, W., *Die deutsche Industrie und die Industrialisierung Russlands, 1815–1914*, St Katharinen, 1986.

Kir'ianov, Iu. I., *Zhiznennyi uroven' rabochikh Rossii, konets XIX-nachalo XXv.*, Moscow, 1979.

Kitanina, T. M., *Khlebnaia torgovlia v Rossii, 1875–1914gg.*, Leningrad, 1978.

Kokovtsov, V. N., *Iz moego proshlogo: vospominaniia*, 2 vols., Paris, 1933.

Out of My Past: The Memoirs of Count Kokovtsov, ed. H. H. Fisher, Stanford, 1935.

Kol'tsov, D., 'Rabochie v 1905–1907gg.', in Iu. N. Martov et al., eds., *Obshchestvennoe dvizhenie v Rossii v nachale XX veka*, 4 vols., St Petersburg, 1909–14, vol. 2, part 1, pp. 185–341.

Kondrat'ev, N. D., *Rynok khlebov i ego regulirovanie v voine i revoliutsii*, Moscow, 1922.

Korolev, A. A., 'Iz istorii russkoi voennoi promyshlennosti: vozniknovenie chastnogo patronnogo zavoda', *Uchenye zapiski Tul'skogo gosudarstvennogo pedagogicheskogo instituta, kafedra istorii*, vol. 2, Tula, 1969, pp. 78–98.

'Finansovo-ekonomicheskaia deiatelnost' Tul'skogo patronnogo zavoda, 1899–1907', *Iz istorii Tul'skogo kraia*, Tula, 1972, pp. 26–41.

'Reviziia senatorom N. P. Garinym Tul'skogo patronnogo zavoda', in *Iz istorii Tul'skogo kraia*, Tula, 1972, pp. 54–62.

Krumeich, G., *Armaments and Politics in France on the Eve of the First World War: The Introduction of Three-Year Conscription, 1913–1914*, Leamington Spa, 1984.

Krupina, T. D., 'K voprosu o vzaimootnosheniiakh tsarskogo pravitel'stva s monopoliiami', *Istoricheskie zapiski*, 57, 1956, pp. 144–76.

Kruze, E. E., *Peterburgskie rabochie v 1912–1914gg.*, Moscow-Leningrad, 1961.

Usloviia truda i byta rabochego klassa Rossii v 1900–1914gg., Leningrad, 1981.

Krylov, A. N., *Moi vospominaniia*, 8th edn, Leningrad, 1984.

Kuznetsov, K. A., et al., *Baltiiskii sudostroitel'nyi, 1856–1917*, Leningrad, 1970.

Laverychev, V. Ia., *Po tu storonu barrikad: iz istorii bor'by Moskovskoi burzhuazii s revoliutsii*, Moscow, 1967.

Tsarizm i rabochii vopros v Rossii, Moscow, 1972.

Gosudarstvo i monopolii v dorevoliutsionnoi Rossii, Moscow, 1982.

Liashchenko, P. I., 'Iz istorii monopolii v Rossii', *Istoricheskie zapiski*, 20, 1946, pp. 150–89.

Istoriia narodnogo khoziaistva SSSR, 2 vols., Moscow-Leningrad, 1952.

Lieven, D. C. B., *Russia and the Origins of the First World War*, London, 1983.

Russia's Rulers Under the Old Regime, London, 1989.

Lisovskii, N. M., *Rabochie v voennom vedomstve*, St Petersburg, 1906.

Liubarov, P. E., 'Tret'ia gosudarstvennaia Duma i vopros o strakhovanii rabochikh kazennykh predpriiatii', *Vestnik MGU, istoriia*, 1967, 2, pp. 36–48.

Livshin, Ia. I., 'K voprosu o voenno-promyshlennykh monopoliiakh v Rossii v nachale XX veka', *Voprosy istorii*, 1957, 7, pp. 55–70.

'"Predstavitel'nye" organizatsii krupnoi burzhuazii v Rossii v kontse XIX-nachale XX vv.', *Istoriia SSSR*, 1959, 2, pp. 95–117.

Lohr, B., *Die 'Zukunft Russlands': Perspektiven russischer Wirtschaftsentwicklung und deutsch-russische Wirtschaftsbeziehungen vor dem ersten Weltkrieg*, Wiesbaden, 1985.

Luknitskii, V., 'O vol'nonaemnykh rabochikh artilleriiskikh tekhnicheskikh zavedenii', *Artilleriiskii zhurnal*, 1899, 1, pp. 89–100.

Lur'e, E. S., *Organizatsiia i organizatsii torgovo-promyshlennykh interesov v Rossii*, St Petersburg, 1913.

Lyashchenko, P. I., *History of the Russian National Economy to 1917*, New York, 1949.

McCully, Newton A., *The McCully Report: The Russo-Japanese War, 1904–1905*, Annapolis, Maryland, 1977.

McDaniel, T., *Autocracy, Capitalism and Revolution in Russia*, Berkeley, 1988.

MacDonald, David M., *United Government and Foreign Policy in Russia, 1900–1914*, Cambridge, Mass., 1992.

Macey, D. A. J., 'The peasant commune and the Stolypin reforms: peasant attitudes, 1906–1914', in R. Bartlett, ed., *Land Commune and Peasant Community in Russia*, London, 1990, pp. 219–36.

McKay, J. P., *Pioneers for Profit: Foreign Entrepreneurship and Russian Industrialization, 1885–1913*, Chicago, 1970.

McKean, R. B., *St. Petersburg between the Revolutions: Workers and Revolutionaries, June 1907–February 1917*, London, 1990.

McNeill, W. H., *The Pursuit of Power: Technology, Armed Force and Society since A.D. 1000*, Chicago, 1982.

Maevskii, E., 'Massovoe dvizhenie s 1904 po 1907gg.', in Iu. N. Martov et al., eds., *Obshchestvennoe dvizhenie v Rossii v nachale XX veka*, 4 vols., St Petersburg, 1909–14, vol. 2, part 1, pp. 34–184.

Maksheev, F., *Voenno-administrativnoe ustroistvo tyla armii*, 3 vols., St Petersburg, 1893–5.

Malozemoff, A., *Russian Far Eastern Policy, 1881–1904*, Berkeley, 1958.

Manfred, A. Z., *Obrazovanie russko-frantsuzskogo soiuza*, Moscow, 1975.

Manikovskii, A. A., *Boevoe snabzhenie russkoi armii v mirovuiu voinu 1914–1918gg.*, 2 vols., Moscow-Leningrad, 1930.

Marinov, V. A., *Rossiia i Iaponiia pered pervoi mirovoi voinoi, 1905–1914gg: ocherki istorii otnoshenii*, Moscow, 1974.

Marshall, A. C., and H. Newbould, *The History of Firth's*, Sheffield, 1924.

Materialy po istorii SSSR, vol. 6, Moscow, 1959.

Meerson, G., 'Promyshlennaia depressiia v Rossii, 1906–1909gg.', *Vestnik Kommunisticheskoi Akademii*, 9, 1924, pp. 147–74.

Mehlinger, H. D., and J. M. Thompson, *Count Witte and the Tsarist Government in the 1905 Revolution*, Bloomington, Indiana, 1972.

Mendel'son, L. A., *Teoriia i istoriia ekonomicheskikh krizisov i tsiklov*, 3 vols., Moscow, 1959–64.

Migulin, P. P., *Russkii gosudarstvennyi kredit*, 3 vols., St Petersburg, 1907.

M[ikhailov], V. S., 'Ob organizatsii voennoi promyshlennosti', *Voennaia nauka i revoliutsiia*, 1922, 1, pp. 138–54.

Miller, M., *The Economic Development of Russia, 1905–1914*, London, 1926.

Miliukov, Paul, *Political Memoirs, 1905–1917*, Ann Arbor, 1967.

Milward, A. S., *The German Economy at War*, London, 1967.

War, Economy and Society, 1939–1945, 1987.

Mints, L. E., *Trudovye resursy SSSR*, Moscow, 1975.

Mitel'man M., et al., *Istoriia Putilovskogo zavoda, 1801–1917gg.*, 4th edn, Moscow, 1961.

Monkhouse, Allan, *Moscow, 1911–1933*, London, 1933.

Monopolii v metallurgicheskoi promyshlennosti Rossii, 1900–1917, Moscow, 1963.

Murzintseva, S. V., 'Iz istorii ekonomicheskogo polozheniia rabochikh na predpriiatiakh voennogo i morskogo vedomstv v 1907–1914gg. v Peterburge', *Uchenye zapiski LGU*, 270, 1959, pp. 217–41.

'Izuchenie formirovaniia i sostava rabochikh trubochnogo zavoda po dannym pasportnykh knig, 1907–1941gg.', in *Rabochie Rossii v epokhu kapitalizma: sravnitel'nyi poraionnyi analiz*, Rostov, 1972, pp. 59–68.

'Iz istorii razrabotki antirabochego zakonodatel'stva na zavodakh voennogo i morskogo vedomstv v 1907–1914gg.', in V. V. Mavrodin, ed., *Rabochie oruzheinoi promyshlennosti v Rossii i russkie oruzheiniki v XIX-nachale XXv.*, Leningrad, 1976, pp. 101–12.

Nachalo pervoi russkoi revoliutsii, ianvar' – mart 1905g., Moscow, 1955.

Nish, I., *The Origins of the Russo-Japanese War*, London, 1985.

Nolde, B. E., *Russia in the Economic War*, New Haven, 1928.

O'Brien, P. K., 'The costs and benefits of British imperialism, 1846–1914', *Past and Present*, 120, 1988, pp. 163–200.

Ocherki istorii SSSR, 1905–1907, Moscow, 1955.

Ocherki istorii tekhniki v Rossii, 1861–1917gg., Moscow, 1973.

Offer, A., *The First World War: An Agrarian Interpretation*, Oxford, 1989.

Okun', S. B., ed., *Putilovets v trekh revoliutsiiakh: sbornik materialov po istorii Putilovskogo zavoda*, Leningrad, 1933.

Overy, R., 'Hitler's war and the German economy: a reinterpretation', *Economic History Review*, 35, 1982, pp. 272–91.

Owen, T. C., *The Corporation under Russian Law, 1800–1917: A Study in Tsarist Economic Policy*, Cambridge, 1991.

Ozerov, I. Kh., *Ekonomicheskaia Rossiia i ee finansovaia politika*, St Petersburg, 1905.

Kak raskhoduiutsia v Rossii narodnye dengi, Moscow, 1907.

Gornye zavody Urala, Moscow, 1910.

Na temy dnia: k ekonomicheskomu polozheniiu Rossii, St Petersburg, 1912.

Pearton, M., *The Knowledgeable State: Diplomacy, War and Technology since 1870*, London, 1982.

Peck M. J., and F. M. Scherer, *The Weapons Acquisition Process: An Economic Analysis*, Boston, 1962.

Perrins, M., 'The Council for State Defence, 1905–1909: a study in Russian bureaucratic politics', *Slavonic and East European Review*, 58, 1980, pp. 370–98.

Pintner, W. M., 'The burden of defense in imperial Russia, 1725–1914', *Russian Review*, 43, 1984, pp. 231–59.

'Russian military thought: the western model and the shadow of Suvorov', in P. Paret, ed., *Makers of Modern Strategy*, New York, 1986, pp. 354–75.

Pogrebinskii, A. P., 'Komitet po zheleznodorozhnym zakazam i ego likvidatsiia v 1914g.', *Istoricheskie zapiski*, 83, 1969, pp. 233–43.

Polikarpov, V. V., 'Iz istorii voennoi promyshlennosti v Rossii, 1906–1917gg.', *Istoricheskie zapiski*, 104, 1979, pp. 123–67.

'Gosudarstvennoe proizvodstvo vooruzheniia v Rossii nachalo XXv. (istoriografiia voprosa)', *Istoriia i istoriki (1982–3)*, Moscow, 1987, pp. 16–37.

Polivanov, A. A., *Iz dnevnikov i vospominanii po dolzhnosti voennogo ministra i ego pomoshchnika, 1907–1916gg.*, Moscow, 1924.

Pollard S., and P. L. Robertson, *The British Shipbuilding Industry, 1870–1914*, Cambridge, Mass., 1979.

Pol'ner, T. I., *Obshchezemskaia organizatsiia na Dal'nem Vostoke*, Moscow, 1908.

Prokopovich, S. N., *Voina i narodnoe khoziaistvo*, Moscow, 1918.

Ramer, S. C., 'The zemstvo and public health', in T. Emmons and W. Vucinich, eds., *The Zemstvo in Russia: An Experiment in Local Self-Government*, Stanford, 1982, pp. 279–314.

Rashin, A. G., *Formirovanie rabochego klassa Rossii*, Moscow, 1958.

Reichman, H., *Railwaymen and Revolution*, Berkeley, 1989.

Reikhardt, V. V., 'Partiinye gruppirovki i predstavitel'stvo interesov krupnogo kapitala v 1905–1906gg.', *Krasnaia letopis'* 1930, 6, pp. 5–39.

Reshetar, J., *The Ukrainian Revolution*, Princeton, 1952.

Revoliutsiia 1905–1907gg. v Latvii: dokumenty i materialy, Riga, 1956.

Revoliutsionnoe dvizhenie v Rossii vesnoi i letom 1905g., aprel'-sentiabr', Moscow, 1957.

Revoliutsionnoe dvizhenie v Tul'skoi gubernii 1905–1907gg.: sbornik dokumentov i materialov, Tula, 1956.

Rice, C., *Russian Workers and the Socialist-Revolutionary Party through the Revolution of 1905–1907*, London, 1988.

Rieber, A. J., *Merchants and Entrepreneurs in Imperial Russia*, Chapel Hill, 1982.

Rödiger, A. F., 'Istoriia moei zhizni', *Voenno-istoricheskii zhurnal*, 1990, 6, pp.82–7.

Romanov, B. A., *Ocherki diplomaticheskoi istorii russko-iaponskoi voiny*, Moscow-Leningrad, 1955.

ed., *Rabochii vopros v komissii V. N. Kokovtsova v 1905g.*, Moscow, 1926.

'Konets russko-iaponskoi voiny', *Krasnyi arkhiv*, 28, 1928, pp. 182–204.

Roosa, R. A., 'Russian industrialists and "state socialism", 1906–1917', *Soviet Studies*, 23, 1972, pp. 395–417.

Ropponen, R., *Die Kraft Russlands: wie beurteilte die politische und militarische Führung der europäischen Grossmächte in der Zeit von 1905 bis 1914 die Kraft Russlands?*, Helsinki, 1968.

Rozenfel'd Ia. S., and K. I. Klimenko, *Istoriia mashinostroeniia SSSR*, Moscow, 1961.

Rummel', Iu. V., *Otechestvennyi flot kak sredstvo oborony i mezhdunarodnoi politiki*, St Petersburg, 1907.

Rybnikov, A. A., *Mel'kaia promyshlennost' Rossii*, Moscow, 1922.

Sarab'ianov, B. N., *Metallopromyshlennost' Rossii*, Moscow, 1921.

Sarkesian, S. C., ed., *The Military Industrial Complex: A Reassessment*, Beverly Hills, 1972.

Savich, N. V., 'Morskie raskhody i sudostroitel'naia programma', *Novyi ekonomist*, 1914, 5, pp. 4–7.

Savvin, N. N., *K voprosu o potreblenii metalla i metallicheskikh izdelii v Rossii*, St Petersburg, 1913.

Savin, N., 'The machine industry', in A. Raffalovich, ed., *Russia: Its Trade and Commerce*, London, 1918, pp. 200–16.

Scherer, F. M., *The Weapons Acquisition Process: Economic Incentives*, Cambridge, Mass., 1962.

Schmidt, C., ed., *The Economics of Military Expenditure*, London, 1987.

Sef, S. E., ed., *Burzhuaziia v 1905g. po neizdannym arkhivnym materialiam*, Moscow, 1926.

Semanov, S. N., *Peterburgskie rabochie nakanune pervoi russkoi revoliutsii*, Moscow, 1966.

Semenev-Tian-Shanskii, A. P., *O napravlenii v razvitii russkogo flota*, St Petersburg, 1907.

Shanin, T., *Russia as a 'Developing Society': Volume One, The Roots of Otherness*, London, 1985.

Shatsillo, K. F., 'Formirovanie finansovogo kapitala v sudostroitel'noi promyshlennosti iuga Rossii', in M. P. Viatkin, ed., *Iz istorii imperializma v Rossii*, Moscow-Leningrad, 1959, pp. 26–56.

'Monopolii i stroitel'stvo podvodnogo flota v Rossii nakanune i v period pervoi mirovoi voiny', *Vestnik MGU, istoriia*, 1960, 3, pp. 27–42.

'Inostrannyi kapital i voenno-morskie programmy Rossii nakanune pervoi mirovoi voiny', *Istoricheskie zapiski*, 69, 1961, pp. 73–100.

Russkii imperializm i razvitie flota nakanune pervoi mirovoi voiny, 1906–1914gg., Moscow, 1968.

'O disproportsii v razvitii vooruzhennykh sil Rossii nakanune pervoi mirovoi voiny, 1906–1914', *Istoricheskie zapiski*, 83, 1969, pp. 123–36.

Rossiia pered pervoi mirovoi voinoi: vooruzhennye sily tsarizma v 1905–1914gg., Moscow, 1974.

'Poslednie voennye programmy Rossiiskoi imperii', *Voprosy istorii*, 1991, 7–8, pp. 224–33.

Shchegolev, P. E., ed., *Padenie tsarskogo rezhima*, 7 vols., Leningrad, 1924–7.

Shebaldin, Iu. N., 'Gosudarstvennyi biudzhet tsarskoi Rossii', *Istoricheskie zapiski*, 65, 1959, pp. 163–90.

Shelymagin, I. I., *Zakonodatel'stvo o fabrichno-zavodskom trude v Rossii v 1900–1917gg.*, Moscow, 1952.

Shepelev, L. E., *Akstionernye kompanii v Rossii*, Leningrad, 1973.

Tsarizm i burzhuaziia vo vtoroi polovine XIX veke, Leningrad, 1981.

Tsarizm i burzhuaziia v 1904–1914gg., Leningrad, 1987.

Shidlovskii, S. I., *Vospominaniia*, Berlin, 1923.

Shpolianskii, D. I., *Monopolii ugol'no-metallurgicheskoi promyshlennosti iuga Rossii v nachale XX veka*, Moscow, 1953.

Shteinfel'd, N., 'Politika kazennykh zakazov', *Narodnoe khoziaistvo*, 1902, 8, pp. 149–54.

Shuster, U. A., *Peterburgskie rabochie v 1905–1907gg.*, Leningrad, 1976.

Sidorov, A. L., 'Otnosheniia Rossii s soiuznikami i inostrannye postavki vo vremia pervoi mirovoi voiny, 1914–1917gg.', *Istoricheskie zapiski*, 15, 1945, pp. 128–79.

Finansovoe polozhenie Rossii v gody pervoi mirovoi voiny, Moscow, 1960.

Istoricheskie predposylki Velikoi Oktiabr'skoi sotsialisticheskoi revoliutsii, Moscow, 1970.

Ekonomicheskoe polozhenie Rossii v gody pervoi mirovoi voiny, Moscow, 1973.

ed., 'Finansovoe polozhenie tsarskogo samoderzhaviia v period russko-iaponskoi voiny i pervoi russkoi revoliutsii', *Istoricheskii arkhiv*, 1955, 2, pp. 120–49.

'Iz istorii podgotovki Rossii k pervoi mirovoi voine', *Istoricheskii arkhiv*, 1962, 2, pp. 120–55.

Simms, J. Y., 'The crisis in Russian agriculture at the end of the nineteenth century: a different view', *Slavic Review*, 36, 1977, pp. 377–98.

Smith, Merritt Roe, *The Harpers Ferry Armory and the New Technology: The Challenge of Change*, Ithaca, 1977.

Soboleff, M., 'Foreign trade of Russia', in A. Raffalovich, ed., *Russia: Its Trade and Commerce*, London, 1918, pp. 298–328.

Spear, Raymond, *Report on the Russian Medical and Sanitary Features of the Russo-Japanese War to the Surgeon General, U.S. Navy*, Washington, 1906.

Spring, D. W., 'Russia and the Franco-Russian Alliance, 1905–1914: dependence or interdependence', *Slavonic and East European Review*, 66, 1988, pp. 564–92.

Stenogramma soveshchaniia o polozhenii metallurgicheskoi i mashinostroitel'noi promyshlennosti, mai 1908, St Petersburg, 1908.

Stone, N., *The Eastern Front, 1914–1917*, London, 1975.

Strumilin, S. G., *Statistiko-ekonomicheskie ocherki*, Moscow, 1958.

Subbotin, Iu. N., 'Iz istorii voennoi promyshlennosti Rossii kontsa XIX-nachala XXv., *Vestnik LGU*, 20, 1973, 3, pp. 45–52.

Sukhomlinov, V. A., *Vospominaniia*, Berlin, 1924.

Surh, G. D., *1905 in St Petersburg: Labour and Government*, Stanford, 1989.

Sylla, R., and G. Toniolo, eds., *Patterns of European Industrialization: The Nineteenth Century*, London, 1991.

Tarnovskii, K. N., 'Kustarnaia promyshlennost' i tsarizm, 1907–1914gg.', *Voprosy istorii*, 1986, 7, pp. 33–46.

Torpan, N. I. 'Finansovo-monopolisticheskie gruppirovki v voennoi promyshlennosti na territorii Estonii v 1911–1917gg.', *Isvestiia AN Estonskoi SSR, obshchestvennye nauki*, 1984, 2, pp. 112–23; 3, pp. 228–39.

Trebilcock, R. C., 'Legends of the armaments industry', *Journal of Contemporary History*, 5, 1970, pp. 3–19.

'British armaments and European industrialization', *Economic History Review*, 26, 1973, pp. 254–72.

'War and the failure of industrial mobilization: 1899 and 1914', in J. Winter, ed., *War and Economic Development*, Cambridge, 1975, pp. 139–64.

The Vickers Brothers: Armaments and Enterprise, London, 1977.

Trudy pervogo s"ezda predstavitelei metalloobrabatyvaiushchei promyshlennosti, Petrograd, 1916.

Trudy soveshchanii po izgotovleniiu korpusov 3-dium. granat, Moscow, 1916.

Tsukernik, A. L., 'Iz istorii monopolizatsii zheleznogo rynka v Rossii', *Istoricheskie zapiski*, 42, 1953, pp. 160–201.

Sindikat 'Prodamet' 1902–1914gg.: istoriko-ekonomicheskii ocherk, Moscow, 1959.

Tsybul'skii, V. A., 'Sestroretskie rabochie v revoliutsii 1905–1907gg.', in Iu. D. Margolis, ed., *Novoe o revoliutsii 1905–1907gg. v Rossii*, Moscow, 1989.

Tugan-Baranovskii, M. I., *K luchshemu budushchemu*, Petrograd, 1912.

Tukholka, V. L., 'Zheleznye rudy', in *Bogatstva SSSR*, vol. 3, Moscow, 1925.

Vainshtein, A. L., *Narodnoe bogatstvo i narodnokhoziaistvennoe nakoplenie predrevoliutsionnoi Rossii*, Moscow, 1960.

Vankov, S. N., 'O normalizatsii metalloobrabatyvaiushchei promyshlennosti', *Nauchno-tekhnicheskii vestnik*, 1921, 4–5, pp. 1–18.

'O sostoianii nashei metalloobrabatyvaiushchei promyshlennosti k nachalu 1914 g. i vo vremia voiny', *Nauchno-tekhnicheskii vestnik*, 1921, 6, pp. 1–18.

Varzar, V., 'Factories and workshops', in A. Raffalovich, ed., *Russia: Its Trade and Commerce*, London, 1918, pp. 105–64.

'Machine industry', in A. Raffalovich, ed., *Russia: Its Trade and Commerce*, London, 1918, pp. 200–26.

Verner, A., *The Crisis of Russian Autocracy: Nicholas II and the 1905 Revolution*, Princeton, 1990.

Viatkin, M. P., *Gornozavodskii Ural v 1900–1917gg.*, Moscow-Leningrad, 1965.

Vinogradoff, E., 'The Russian peasantry and the elections to the Fourth State Duma' in L. H. Haimson, ed., *The Politics of Rural Russia, 1907–1914*, New York, 1978, pp. 219–60.

Voennaia entsiklopediia, 18 vols., St Petersburg/Petrograd, 1911–15.

Volobuev, P. V., and V. Z. Drobizhev, 'Iz istorii goskapitalizma v nachal'nyi period sotsialisticheskogo stroitel'stva v SSSR', *Voprosy istorii*, 1957, 9, pp. 107–22.

Voprosy istorii kapitalisticheskoi Rossii, Sverdlovsk, 1972.

Vorob'ev, N. Ia., *Ocherki po istorii promyshlennoi statistiki v dorevoliutsionnoi Rossii i SSSR*, Moscow, 1961.

Voznesenskii, A. P., 'O voennom khoziaistve', *Obshchestvo revnitelei voennykh znanii*, 1906, vol. 1, pp. 97–123.

Vserossiiskaia politicheskaia stachka v oktiabre 1905g., part 1, Moscow, 1955.

Vysshii pod"em revoliutsii 1905–1907gg: vooruzhennye vosstaniia noiabr'-dekabr' 1905g., part 2, Moscow, 1955.

Webb, S. L., 'Tariffs, cartels, technology and growth in the German steel industry', *Journal of Economic History*, 40, 1980, pp. 309–29.

Weber, E., *Peasants into Frenchmen*, London, 1977.

Weber, M., 'Zur Lage der bürgerlichen Demokratie in Russland', in W. J. Mommsen and D. Dahlmann, eds., *Max Weber: Zur Russischen Revolution von 1905*, Tübingen, 1989, pp. 71–280.

Westwood, J., 'The railways', in R. W. Davies, ed., *From Tsarism to the New Economic Policy*, London, 1990, pp. 169–88.

Wheatcroft, S. G., 'Crises and the condition of the peasantry in late imperial Russia', in E. Kingston-Mann and T. Mixter, eds., *Peasant Economy, Culture and Politics of European Russia, 1800–1921*, Princeton, 1991, pp. 128–72.

Wildman, Allan, *The End of the Russian Imperial Army: The Old Army and the Soldiers' Revolt*, Princeton, 1980.

Witt, P. C., 'Reichsfinanzen und Rüstungspolitik, 1898–1914', in H. Schottelius and W. Deist, eds., *Marine und Marinepolitik im kaiserlichen Deutschland, 1871–1914*, Düsseldorf, 1972, pp. 156–77.

Workmen's Insurance and Compensations Systems in Europe, 2 vols., Washington, 1911.

Wright, Quincy, *The Study of War*, Chicago, 1940.

Zaionchkovskii, A. M., *Podgotovka Rossii k mirovoi voine v mezhdunarodnom otnoshenii*, Moscow, 1926.

Podgotovka Rossii k imperialisticheskoi voine: ocherki voennoi podgotovki i pervona-chal'nykh planov, Moscow, 1926.

Zaionchkovskii, P. A., *Samoderzhavie i russkaia armiia na rubezhe XIX–XX stoletii, 1881–1903*, Moscow, 1973.

Zapiska soveta s"ezdov o merakh k pod"emu otechestvennoi zheleznoi promyshlennosti i mashinostroeniia, St Petersburg, 1908.

Zav'ialov, S. I., *Izhorskii zavod*, 2 vols, Leningrad, 1976.

Zhdanov, V. I., *Dovoennaia moshchnost' metallopromyshlennosti i ee znachenie v ekonomike strany*, Moscow, 1925.

Zhilin, A., 'Bol'shaia programma po usileniiu russkoi armii', *Voenno-istoricheskii zhurnal*, 1974, 7, pp. 90–7.

Zhilin, P. A., *Russkaia voennaia mysl'*, Moscow, 1986.

Ziv, V. S., *Inostrannye kapitaly v russkoi gornozavodskoi promyshlennosti*, Petrograd, 1917.

Zvegintsev, A., 'The Duma and state defence', *Russian Review*, 1, 1912, pp. 49–63.

Zyr'ianov, P. N., 'Petr' Arkad'evich Stolypin', *Voprosy istorii*, 1990, 6, pp. 54–75.

Index

Cambridge Russian, Soviet and Post-Soviet Studies